AF476990

Wildlife Photographer of the Year

PORTFOLIO TWO

Picture Editor
PETER WILKINSON FRPS

Project Co-ordinator
HELEN GILKS

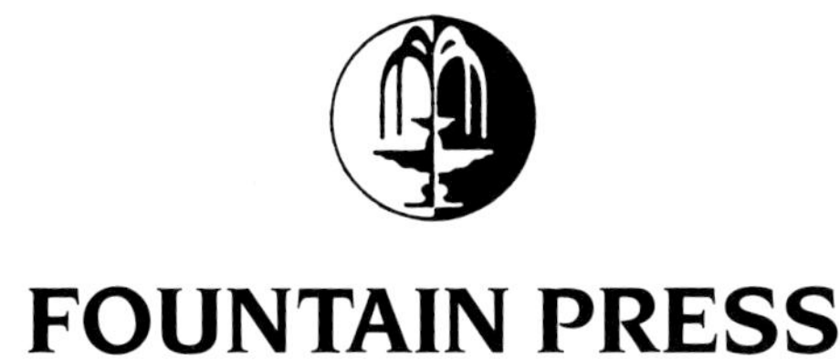

FOUNTAIN PRESS

Published by
FOUNTAIN PRESS LIMITED
Queensborough House
2 Claremont Road
Surbiton
Surrey
KT6 4QU
ENGLAND

COPYRIGHT
FOUNTAIN PRESS 1993

Design & Layout
by Grant Bradford

Typeset in Novarese Medium Italic
by Crowborough Typesetters

Colour Reproduction and Printing
by Regent Publishing Services Ltd.
Hong Kong

ISBN 0 86343 306 5

Contents

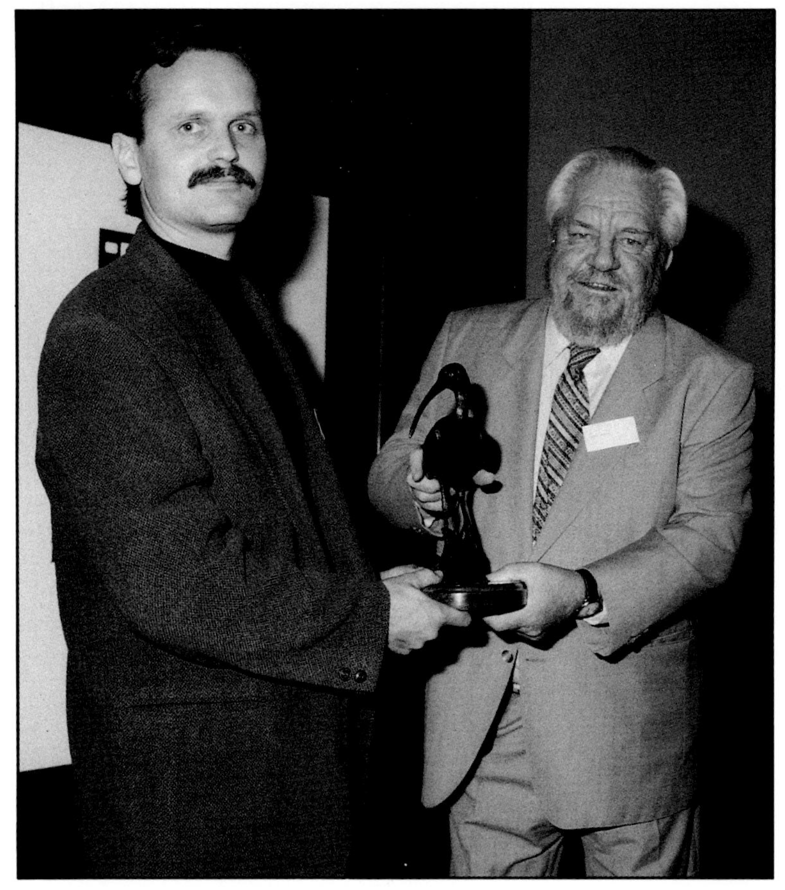

**Gerald Durrell presents the British Gas Award for
Wildlife Photographer of the Year to André Bärtschi.**

Foreword

In days of yore, having your photograph taken was something of a torture. Firstly, you and your wife and lace-encrusted children had to dress up in your best clothes and you had to be arranged symmetrically with a potted palm as a background. Then you had to stand immobile for an inordinate length of time, clasping your bowler hat to your bosom while the photographer fiddled with his camera. Eventually, there was a blinding flash and you and your beloved were immortalised in a slightly blurred picture on a piece of cardboard. Slowly, however, things got better and the camera moved outside the confines of the studio. Then, wonder of wonders, they started to photograph wild animals.

I remember how thrilled I was to get the early books of Cherry and Richard Kearton. True, most of the pictures looked as though they had been taken through a bridal veil, but there was an undeniable oyster catcher standing by its eggs. What more could one ask?

Now the camera has become like the eyes of one of the great animal artists such as Wolf or Audubon, freezing in a magical instant the subtle workings of nature, whether it is a school of fish hanging like a coloured living curtain against a coral reef, the pleated feathers of a bird's wing in flight, or a whale bursting from the depths of the ocean in a bouquet of spray. Now we can marvel at the extraordinary fidelity with which the camera can capture for us these entrancing moments of nature, but never let us forget that, however good the camera equipment, it is the brain behind the camera that knows how to compose the picture and, moreover, knows instinctively the right moment to take the picture. Looking at these startling and wonderful photographs, you will find it hard to choose whose is best. You can only congratulate them all on their brilliance, and thank them for the permanent pleasure they have provided for us.

Gerald Durrell

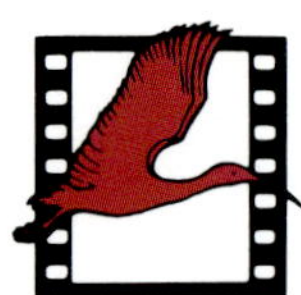

British Gas

Wildlife Photographer of the Year

1992

Editorial

This book displays the winning and commended entries in the Wildlife Photographer of the Year 1992 Competition, an annual event organised by BBC WILDLIFE Magazine and The Natural History Museum and sponsored by British Gas. The competition was first run in 1965 by BBC WILDLIFE's predecessor *Animals* magazine, and in 1984 BBC WILDLIFE joined forces with The Natural History Museum to find a sponsor for the event. After four years association with Prudential and one with Kodak, the magazine and museum entered into a partnership with British Gas, whose sponsorship since 1990 has enabled the competition to develop to the high profile that it now enjoys.

The Competition

This is now the largest and most prestigious event of its kind in the world, attracting more than 10,000 entries from professional and amateur photographers worldwide. It is a truly international event, and in 1992, entries came from 42 different countries (photographers from 19 countries are represented in this book).

Entries (which must be colour slides) compete for a winner and runner-up cash prize in each category. Where competition for the top places is particularly fierce, a specially commended, or third place, is sometimes

Winners 1984-1991

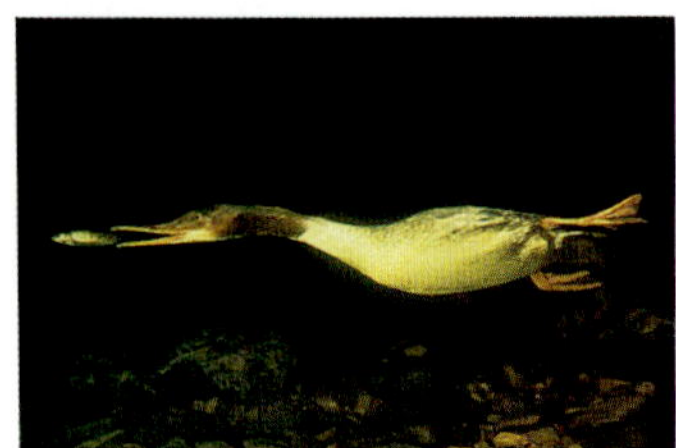

1984
Richard & Julia Kemp
United Kingdom

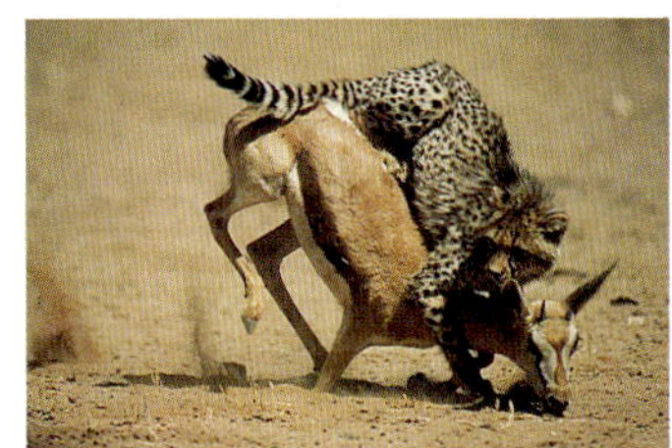

1985
Charles G. Summers Jnr.
United States of America

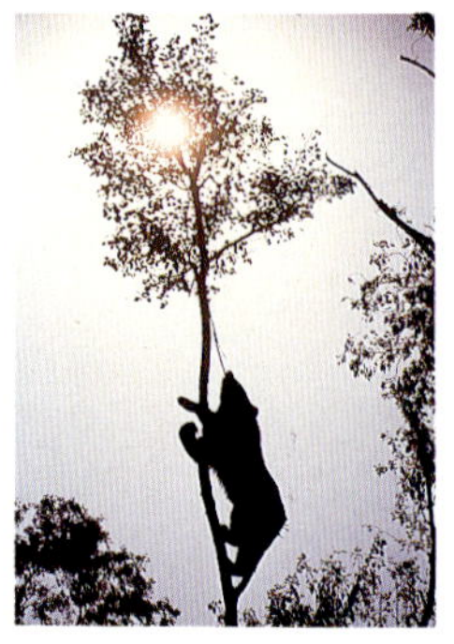

1986
Rajesh Bedi
India

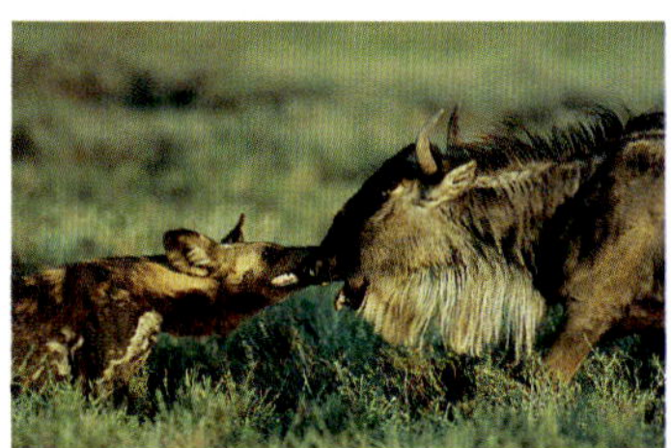

1987
Jonathan Scott
United Kingdom

awarded. Other entries which reach the very last stages of the judging are highly commended and included in the exhibition either as cibachrome prints or in an audio-visual display.

Awards ceremony and exhibitions

Each year at the end of November, the prize-winners gather at The Natural History Museum for an awards ceremony, which is compered by Barry Paine. In 1992 Gerald Durrell presented the British Gas Awards for the overall winners of the junior as well as for the main competition. Simon King presented the Eric Hosking Award and the prizes for the junior winners. The other category prizes were presented by Heather Angel, Chris Baines, Neil Chalmers, Nick Davies, Lee Durrell, Anthony Huxley, Shirley McGreal, Virginia McKenna, Bill Oddie, Andrew Sachs, Keith Shackleton, Tony Soper and Ralph Steadman. The awards ceremony marks the opening of the exhibition at The Natural History Museum where it remains on display for several months. Two further sets of the exhibition tour the UK visiting some 24 different galleries, museums and nature centres. Additional sets of the 1992 exhibition have been exhibited in The Hague, Holland; Bourges, France; Berlin, Germany; Sydney, Australia; and Houston, USA prior to national tours in these countries.

Bruce Coleman
Director of the Bruce Coleman Agency

Dr. Giles Clarke
Head of exhibition planning at The Natural History Museum

Rosamund Kidman Cox
Editor of BBC WILDLIFE Magazine

Amanda Nevill
Secretary of the Royal Photographic Society

Bruce Pearson
Artist and Biologist

Jonathan Scott
Photographer and Artist

Pedro Silmon
Art Editor of The Sunday Times Magazine

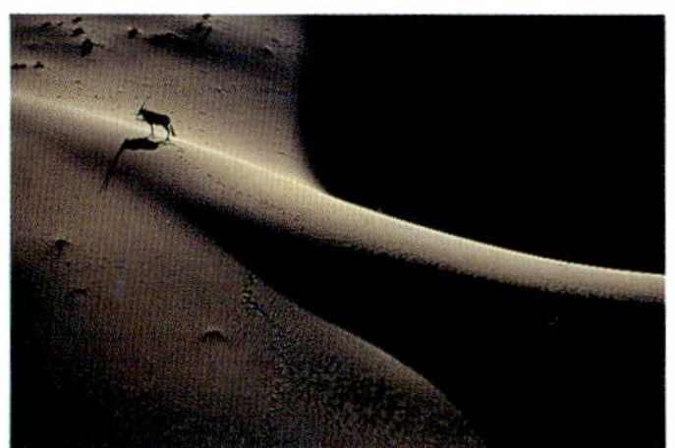

1988
Jim Brandenburg
United States of America

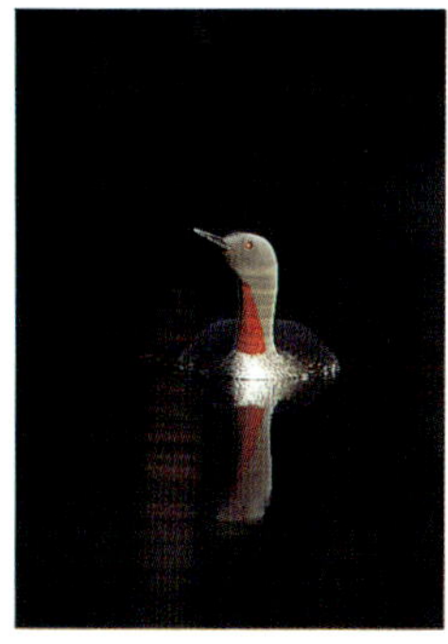

1989
Jouni Ruuskanen
Finland

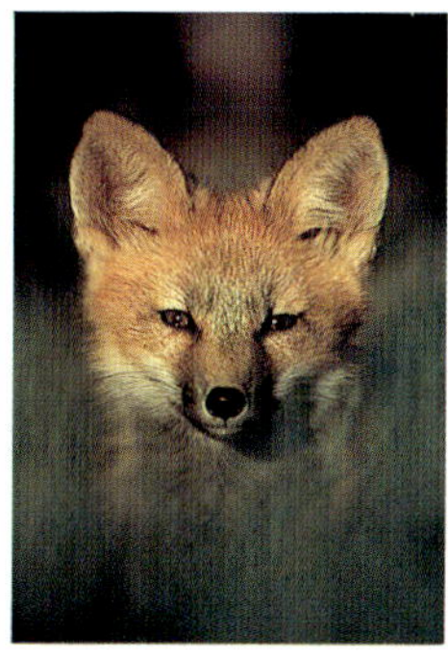

1990
Wendy Shattil
United States of America

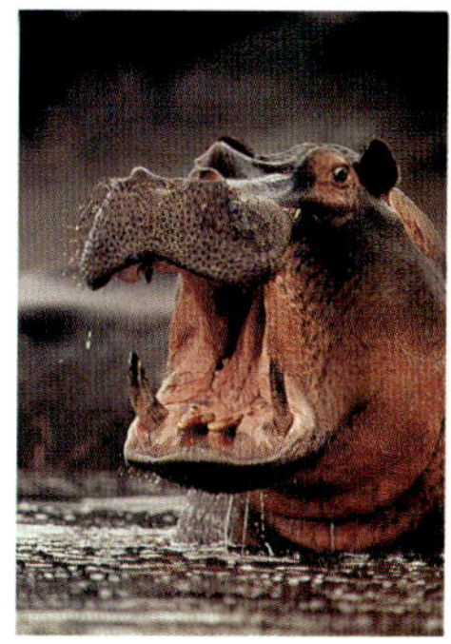

1991
Frans Lanting
The Netherlands

Wildlife *Photographer* of the Year

The British Gas Award for Wildlife Photographer of the Year was given for the individual image judged to be the most striking and memorable of all the photographs entered for the competition. The 1992 winner, André Bärtschi, received the British Gas Award - a bronze sculpture of a scarlet ibis and a cheque.

André Bärtschi

André Bärtschi first took up photography when studying interior and industrial design in Zurich. While developing his skills, he supported himself by working at Zurich Zoo caring for its collection of big cats, amphibians and reptiles. André now works full time as a photographer, specialising in the natural history of rainforests. He has photographed in Costa Rica, Venezuela, Ecuador and Bolivia but his favourite site is the Manu Biosphere Reserve in Peru, where his winning picture was taken. In October 1992, *Peru's Amazonian Eden - Manu Biosphere Reserve*, illustrated with André's photographs, was published.

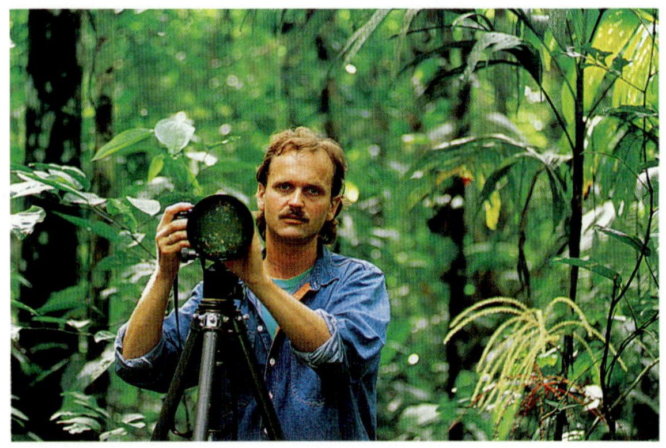

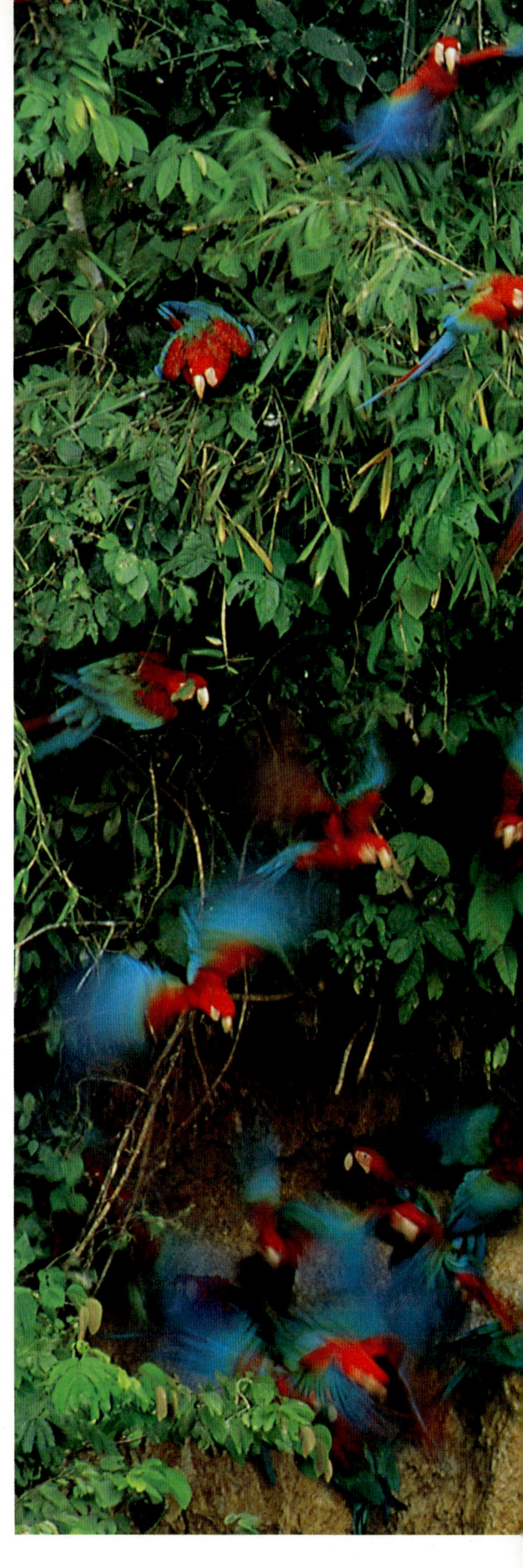

André Bärtschi
Liechtenstein
WILDLIFE PHOTOGRAPHER
OF THE YEAR 1992

Red-and-Green and Scarlet Macaws

"The birds had gathered on the bank to feast on clay in Manu Biosphere Reserve, Peru. Scientists believe that the minerals may help macaws and other parrots neutralise the toxins they take in every day while feeding on poisonous seeds and leaves."

Nikon F4 with 400mm lens; tripod; f4 at 1/30 sec; Fujichrome Velvia

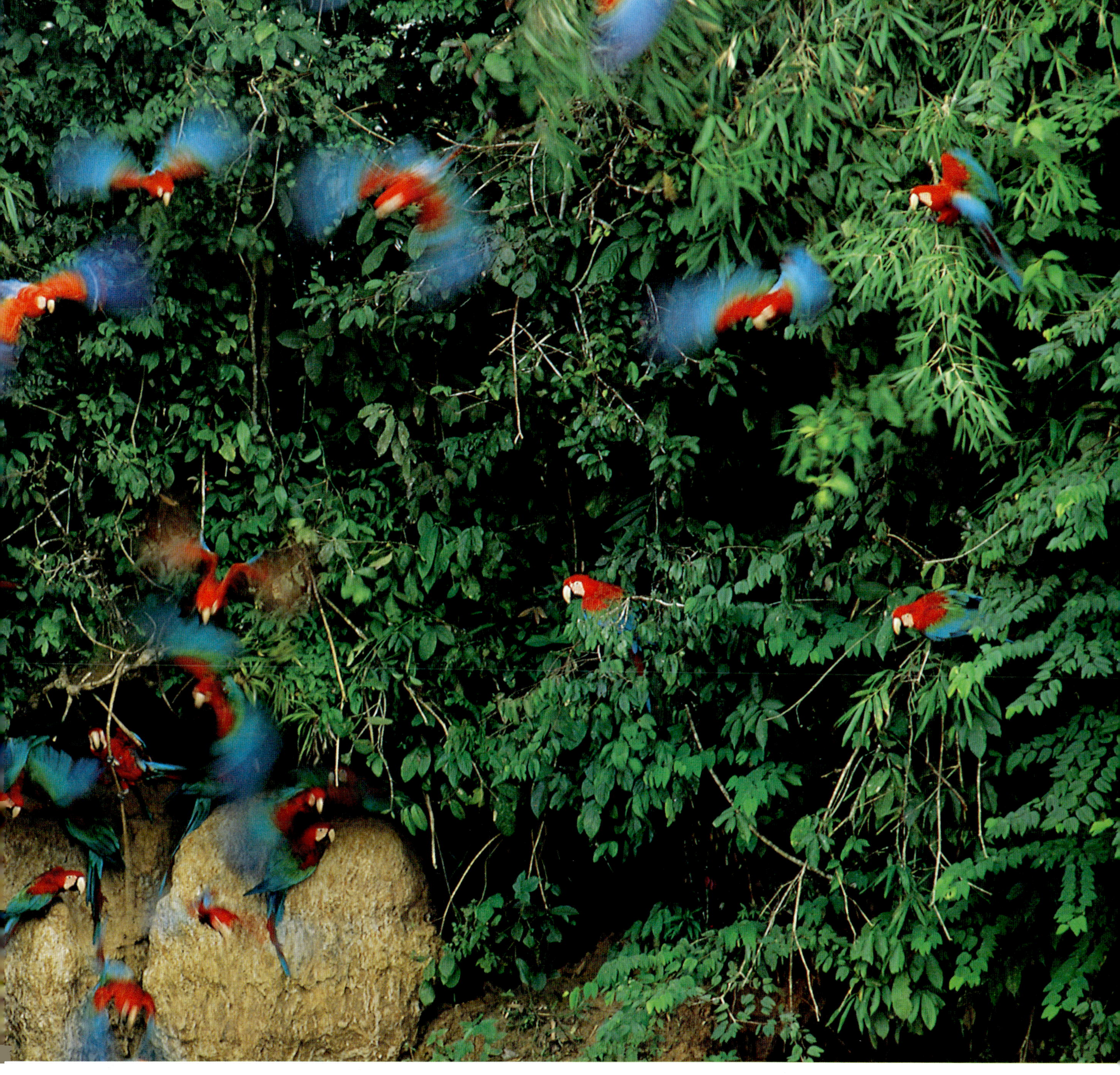

The Eric Hosking Award

- WINNER -

This award was introduced in 1991, in memory of Eric Hosking who was probably Britain's most famous wildlife photographer and a supporter of this competition since it was first run in 1965. It is given for the best portfolio of pictures submitted by a photographer aged 26 years or under.

Neil McIntyre

The winner for the second year running, Neil McIntyre, comes from the Highlands of Scotland. He concentrates almost exclusively on the area around his home in Strathspey, believing that, to do justice to plants and animals, it is best to photograph them over a period of years rather than months.

Neil McIntyre
United Kingdom
WINNER

Mountain Hare

"The hares were on top of one of the hills in the Monadliath Mountains, 2,500 feet up. When approached, they ran up the hill. Positioning myself among some rocks, I waited, and after about an hour, I saw the hares starting to move back down. This was the one that came the closest."

Canon T90 with 400mm lens; tripod; f8 at 1/500 sec; Fujichrome Velvia

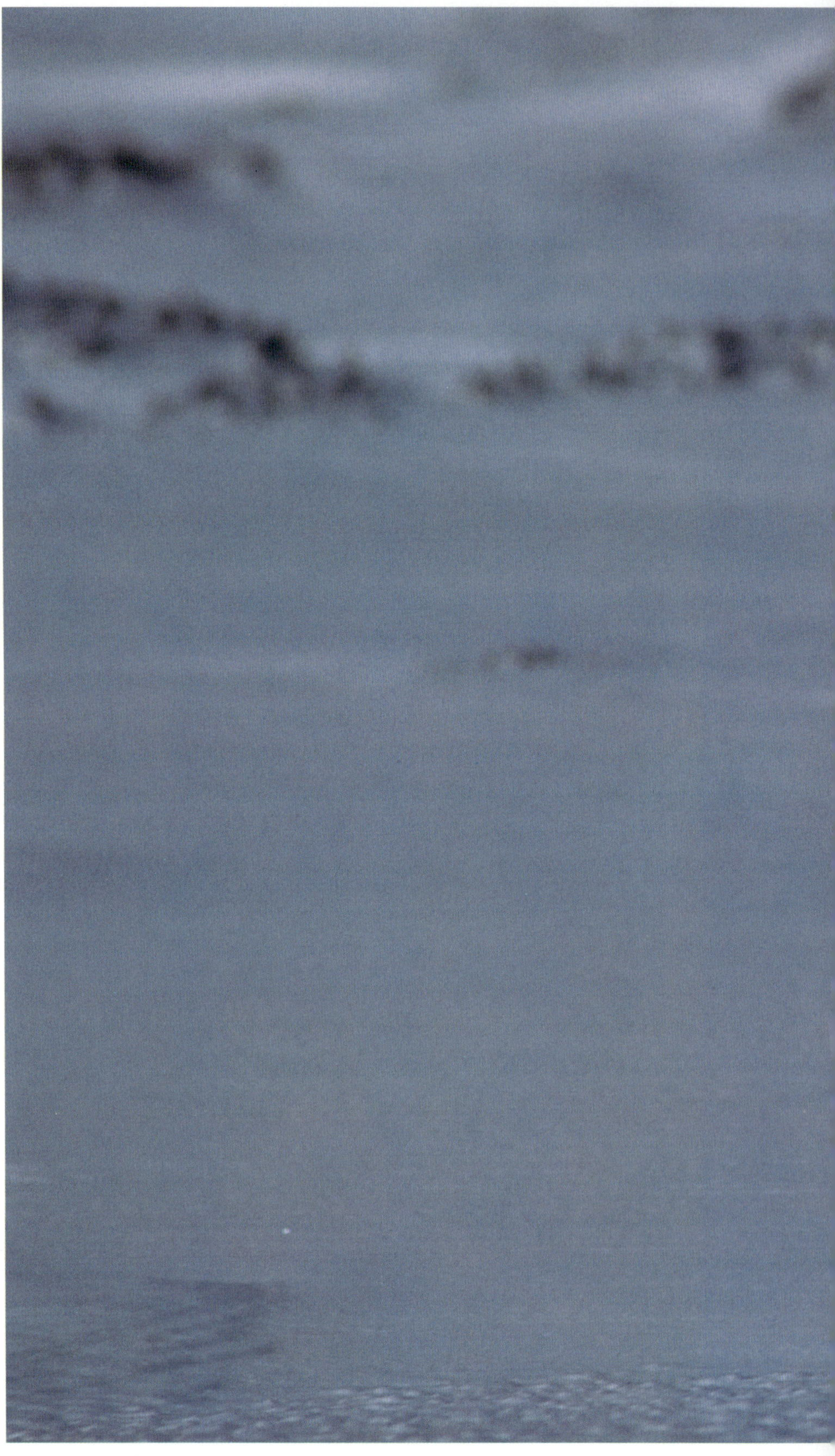

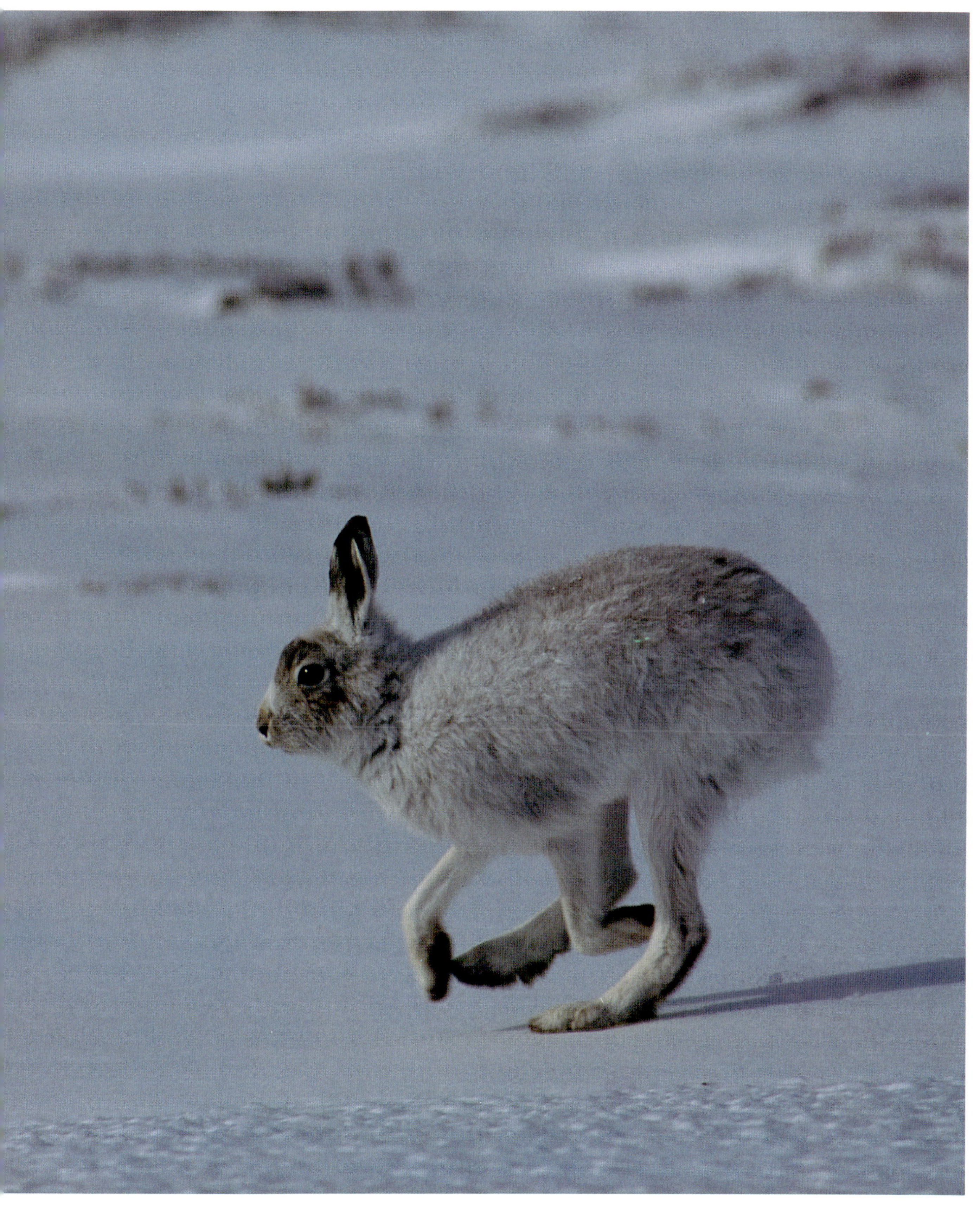

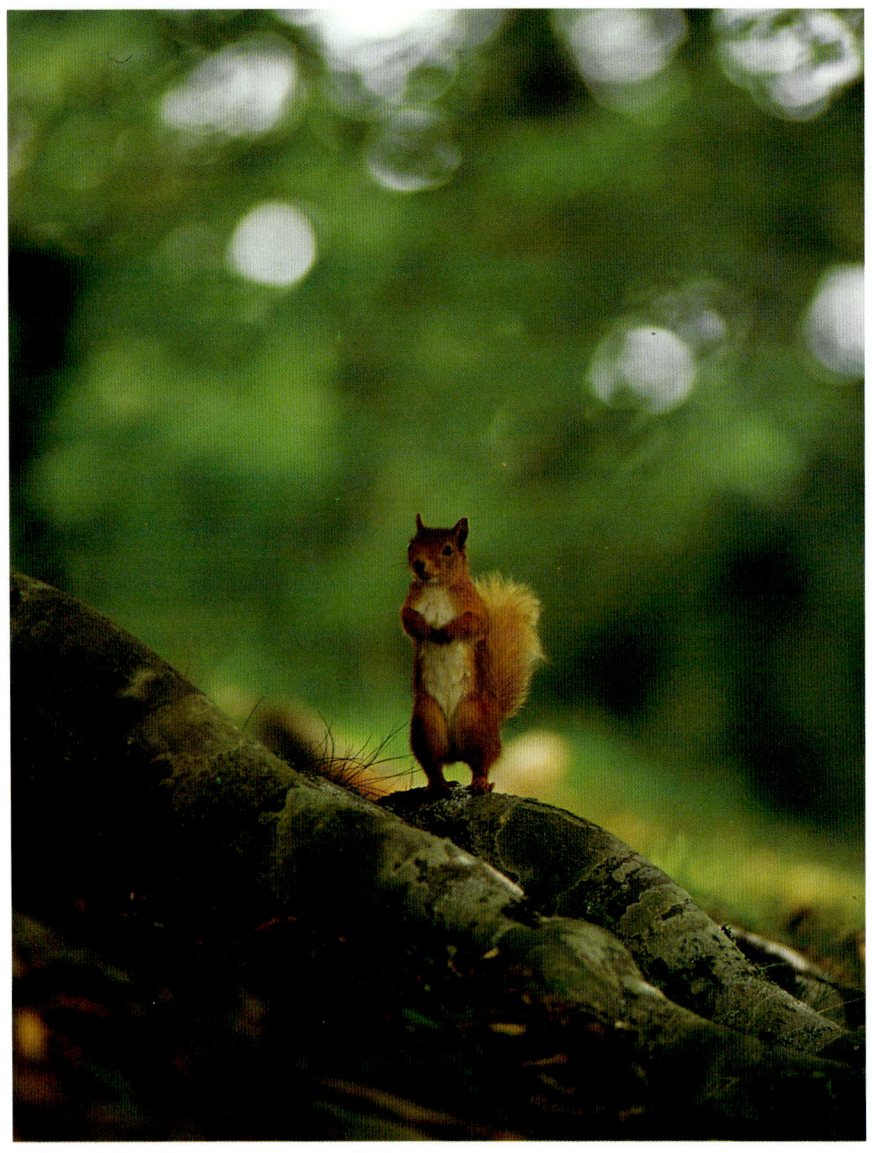

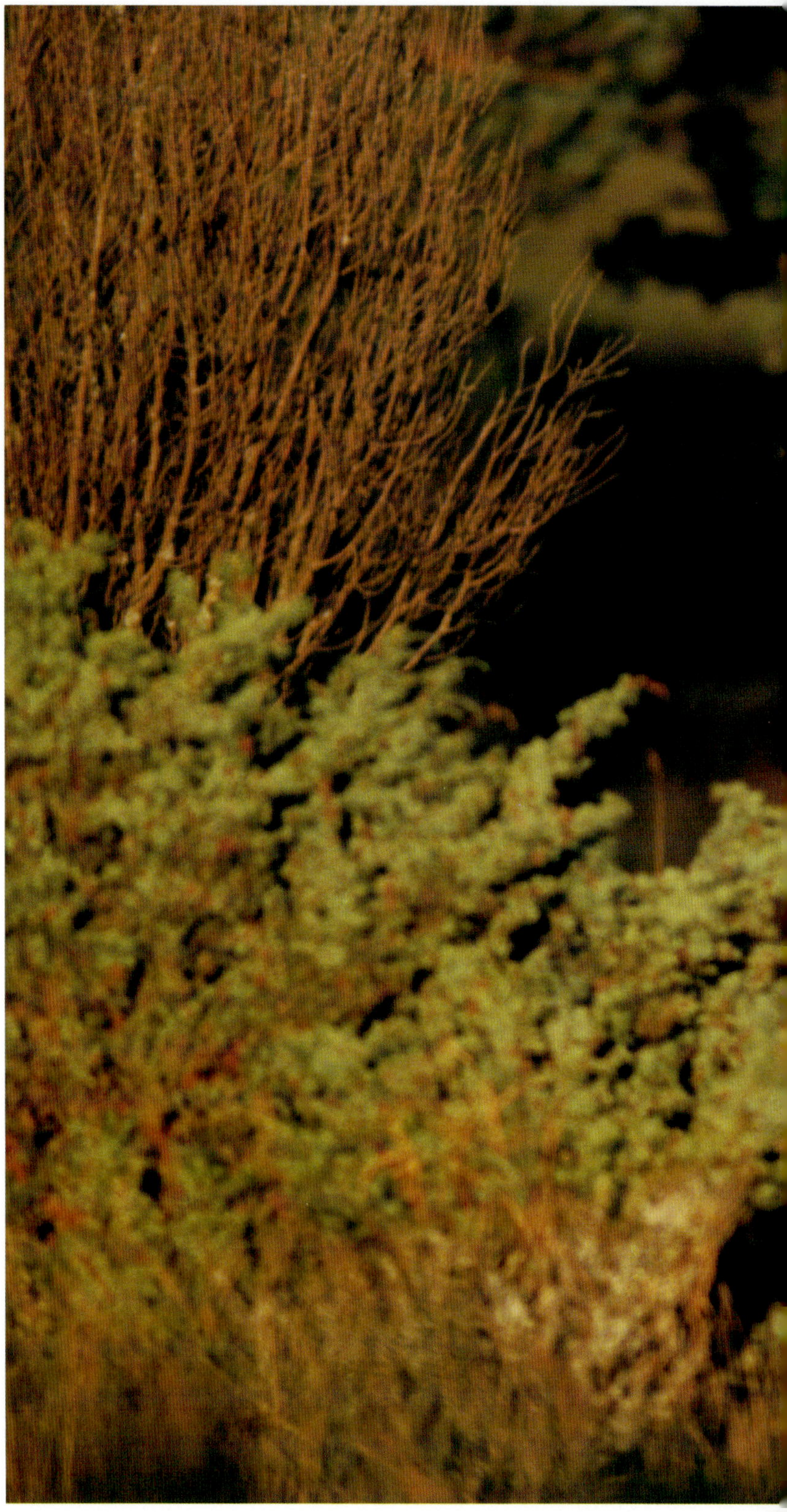

Neil McIntyre
United Kingdom
WINNER

Red Squirrel

*"I have often seen squirrels stand
upright but usually only for a
few seconds. For some reason,
this one stood for a full minute -
perhaps it was just curious - and
gave me a great opportunity
to take what is one of my
favourite pictures."*

Canon T90 with 400mm lens; tripod;
f4 at 1/60 sec;
Fujichrome Professional 100

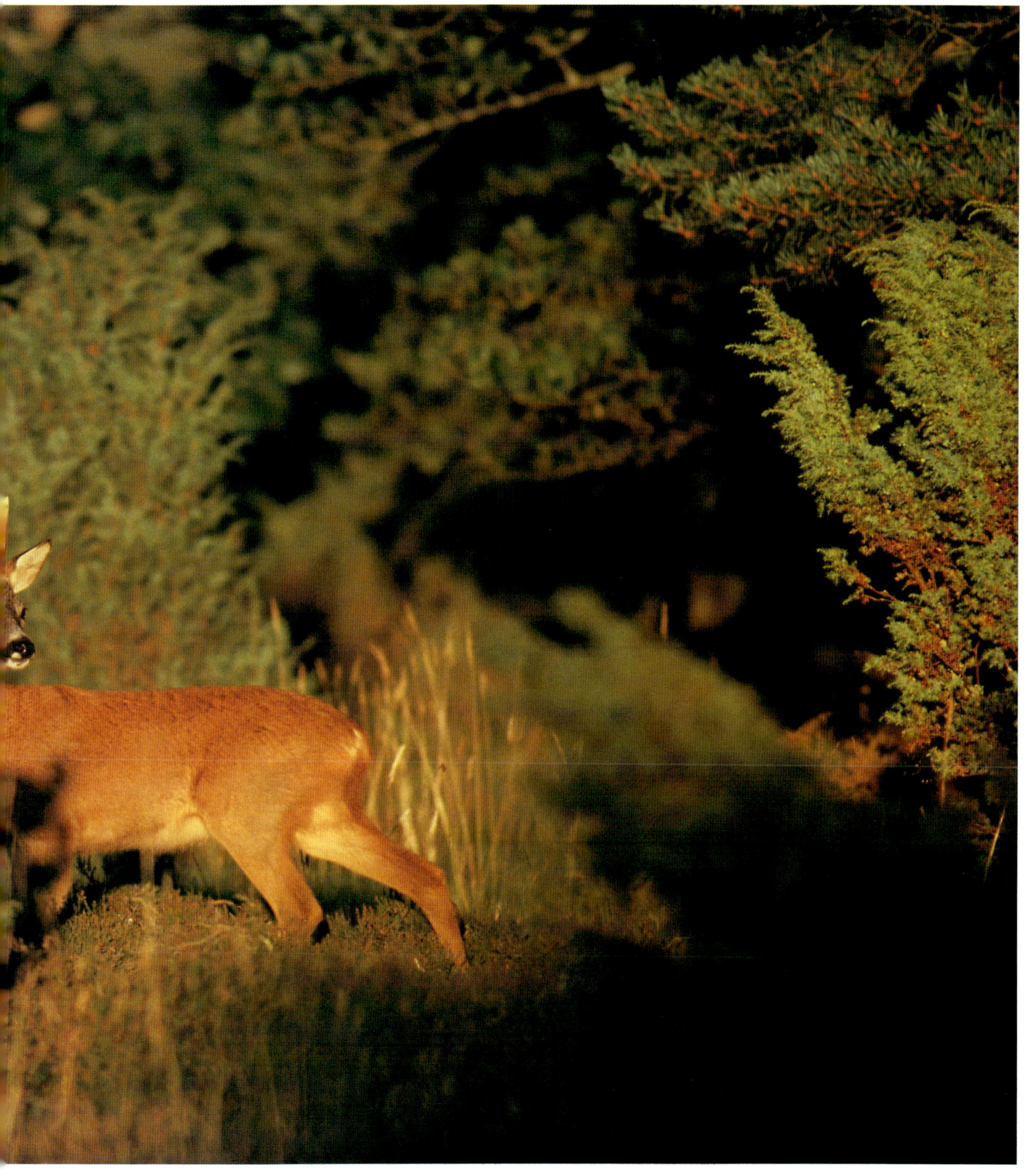

Neil McIntyre
United Kingdom
WINNER

Roe Deer buck

''I saw this roe deer buck at the
edge of a pine wood late one
evening. For once, everything
seemed to work, the buck walked
right into the clearing, stopped
and looked back. It was ideal
light, which disappeared literally
minutes after I had taken
the picture.''

Canon T90 with 400mm lens; tripod;
f4 at 1/60 sec;
Fujichrome Professional 100

Neil McIntyre
United Kingdom
WINNER

Caledonian Pine Trees at sunset

"Looking for something to photograph against a beautiful red sun slowly setting, I saw these pine trees on the other side of the river Druie. I carry a pair of waders in my jeep which come in handy to cross rivers quickly. Once on the other side, it was just a matter of getting in the right position."

Canon T90 with 50-135mm zoom lens; tripod; f11 at 1/250 sec; Fujichrome Velvia

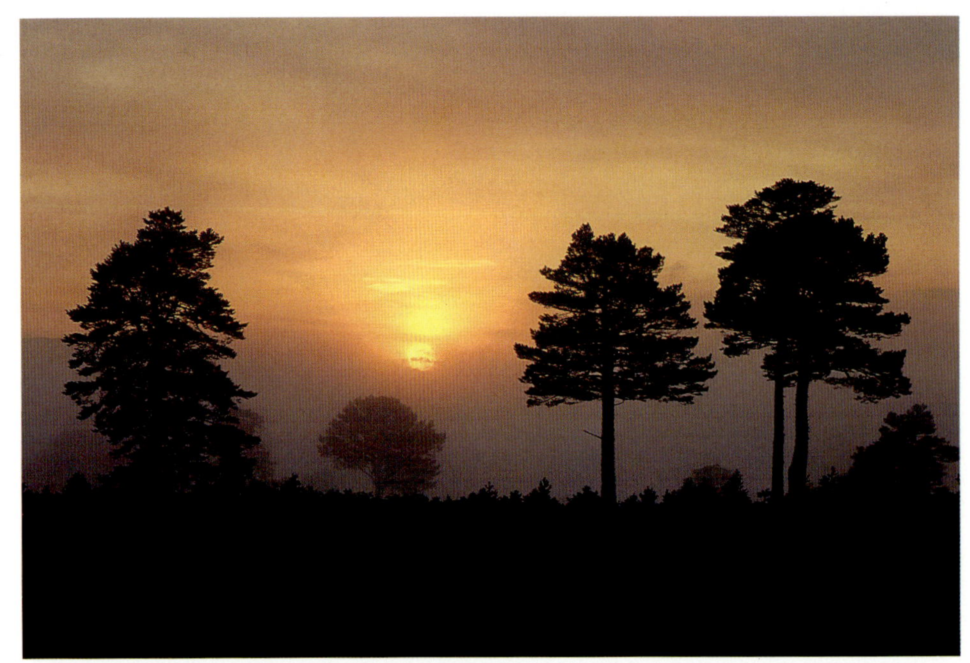

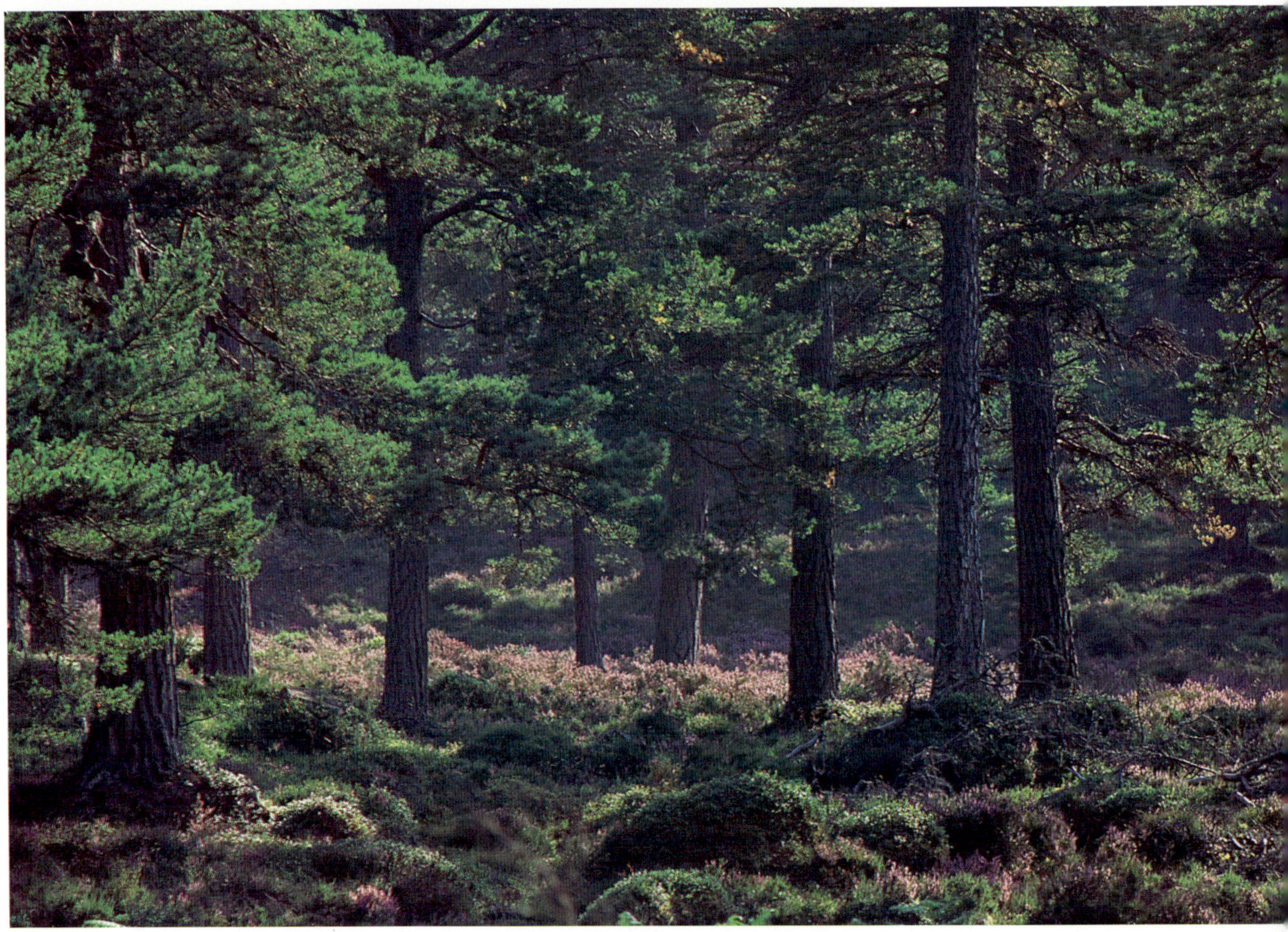

Neil McIntyre
United Kingdom
WINNER

Ancient Caledonian pine forest

"The old pine forests are fascinating places, not just for animals but also because of the trees themselves - they are a photographer's dream. In August the heather is in bloom and much of the forest is covered with a lovely purple colour; I wanted that to play an important part in the picture."

Canon T90 with 400mm lens; tripod; f11 at 1/45 sec; Fujichrome Velvia

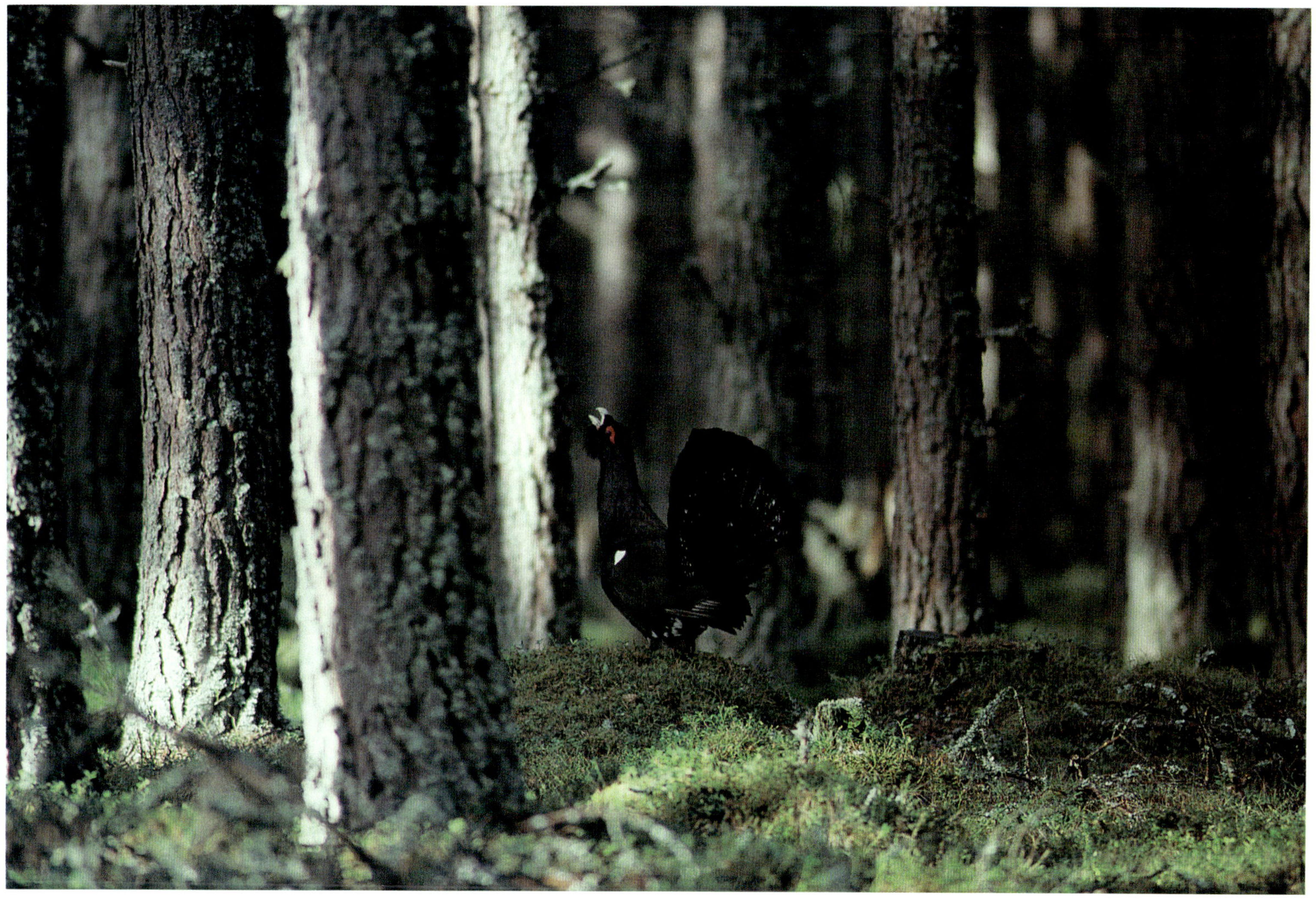

Neil McIntyre
United Kingdom
WINNER

Cock Capercaillie
displaying

*"Capercaillie are one of my
favourite birds and are
fascinating to watch, and so
getting up at three in the
morning to get to my hide before
first light was not too much of a
trial. Unfortunately, this species
is in serious decline in Scotland -
one estimate puts their numbers
at as few as 2,000."*

Canon T90 with 400mm lens; tripod;
hide; f4 at 1/125 sec; Fujichrome
Professional 100 uprated to 200

The Eric Hosking Award
- RUNNER UP -

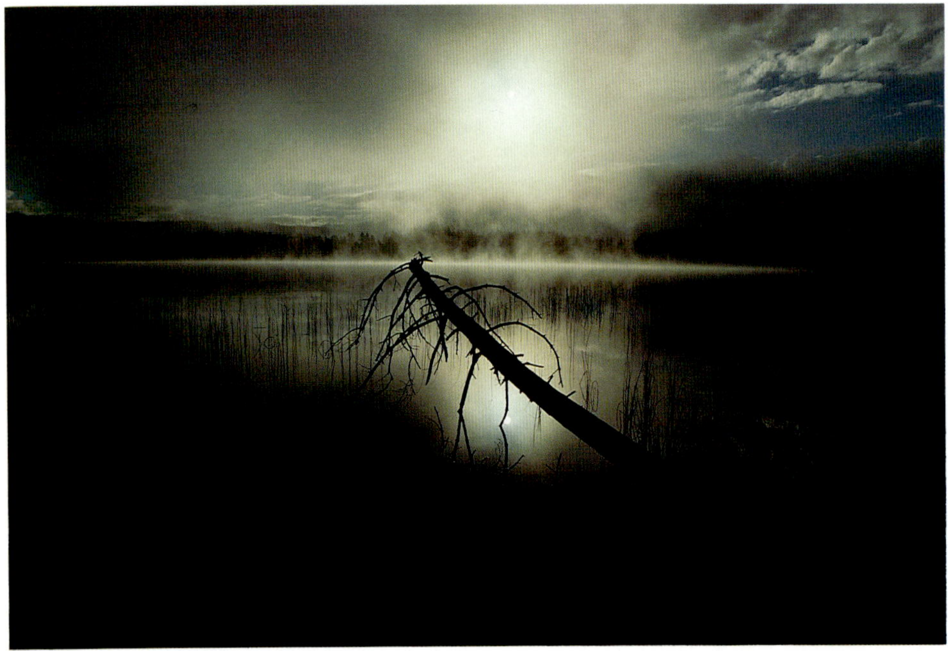

Asgeir Helgestad
Norway
RUNNER-UP

Sunrise over Lake Gjomle

"I often go to this lake on cold summer mornings to see the mist rising from the water as the sun comes up. It is amazing to sit beside the lake and hear the black-throated diver calling from out of the mist."

Canon T90 with 24mm lens; polarising filter

Asgeir Helgestad
Norway
RUNNER-UP

Golden Eagle

"Over the past five years, I have spent some 1,500 hours photographing golden eagles. In winter I put out carrion in the hope of attracting them. All this has to be done at night and I am in my hide from early morning until dusk so as not to disturb these shy birds. In this shot the eagle, with its spread wings, seems to be sovereign of the mountain forest."

Canon T90 with 80-200mm zoom lens; tripod; Kodachrome 64

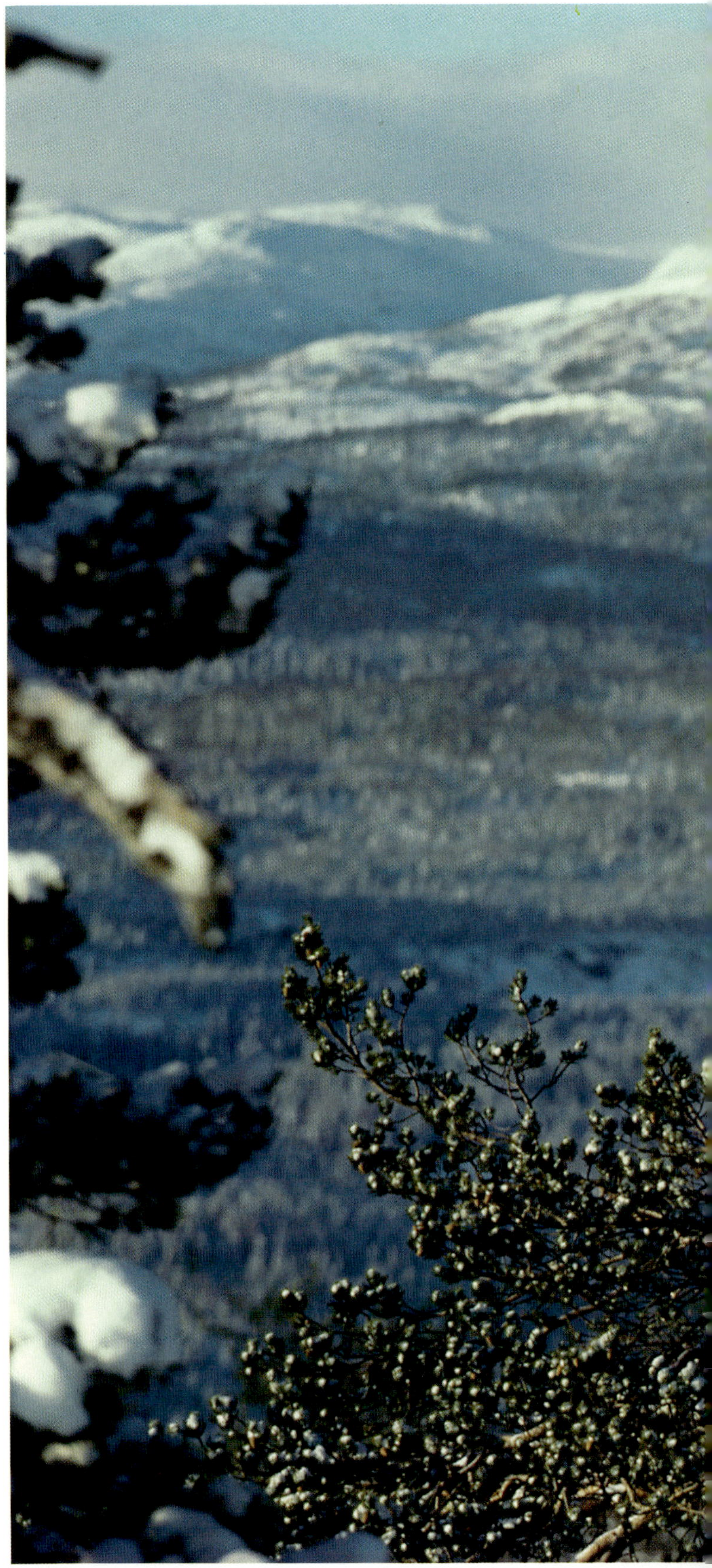

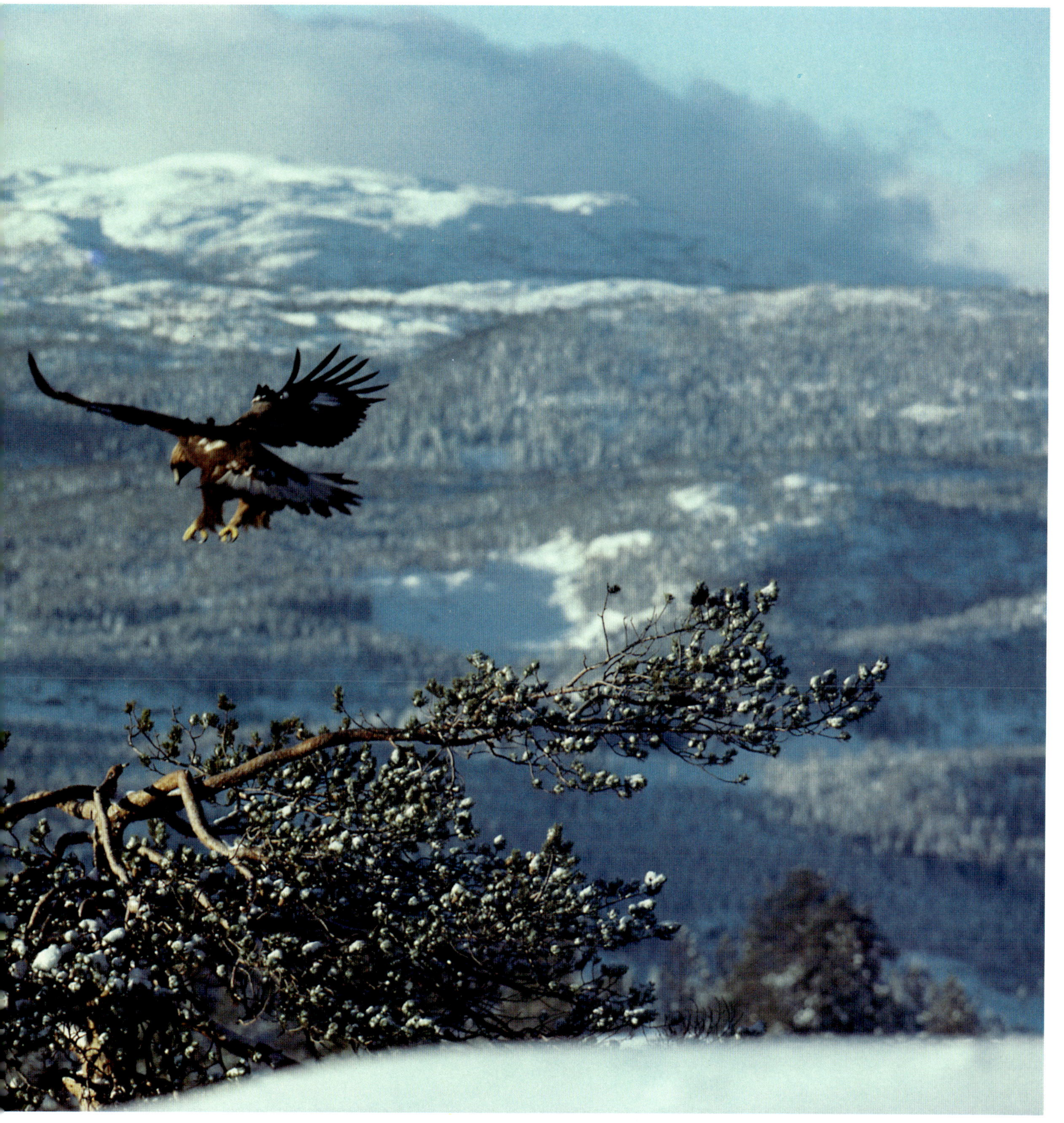

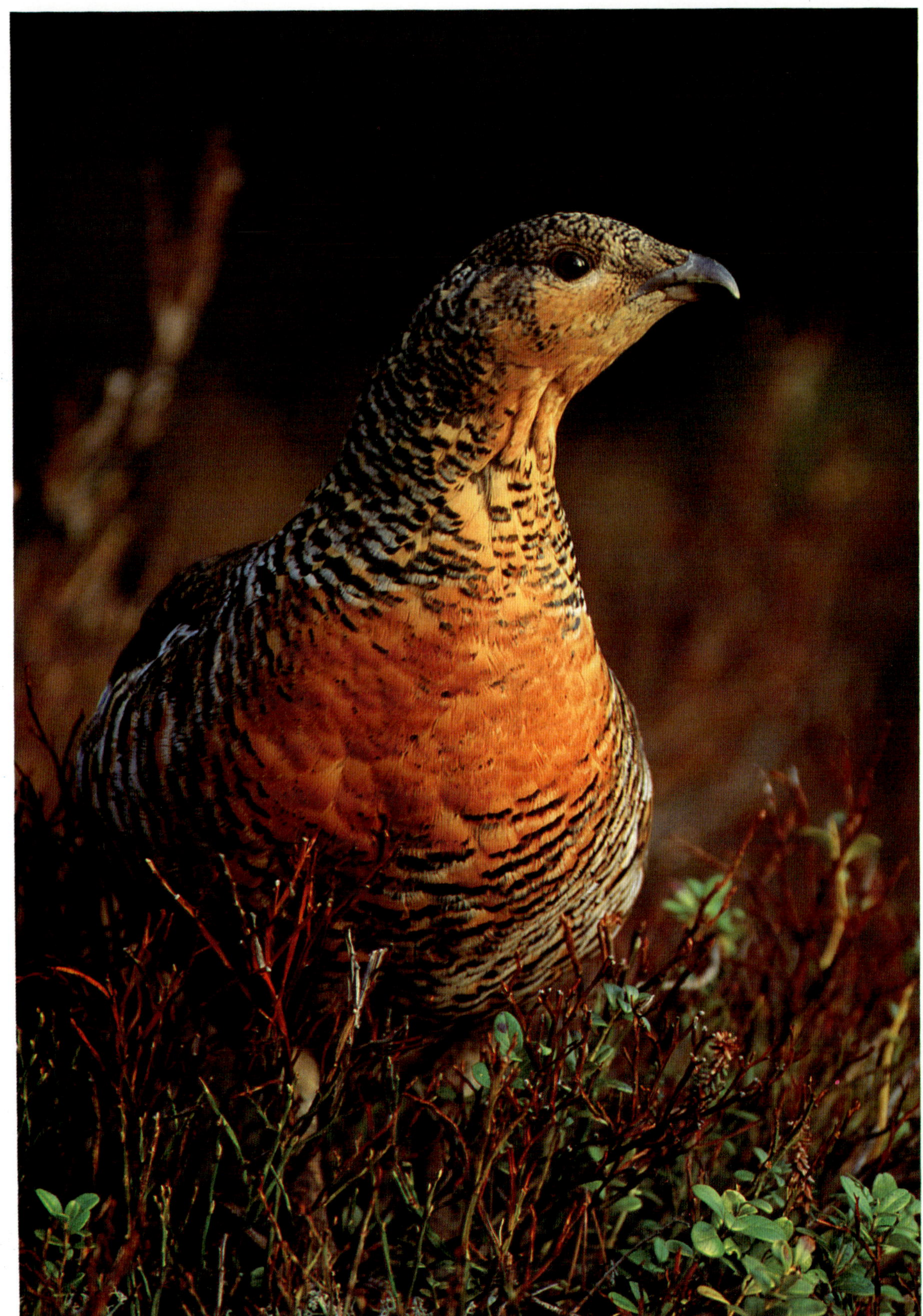

Asgeir Helgestad
Norway
RUNNER-UP

Capercaille hen at the lek

*"This picture is important to me
- it shows one of the losers of
Norwegian forestry policy. It is
the last picture I got at a
capercaille lek which I visited for
many years. When I heard the
trees there were to be felled I
pleaded with the landowner and
chief forester but to no avail.
Most of the leks I know have now
been clear felled."*

Canon T90 with 300mm lens and ×1.4
converter; tripod; f4.5 at 1/6 sec;
Fujichrome Velvia

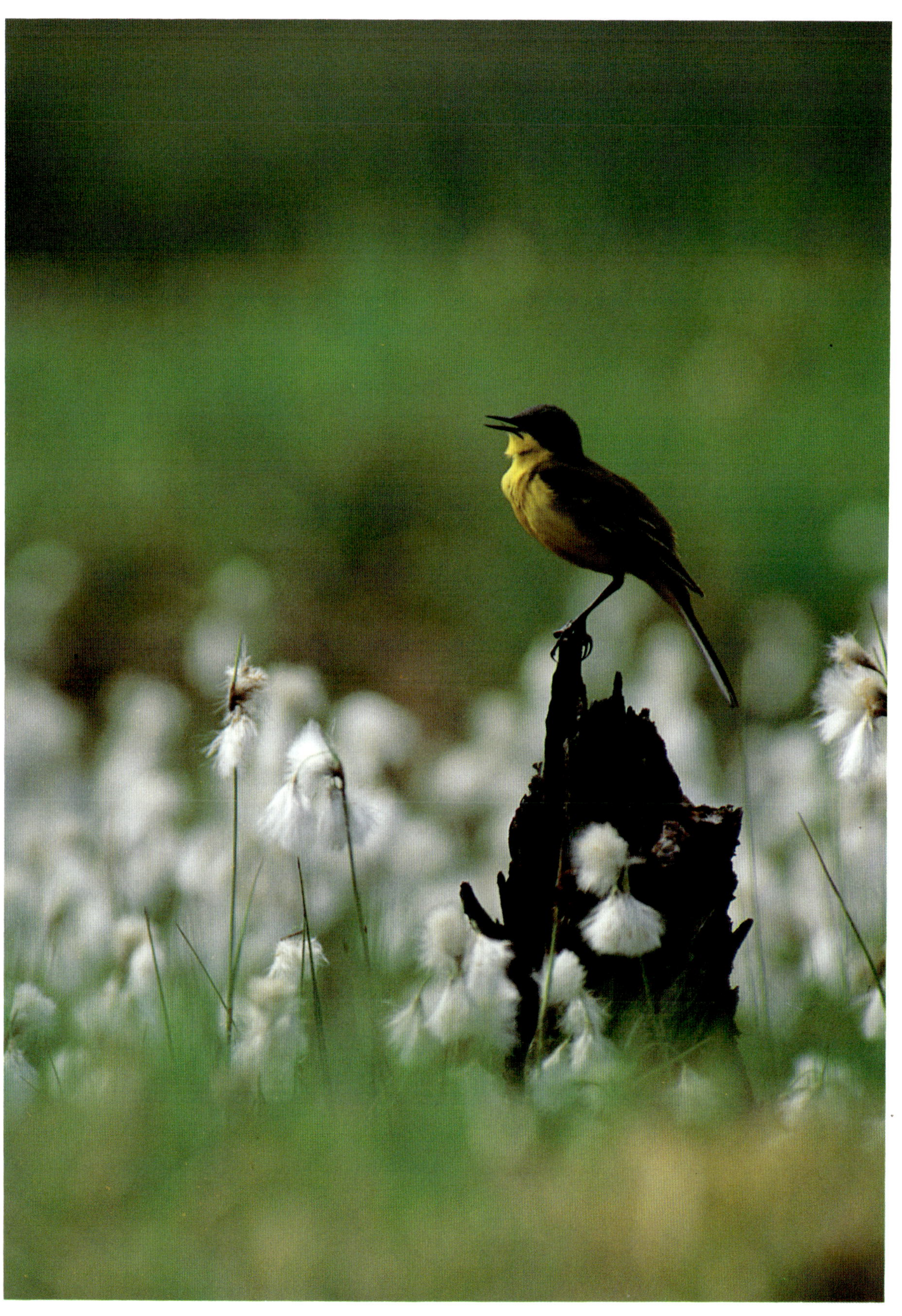

Asgeir Helgestad
Norway
RUNNER-UP

Yellow Wagtail singing

''I encountered this yellow
wagtail early one morning while
hoping to photograph deer
drinking at the lake. Returning
the next morning, I saw it again,
and was lucky to get this shot of
it singing among cotton grass.''

Canon T90 with 300mm lens and ×2
converter; tripod; f6.7 at 1/30 sec;
Fujichrome Velvia

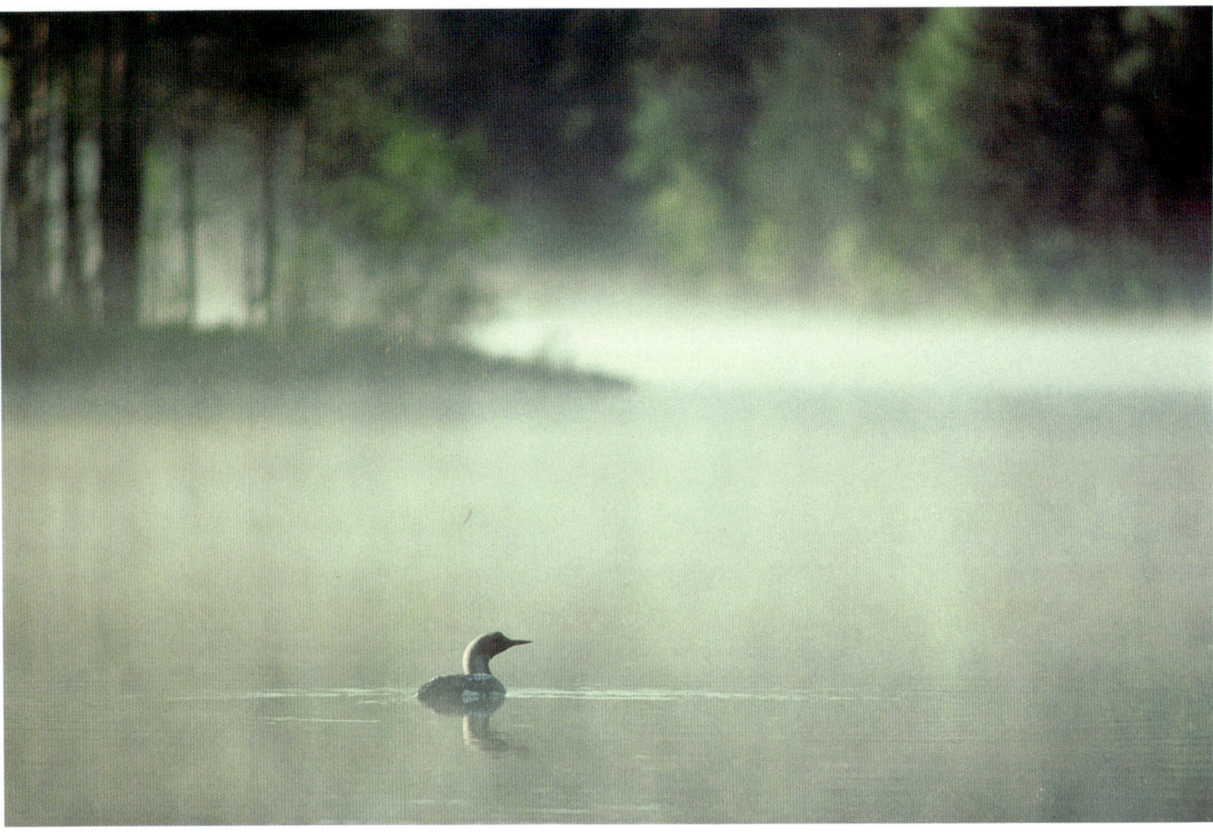

Asgeir Helgestad
Norway
RUNNER-UP

Black-throated Diver

"Usually, black-throated divers stay in the middle of the lake, and so to photograph them I made a model of one and placed it in the water. When I imitated its call, one came to see who the new rival was and started diving round the model. In the water, divers are less shy and I have often swum quite close to them."

Pentax LX with 400mm lens; tripod; Kodachrome 200

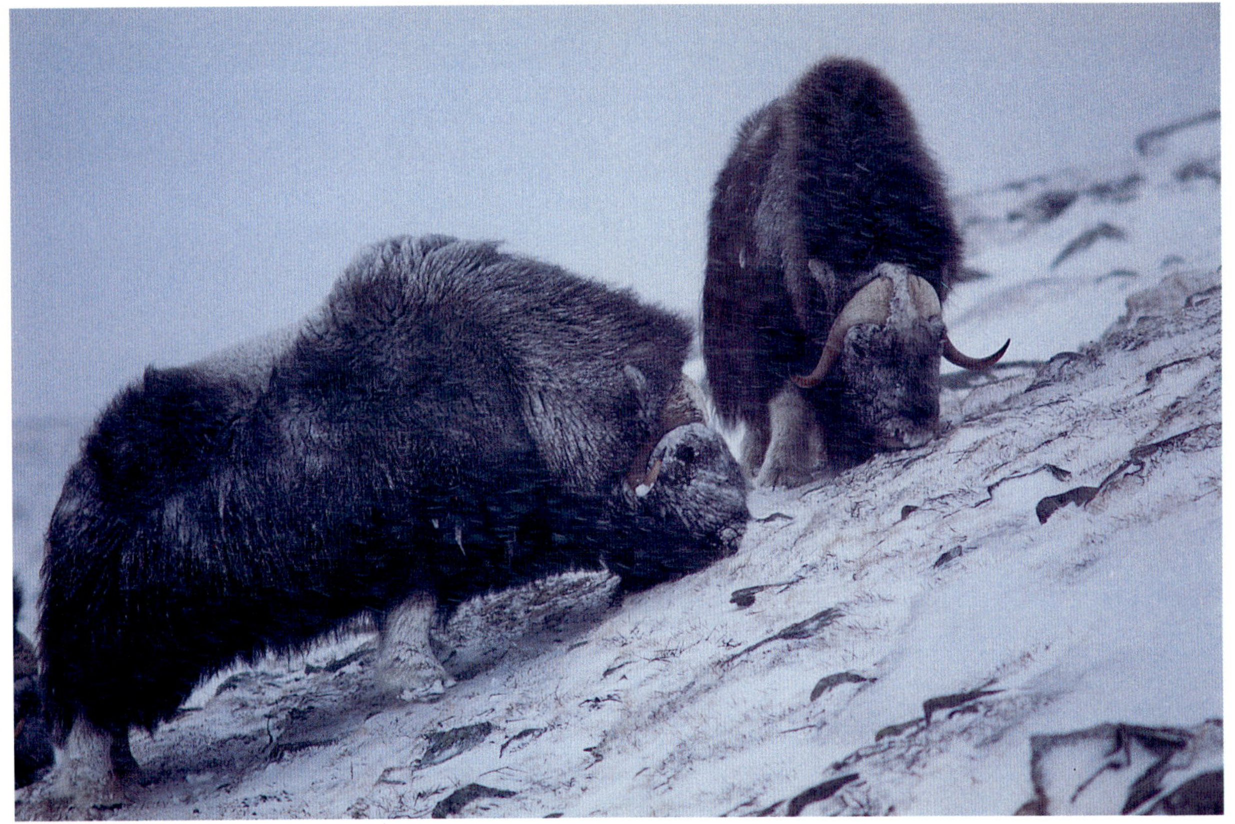

Asgeir Helgestad
Norway
RUNNER-UP

Muskoxen in snowstorm

"After photographing muskoxen in summer, I was determined to photograph them in the extreme conditions that they can live in. In February, I got what I wanted - a real snowstorm. It took three days up in the mountain, in Dovrefjell National Park (with my tent falling down in the middle of one dark night) but I eventually found the animals."

Pentax LX with 400mm lens; tripod; Kodachrome 200

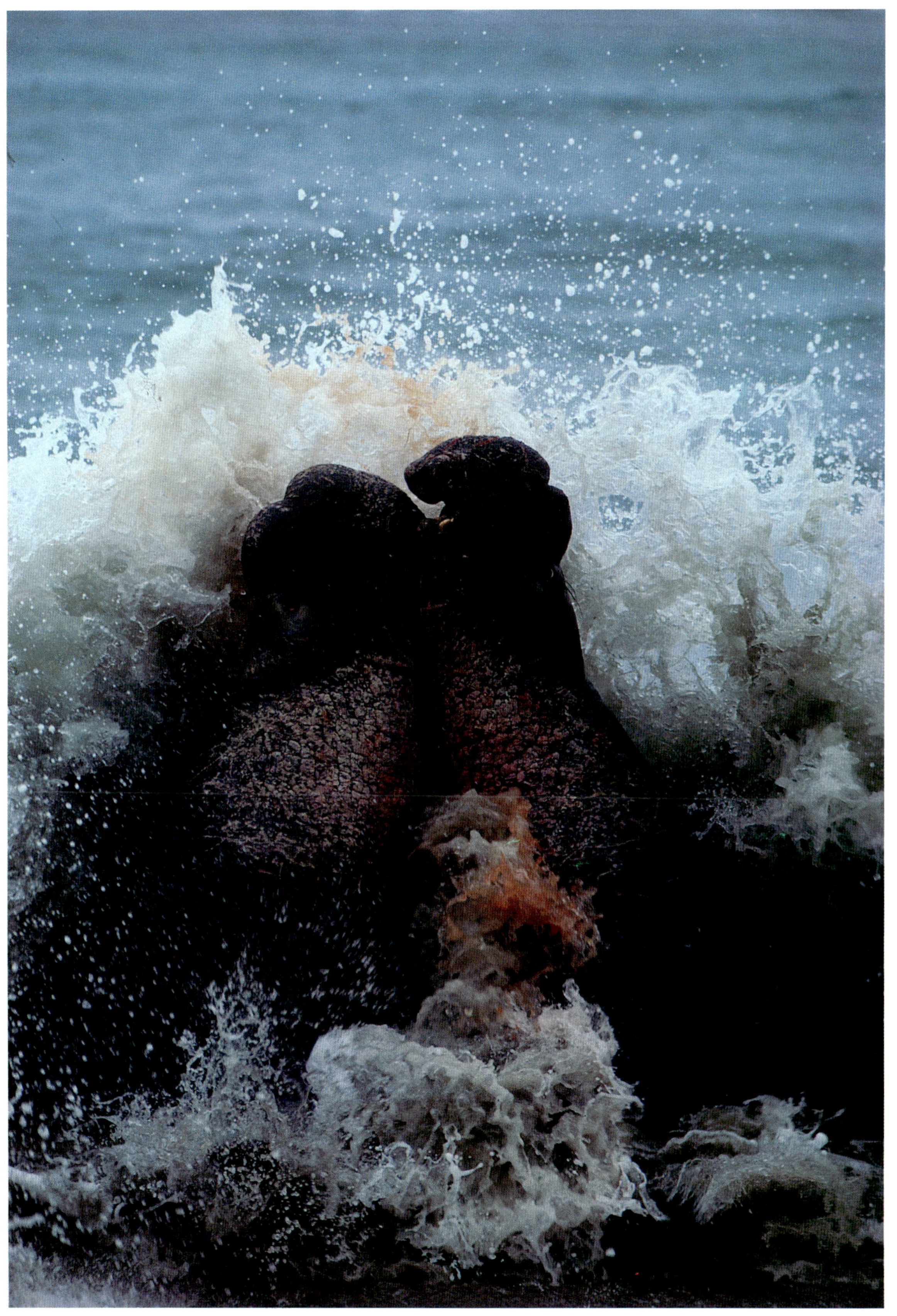

Animal Behaviour
- MAMMALS -

Photographs entered for this category are judged for their interest value as well as their aesthetic appeal and should show mammals actively doing something.

Kennan Ward
United States of America
WINNER

Elephant Seals clash
"Two elephant seal bulls battle in the surf off a beach at Ano Nuevo, California, for a harem of more than a hundred females. This picture captures the moment when the first wave hit them. The struggle between these two high ranking alpha bulls began on shore and ended in the sea. The contest was decided further out at sea, the victorious bull returning to shore to stay with the harem for the mating season."

Nikon FA with 180mm lens;
Kodachrome 64 professional

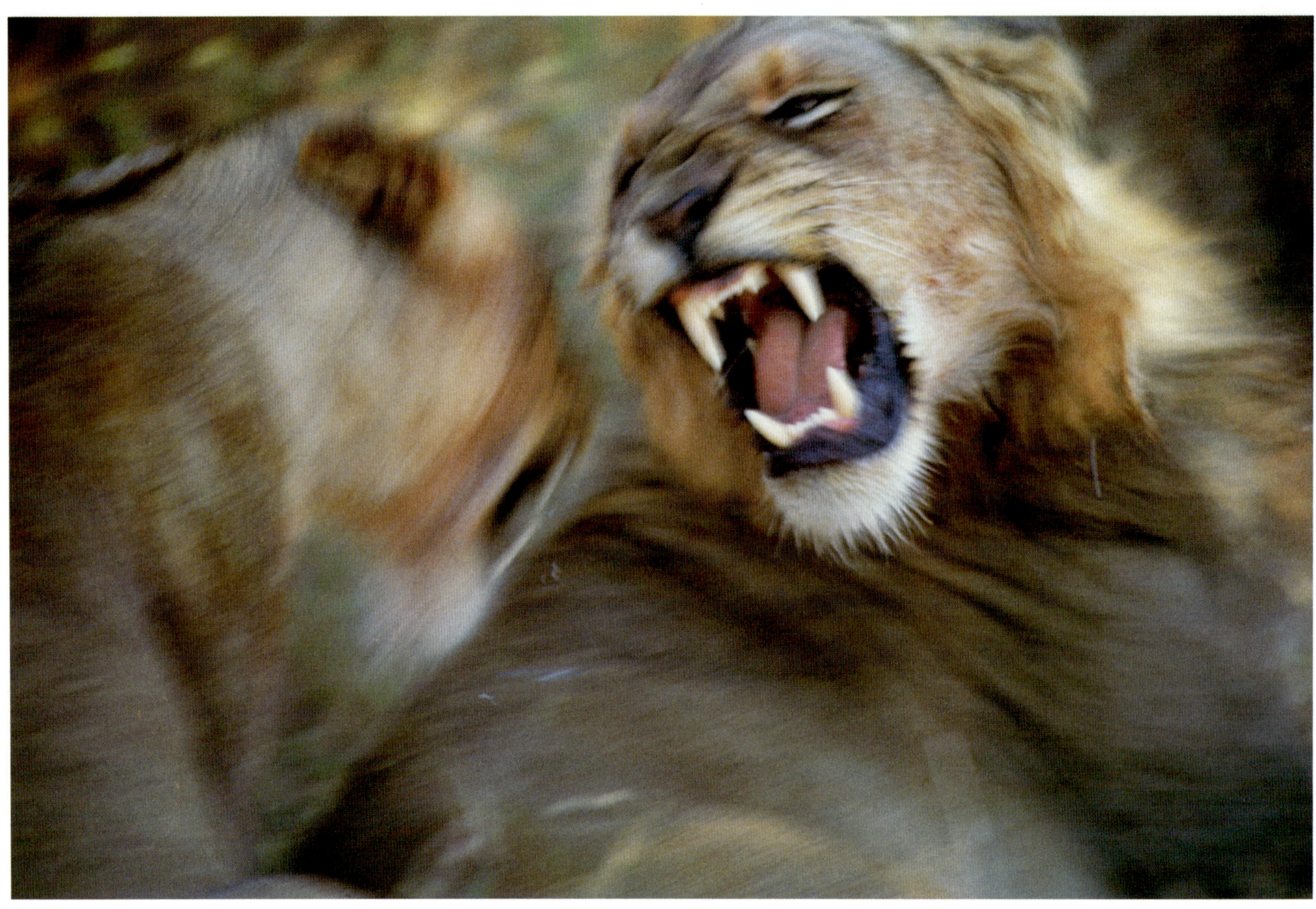

Gerald Hinde
South Africa
RUNNER-UP

Lions fighting

"Competition between members of the pride for meat at a kill can be fierce, especially if a lioness dares to approach a male too closely. On this occasion, males had killed a warthog when two lionesses, which were lying some distance away, approached and tried to knuckle in on the meat. The males took exception and aggressively turned on them."

Canon EOS 1 with 80-200mm lens; beanbag; f2.8 auto; Fujichrome 50

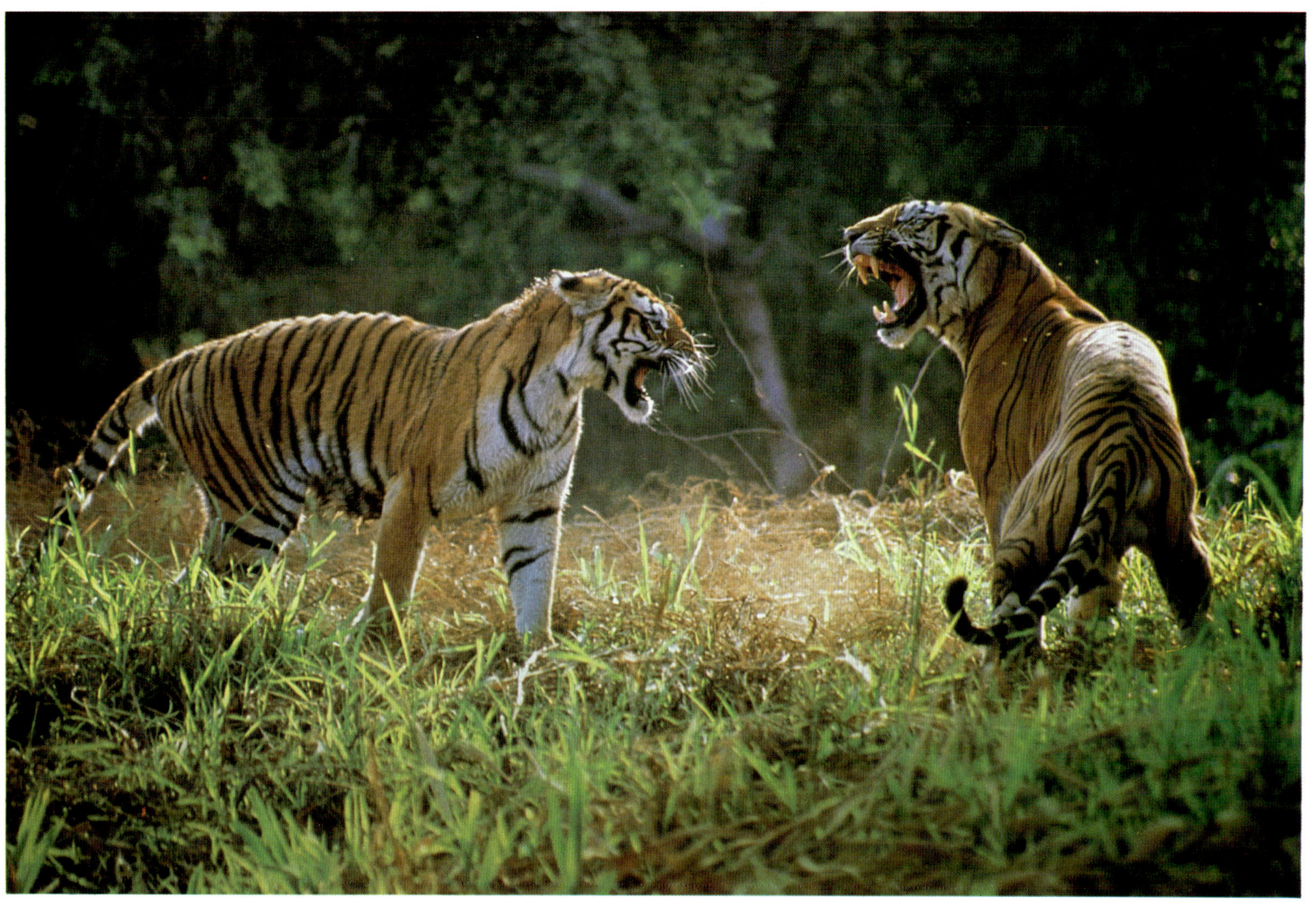

Jagdeep Rajput
India
SPECIALLY COMMENDED

Tigers courting

''Along with other visitors to the
Sariska Tiger Reserve in
Rajasthan, I visited the
waterholes.
Expecting to see herbivores, I was
surprised when these tigers
appeared. The pair snarled at
each other, presumably as part of
their courtship behaviour, then
retreated into the jungle.''

Pentax Super A with 300mm lens; f5.6
at 1/125 sec; Fujichrome 100

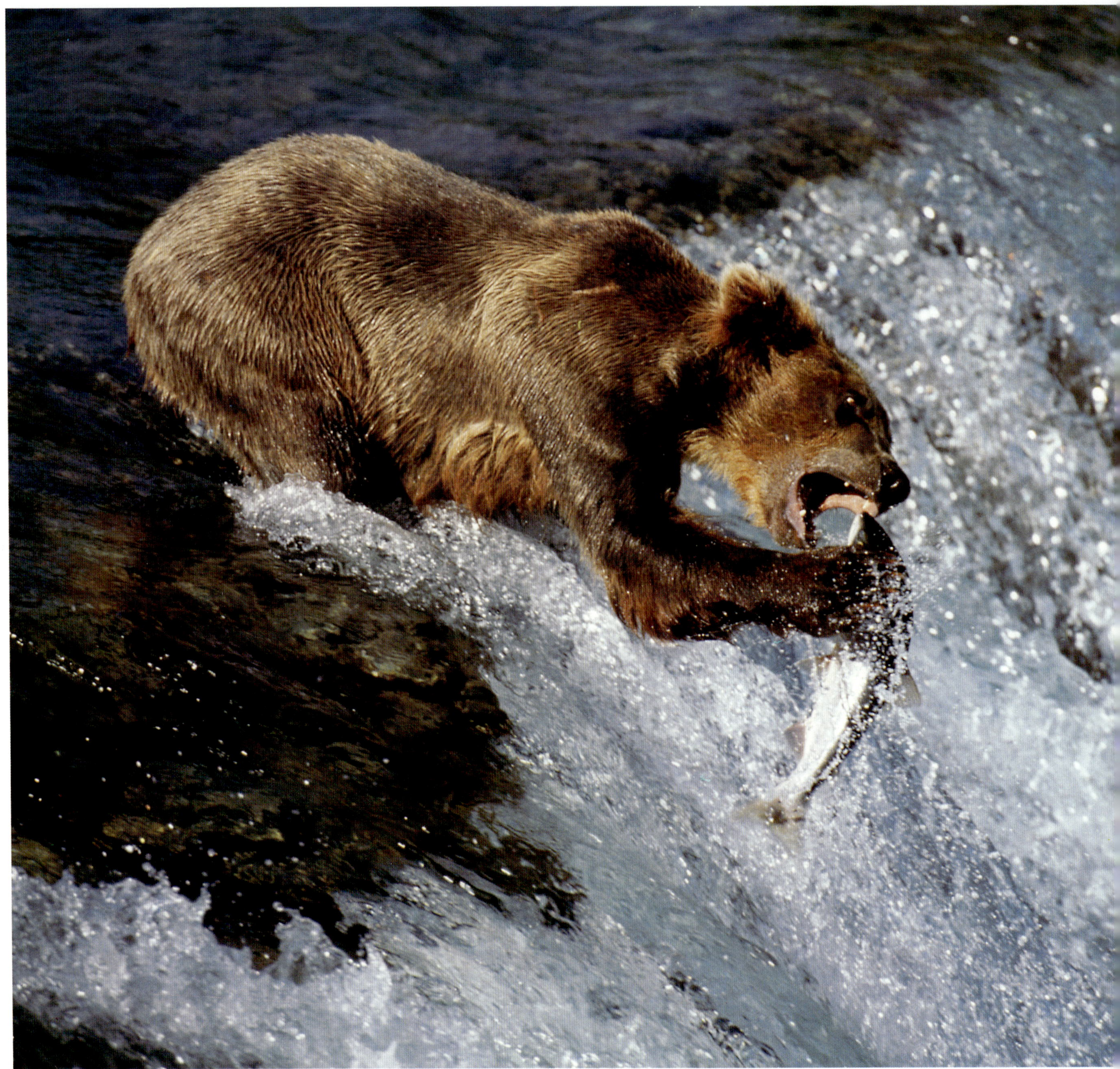

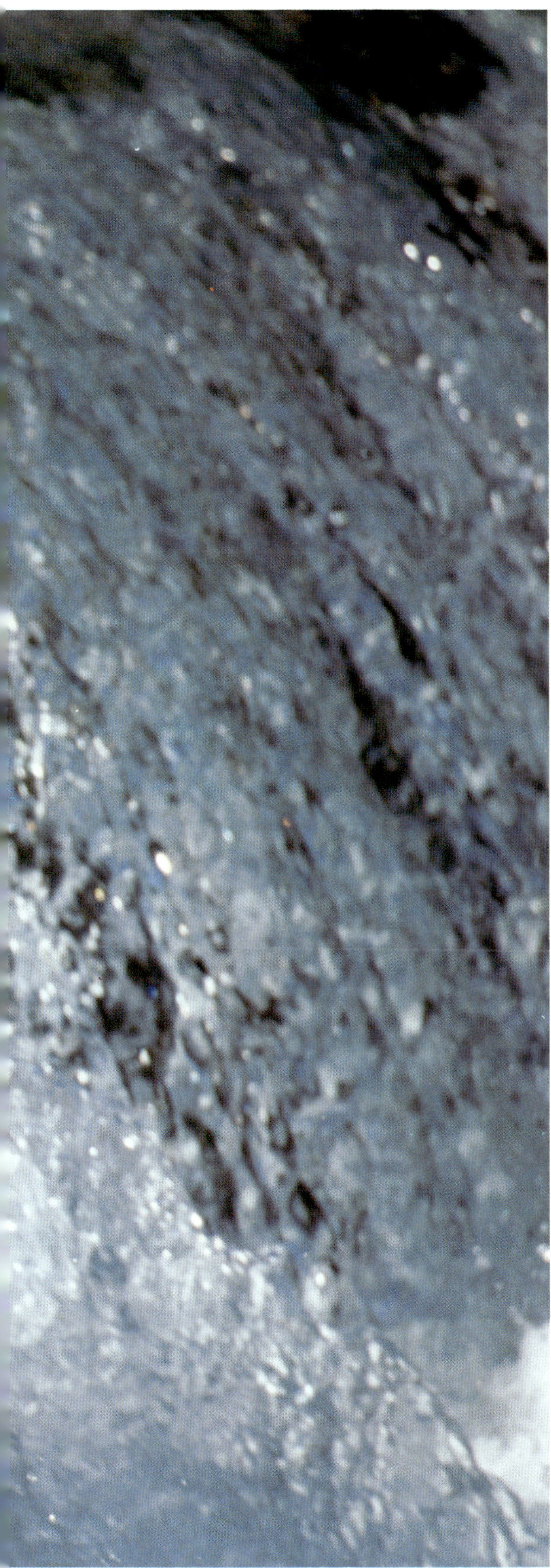

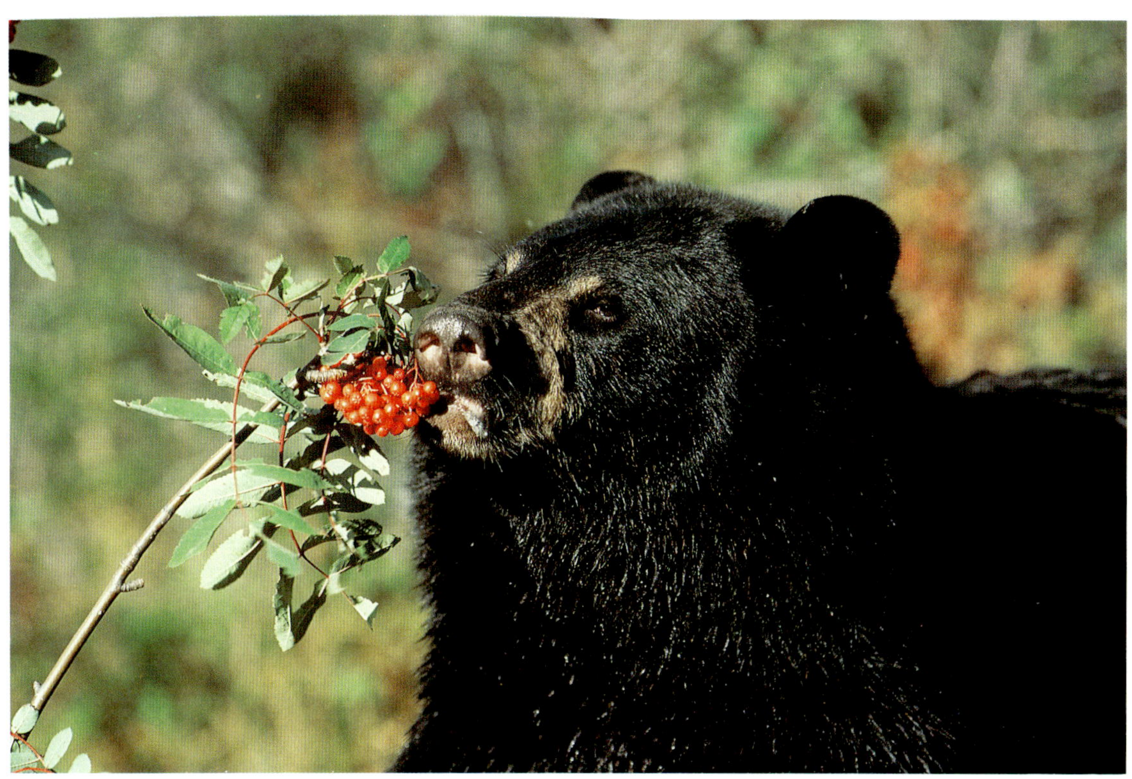

Daniel J. Cox
United States of America
HIGHLY COMMENDED

Black Bear with berries
"*The bear is gorging himself on
the ripe berries of a mountain
ash tree in the northwoods of
Minnesota. At this time
of year, he is fattening up for
hibernation during the long
cold winter.*"

Nikon F3 with 80-200mm lens; tripod;
Kodachrome 64

John Shaw
United States of America
HIGHLY COMMENDED

Fishing Brown Bear
"*The river in Katmai National
Park, Alaska, is a well-known
place to go for brown bears
during the sock-eye salmon run.
At the time I was the leader of a
tour specifically to photograph
the bears. The best light for
photography is around dinner
time but a lot of people don't like
to skip a meal, which left the
action to just a few of us.*"

Nikon F4 with 300mm lens;
Fujichrome 100

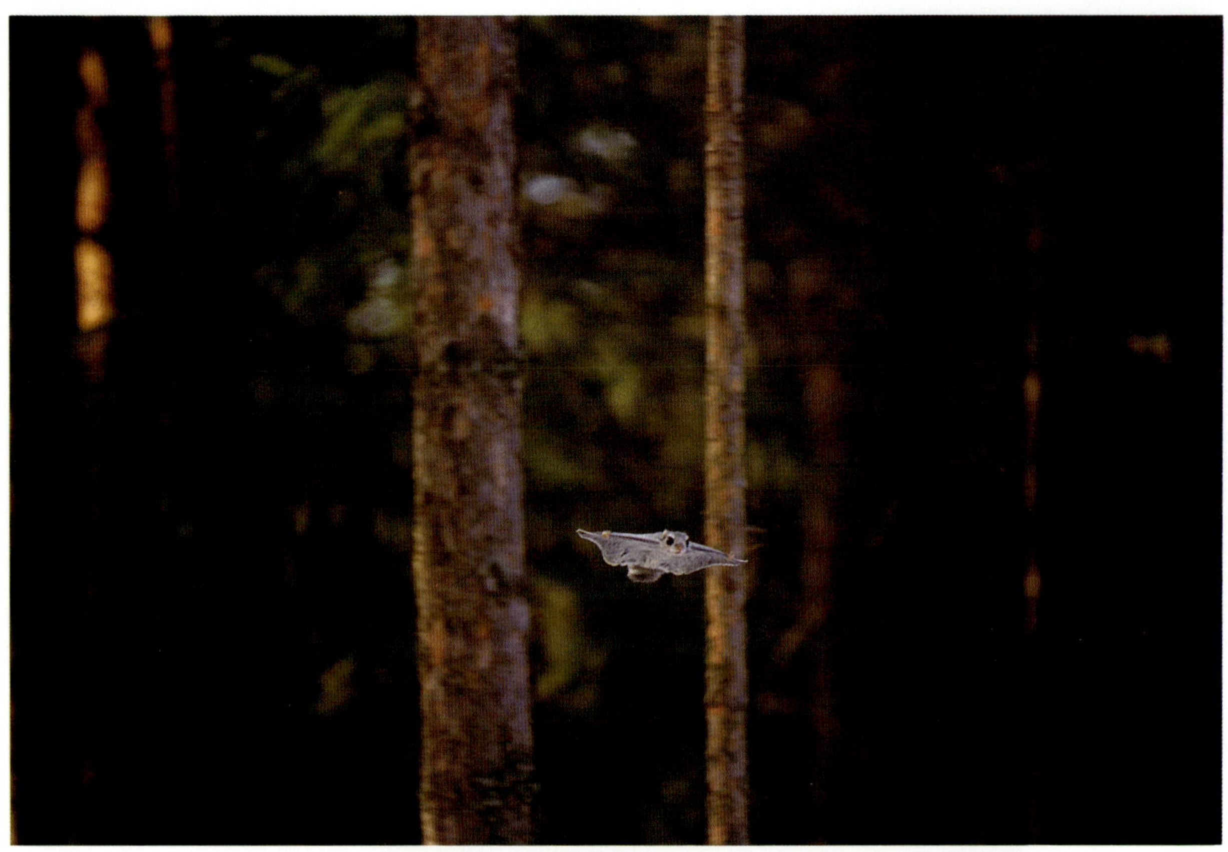

Benjam Pontinen
Finland
HIGHLY COMMENDED

Flying Squirrel

"*During their mating season, I shot pictures of five flying squirrels in the forest. Flying squirrel are exceptional among many wild animals in Finland in that they are not afraid of humans. They would silently fly past me within a metre range, which was fantastic. On Good Friday when this picture was taken, there was still snow about and the squirrel is lit by light reflected from it.*"

Canon EOS with 80-200mm zoom lens; f2.8 at 1/350 sec; Fujichrome RDP 100

Brian Lightfoot
United Kingdom
HIGHLY COMMENDED

Red Squirrel eating nut

"*A neighbour was feeding red squirrels near her house, and they had become quite tame. I put out some nuts on a tree stump in her garden and got in position with the camera focused. This squirrel came for the nut, and I managed to take its picture before it scampered off.*"

Nikon F801 with 500mm lens and x1.4 converter; tripod; Kodachrome 200

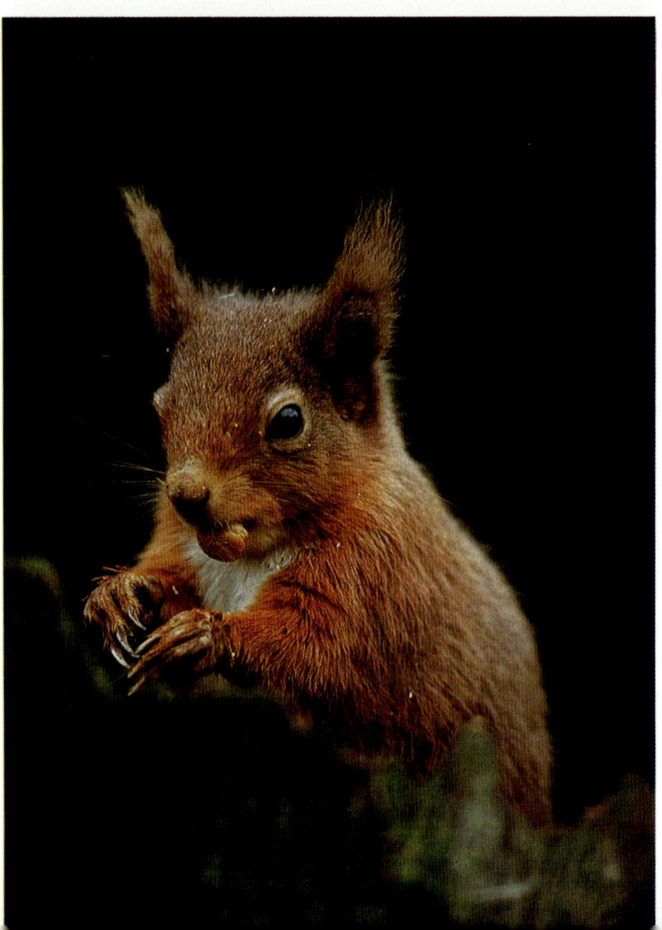

Helmut Pum
Austria
HIGHLY COMMENDED

Hares racing

*''In March, in this part of Austria, the mating season for hares is at its height.
It's an energetic time of fighting and chasing - activity which is becoming harder to photograph as the hares become rarer through industrialisation and increased road traffic.''*

Canon EOS 10 with 300mm lens; f2.8 at 1/125 sec; Fujichrome Velvia

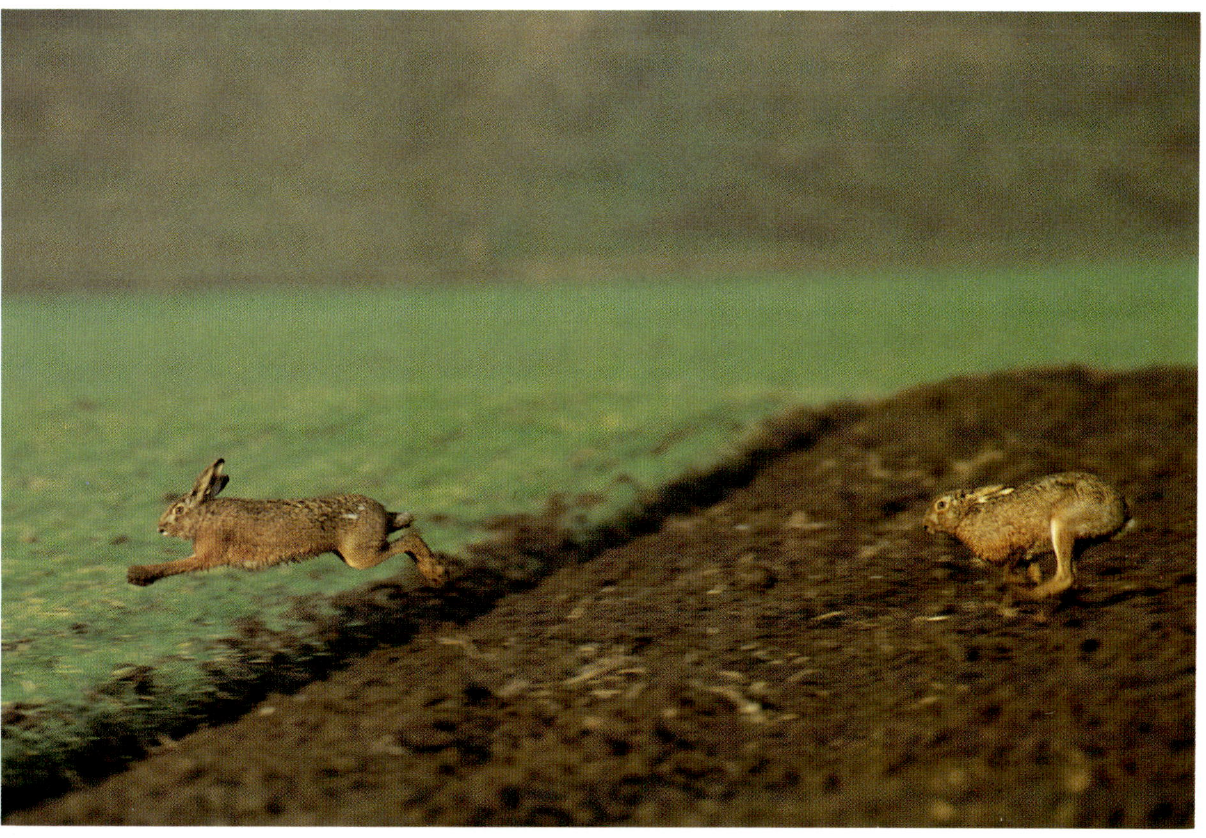

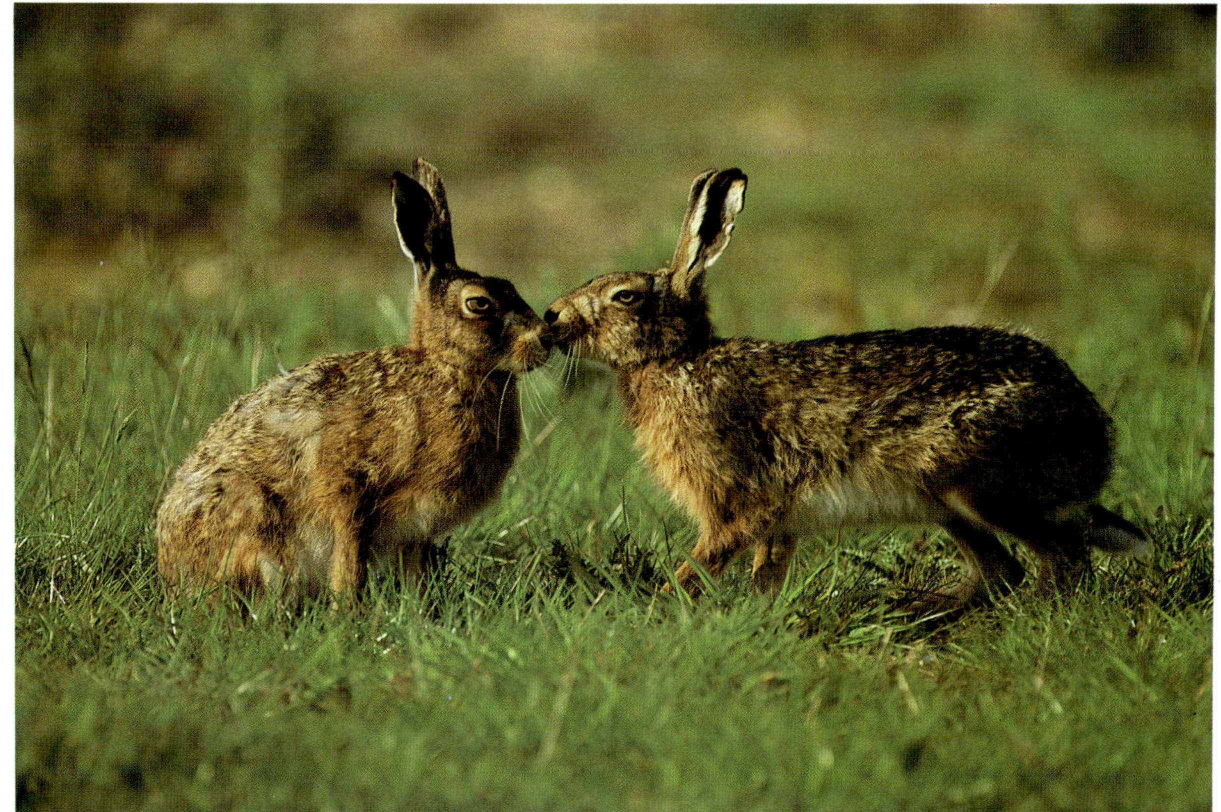

Ernie Janes
United Kingdom
HIGHLY COMMENDED

Brown Hares

''I have been watching a group of hares for more than a year using my car as a hide. I can recognise them as individuals, and they seem to have learnt that I am no threat to them. On this occasion, I had been tracking one particular hare through the viewfinder of my camera for sometime, when another appeared and ran right up to it and touched noses.''

Canon T90 with 500mm lens; beanbag; motordive; f4.5 at 1/180 sec; Kodachrome 64

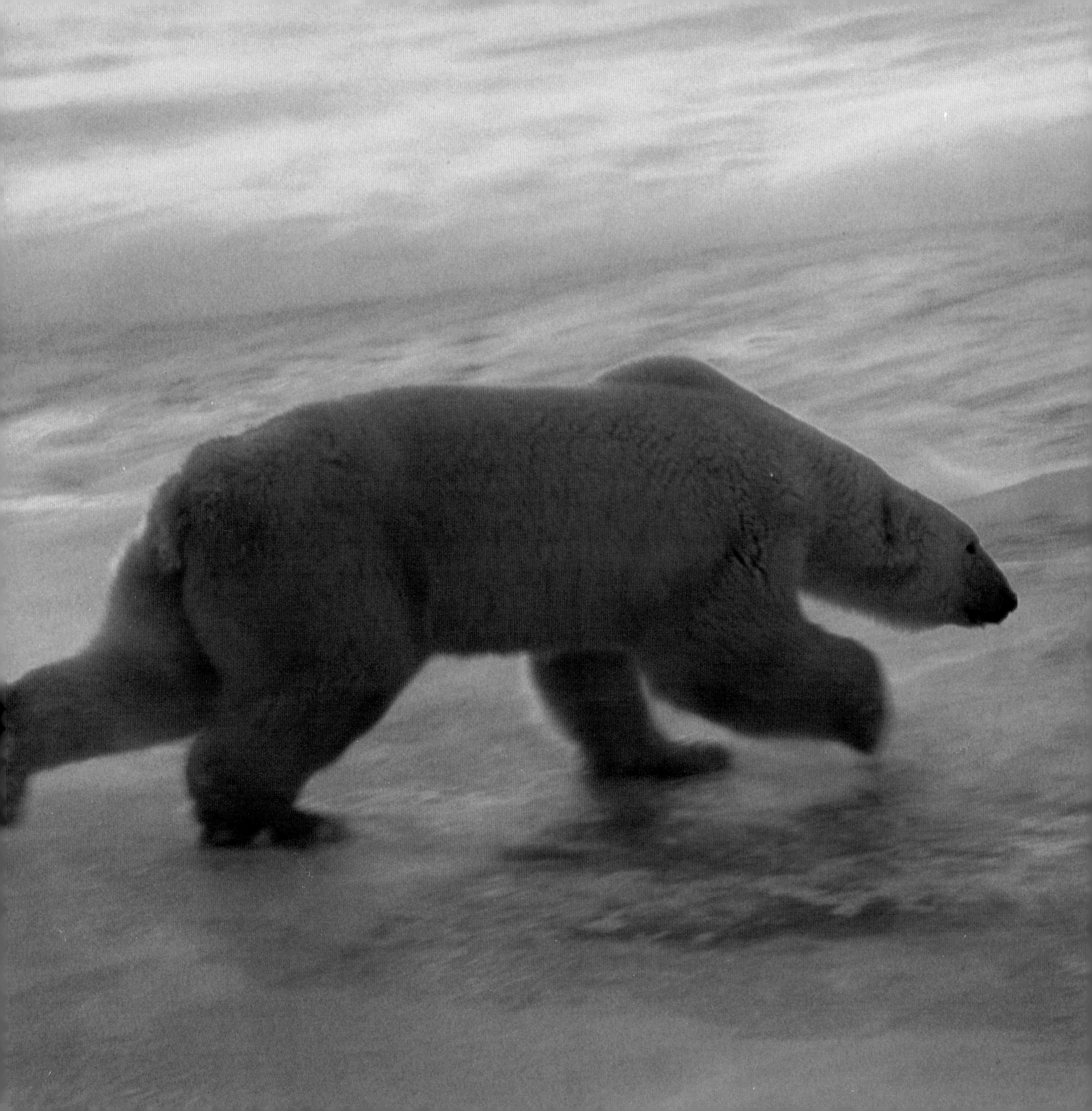

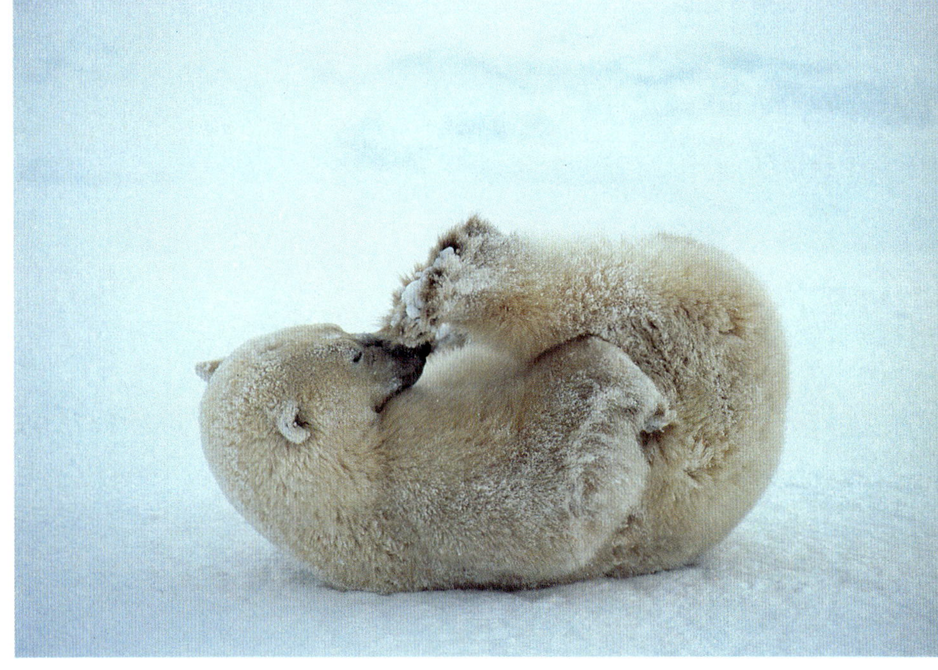

Daniel J Cox
United States of America
HIGHLY COMMENDED

Polar Bear play

"I was photographing polar bears at Hudson Bay in November, when I came across this young bear rolling and playing in the snow."

Nikon F4 with 300mm lens; Kodachrome 64

Cherry Alexander
United Kingdom
HIGHLY COMMENDED

Polar Bear

"Most years I try to spend a week or so on Hudson Bay to photograph the polar bears which gather there, waiting for the bay to freeze so that they can venture out on the ice to hunt seals. On this cold windy day, as the sun was setting, an arctic fox ventured close enough to this bear to provoke him into giving chase for a short distance."

Canon T90 with 300mm lens; beanbag; Kodachrome 64

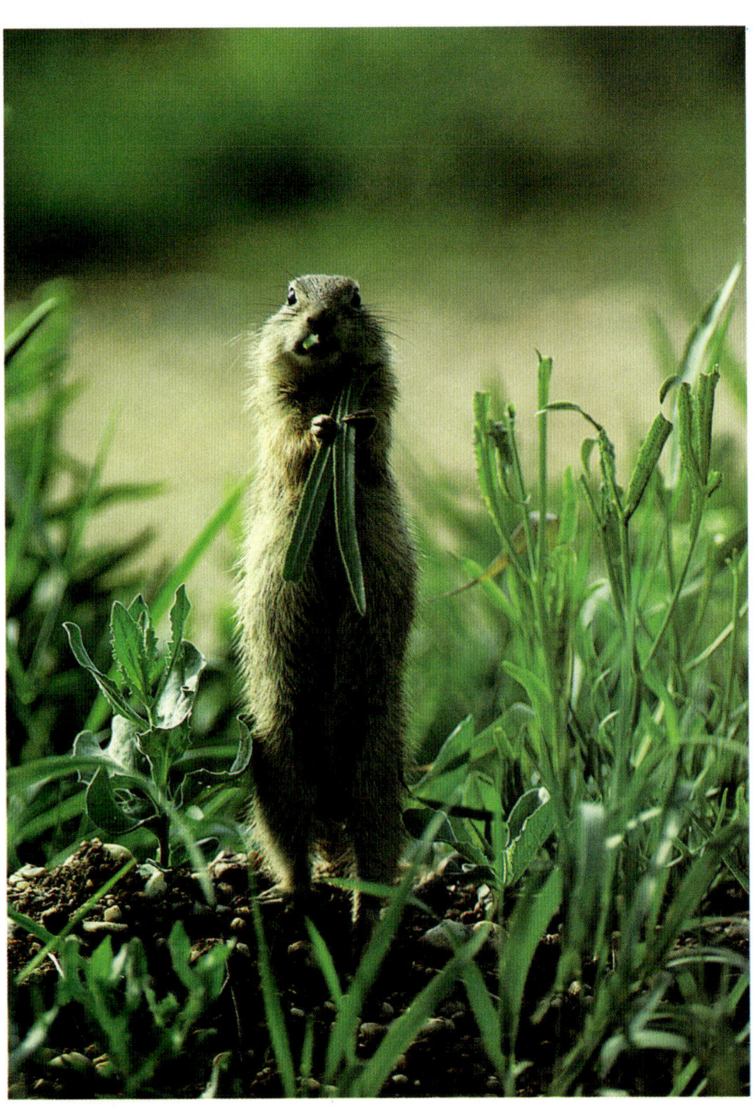

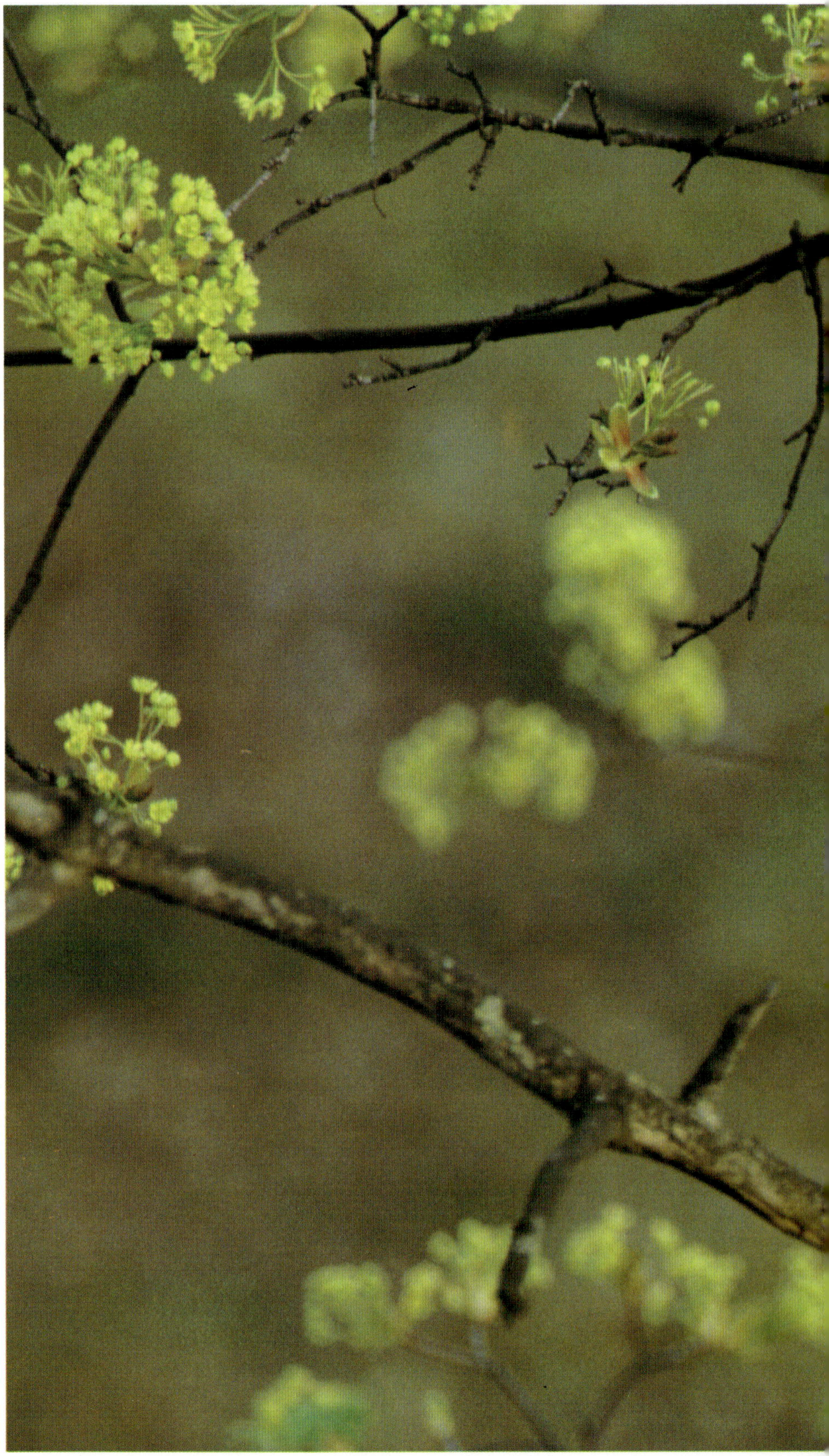

Dietmar Nill
Germany
HIGHLY COMMENDED

Alpine Marmot
*"This photo was a chance shot
taken from my car in the
Neusiedler Sec, in Austria."*

Nikon F4s with 500mm lens;
Kodachrome 64

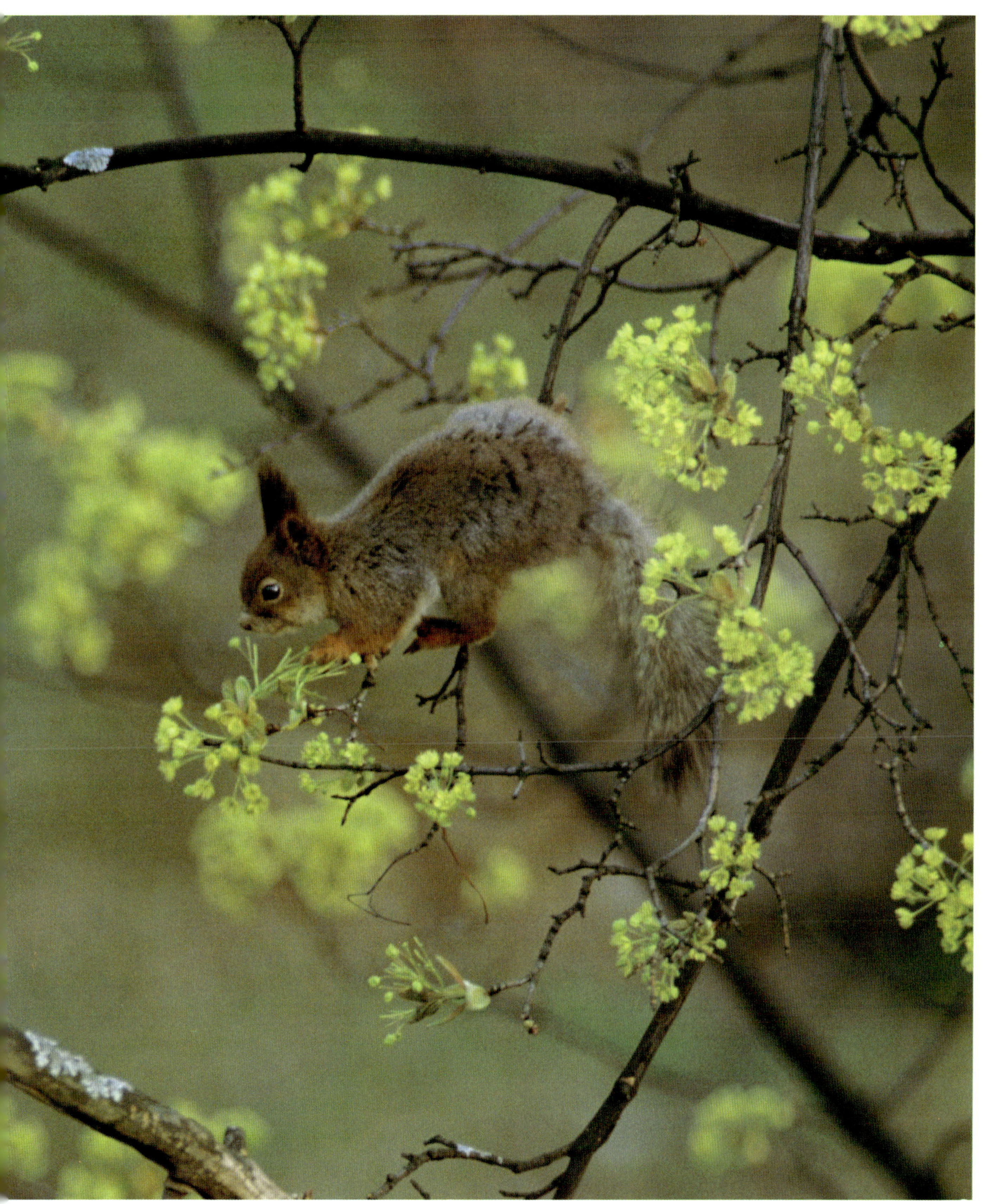

Eero Venhola
Finland
HIGHLY COMMENDED

Foraging Squirrel
"One evening in May, I followed this little fellow for about two hours as it fed on maple shoots. When he finally settled in a good position to be photographed, the branch was swinging. Fortunately there was a short still moment and I got this one sharp picture."

Canon T90 with 80-200mm lens; tripod; f4 at 1/8 sec; Agfa CT100

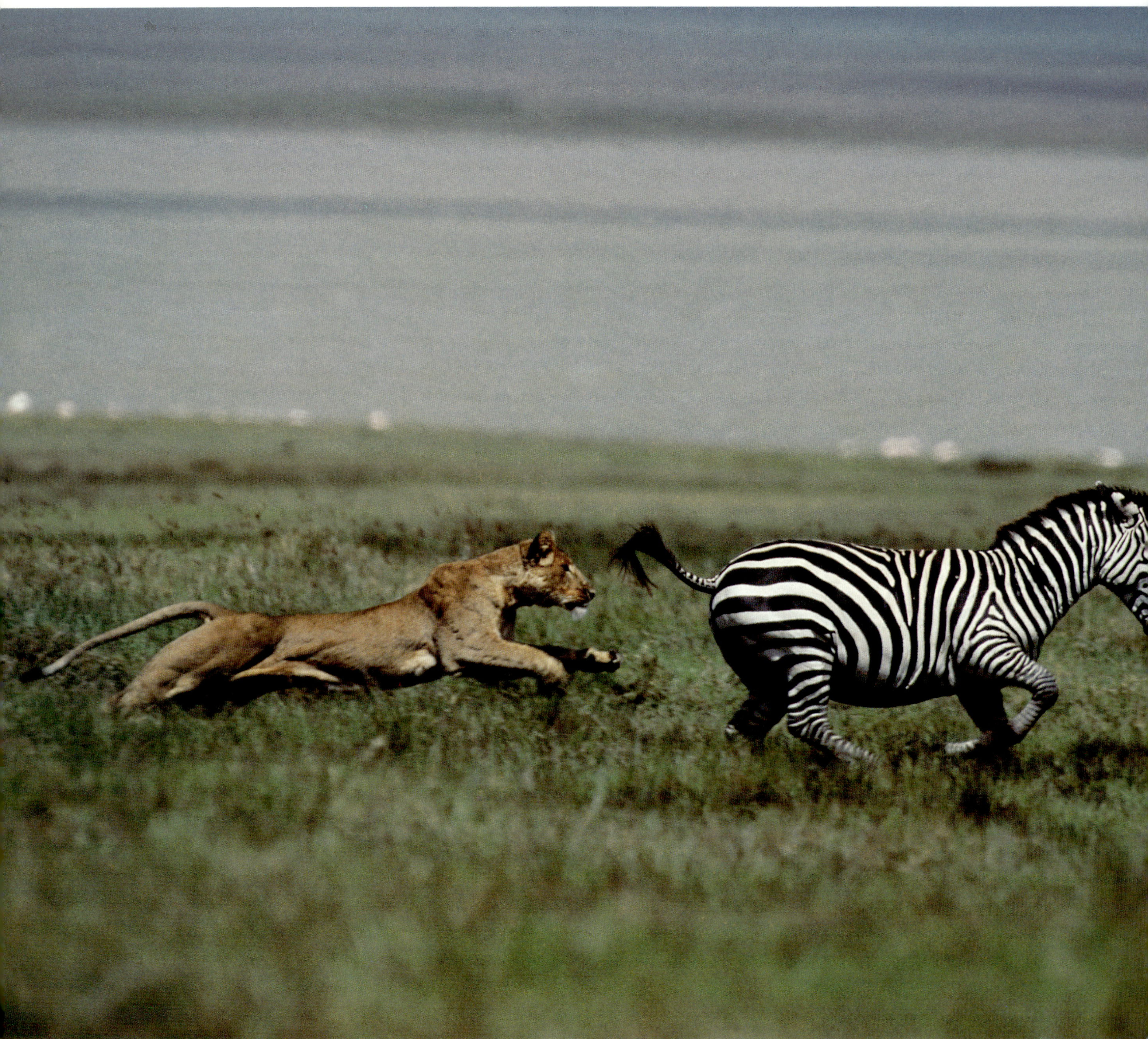

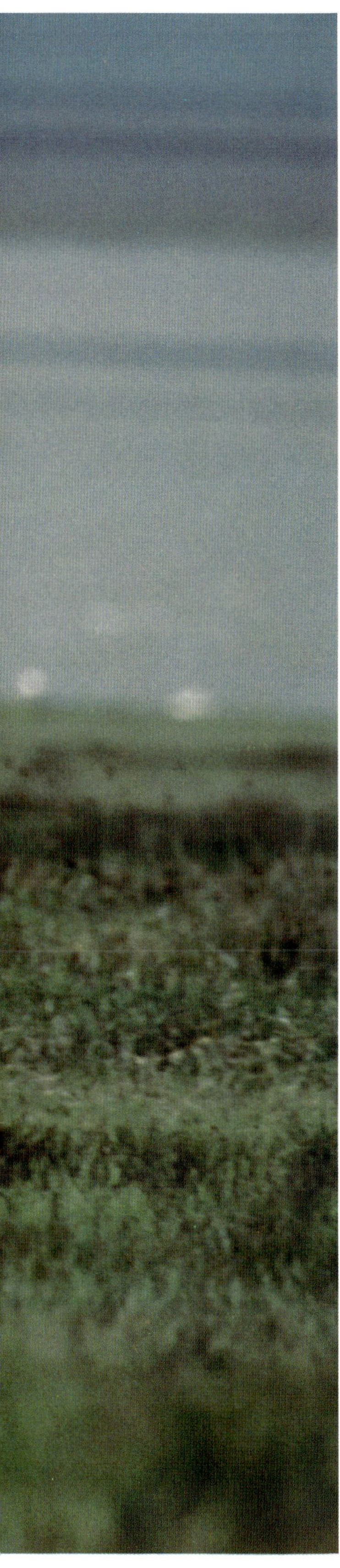

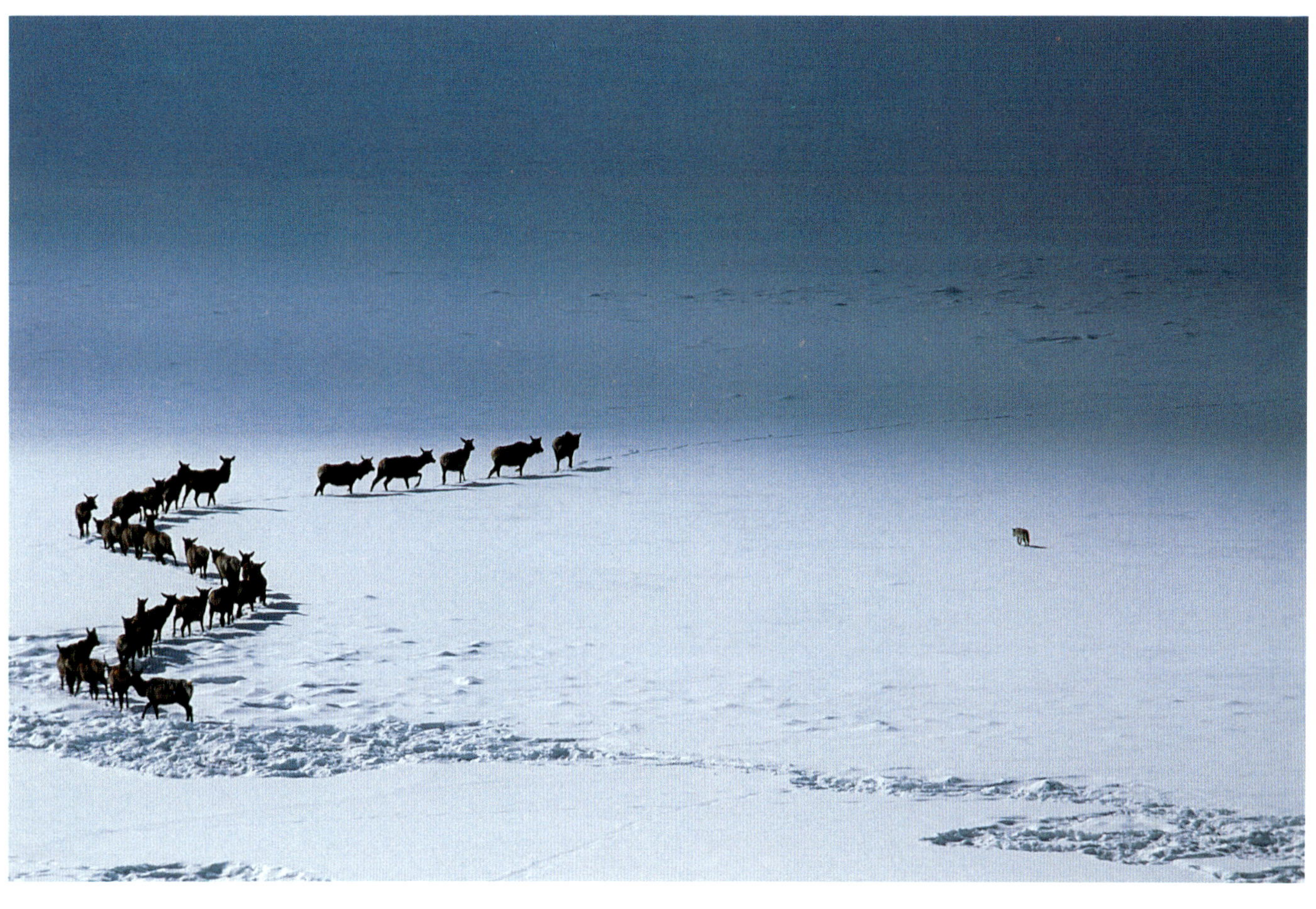

Tom Murphy
United States of America
HIGHLY COMMENDED

Coyote following Elk

*"This herd of elk had spent
the night feeding in the
Lamar Valley, Yellowstone
National Park, pawing the snow
away from the grass. Coyotes
hang around the edges of bison
and elk herds waiting to pounce
on panic-striken mice disturbed
by the grazing animals. Here,
the herd is moving on to new
grazing and a coyote is going
with them."*

Nikon F with 400mm lens; f5.6 at 1/125
sec; Kodachrome 64

Samantha Purdy
United Kingdom
HIGHLY COMMENDED

Lioness hunting Zebra

*"I spent several hours watching
a lioness stalking a herd of zebra
as they headed for a water hole.
She hid in the long grass until
one zebra was almost on her and
then suddenly charged, but the
zebra swerved and just made
its escape."*

Canon EOS1 with 600mm lens; camera
mount on car door; f5.6 at 1/500 sec.
Kodachrome 64

Animal Behaviour

- BIRDS -

Photographs entered in this category are judged for their interest value as well as their aesthetic appeal and should show birds actively doing something.

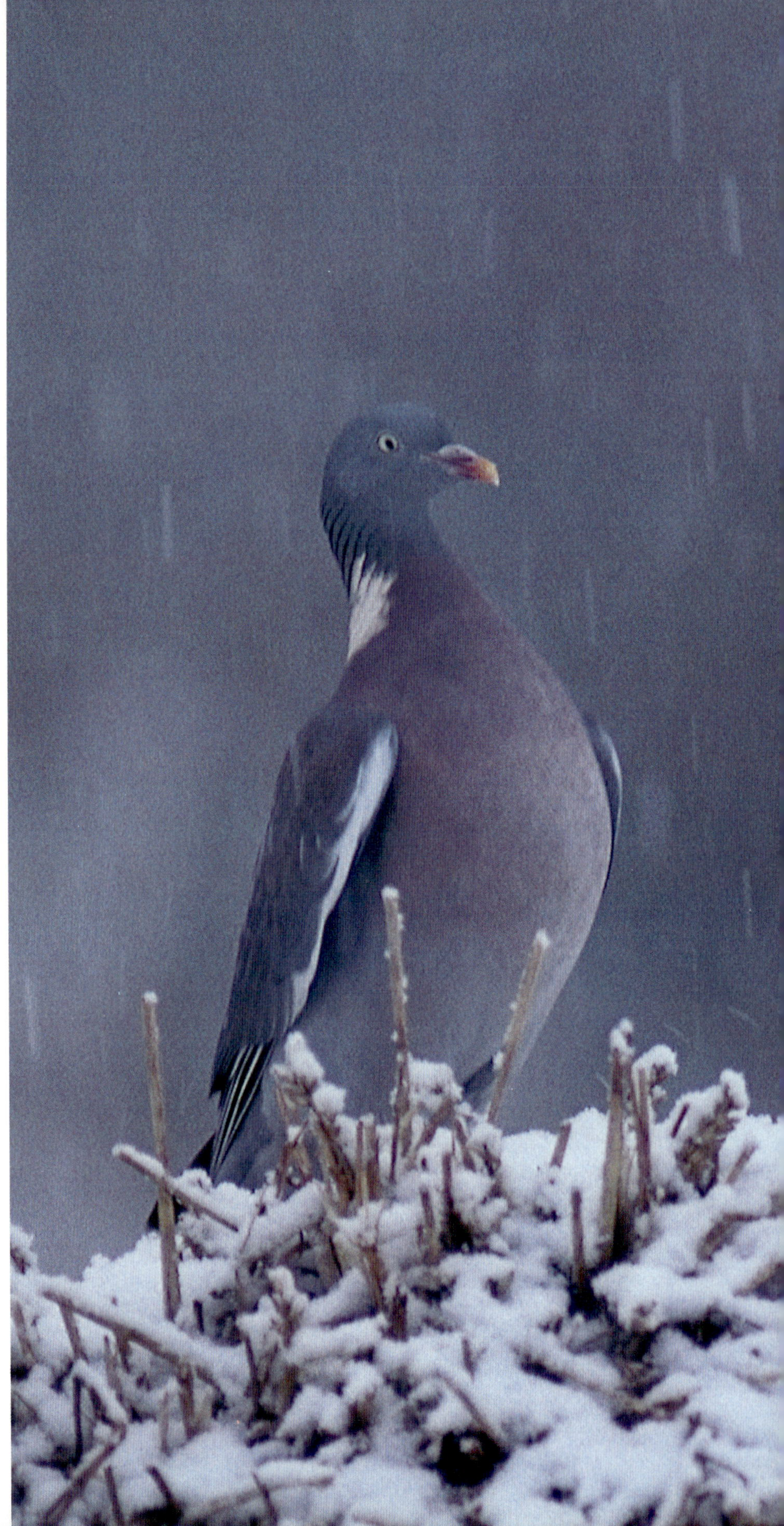

Niall Benvie
United Kingdom
WINNER

Woodpigeons in snow

"Here, two birds are establishing a pecking order on top of a burst straw bale, some 10 yards away from my hide. The picture was taken on one of only five snowy days last winter, and is typical of the sort of marginal conditions I like to work in. More often than not the pictures do not work, but when they do, they usually make very evocative images."

Nikon FM2 with 300mm lens and x1.4 converter; f4 at 1/60 sec; Kodachrome 200

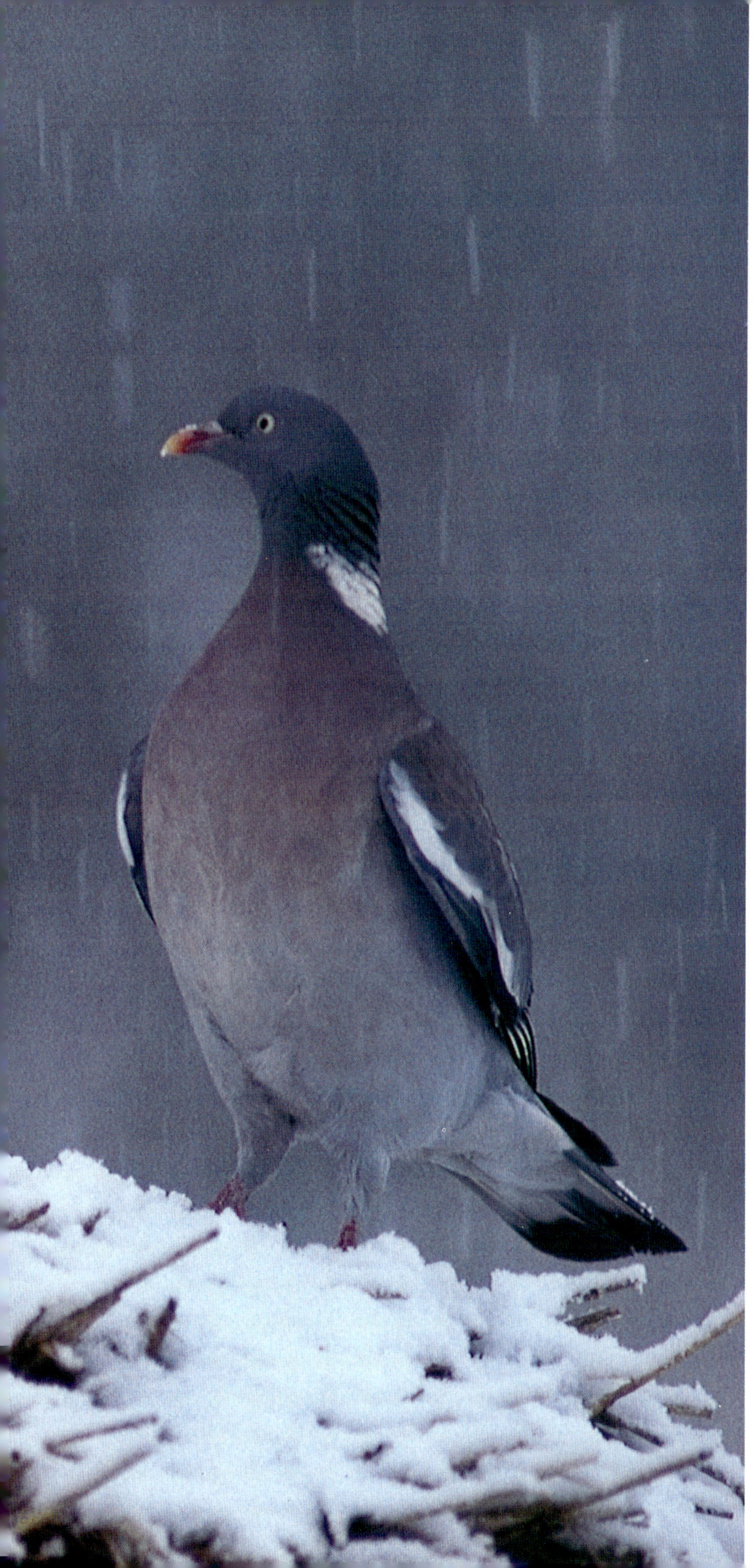

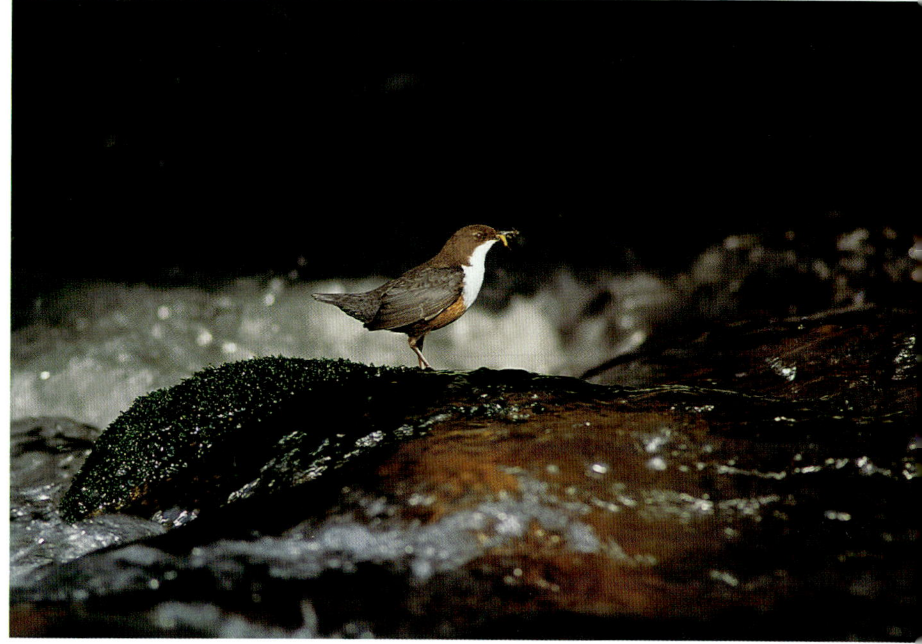

Neil McIntyre
United Kingdom
RUNNER-UP

Dipper

*"The dipper was feeding young
and used this stone on the way to
its nest site under a bridge.
The bridge cast a very dark
shadow and only this stone,
covered with a beautiful green
moss, was suitable to catch the
bird on. I introduced my hide
and waited; the light was perfect
only between five and six o'clock,
and during this time, the dipper
only landed on this stone
about twice."*

Canon T90 with 400mm lens; tripod;
hide; f5.6 at 1/60 sec; Fujichrome Velvia

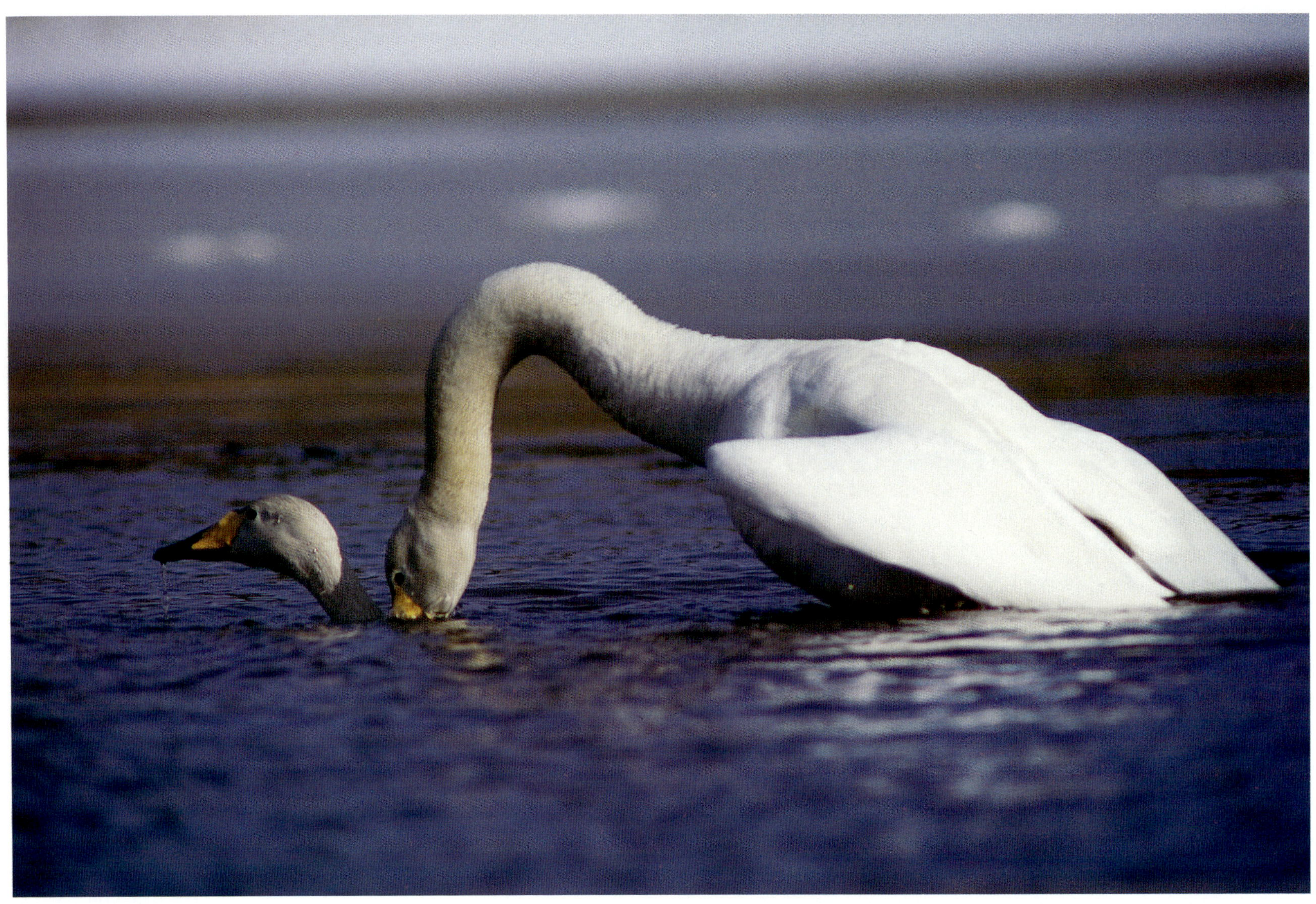

Keijo Penttinen

Finland

HIGHLY COMMENDED

Swans mating

"I took this photograph from a camouflaged hut I built at the edge of the ice cover on the River Sahi, in Joutsa, Central Finland. After several hours spent feeding and preening, the swans started to get amorous. Finally, I was able to get just a few photographs of the mating."

Contax 167 MT with 300mm lens; f5.6 at 1/125 sec; Fujichrome 50

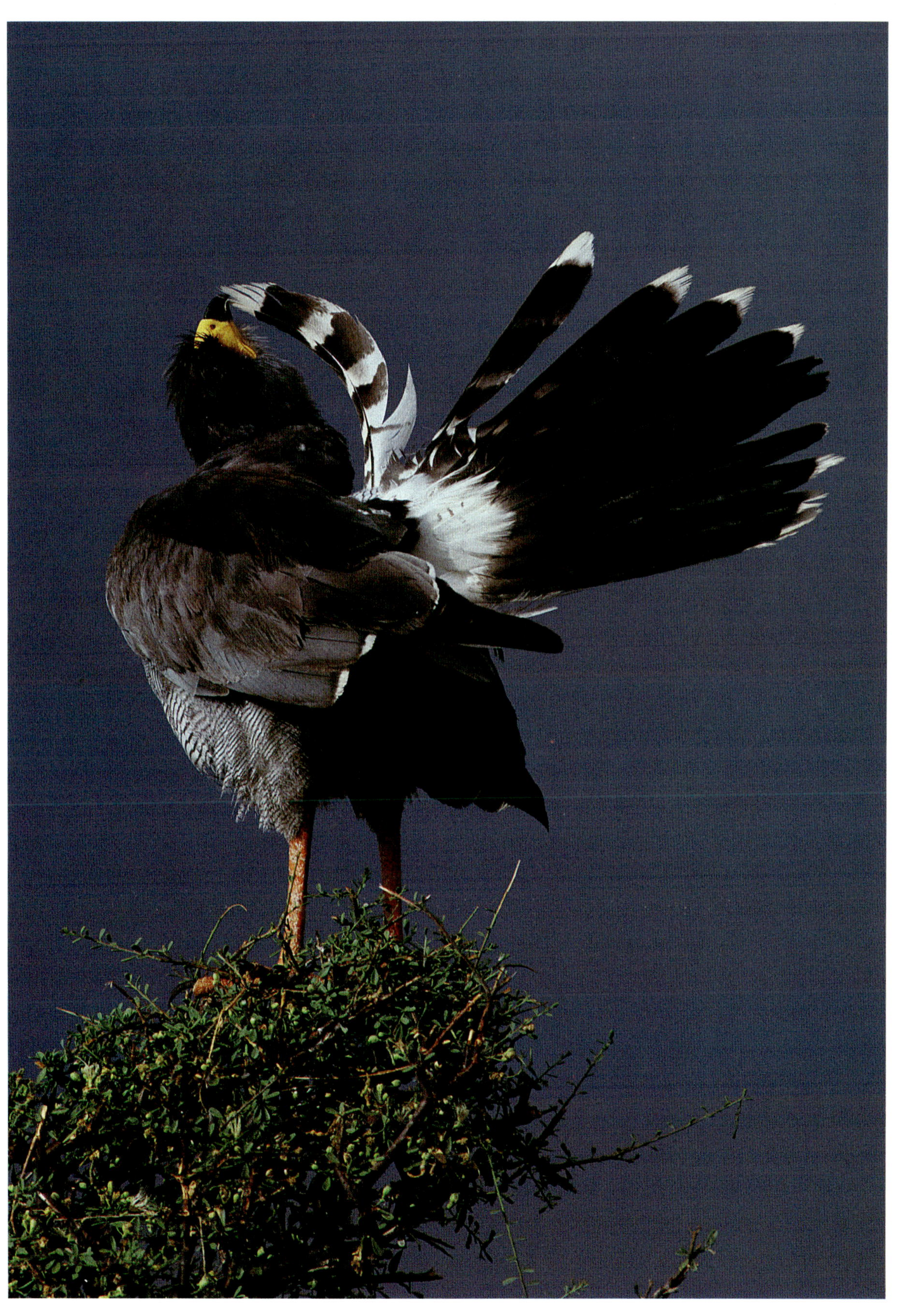

Karl Ammann
Switzerland
HIGHLY COMMENDED

Goshawk preening

''After a thunderstorm in
Samburu, Kenya, this pale, wet
goshawk used the occasion for a
thorough cleaning exercise. I saw
the bird pull it's tail feathers
through its beak, and waited for
the next time it would do this.
When I took the shot I knew it
would be the best of the lot.''

Nikon F4 with 800mm lens; f5.6 at 1/250
sec; Kodachrome 200

Markku K Aikioniemi
Finland
HIGHLY COMMENDED

Siberian Tit

*"Last winter I set up a feeding
station close to my garden, and
soon the birds got used to my
daily photographic visits. This
picture of a Siberian tit shows
typical behaviour - the bird sings
its short calls from a visible
vantage point and then suddenly
flies off to another one."*

Pentax Super A with 300mm lens;
tripod; f4 at 1/125 sec;
Fujichrome Velvia

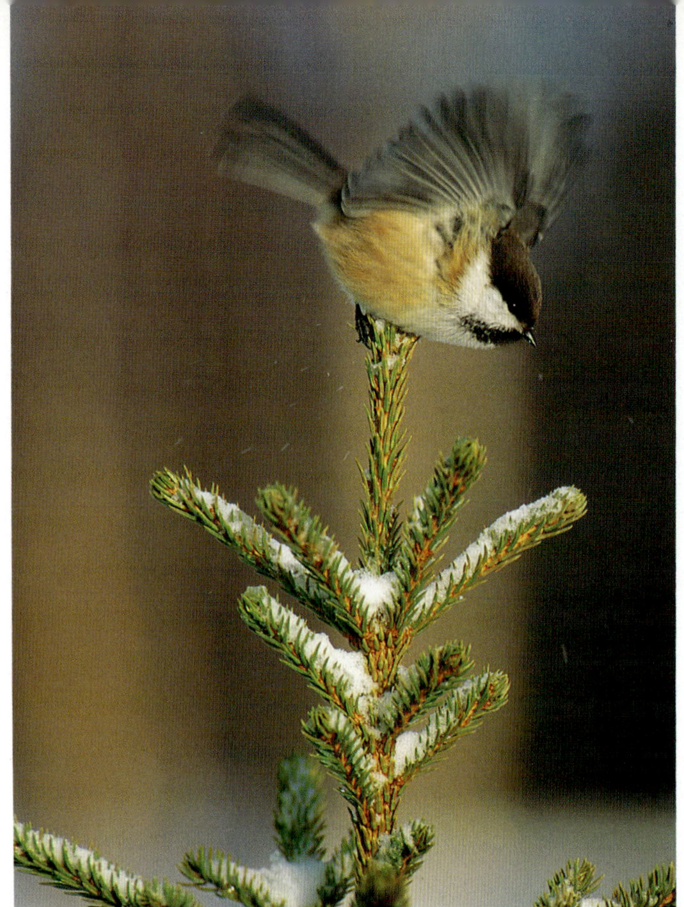

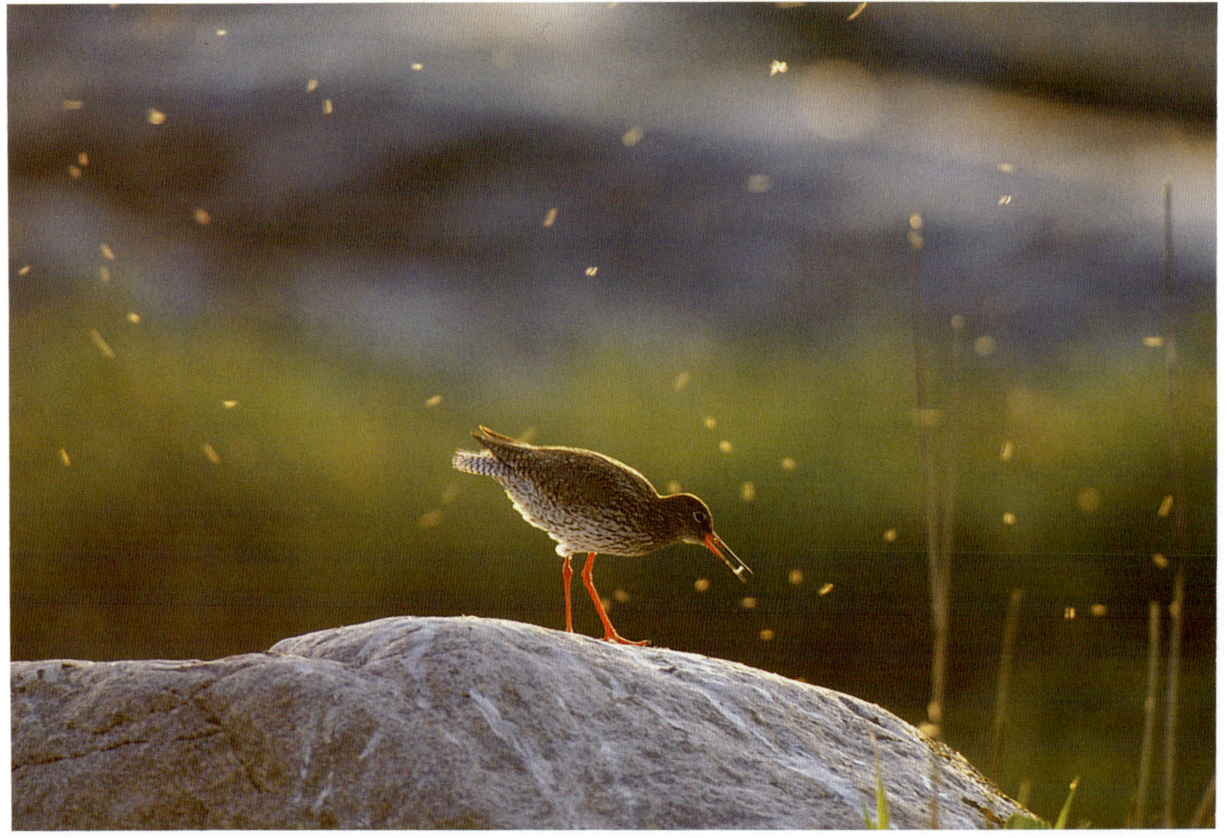

Nils Sundberg
Finland
HIGHLY COMMENDED

Redshank catching flies

*"For the past two years, I have
set up a hide on a small island in
the Baltic Sea to photograph the
redshanks and other birds which
breed there. This year, in May,
I was especially fascinated by the
evening light, and attempted to
photograph the birds backlit as
they fed on swarming flies."*

Canon EOS1 with 300mm lens and
×2 converter; Fujichrome 100

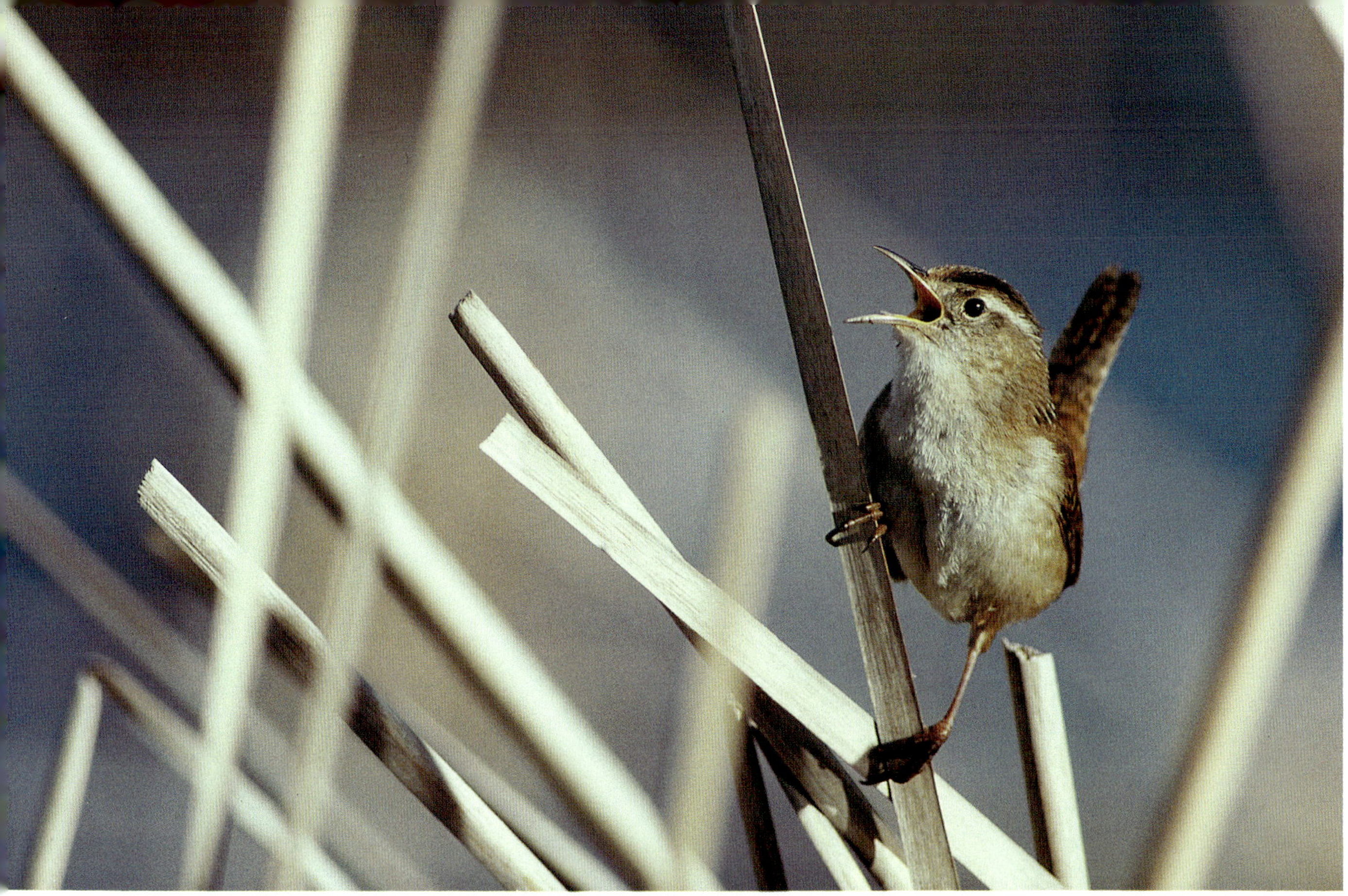

Tim Davis
United States of America
HIGHLY COMMENDED

Marsh Wren

''I watched a marsh wren fly from cat-tail to cat-tail, returning every now and then to the same one. Quickly I set up a hide, got inside and waited for him to return. Here, he is singing hard to attract a mate.''

Nikon F3 with 800mm lens and extension tube; tripod; f8 at 1/250 sec; Fujichrome 100

Richard Chandler
United Kingdom
HIGHLY COMMENDED

Wilson's Phalarope

''Most waders catch flies but only Wilson's phalarope does so while swimming. They move their heads back and forth moorhen-style, constantly changing direction as they see another fly, which makes it difficult to photograph them well. This is one of just four successful pictures out of three rolls of film that I took of the birds while on a photographic trip to California.''

Nikon 801 with 600mm lens and ×1.4 converter; f5.6 auto; Kodachrome 200

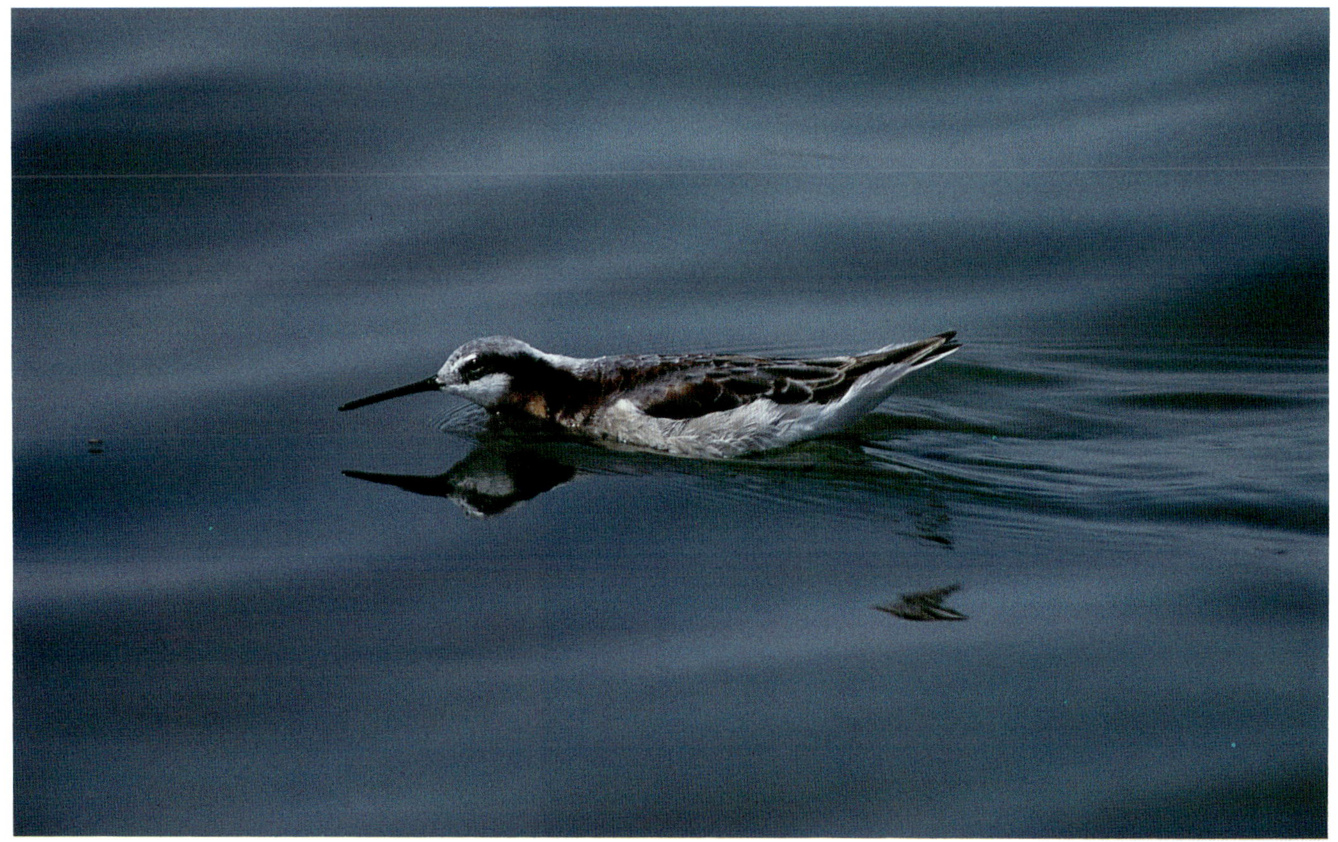

Animal Behaviour
- INSECTS -

Photographs entered in this category are judged for their interest value as well as for their aesthetic appeal and should show insects actively doing something.

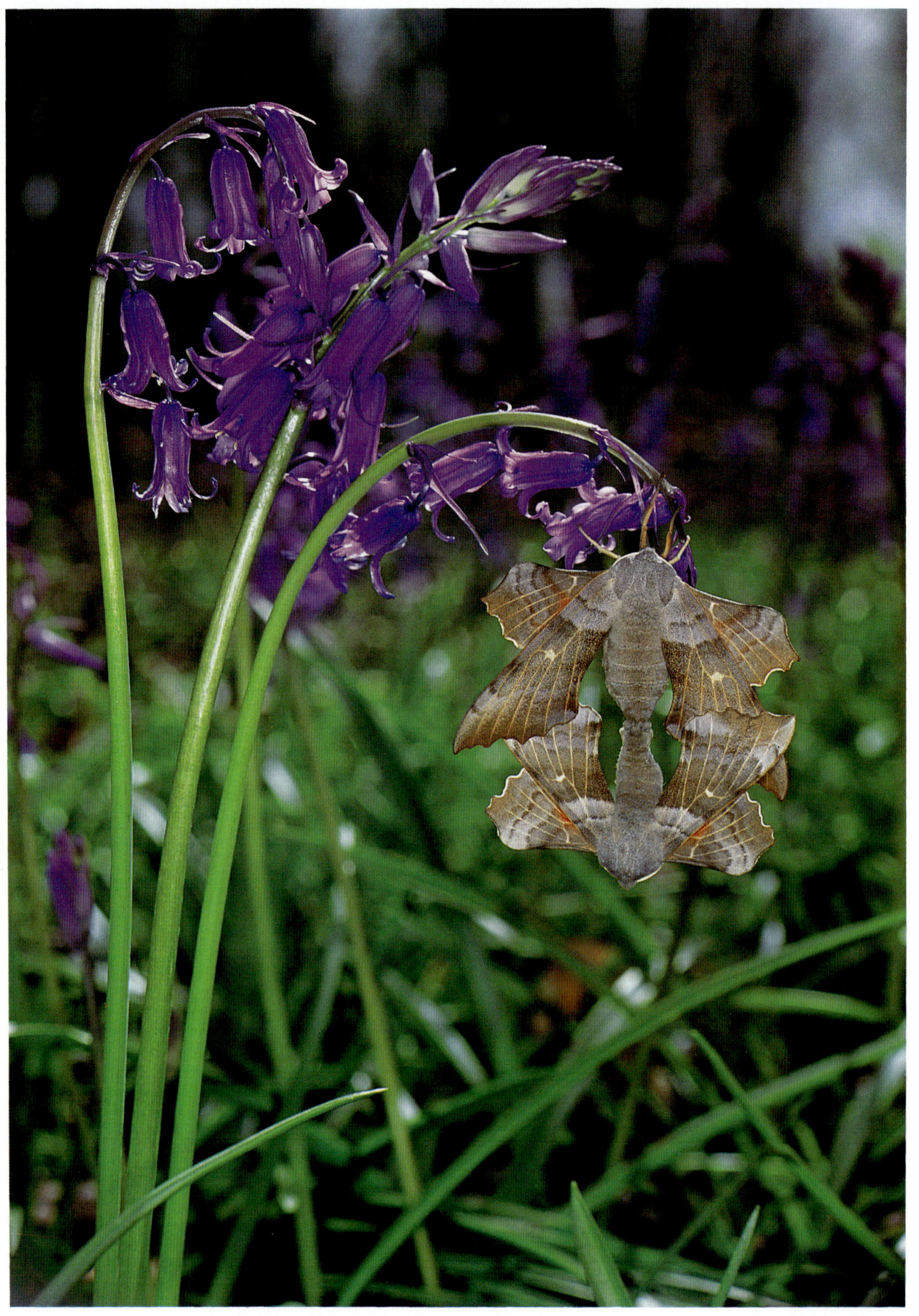

Andy Newman
United Kingdom
WINNER

Hawkmoths and Bluebell

"I was in a local wood trying to photograph deer amongst bluebells when I came across these hawkmoths mating. As the sun was still below the trees, I decided to return later. When I did, the sun was on the wrong side of the moths, so I used a ring flash to fill in. Ironically, I noticed a deer watching my efforts, but by the time I had changed my lens it had moved on."

Canon AE1 Program with 55mm macro lens; flash; monopad; f8 at 1/60 sec; Fujichrome Velvia

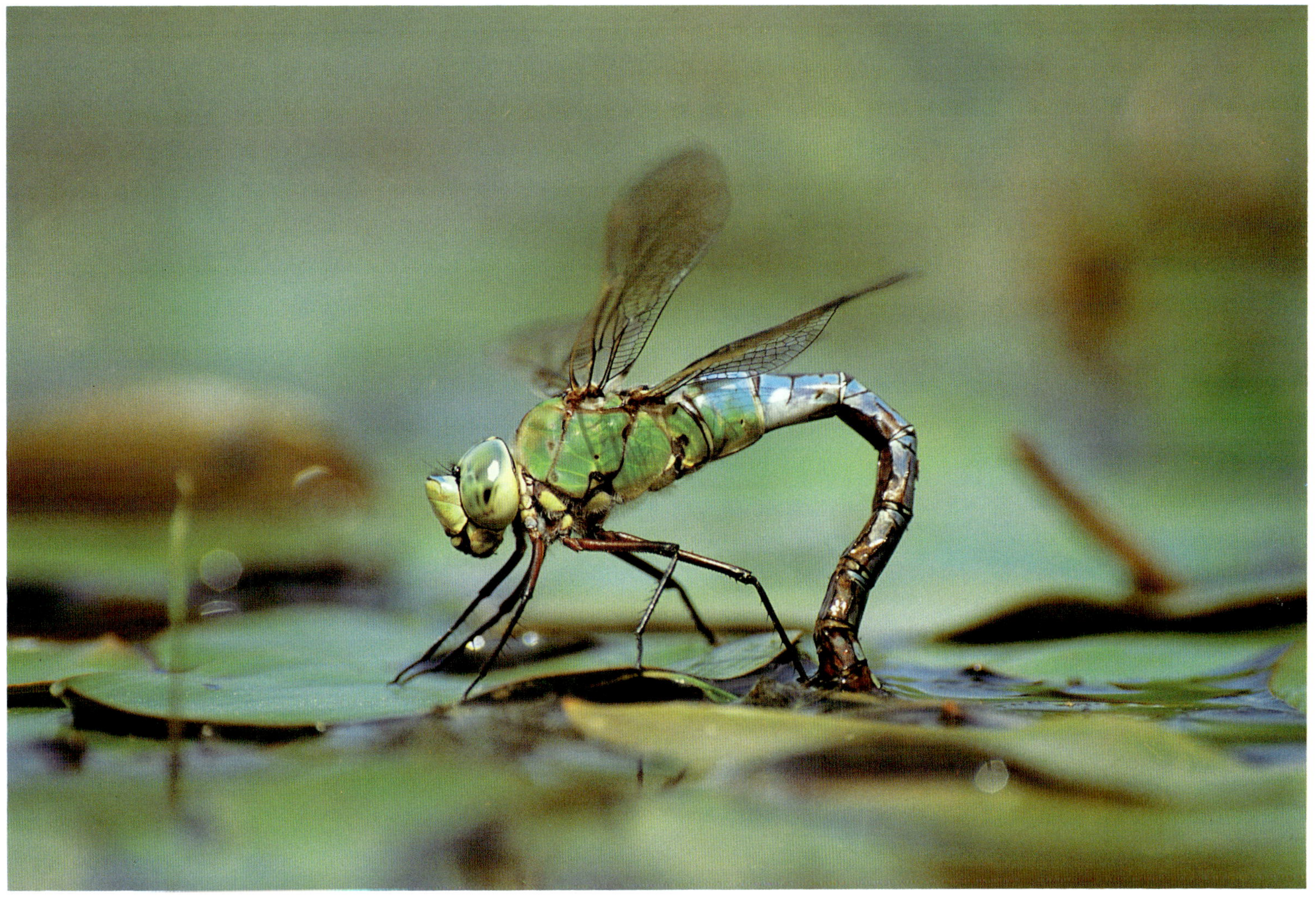

Felix Labhardt
Switzerland
RUNNER-UP

Dragonfly laying eggs
''An Emperor dragonfly **Anax Imperator** lays its eggs on an underwater plant. I took this picture as part of a documentation of the lifecycle of Europe's largest dragonfly. These impressive insects occur near my home, on ponds built 20 years ago specially for the conservation of amphibians and rare flowers.''

Minolta Dynax 7000i with 75-300mm lens and .37 diopter; tripod; f8 auto; Fujichrome 100

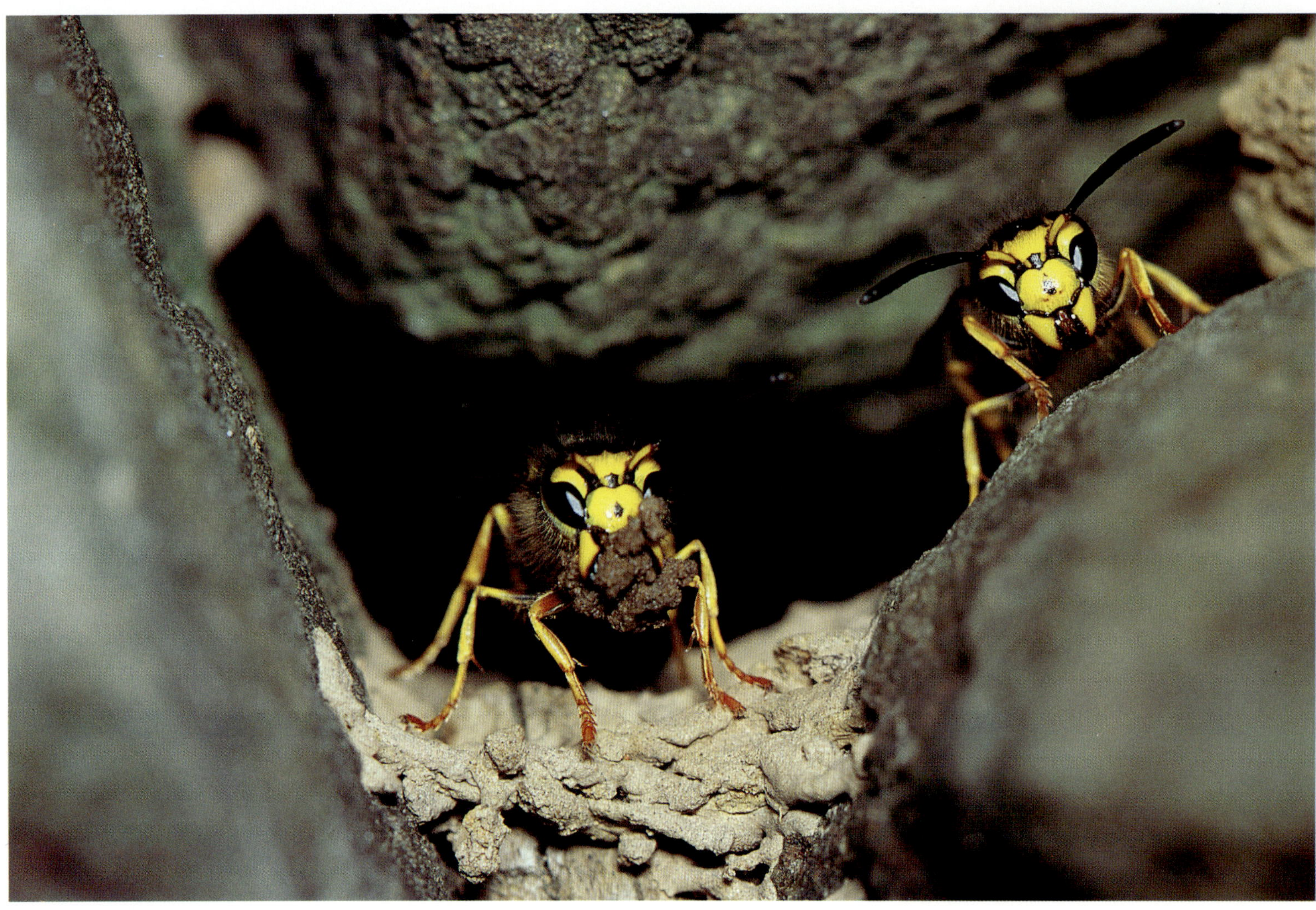

Gerry Ellis
United States of America
HIGHLY COMMENDED

Hornets

"Despite my wife's alarm, I let a hornets' nest develop within a few feet of our backdoor in Portland, Oregon. It provided dozens of opportunities to take behaviour shots. Here the hornets are clearing mud from underground excavations to provide new space for the growing colony."

Nikon F4 with 105mm lens;
Fujichrome Velvia

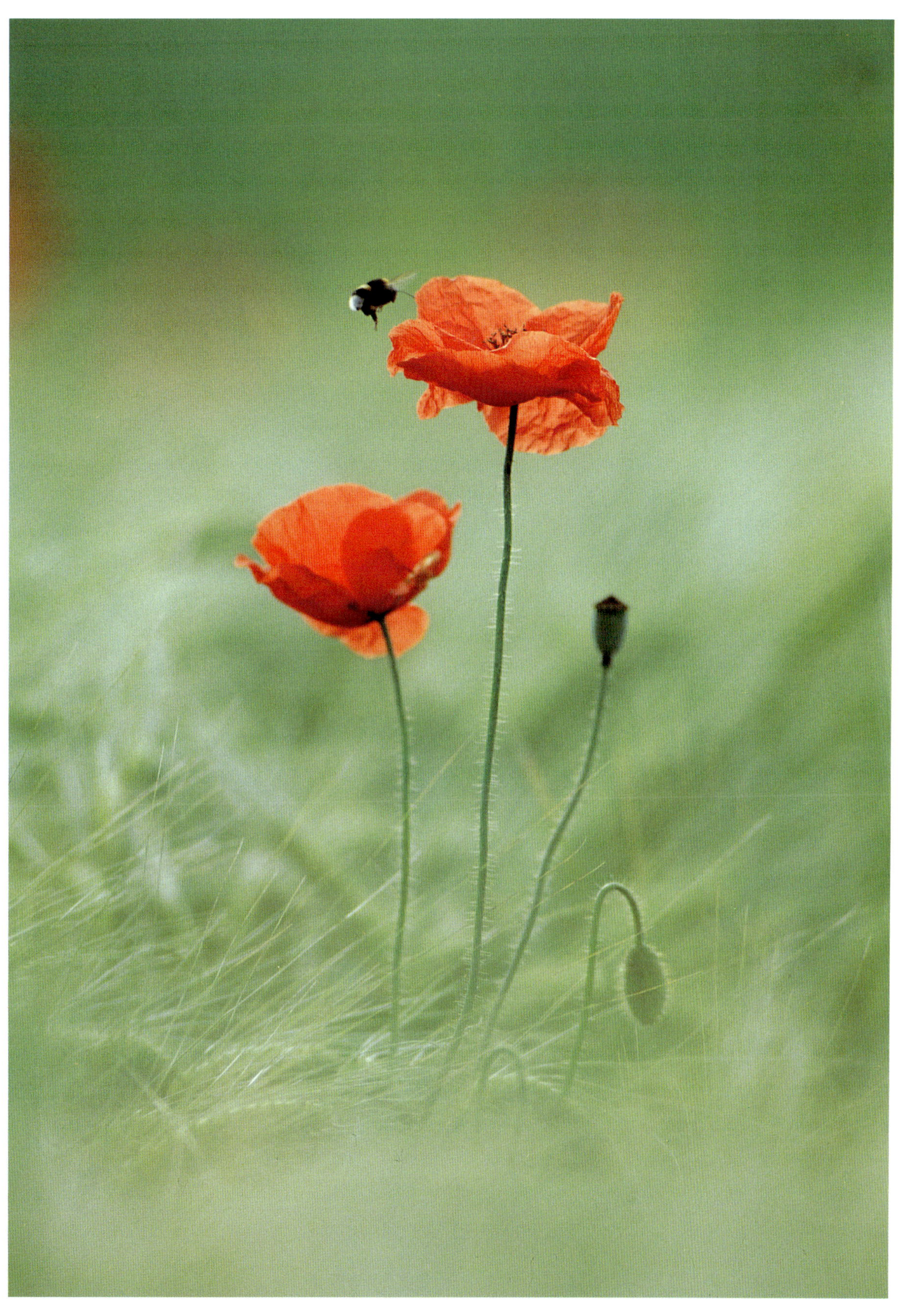

Herbert Kehrer
Germany
HIGHLY COMMENDED

Bee and Poppies

''I was photographing poppies in a grain field near Stuttgart when a bumble bee approached. Since bees collect nectar and therefore pollinate flowers, I thought this would make an interesting shot of nature in action. I chose a short exposure time to ensure that both bee and poppy were sharp.''

Nikon F3 with 500mm lens; tripod; f4 at 1/500 sec; Fujichrome RD 100

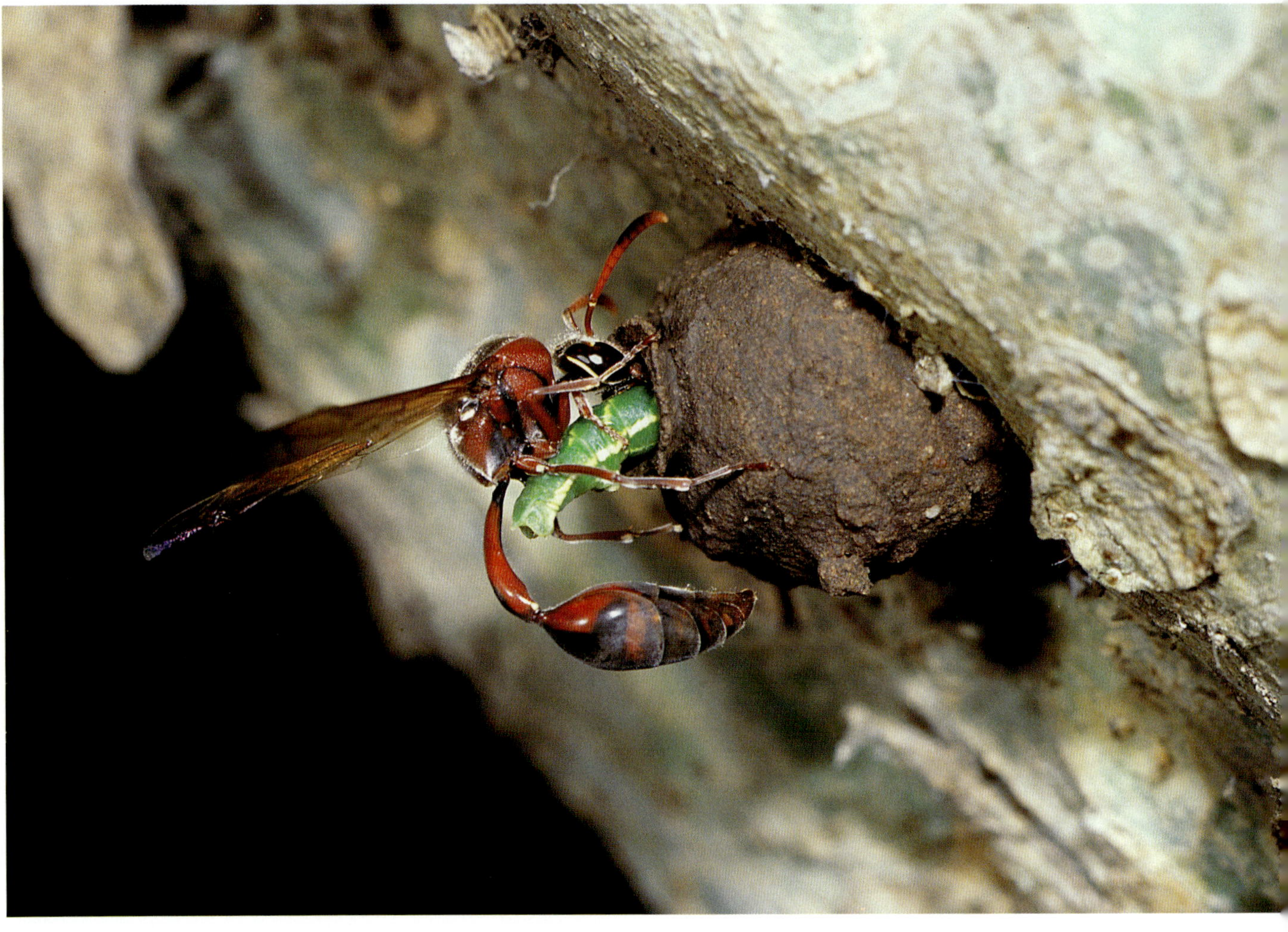

Alan Weaving
South Africa
HIGHLY COMMENDED

Eumenid Wasp provisioning nest

"While studying the nesting behaviour of solitary wasps, I came across this **Delta hottentottoum** which had almost finished building her mud nest. I set up my camera on a tripod, positioned two flashguns and waited for it to return. On this occasion the wasp had a large caterpillar that took a few seconds to get into the nest, giving me enough time to take several frames. It seemed quite unperturbed by my presence."

Nikon FE2 with 105 mm macro lens; tripod; flash; f16 at 1/250 sec; Fujichrome 100

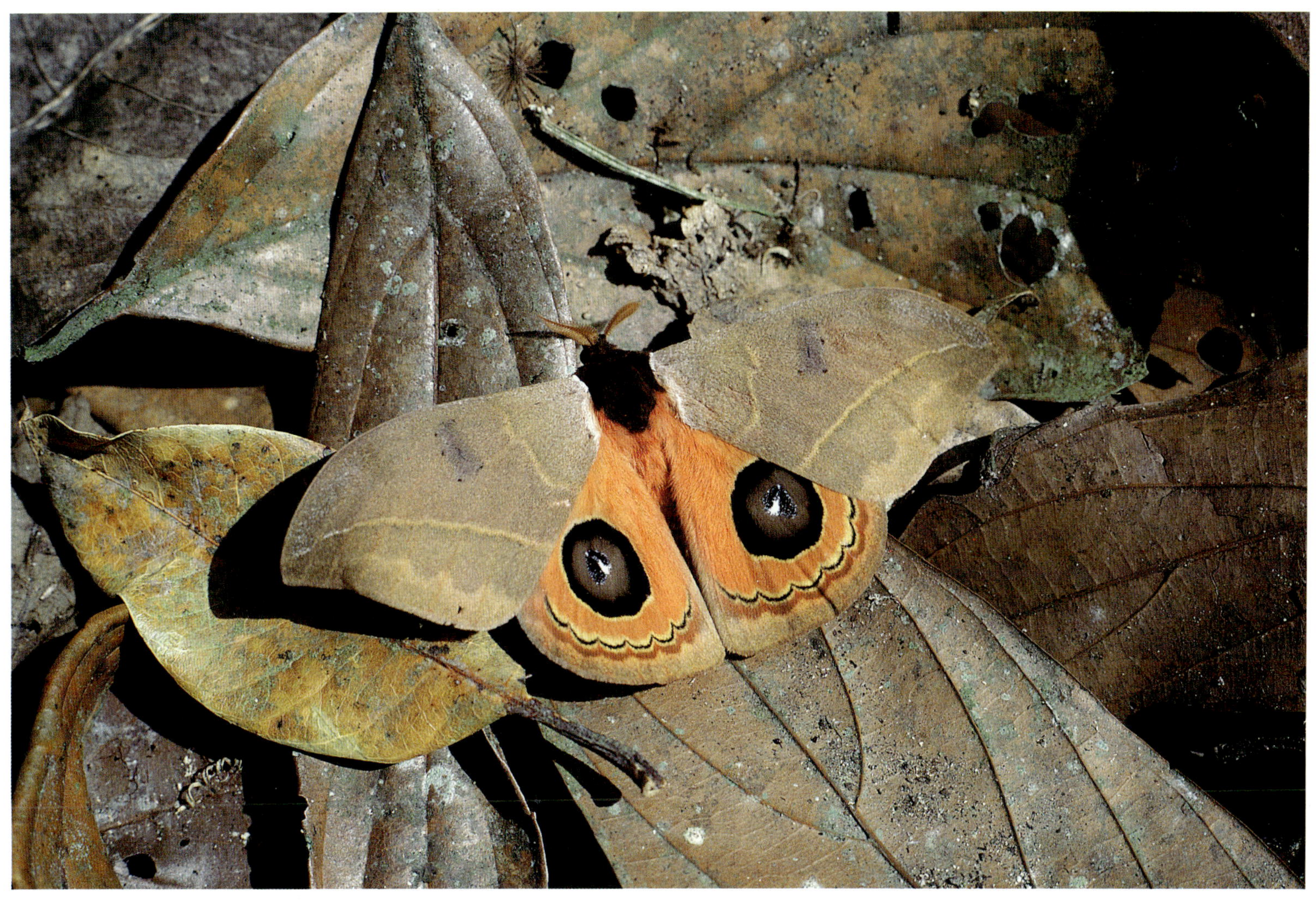

Antonio Manzanares
Spain
HIGHLY COMMENDED

Moth flashing eye-spots
"The moth was photographed during as visit to the Henri Pitier National Park in Venezuela. I was down on the leaf litter photographing a small flower when I noticed this **Antomeris** *moth showing his eye-spots as if to say `Be careful, here I am.''*

Olympus OM4 with 90mm macro lens; flash; f16; Kodachrome 64

Animal Behaviour
- ALL OTHERS -

Photographs entered in this category are judged for their interest value as well as their aesthetic appeal and can show any animal (excluding birds, mammals and insects) actively doing something.

David F Toney
United States of America
WINNER

Jumping Spider and Spiderlings

"This female jumping spider, **Phidippus audax**, *wove two parallel webs in which to lay her eggs. Here she stands at the top of the web above the spiderlings inside.*
For eight years, I have been photographing many different species of spider in my backyard, trying to capture interesting behaviour shots. I use a single flash on the camera most of the time to simulate natural light."

Nikon F4s with 105mm lens; extension tubes; tripod; flash; f16 at 1/8 sec; Kodachrome 64

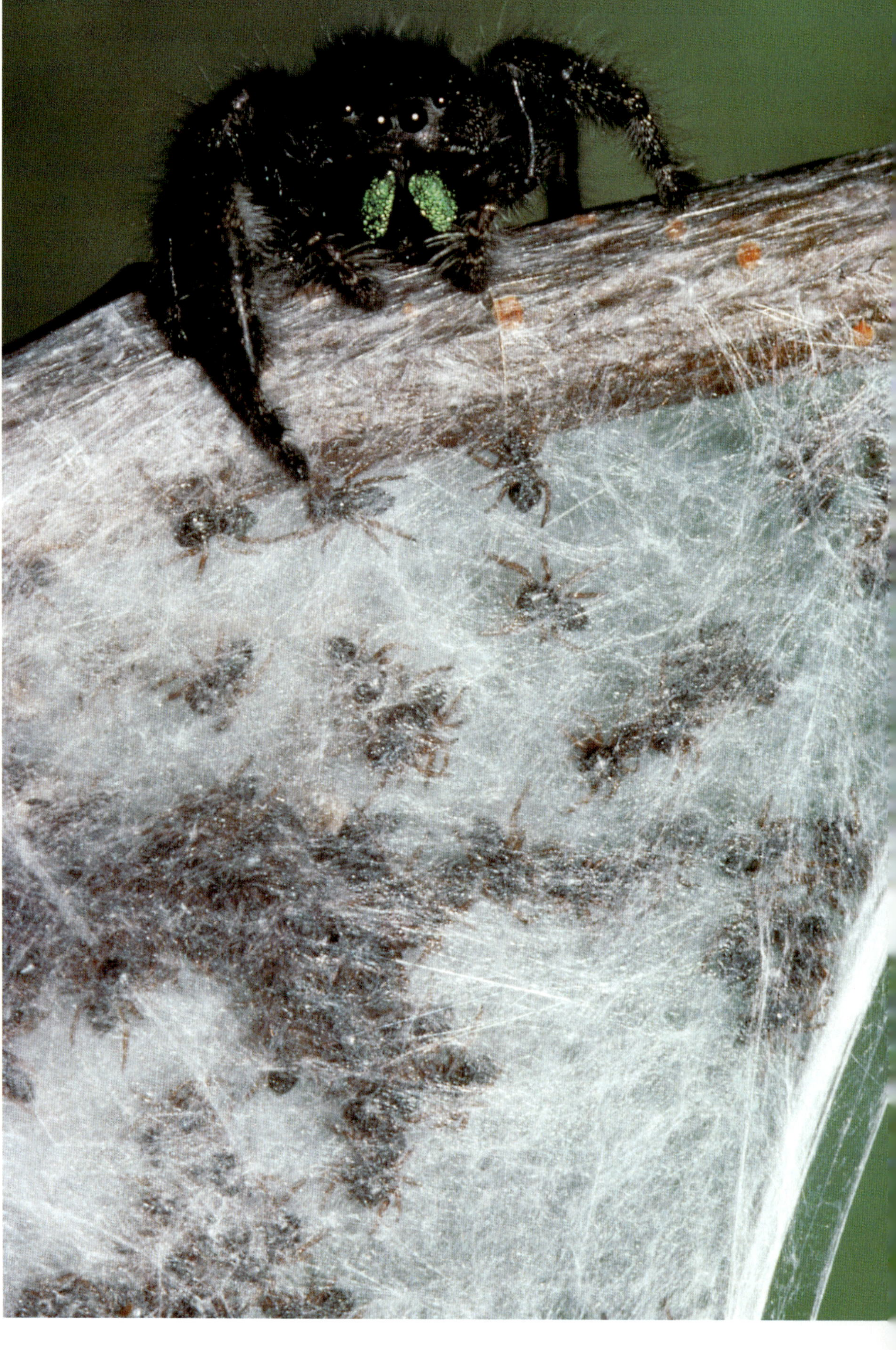

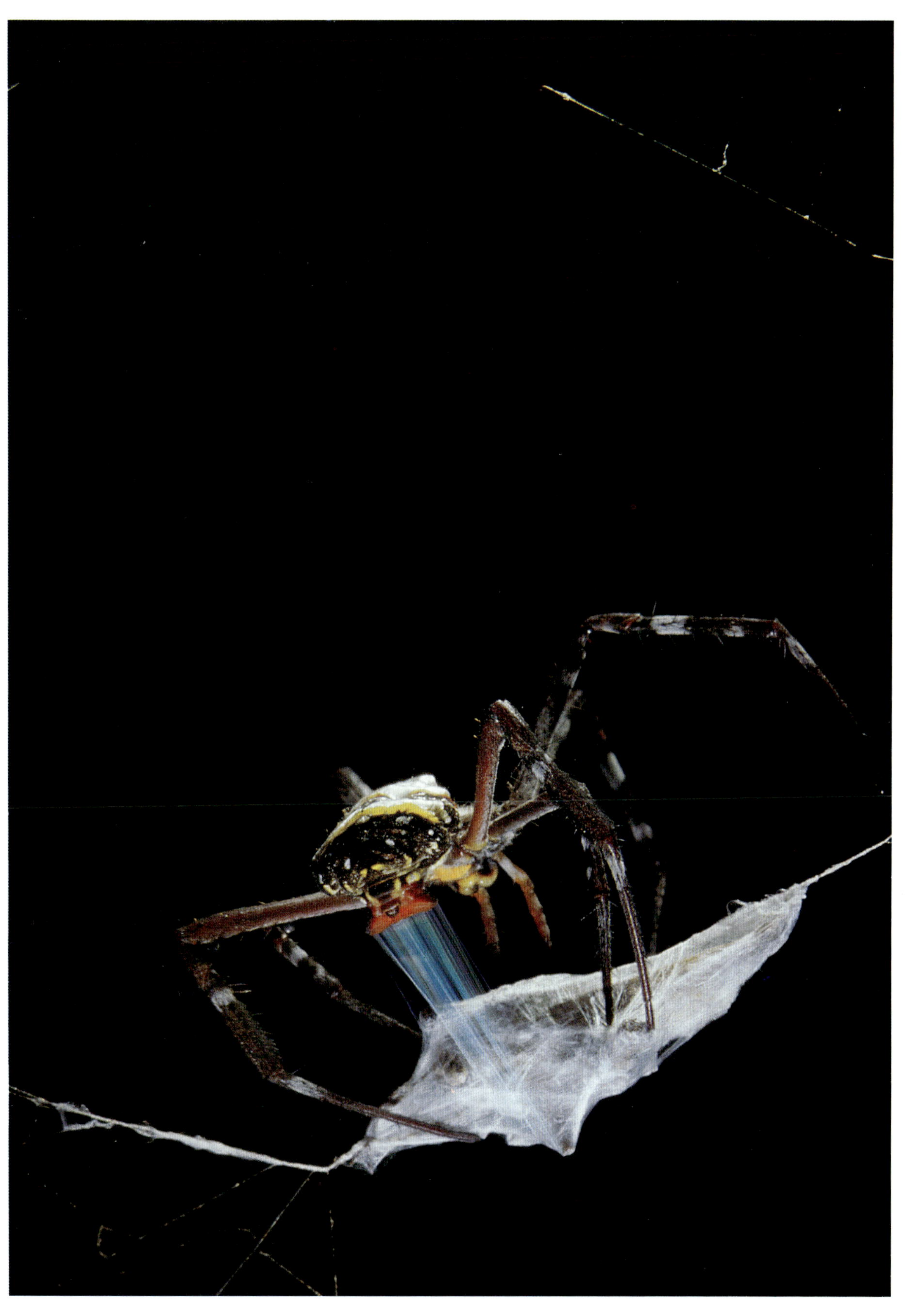

Vivek R Sinha
India
RUNNER-UP

Spider spinning

''*My photo shows an agriope spider in the process of capturing a grasshopper. The spider sprays jets of liquid protein from its spinnerets over its prey. The liquid hardens into silk strands and in no time the spider has its prey trussed up in sheets of silk like a mummy.*''

Nikon FA with 105mm lens; tripod; f32 at 1/250 sec; Fujichrome 100

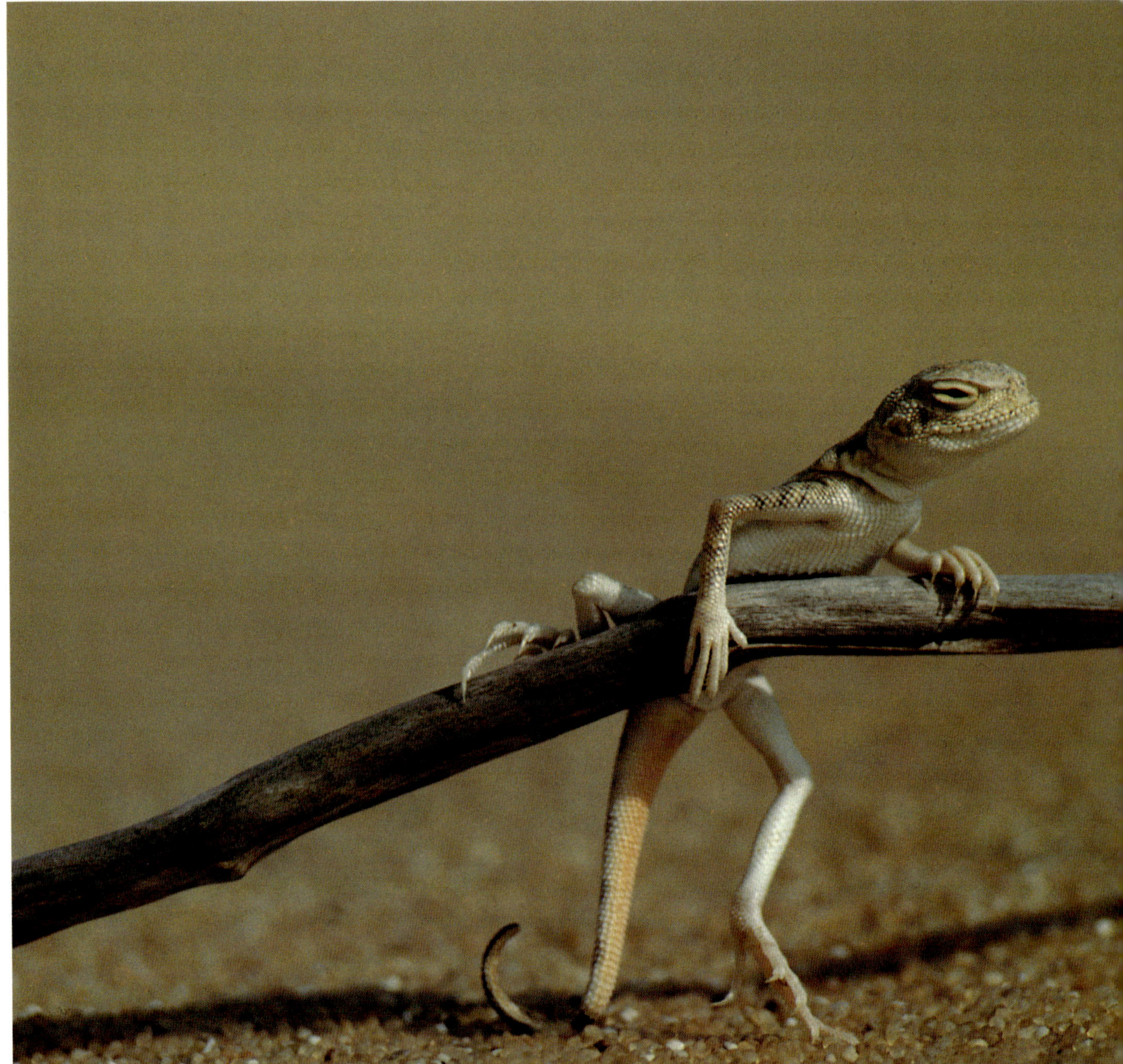

Bill Ross
United Kingdom
HIGHLY COMMENDED

Lounge Lizard

''In the heat of the day in eastern
Saudi Arabia, this lizard
climbed onto a twig to get up off
the hot sand and to benefit from
any cooling breeze.
Unfortunately, the only way to
take this picture was to lie on the
very hot ground myself!''

Minolta XD7 with 75-205mm zoom
lens; Kodachrome 64

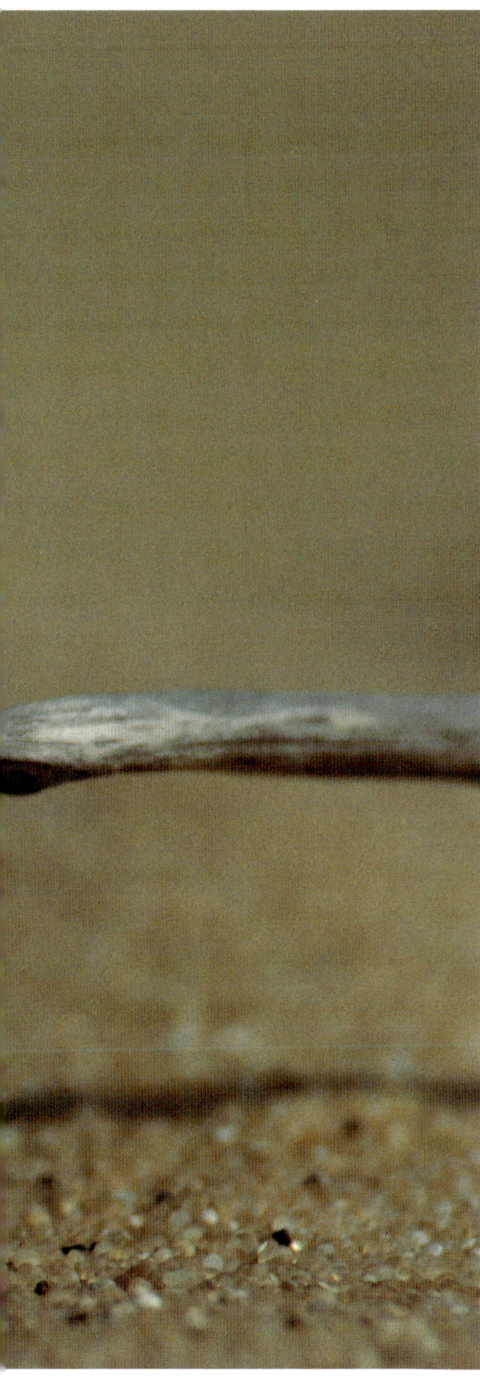

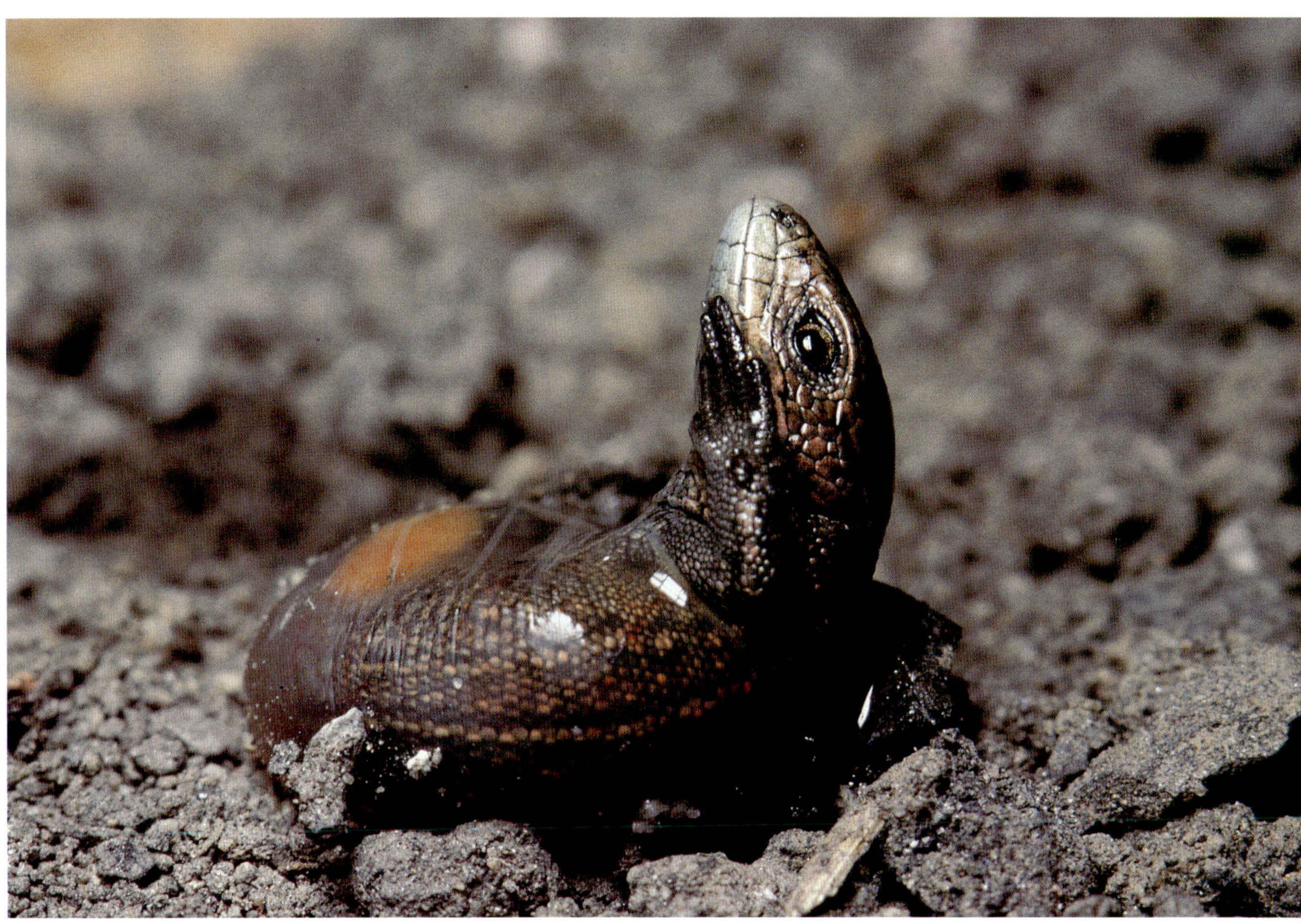

Laurie Campbell
United Kingdom
HIGHLY COMMENDED

Common Lizard hatching

"I was searching among some
rocks for slow worms when
I came across some newly-born
lizards. I rushed back to my car
to get a flash and when
I returned only one was still
there - in the last stages of
breaking out of the membrane
surrounding it."

Nikon F3 with 105mm macro lens; flash;
f16 at 1/60 sec; Kodachrome 64

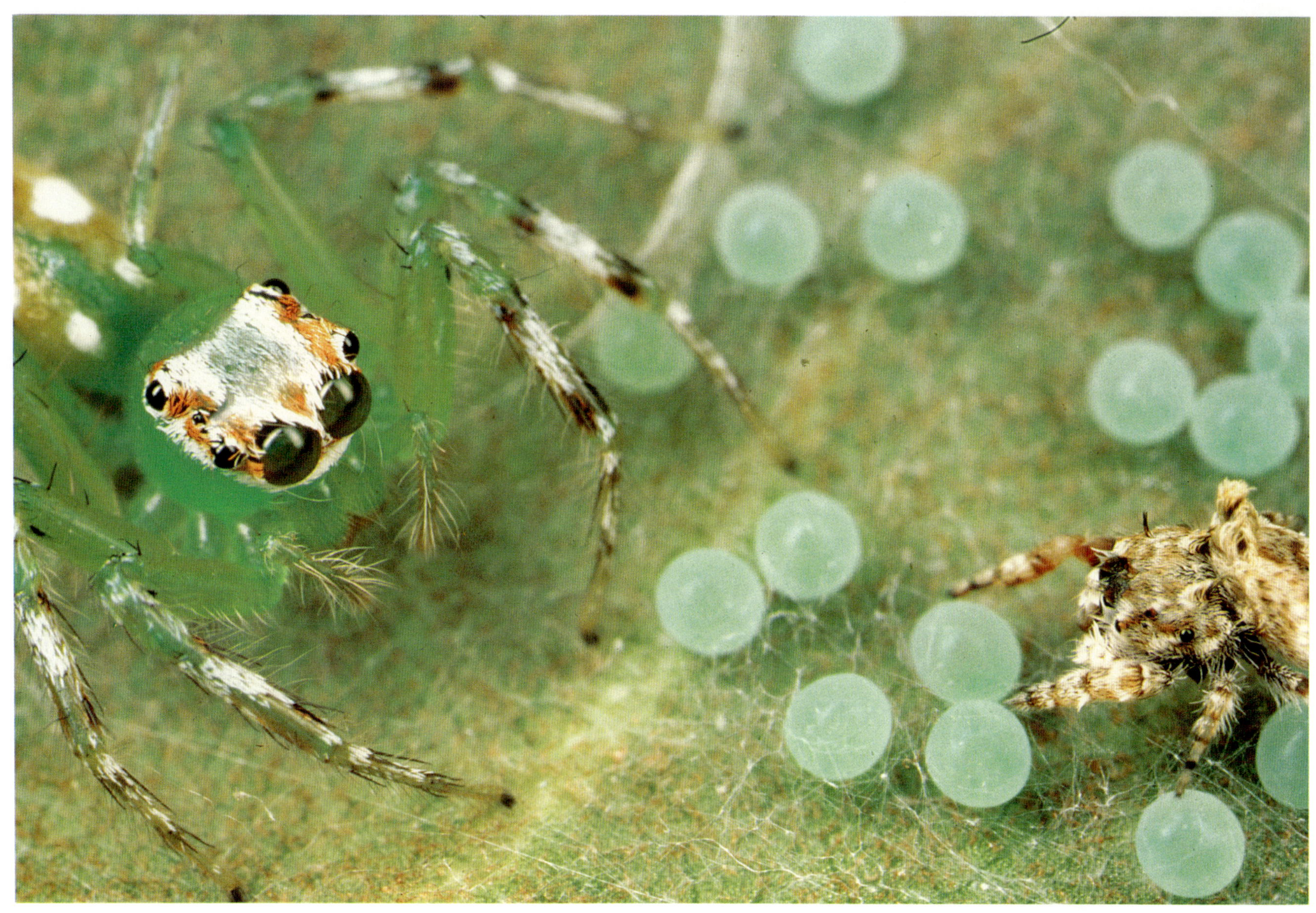

Mark Moffet
United States of America
HIGHLY COMMENDED

Spider thief
''A dust-speck spider invades the
nest of another species of
jumping spider, intent on
stealing an egg.
The mother on guard is confused
because the invader looks just
like a speck of dust. The picture
was taken in a clump of bamboo
in Sri Lanka.''

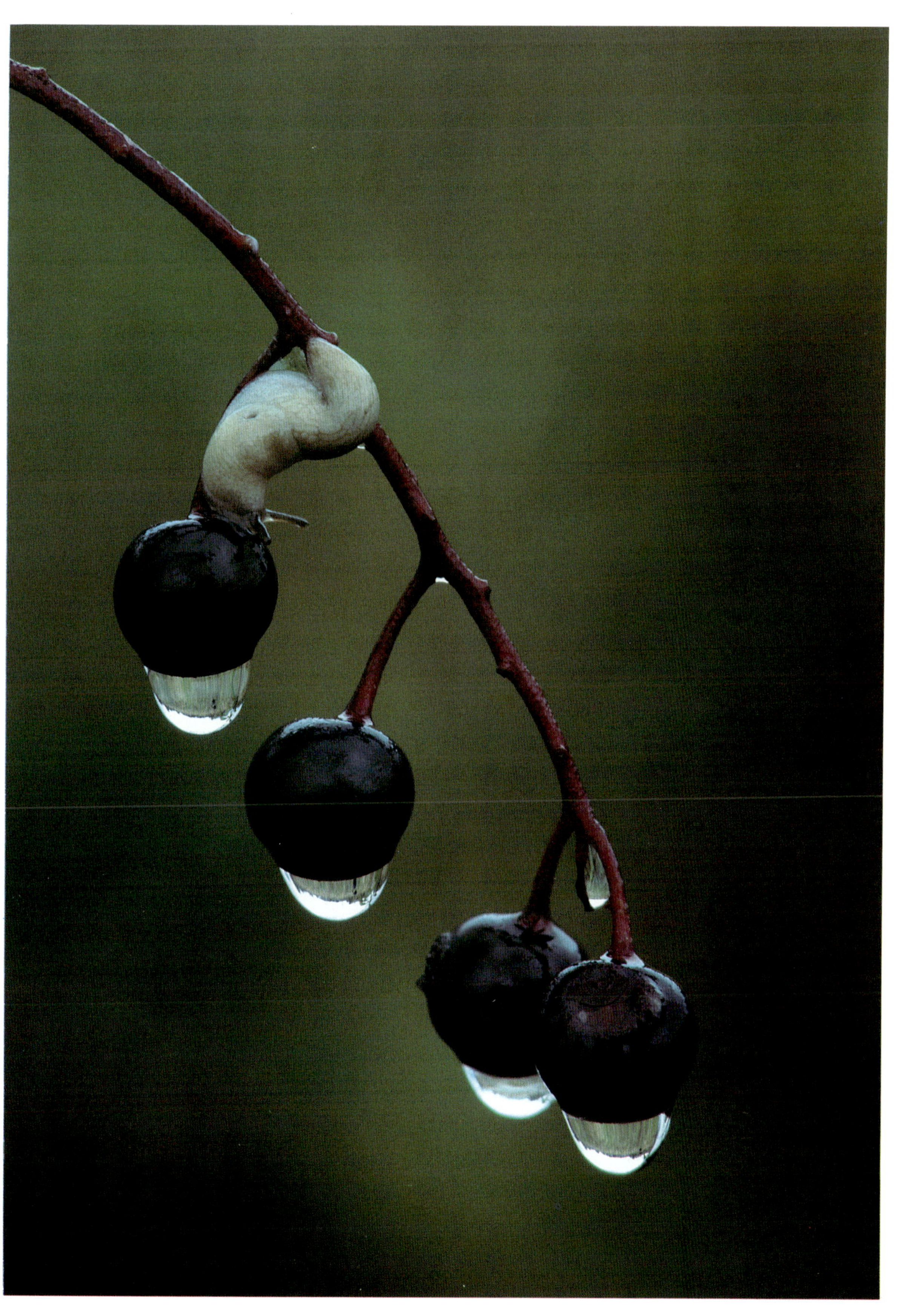

Jorma Peiponen
Finland
HIGHLY COMMENDED

***Slug and
Bird Cherry berries***
*''I photographed this slug
Deroceras agreste moving over
some bird cherry berries in a
meadow that is one of my
favourite places for
photography.''*

Nikon F3 with 200mm macro lens;
tripod; f16 at 1 sec; Kodachrome 64

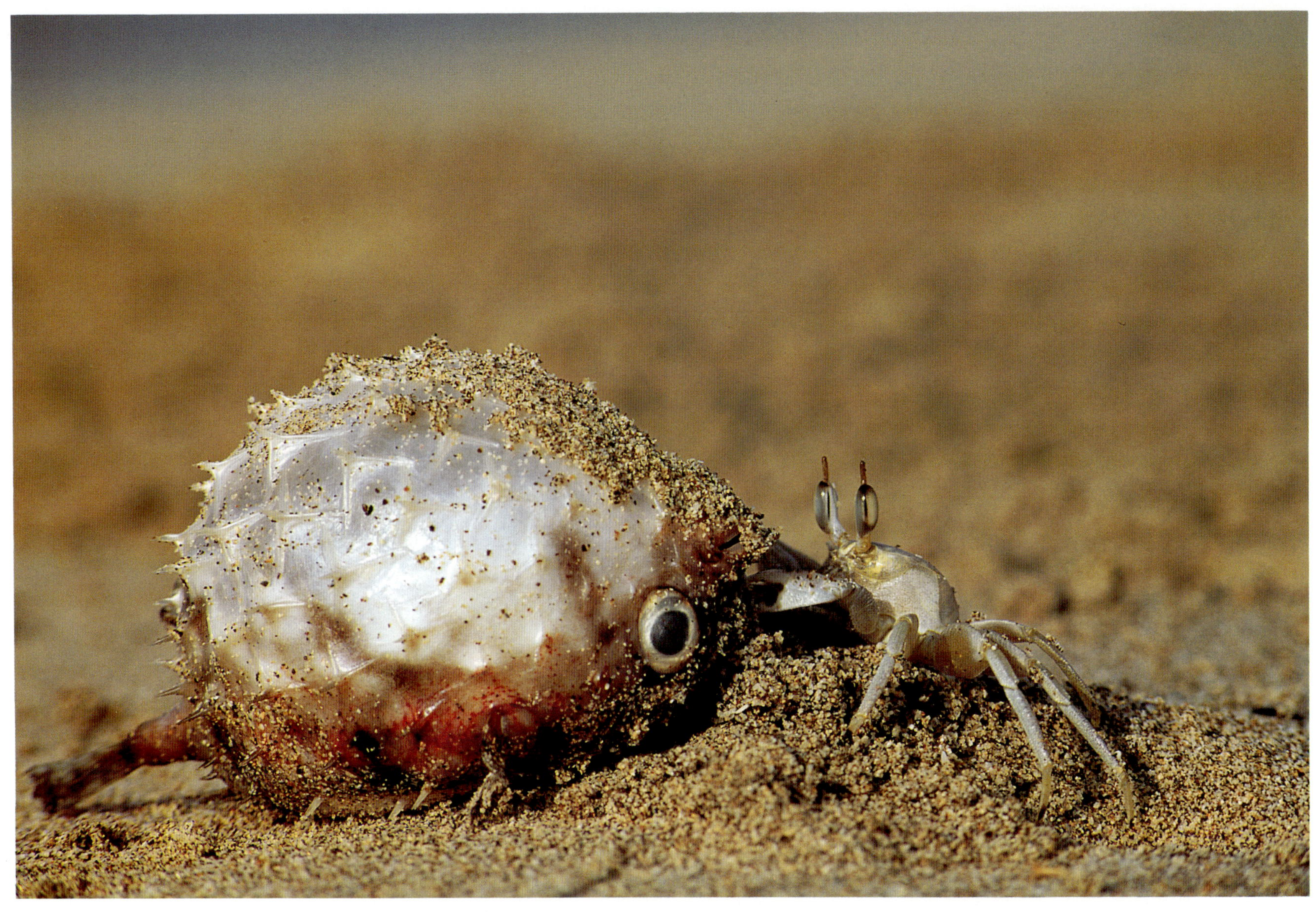

Mike Hill
United Kingdom
HIGHLY COMMENDED

Ghost Crab feeding

*"While staying in Oman, I had noticed that the ghost crabs were feeding on dead pufferfish washed up on the beach.
I looked for a dead fish which was near a crab hole, then lay down on the sand and waited for the crab to appear."*

Nikon F4 with 24-50mm lens; f16 at 1/60 sec; Kodachrome 64

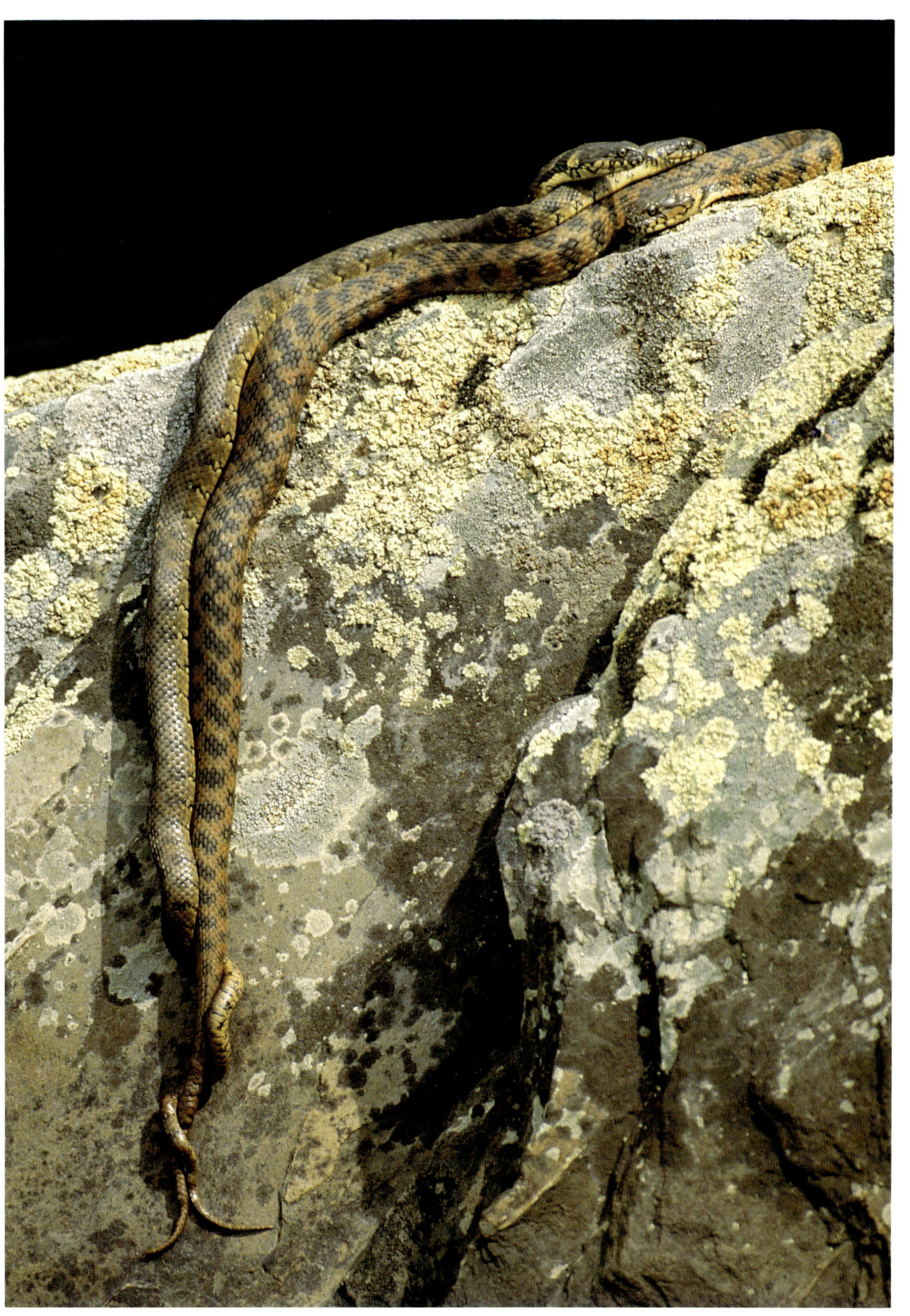

Felix Labhardt
Switzerland
HIGHLY COMMENDED

Viperine snakes mating

"I came upon these viperine snakes, **Natrix maura** in Extremadura in Spain. The snakes mate soon after rousing from hibernation, on sunny days in April or May. The male lies head to head and parallel with the larger female, and often the mating pair is joined by several other males interested in the same female, creating a ball of snakes."

Minolta X-500 with 600mm lens; tripod; Fujichrome RD100

The World In Our Hands

Photographs for this category must illustrate in a symbolic or graphic way our dependence on the natural world or our capability of inflicting harm on it.

Guy Hobbs
United Kingdom
WINNER

Elephant Trophy

"This elephant head was mounted on the lounge wall of the Safari Lodge Hotel near Hwange National Park, Zimbabwe, long before the concern over the future of African elephants became such a sensitive international issue. At the time I was taking pictures for a book 'The Presidential Herd' written by a local game safari operator. The herd regularly come to the waterhole in front of the hotel to drink."

Nikon FM2 with wide angle lens; tripod; flash; Fujichrome 100

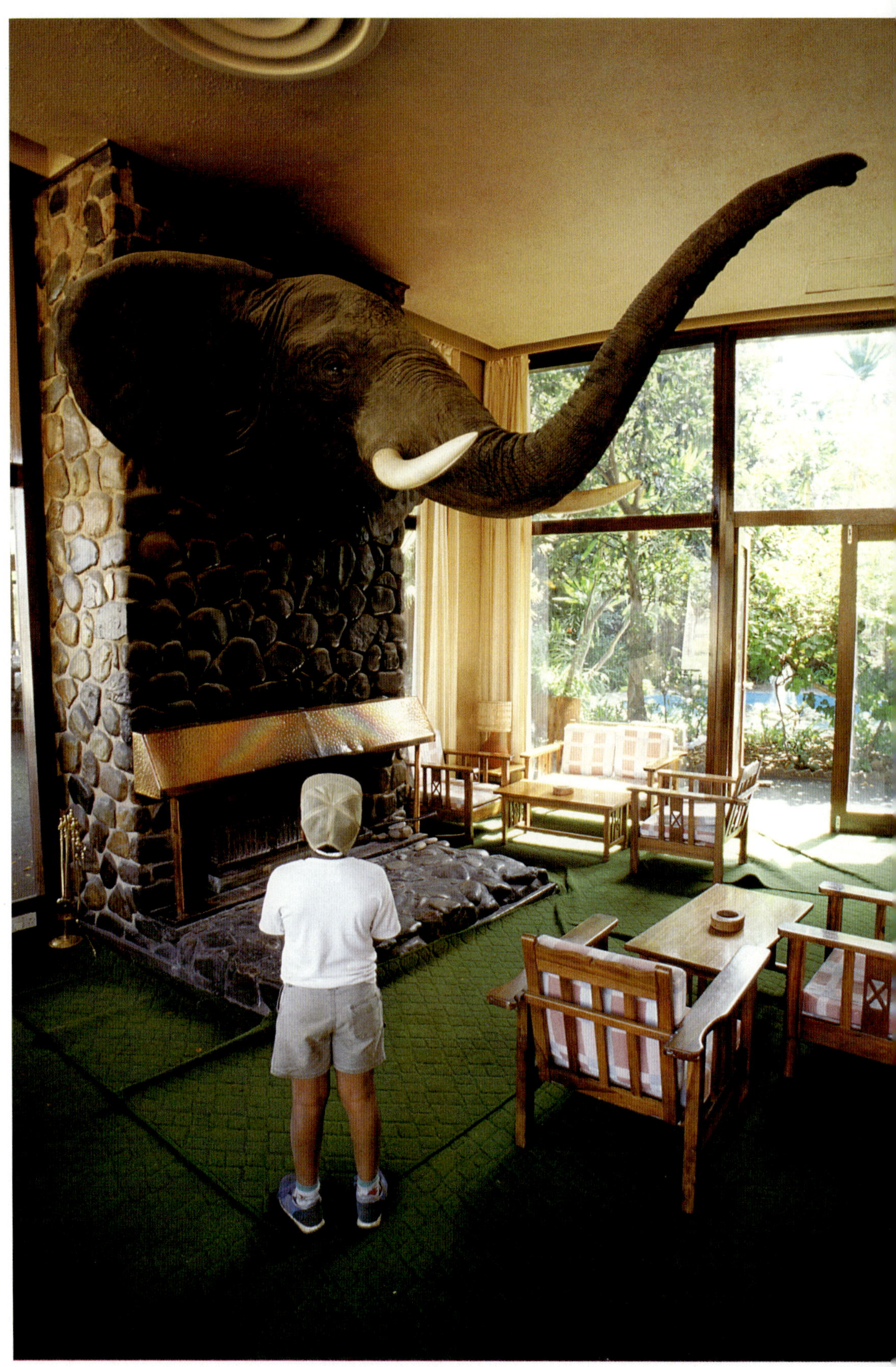

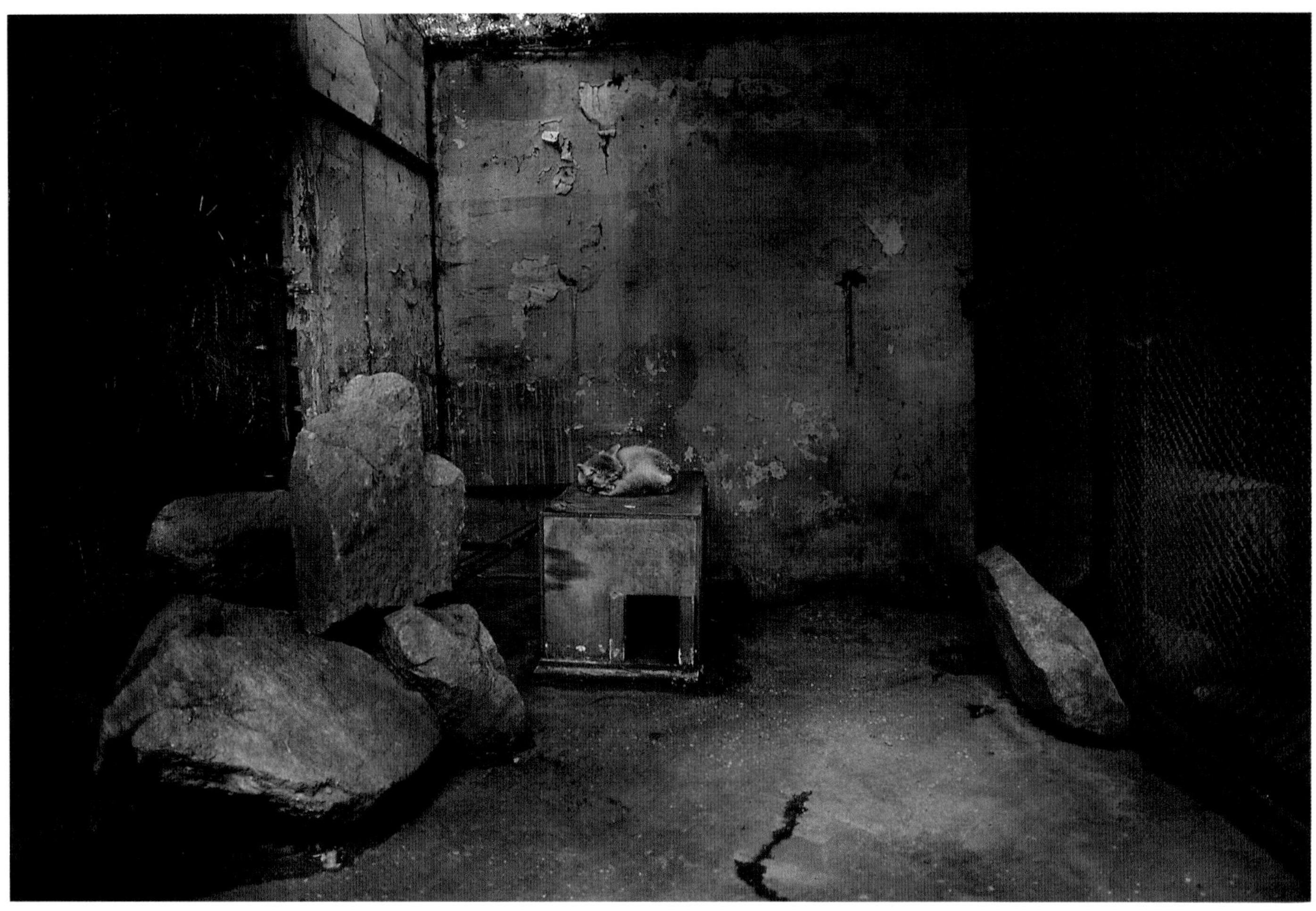

Richard Packwood
United Kingdom
RUNNER-UP

Fox in Bratislava Zoo

*''On a trip throughout Eastern
Europe I began visiting zoos,
determined to photograph
whatever possible and to give the
results to 'Zoo Check'.
This corsac fox was one of the
saddest sights; in his dark, damp
enclosure it seemed that he had
been forgotten about for years.
The lighting was so low that
I almost didn't take any
photographs. In an effort to
remain discreet I didn't use a
tripod but braced my camera
against the bars of the cage.''*

Nikon F4 with 20mm lens; 1/15 sec at
f2.8; Kodachrome 64

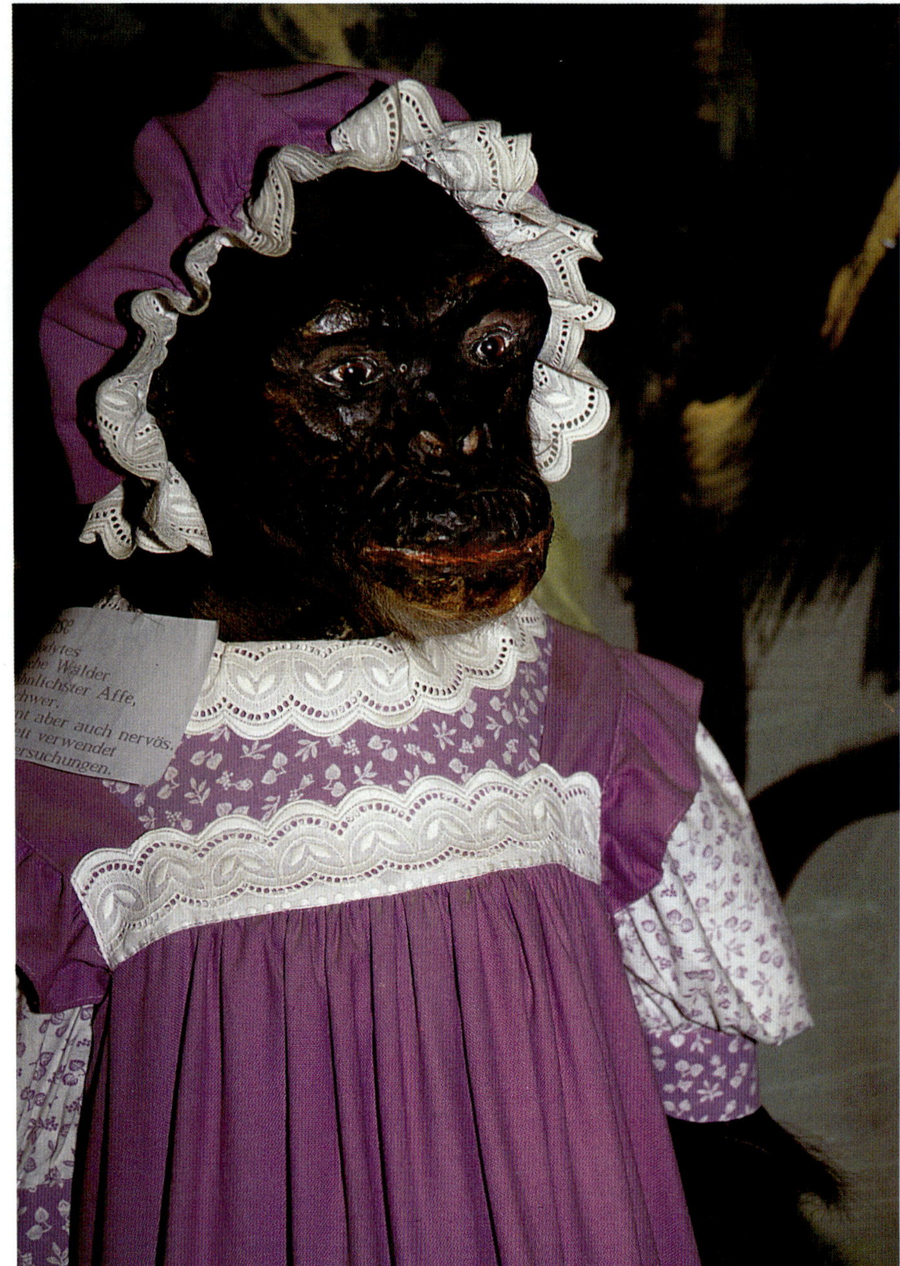

Martin Wendler
Germany
HIGHLY COMMENDED

Stuffed Chimp

"I take pictures to document the
illegal and legal animal trade
and the movement of endangered
species from Africa to Europe.
This stuffed chimpanzee was
exhibited in the Hunting
Museum, Bavaria, as a
gimmick to make money."

Canon EOS 1 with 35-135mm zoom
lens; Fujichrome RD 100

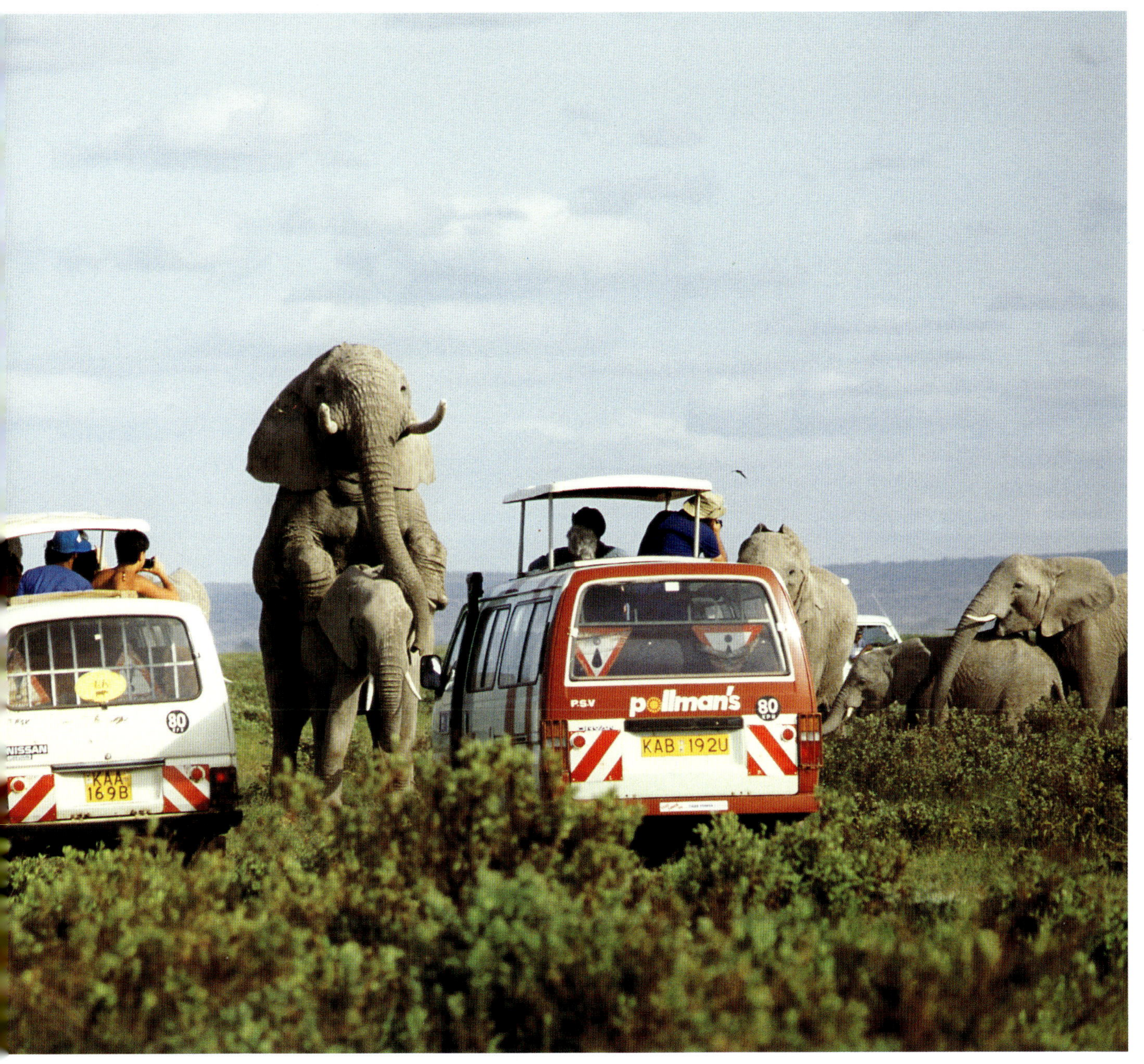

Hanne Lindemann
Denmark
HIGHLY COMMENDED

Tourist intrusion

"When these elephants started to
mate, I was annoyed that the
mini buses were in the way.
Then I realized I could take an
interesting photograph showing
how elephants go on with
their lives, even with
tourists watching."

Nikon 801s with 100-300mm zoom lens;
Fujichrome 100

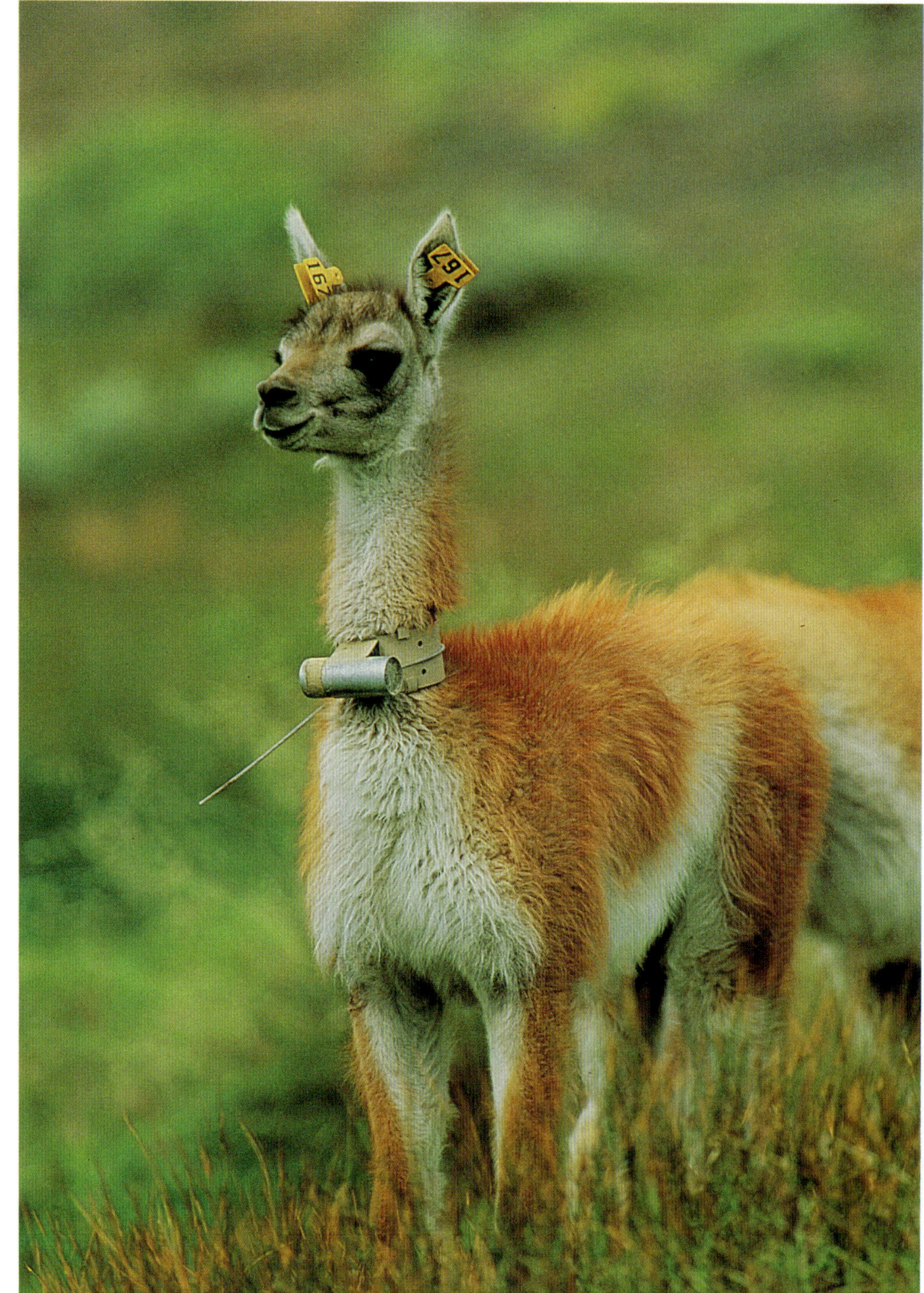

Konrad Wothe
Germany
HIGHLY COMMENDED

Guanaco

"I was angry when I discovered
that nearly 25 percent of all
young animals in a herd of
guanacos were burdened with
radio-tracking collars. Surely,
one collar per herd would be
enough to track their movements
in the Paine National Park,
Chile. The money saved could
be used to save many acres
of rainforest."

Canon EOS 1 with 300mm lens; 1/400
sec at f4; Fujichrome 100

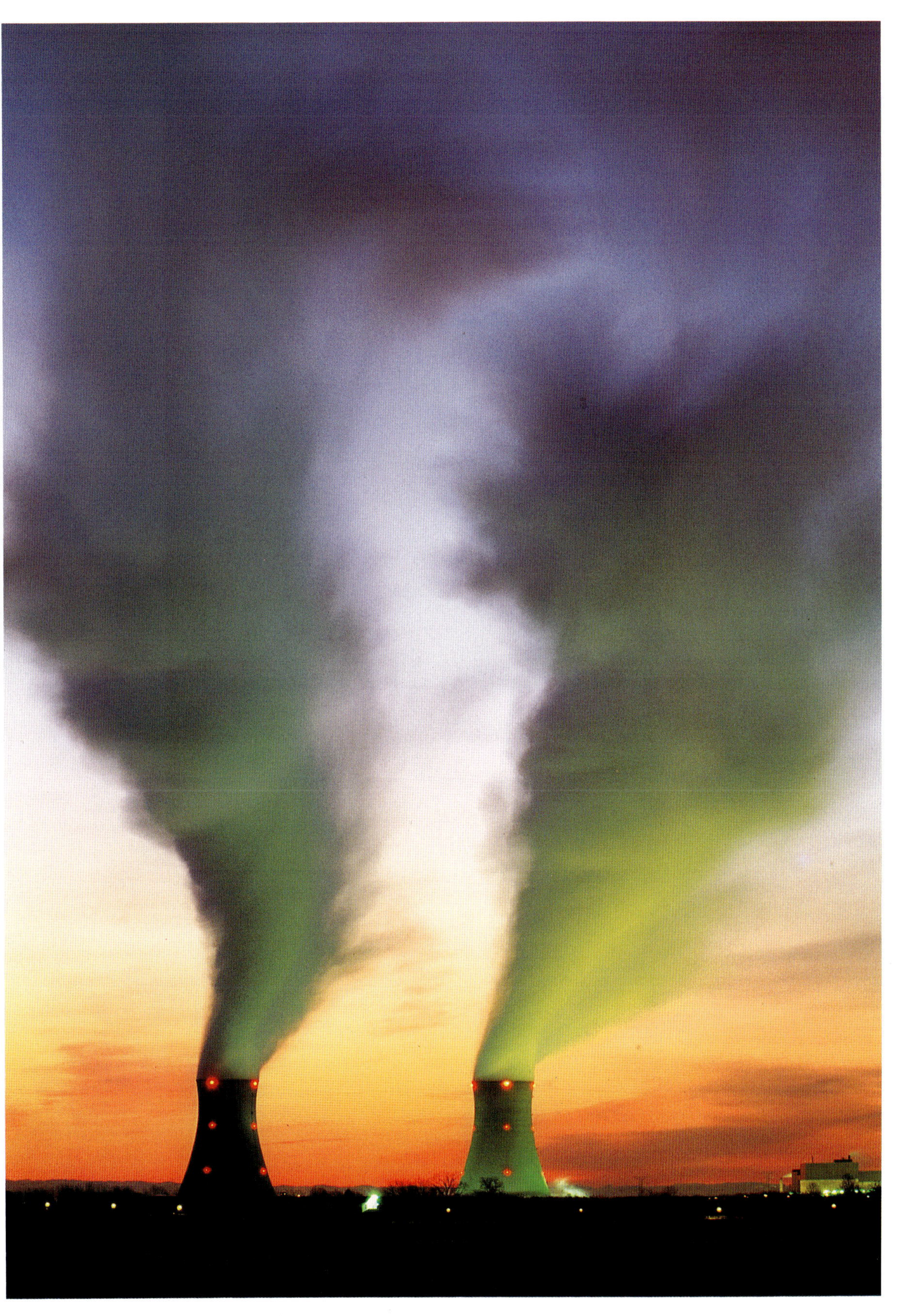

Janet Haas
United States of America
HIGHLY COMMENDED

Nuclear Cooling Towers

''*This picture was taken one bitterly cold morning in Monroe, Michigan. I was attracted by the steam rising in enormous columns from the cooling towers.*''

Nikon 8008 with 55mm lens; tripod; 30 secs at f.4; Fujichrome 100

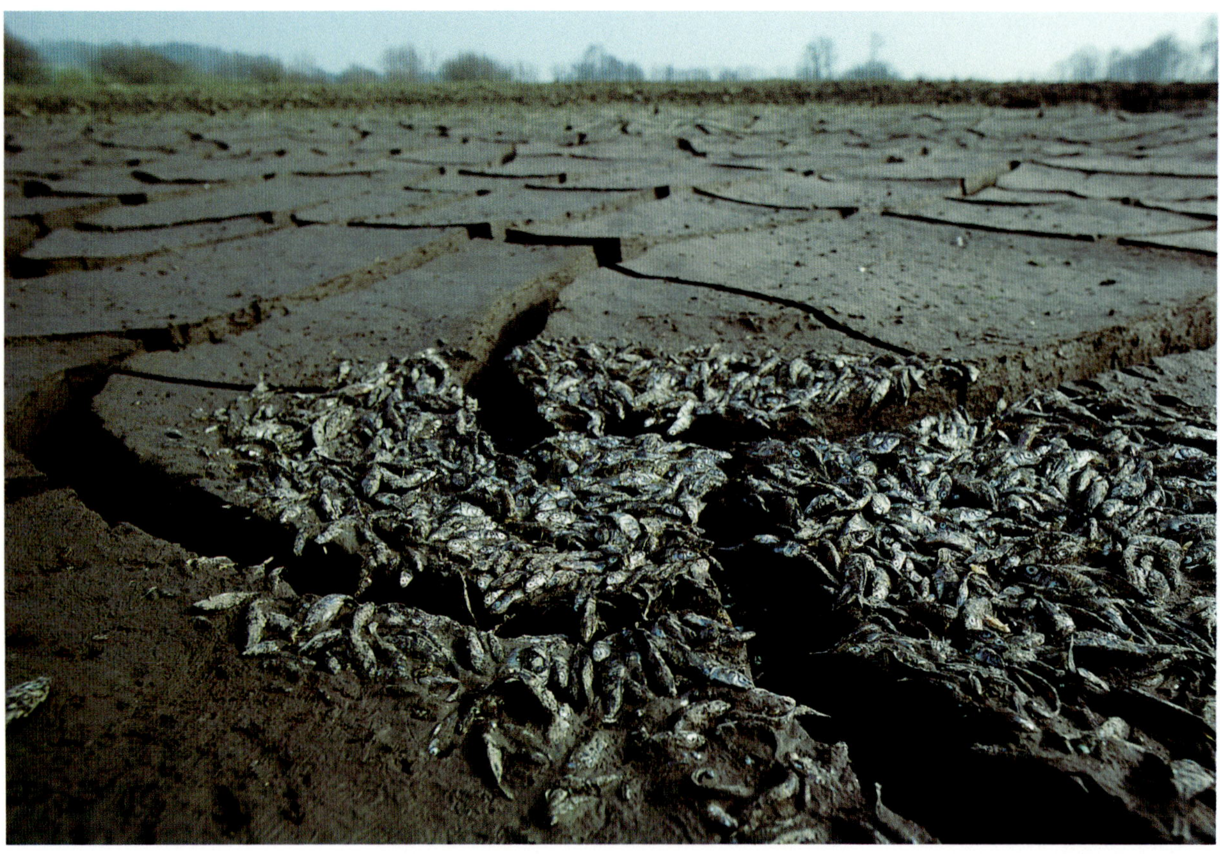

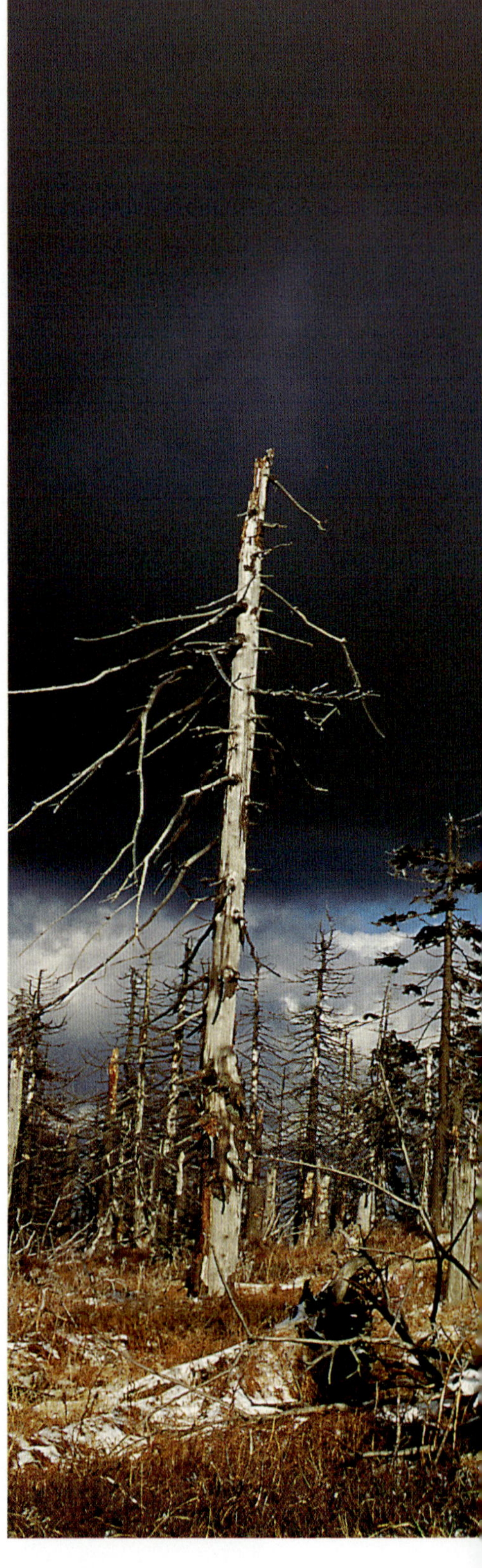

Robin Bush
United Kingdom
HIGHLY COMMENDED

Demise of a river
"I had watched my local river,
the Misbourne near Amersham,
decline over many months, and
so it was just a case of waiting for
a sunny day last February to get
a good picture. The fish are
stickleback which died as the
water level declined to nothing."

Canon F1 NAE with 20mm lens; tripod;
f16 at 1/15 sec; Kodachrome 64

Richard Packwood
United Kingdom
HIGHLY COMMENDED

Acid rain damage
"During summer 1991
I travelled extensively in Eastern
Europe taking photographs. I
particularly wanted to see the
spruce forests on the border
between Czechoslovakia and
Poland, which have been
decimated by acid rain. After a
lengthy walk in dull wet weather
I reached the area where the
devastation is worst - just when
the cloud cover gave way to
dramatic light."

Nikon F4 with 20mm lens; f11 at
1/60 sec; Fujichrome Velvia

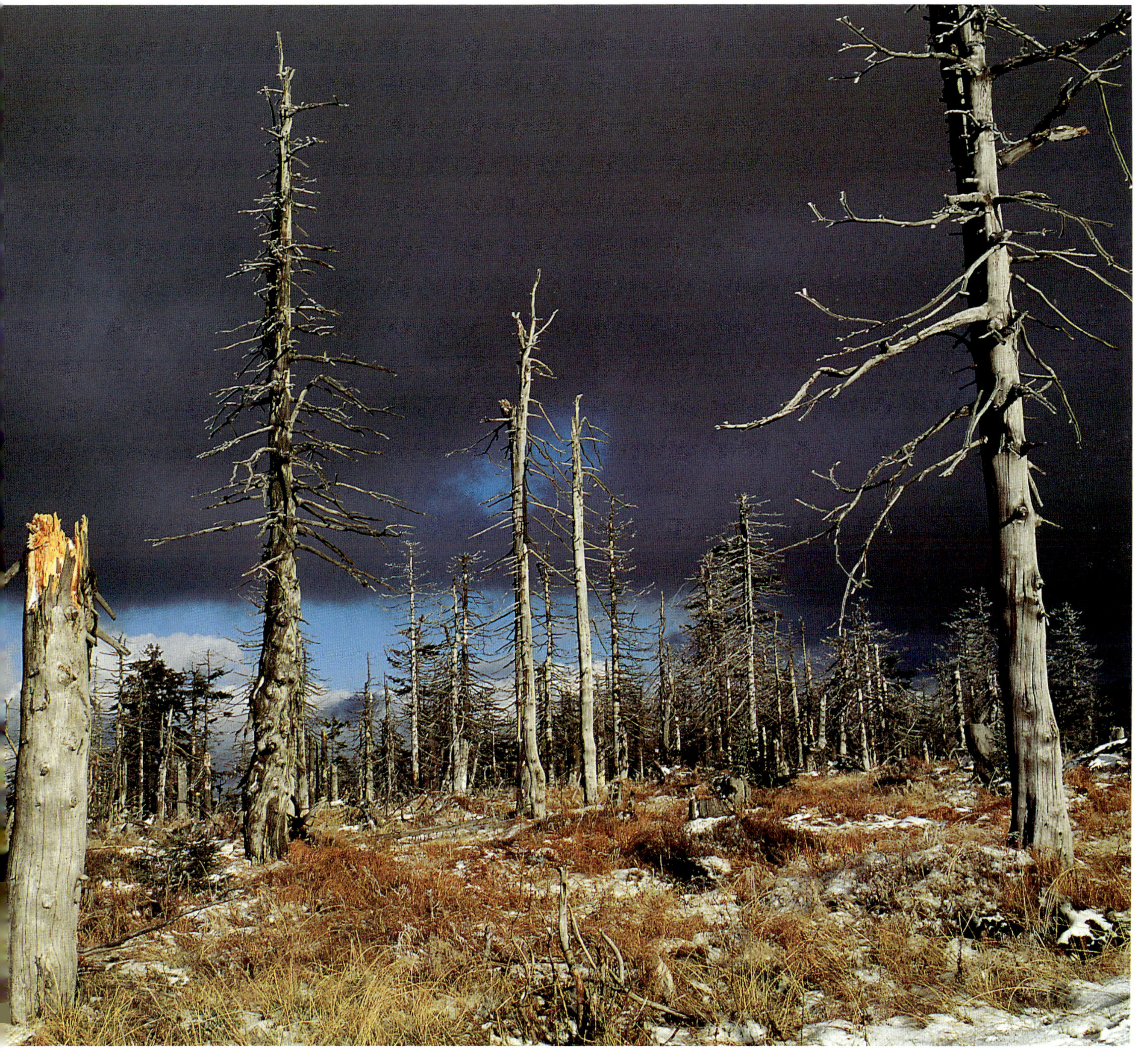

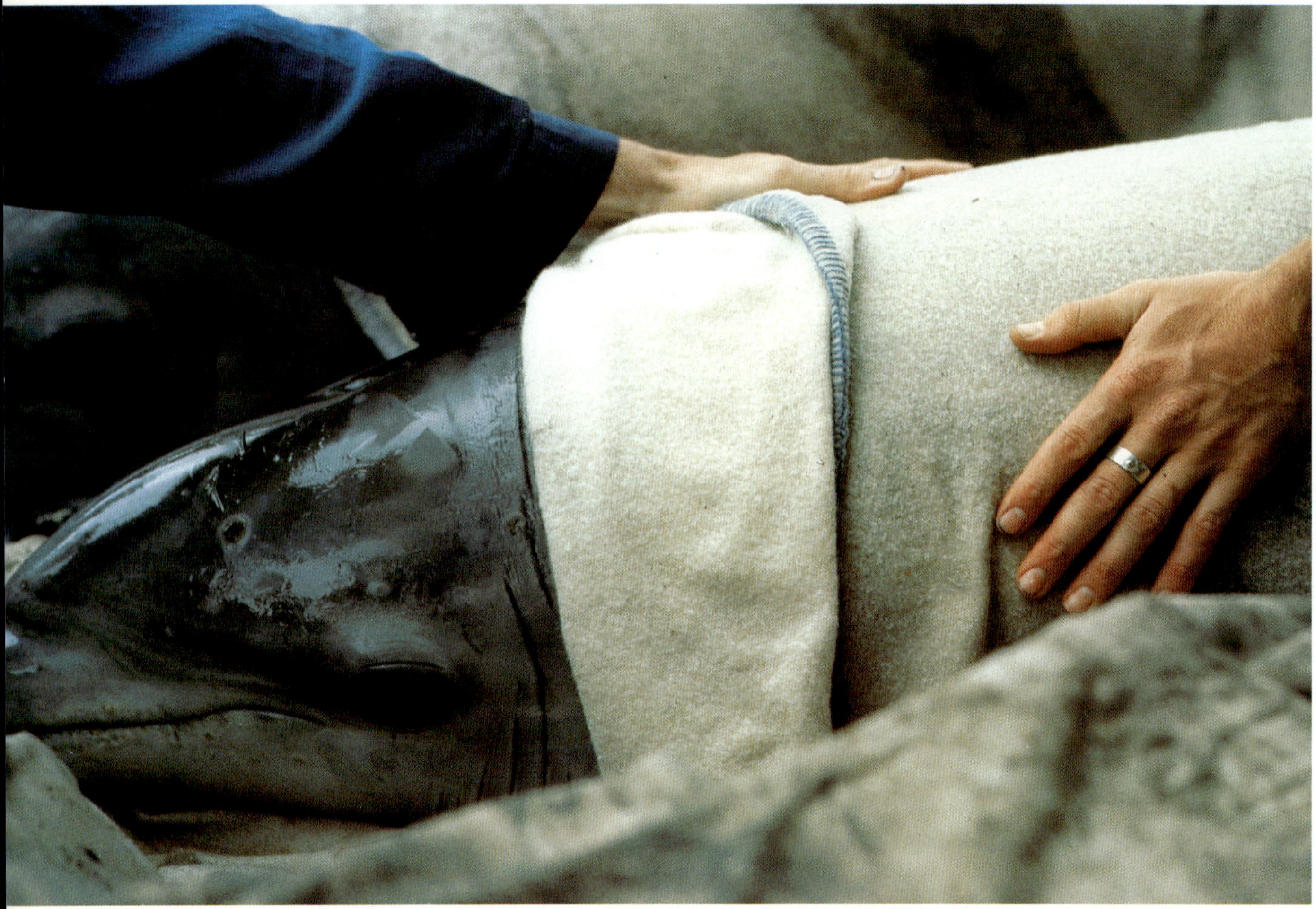

Robert Garvey
Australia
HIGHLY COMMENDED

Dolphin rescue

*"A pod of dolphins swam into the
upper reaches of the Peel Inlet,
south of Perth, and were
stranded by the outgoing tide.
Dozens of volunteers spent the
day looking after them until they
could be transported by trailer to
deep water. Here a rescuer
comforts one of the dolphins
which is covered in wet blankets
to keep its skin moist."*

Canon T90 with 85mm lens; f5.6 at
1/60 sec; Kodachrome 64 Professional

Gary Lee Lackie
United States of America
HIGHLY COMMENDED

Pacific Loon hooked

*"This pacific loon was hooked by
someone fishing for trout on
Lake Campbell near Anchorage.
Luckily, the line wasn't very
heavy, and the loon was able to
break it. As far as I know, the
bird survived the experience and
was one of a pair I watched
successfully raise two chicks the
next year."*

Canon F1n with 400mm lens and ×1.4
converter; monopod; f4 at 1/250 sec;
Fujichrome 100

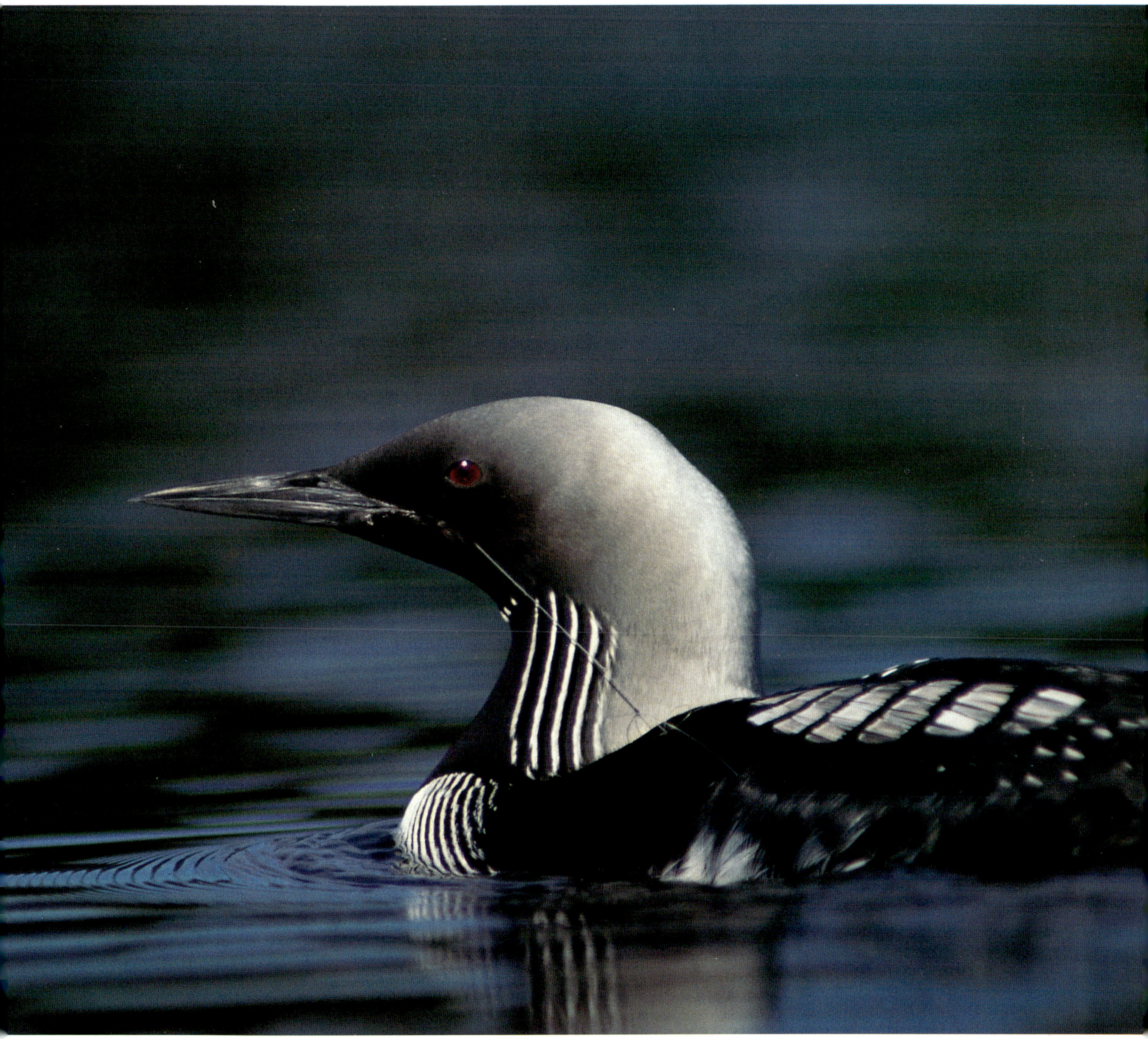

Endangered Wildlife

Pictures in this category must show plants or animals which are listed as endangered at a national or international level.

Joanna Van Gruisen
United Kingdom
WINNER

Asiatic Wild Asses

"There may be only 1000 left of this particular subspecies of wild ass, **Equus hemionus khur**, living almost exclusively in the sanctuary of the Little Rann of Kutch, where this photograph was taken.

Bachelor groups, such as this one, are often playful, hence the raised tail of the lead animal and the apparent neck biting of the animal second from the right.

Because of lack of cover, the animals are difficult to approach. On this day, six or seven hours were spent on foot moving with the herd, and even then I was not able to get within 200 feet."

Nikon F4 with 600mm lens; tripod; f11 at 1/250 sec; Kodachrome 64

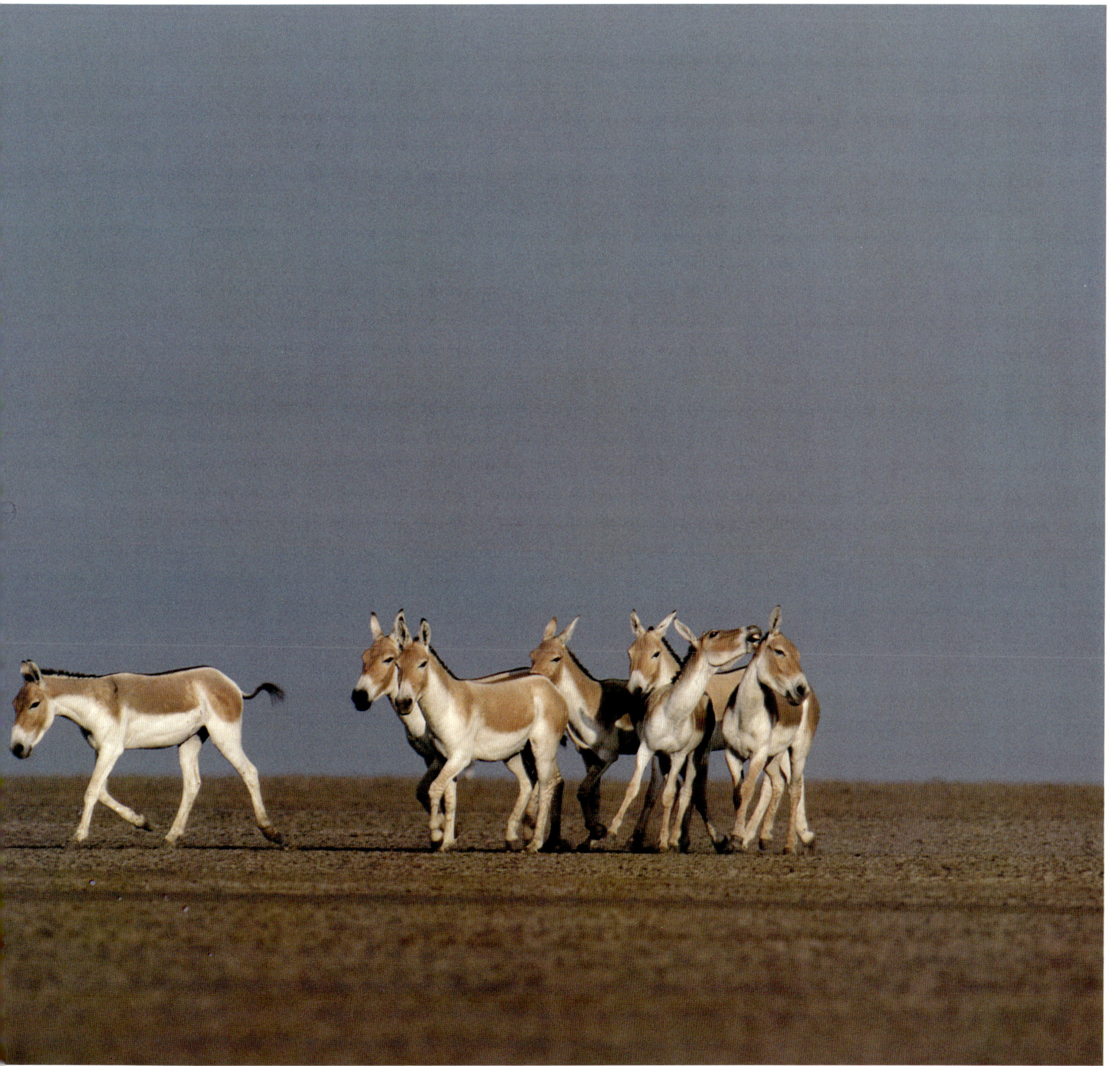

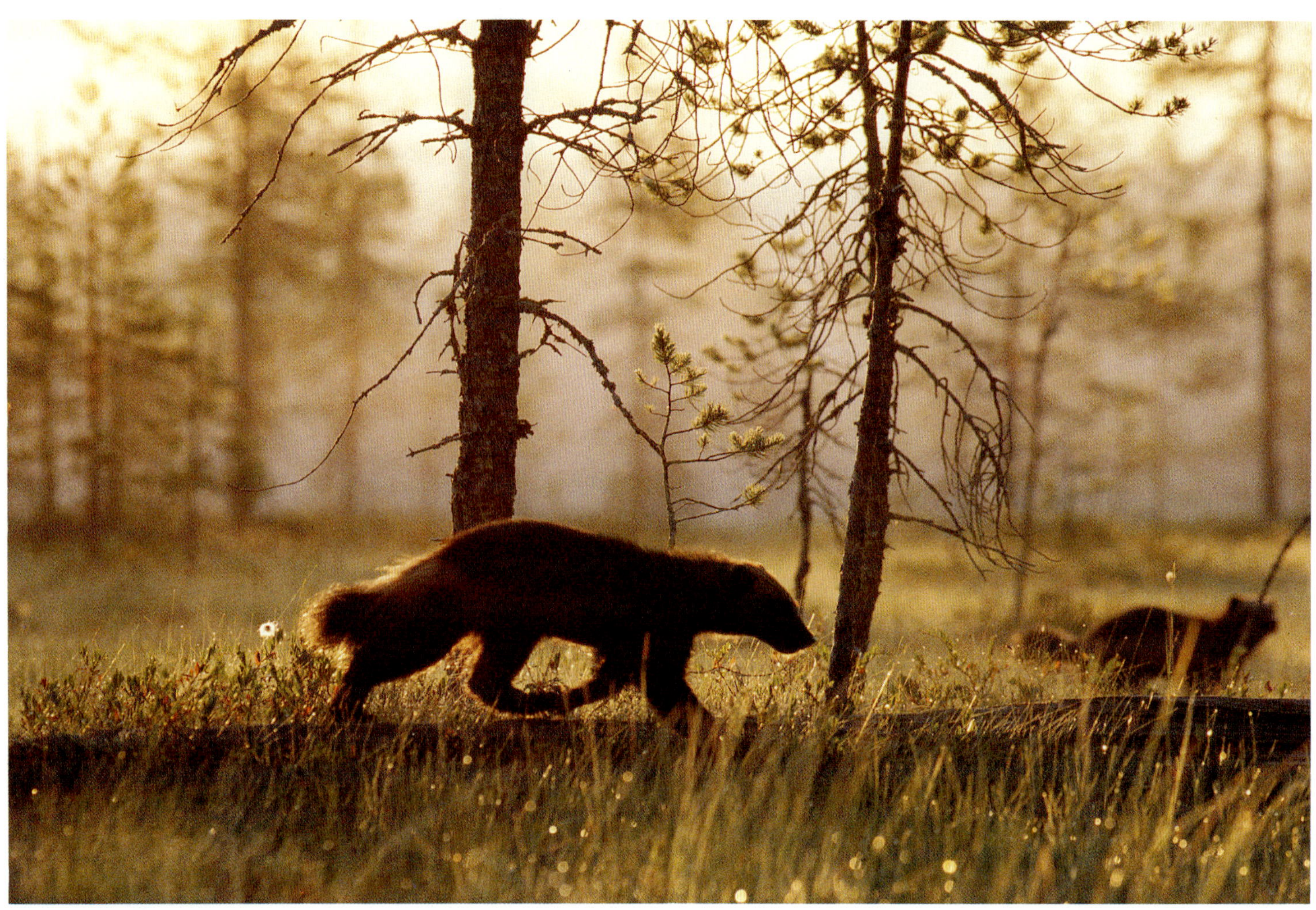

Antti Leinonen

Finland

RUNNER-UP

Wolverine in the summer

"After a winter without seeing
wolverines I started to see them
occasionally during the spring
and summer. Then one early
morning at the end of July, three
young wolverines came close to
my hide. They were about six
months old and seemed to be
independent of their mother.
Perhaps they were the only
wolverines born in Finland that
year - my hide is positioned
four kilometres from the
Russian border."

Canon T90 with 300mm lens; 1/500 sec;
Fujichrome 400 Professional

66

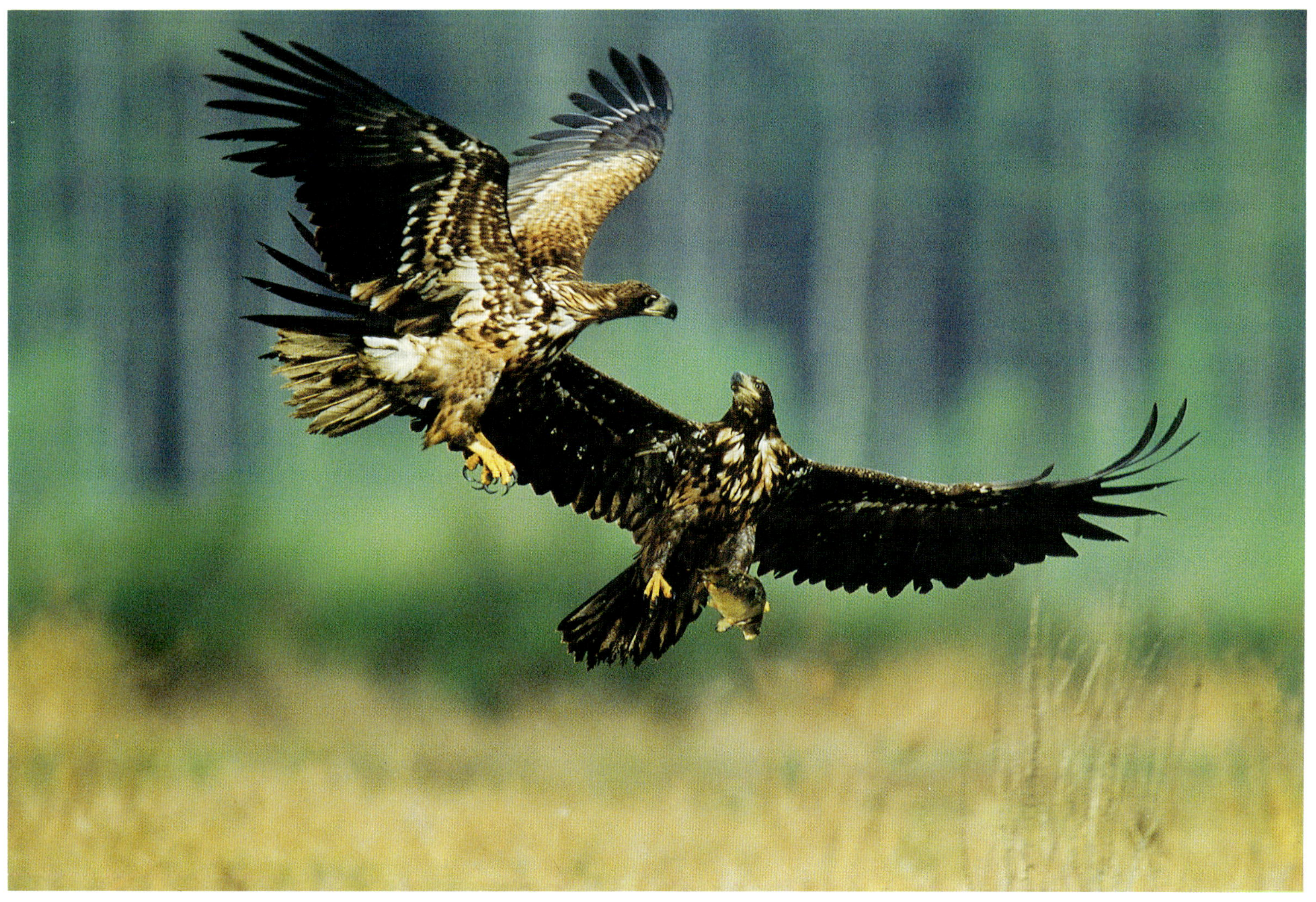

Konrad Wothe
Germany
HIGHLY COMMENDED

White-Tailed Eagles
"The Muritz National Park in Germany is the best place to see rare white-tailed eagles, probably because there are a number of fish farms nearby where the birds are tolerated. I set up a hide at a favourite fishing site and waited there from before sunrise until after sunset over a period of two weeks. Here you can see one eagle trying to steal another's fish."

Canon EOS 1 with 600mm lens and x1.4 converter; tripod; Fujichrome 100

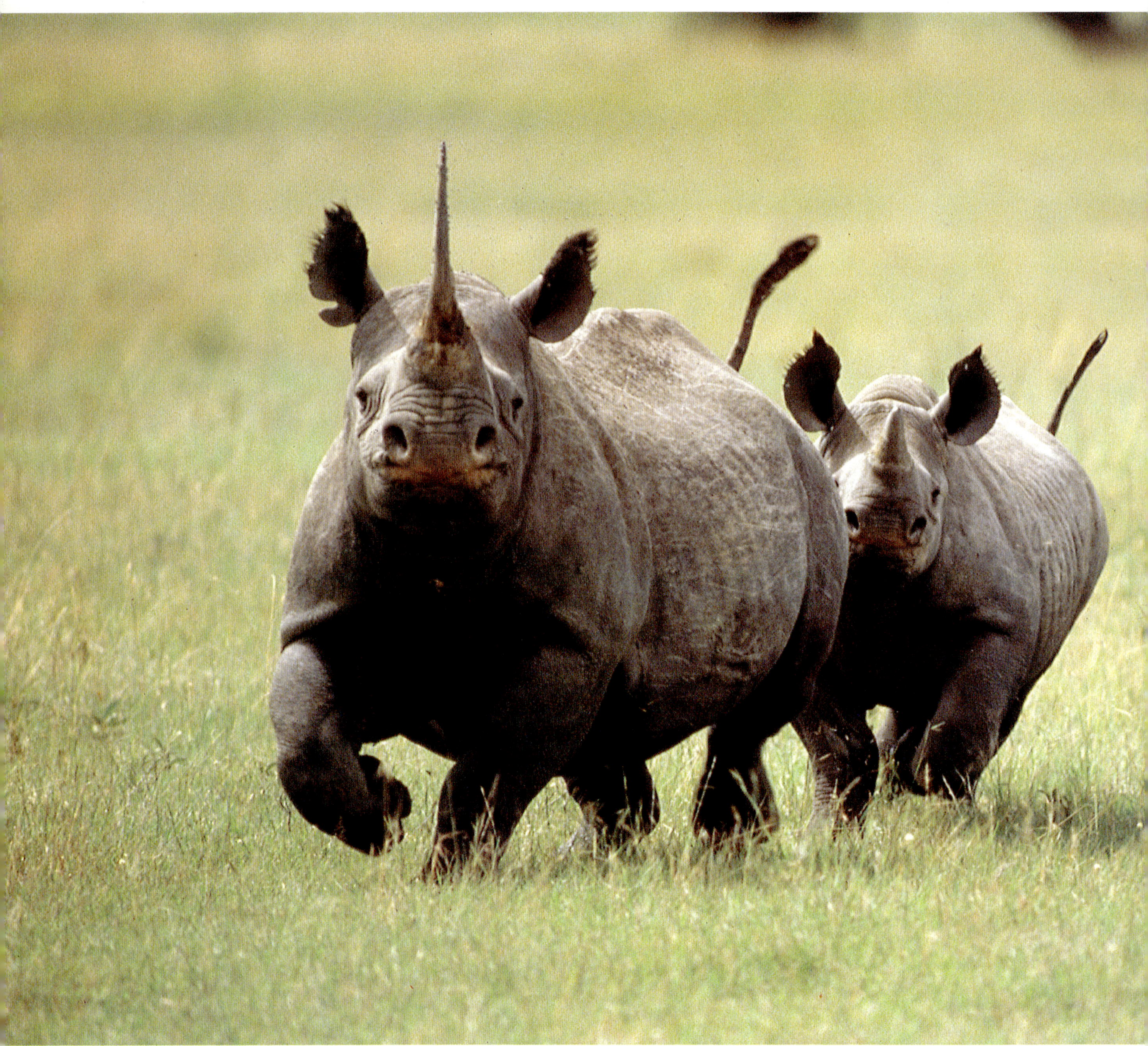

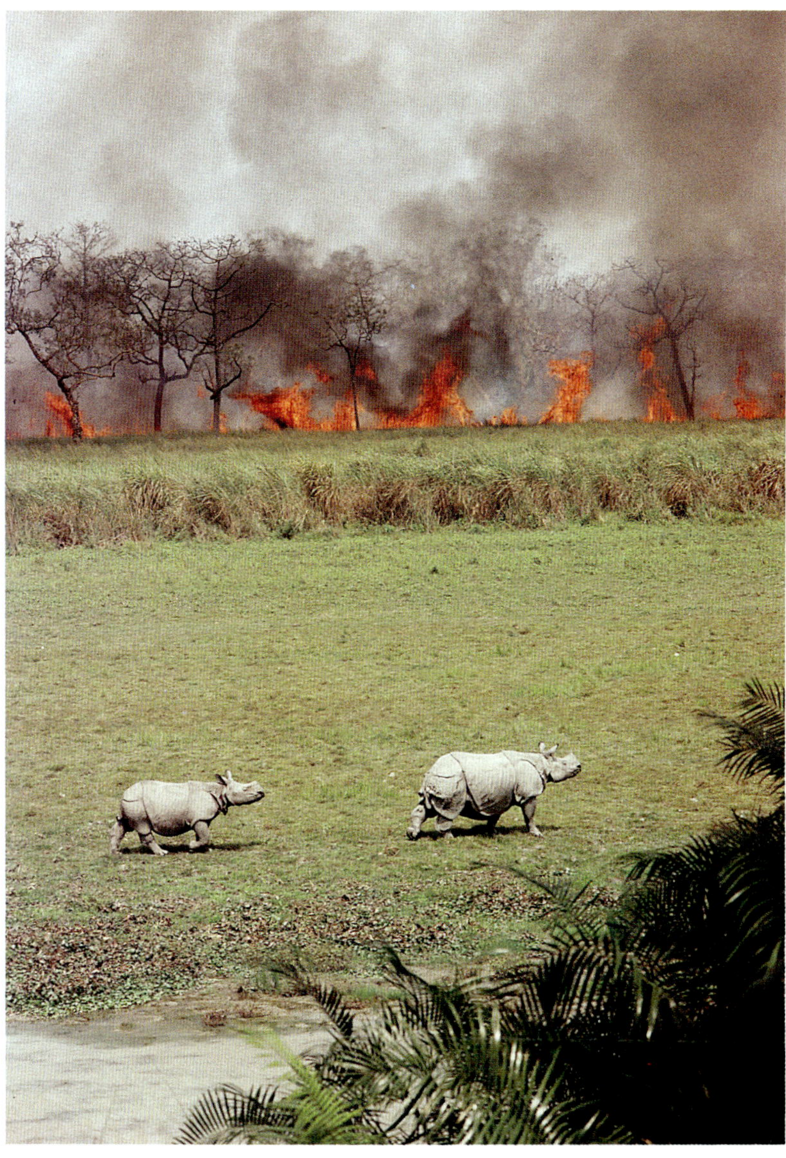

Renee Lynn
United States of America
HIGHLY COMMENDED

Rhinos charging

*"The declining population due to
poaching can make finding a
black rhino in the wild quite a
challenge. They are shy and
elusive and spend a lot of time
hidden in bushy areas.
On seeing my vehicle, this
mother and baby quickly
retreated, although ten minutes
later they came bounding out of
the bush at full speed.
I managed to take five frames
before we had to drive out
of the way."*

Nikon F4 with 500mm lens; f4 at 1/350
sec; Fujichrome 100

Kushal Mookerjee
India
HIGHLY COMMENDED

Indian Rhinos

*"I came upon this scene while
travelling through the Kaziranga
National Park in Assam. Fires
are made to maintain the
grassland habitat that the Indian
rhinocerosos depends on."*

Nikon FM2 with 80-200mm lens;
Kodachrome 64

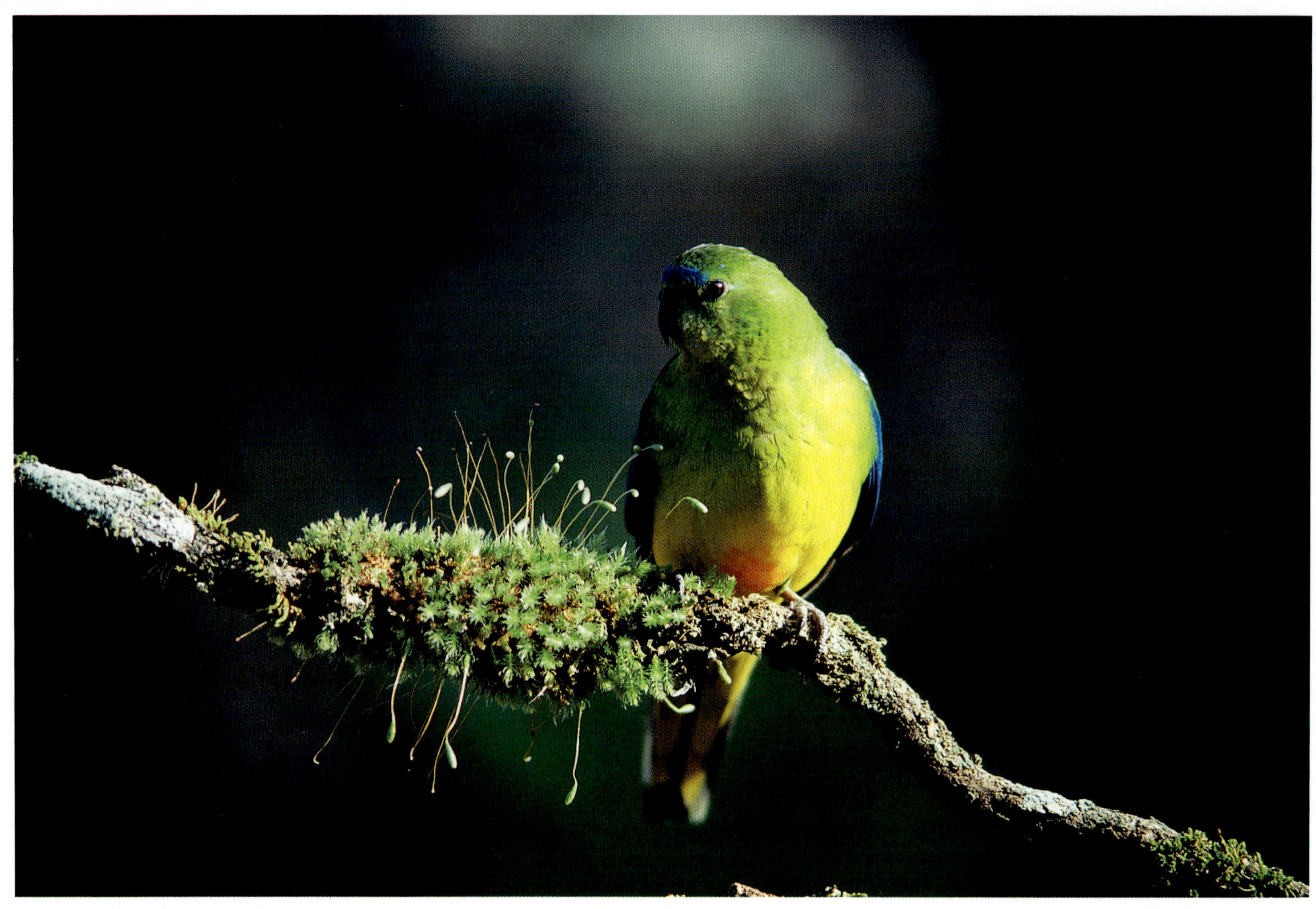

Dave Watts
United Kingdom
HIGHLY COMMENDED

Orange-bellied Parrot

*''After collecting seeds on a
button grass plain during a wild
rainstorm, this male parrot
perched near its nest chamber.
I took this in Tasmania from a
hide on a specially built wooden
tower 25 feet high.''*

Nikon FE with 80-200mm zoom lens;
tripod; Kodachrome 64

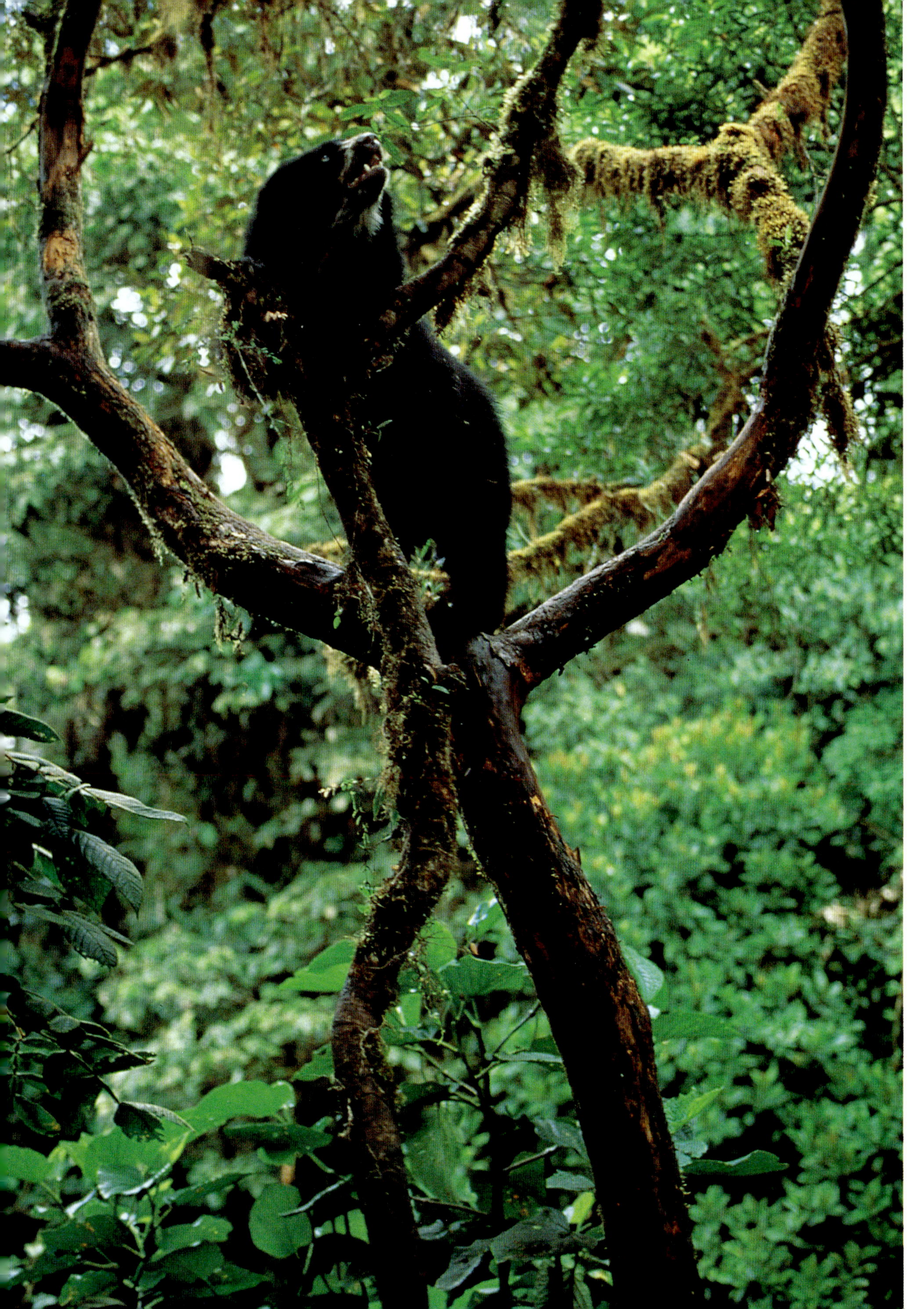

Mark Moffett
United States of America
HIGHLY COMMENDED

Spectacled Bear
*"The spectacled bear is a
genuine canopy animal. This
one is stripping vegetation from
the treetops in La Planada
Reserve, Colombia."*

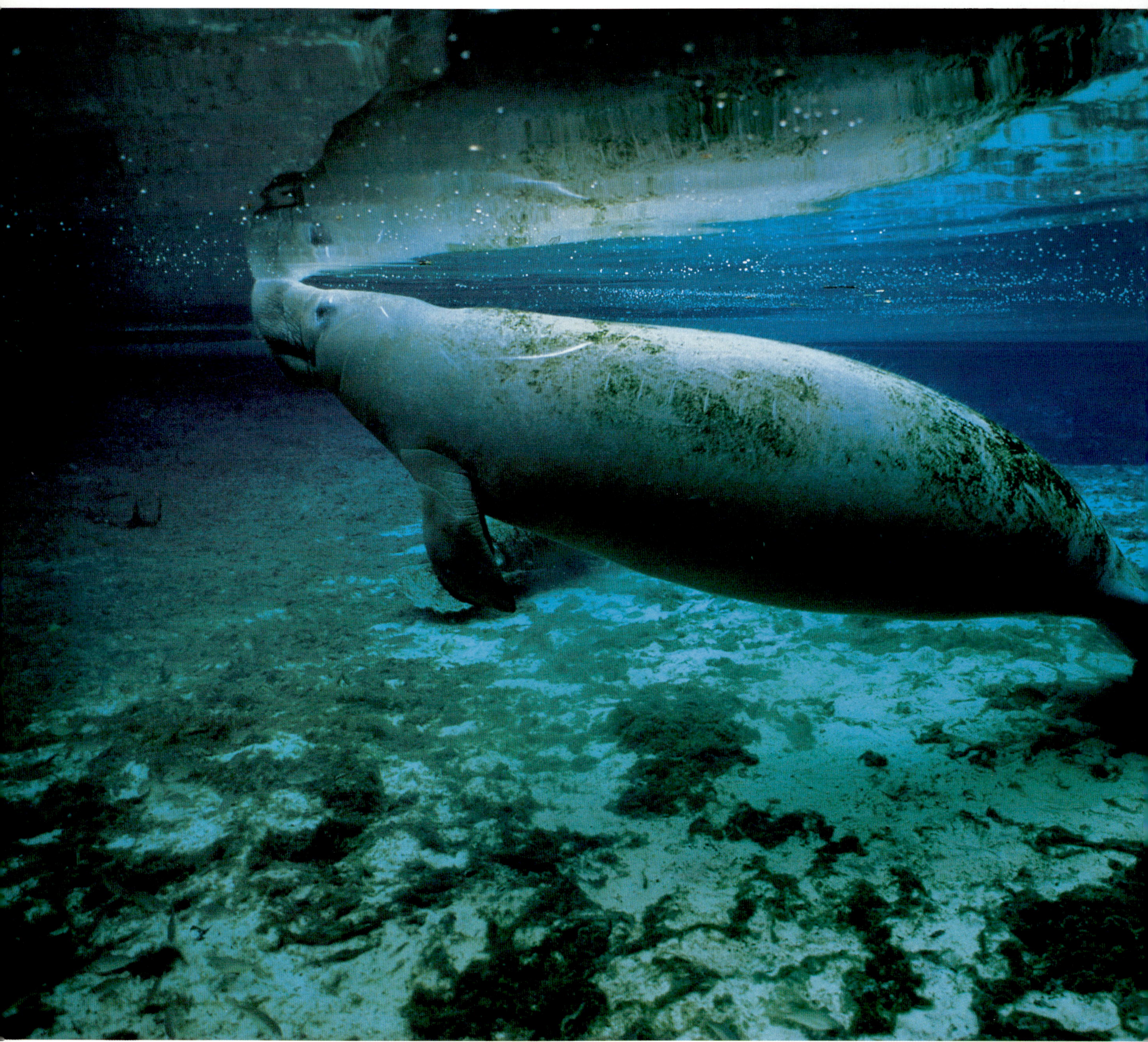

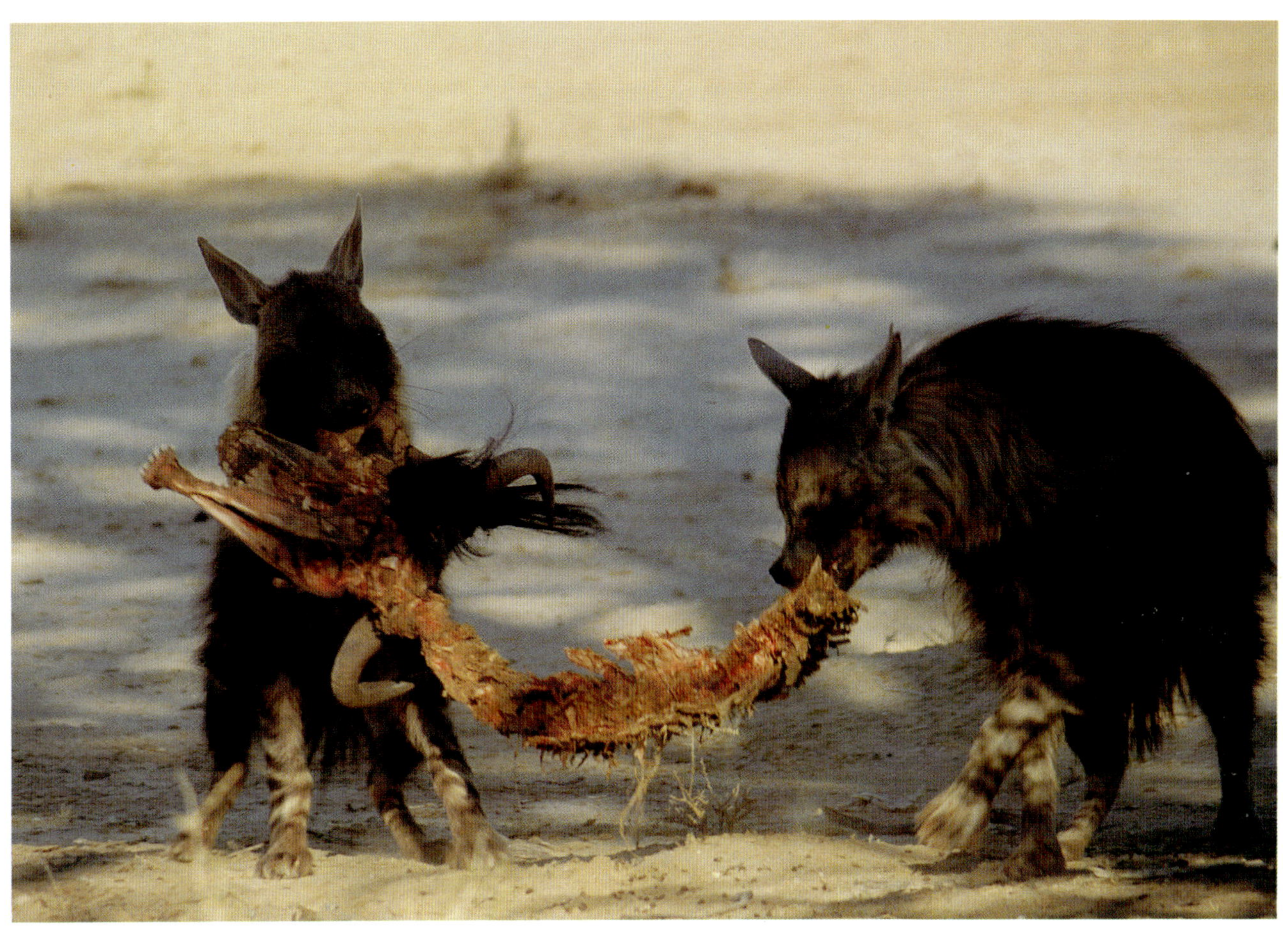

Jill Sneesby
South Africa
HIGHLY COMMENDED

Brown Hyaenas

"Brown hyaenas and jackals had gathered at a kill made by a pride of lions the previous day in the Kalahari Gemsbok Park. The hyeanas broke off large bones from the carcass, disappearing to stash them away before returning for more."

Minolta X700 with 100-500mm lens;
f8/11 at 1/125 sec or 1/250 sec

Daniel J Cox
United States of America
HIGHLY COMMENDED

Manatee

"This West Indian manatee is surfacing for air in a freshwater spring off the Gulf of Mexico coast in Florida."

Nikonos V with 15mm lens;
Kodachrome 64

Primates in Peril

This category was created for the 1992 competition only, to highlight the work of the International Primate Protection League (IPPL). The photographs entered could be portraits or could highlight welfare or conservation issues.

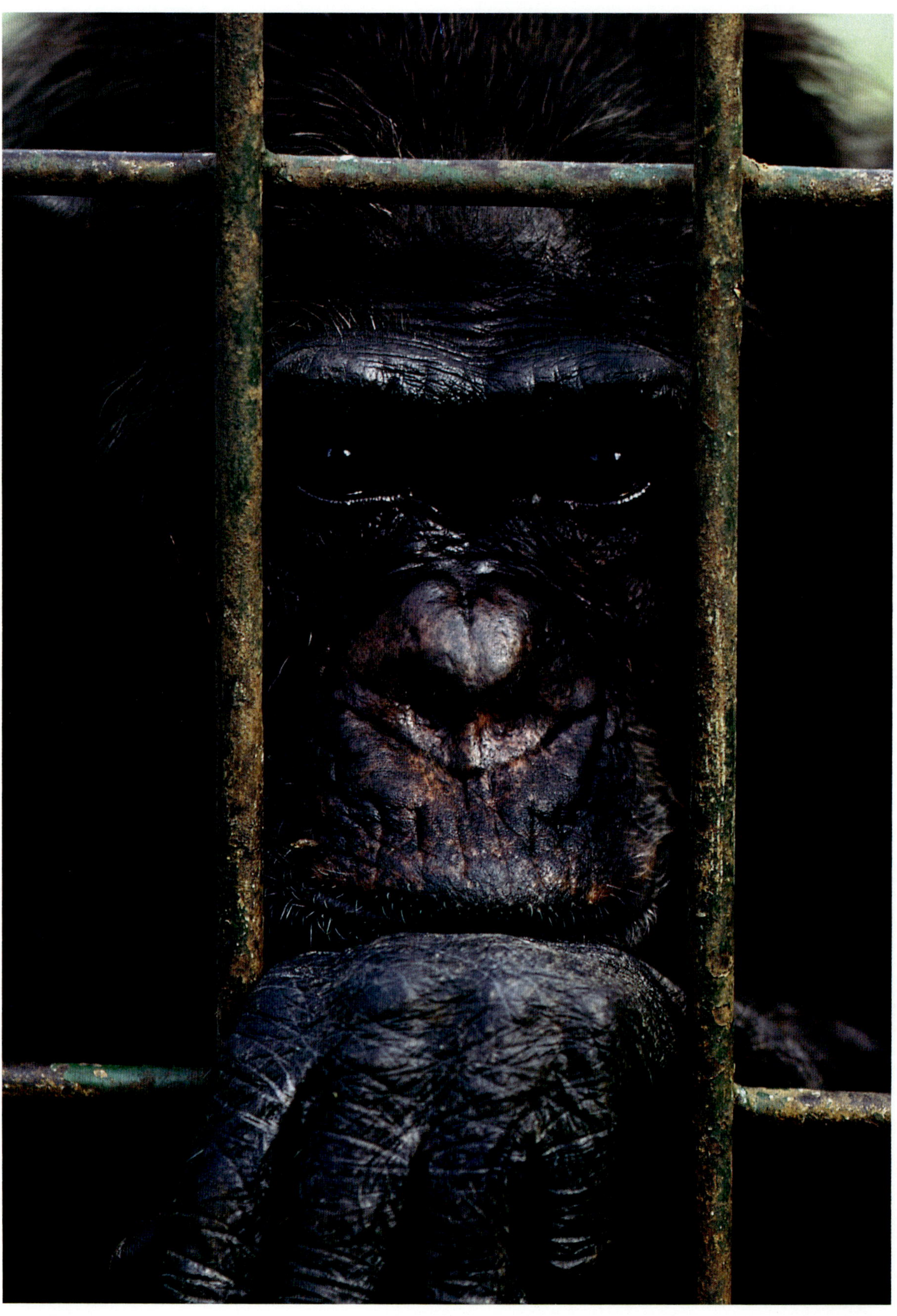

Luis Miguel Ruiz Gordon

Spain

WINNER

Caged Chimp

"This picture was taken in Santillana del Mar's zoo. The cage held a couple of chimpanzees and their young, born in captivity. I was struck by the animal's forceful expression of sadness and resignation."

Nikon FE with 240mm lens; f4.5 at 1/125 sec; Kodachrome 64

Gerry Ellis
United States of America
RUNNER-UP

Young Chimpanzee in transit

"This young chimp was confiscated from poachers and delivered to the Vet Centre at the Karisoke Research Centre near the Virunga Mountains in Rwanda. The chimp was suffering from fright and depression after being violently separated from its mother and family. I took the picture as part of an ongoing project to photograph great apes in the wild and their treatment at the hands of humans."

Nikon F2AS with 85mm lens; f5.6 at 1/30 sec; Fujichrome 50

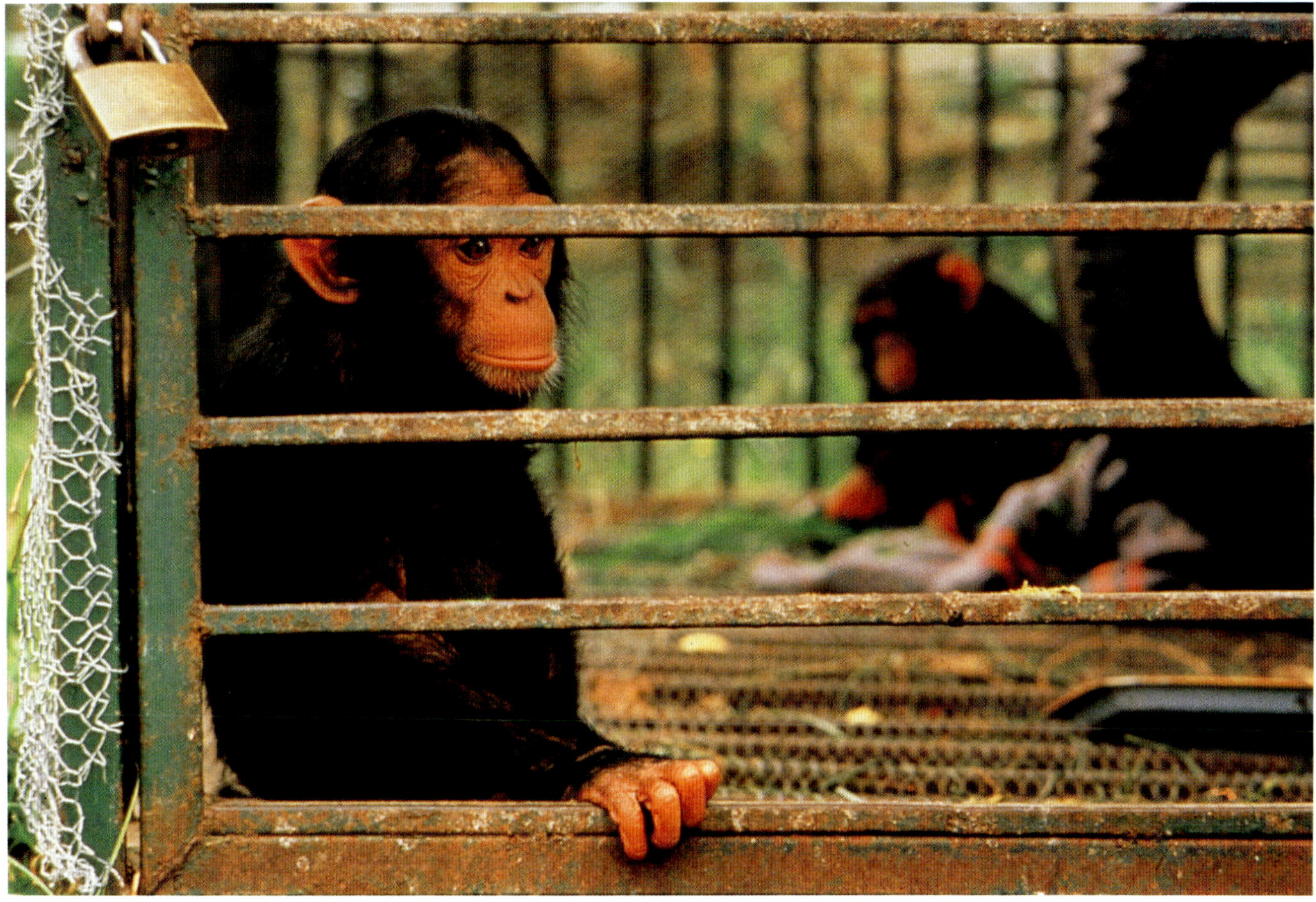

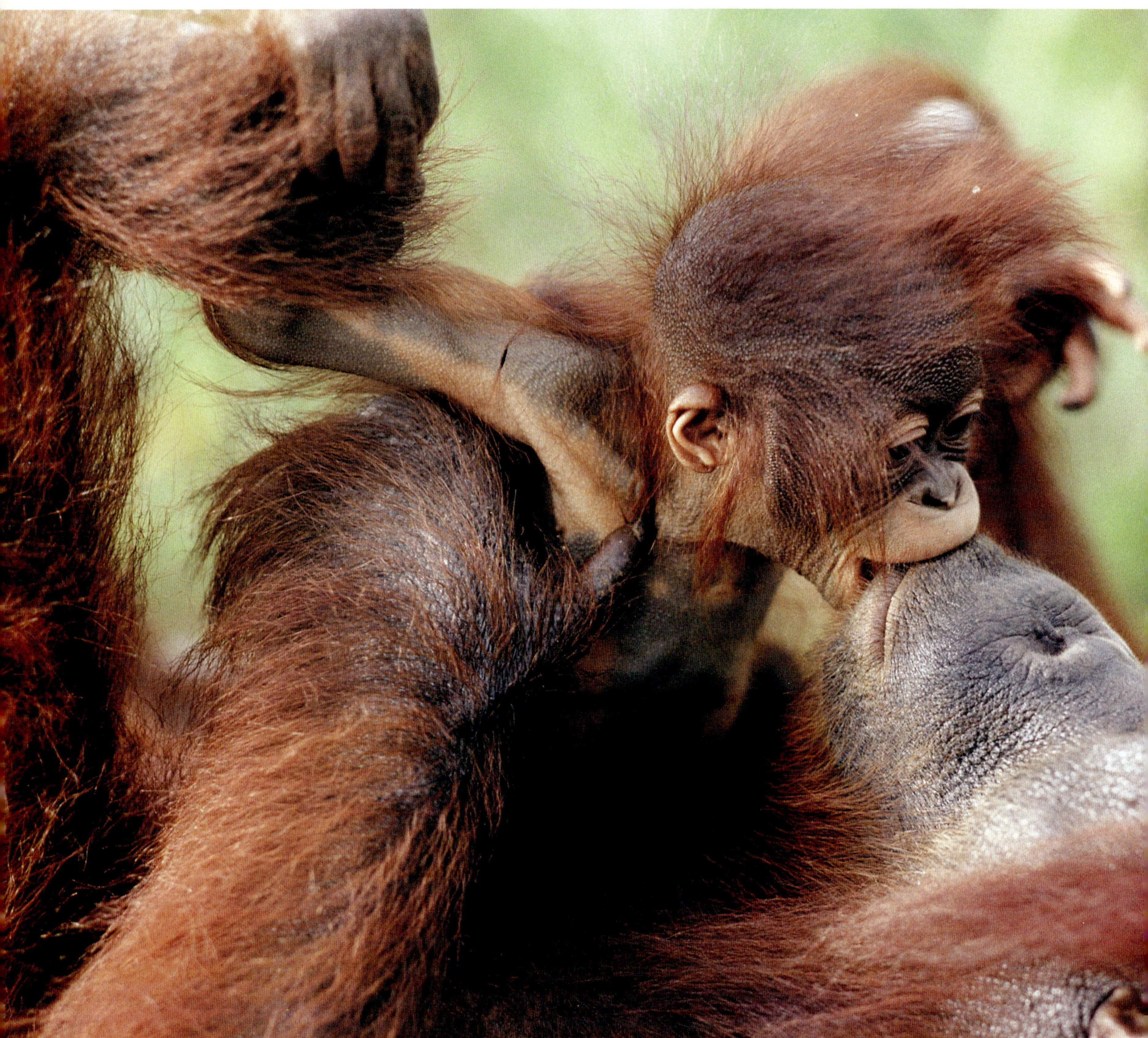

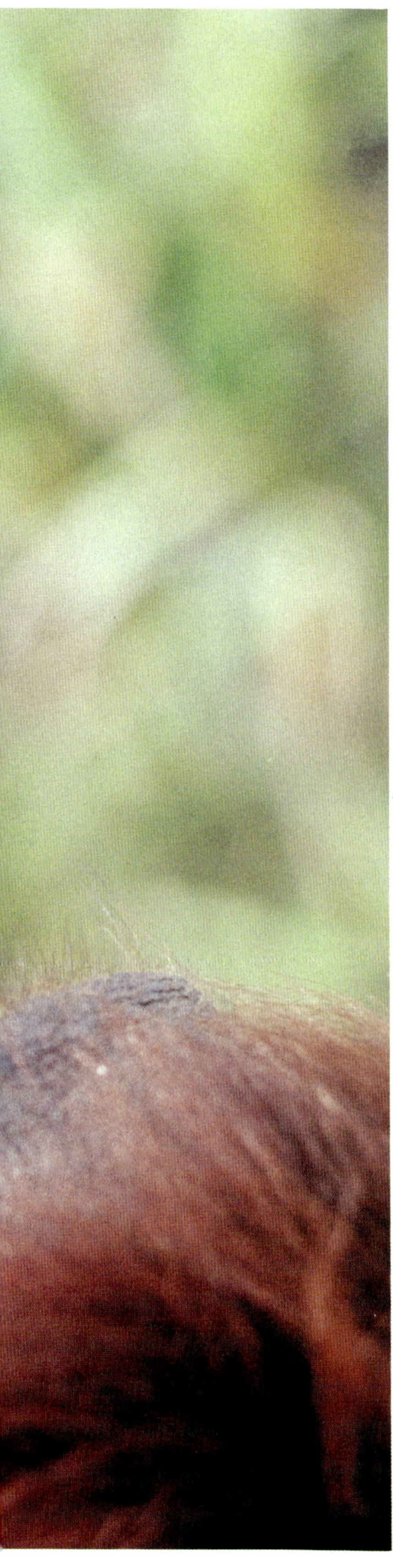

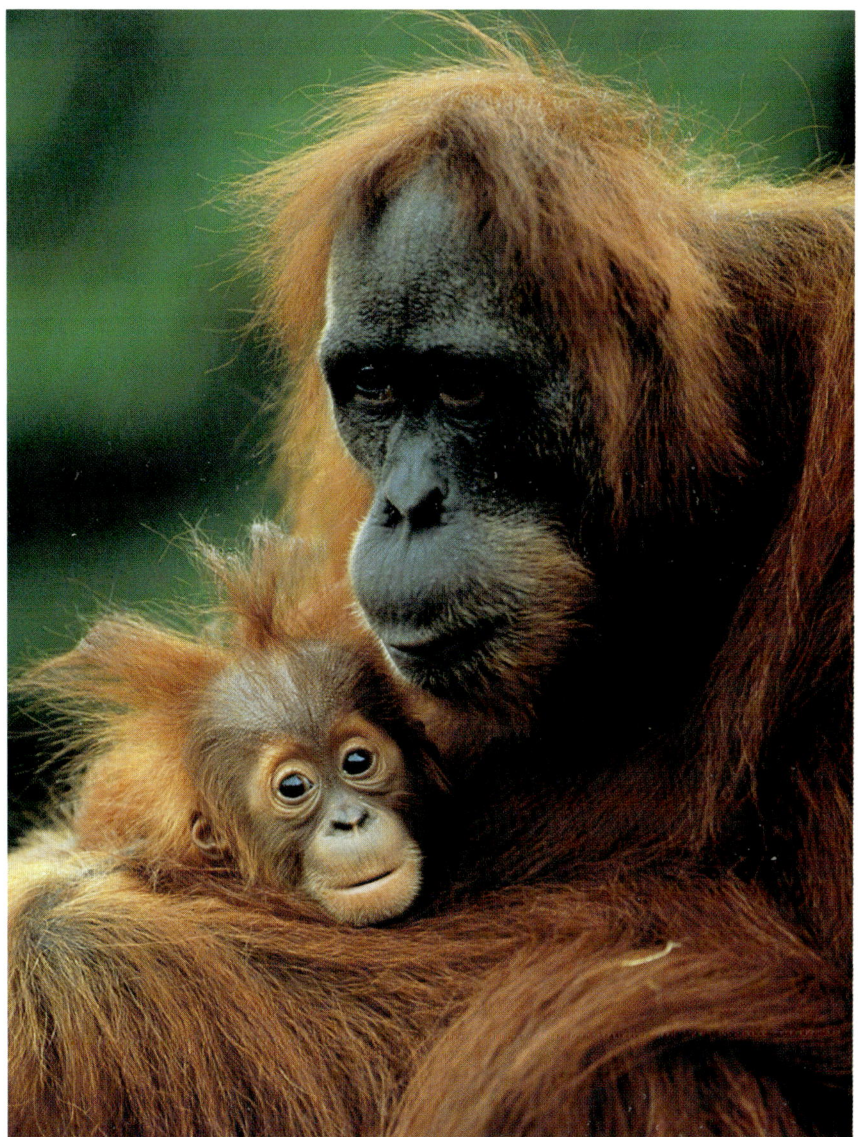

Karl Ammann
Switzerland
HIGHLY COMMENDED

Baby Orang
kissing mother

"Kissing has been observed in chimpanzees as well as Orang-utans, and seems to have pretty much the same meaning as we attribute to it in the human context. The mother orang-utan here was rescued from captivity and is being rehabilitated at Camp Leakey, in Kalimantan, Borneo. Here she can range freely and learn how to behave normally."

Nikon F4 with 80-210mm zoom lens; f5.6 at 1/125 sec; Kodachrome 200

Robert Garvey
Australia
HIGHLY COMMENDED

Orang-utan with baby

"Pusba, a Sumatran orang-utan and her baby were part of an international orang-utan breeding programme at Perth Zoo. Because Pusba was raised in captivity, the zoo was unsure if she would have the skills to mother her infant, but instinct took over."

Canon F1 with 300mm lens; f5.6 at 1/500 sec; Kodachrome Professional 100

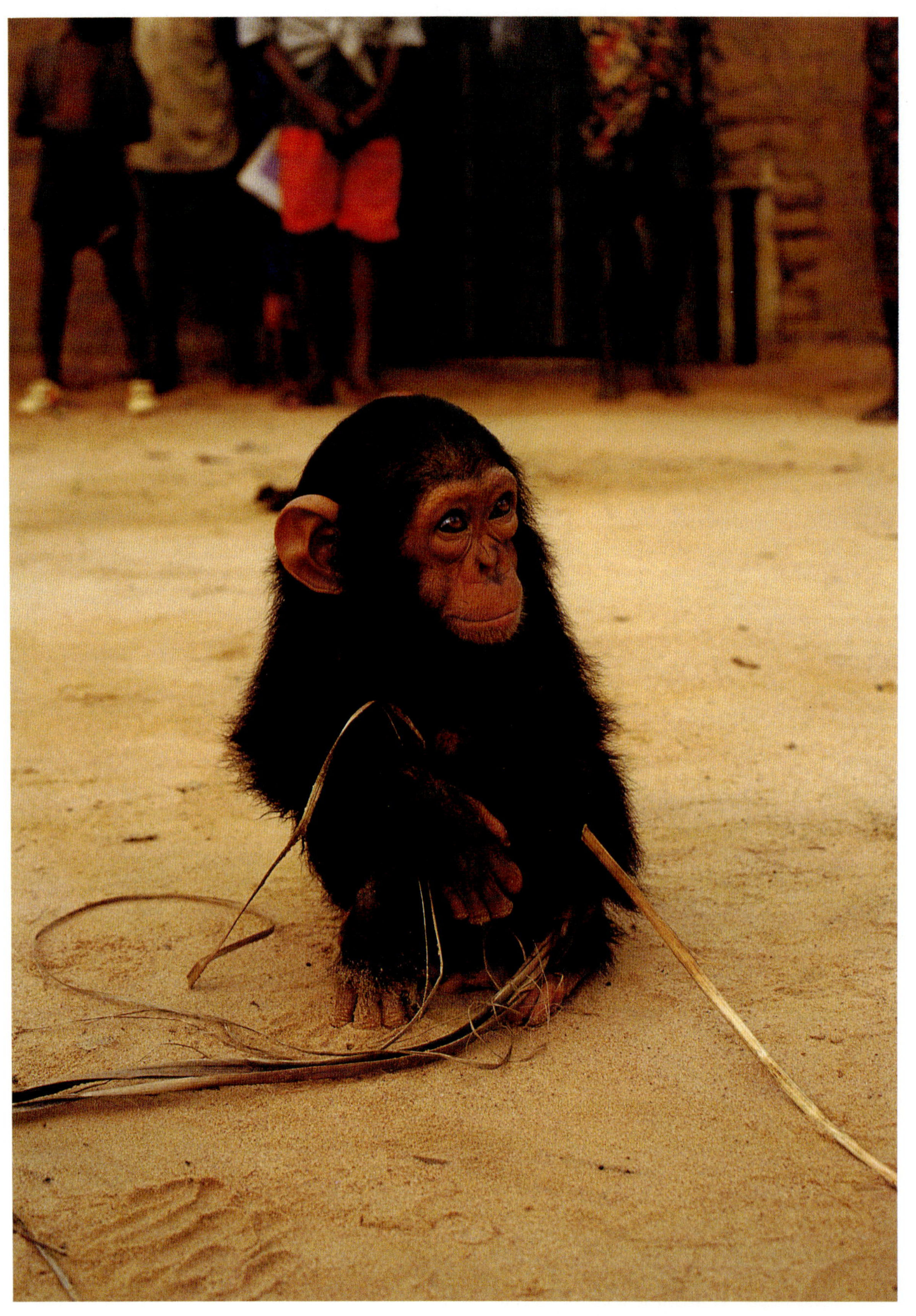

Louise Hartgill
United Kingdom
HIGHLY COMMENDED

Orphaned chimp for sale

"I was staying in a village during an expedition in Northern Congo when I saw this baby chimp for sale. I believe its mother was killed in order to capture it. Being frightened, the chimp was acting aggressively towards the villagers."

Nikon FM2 with 90mm lens;
Fujichrome RDP 100

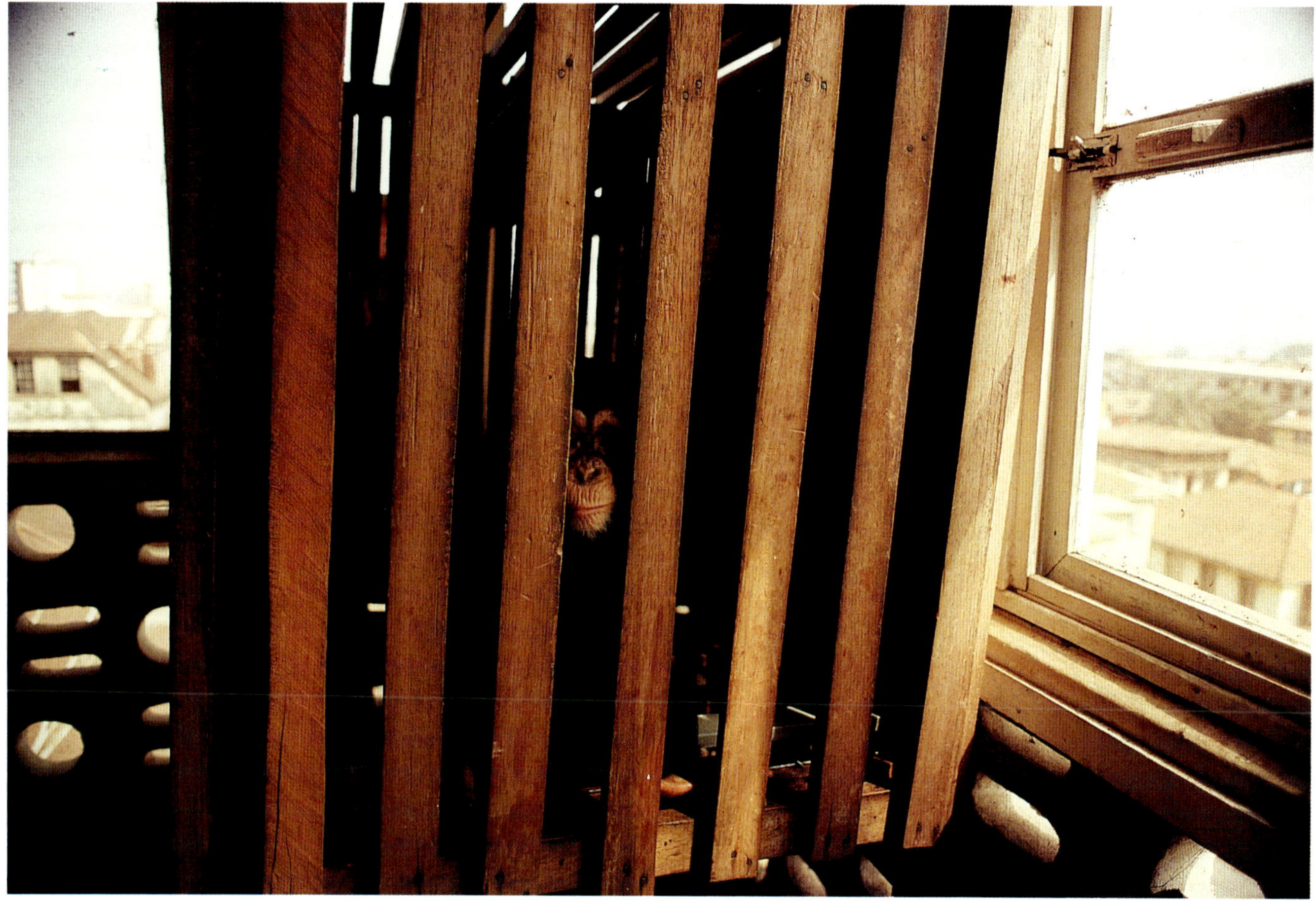

Nick Gordon
United Kingdom
HIGHLY COMMENDED

Chimp for sale

*"An anonymous tip-off led me to
a 'holding station' for chimps in
Freetown, Sierra Leone. The
conditions were deeply upsetting.
The man holding the animals
told me he had been asked to
supply 25 chimps to a company
involved in medical research.
'Big money' he said to me with a
glint in his eye."*

Nikon F3 with 55mm micro lens;
f8 at 1/125 sec; Kodachrome 64

In Praise of Plants

Photographs entered for this category can show plants from a distance or in close-up and should highlight their beauty and/or importance.

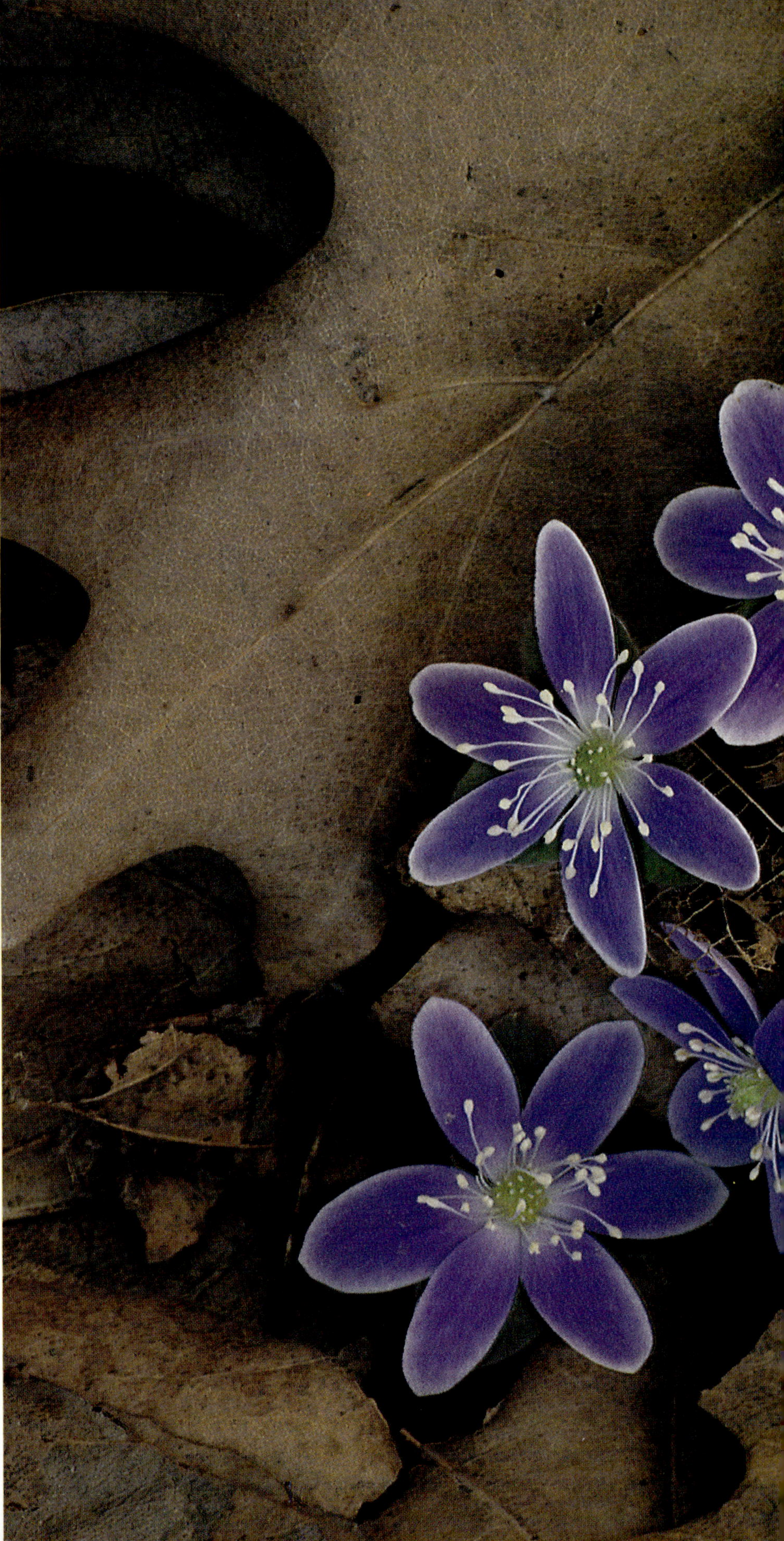

Theresa Thompson
United States of America
WINNER

Round-Lobed Hepatica

*"This clump of round-lobed hepaticas (a member of the buttercup family) were photographed on state land in Highland, Michigan.
I never use flash, and so I selected a composition on a slope with light coming directly on to the flowers. I then placed a diffusing cloth between the subject and the sun."*

Nikon FM2 with 105mm macro lens; tripod; f22 at 3 secs; Kodachrome 25

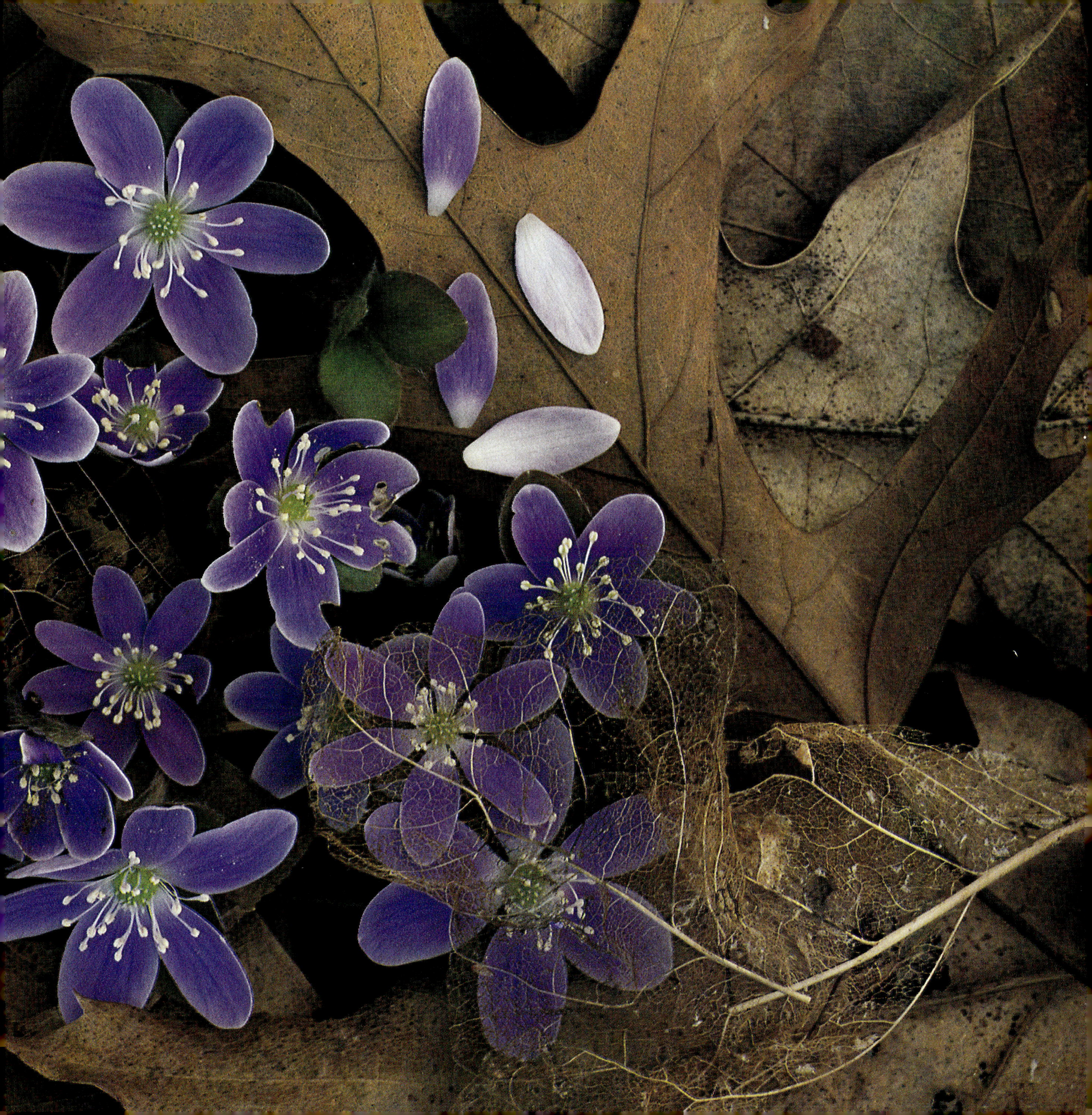

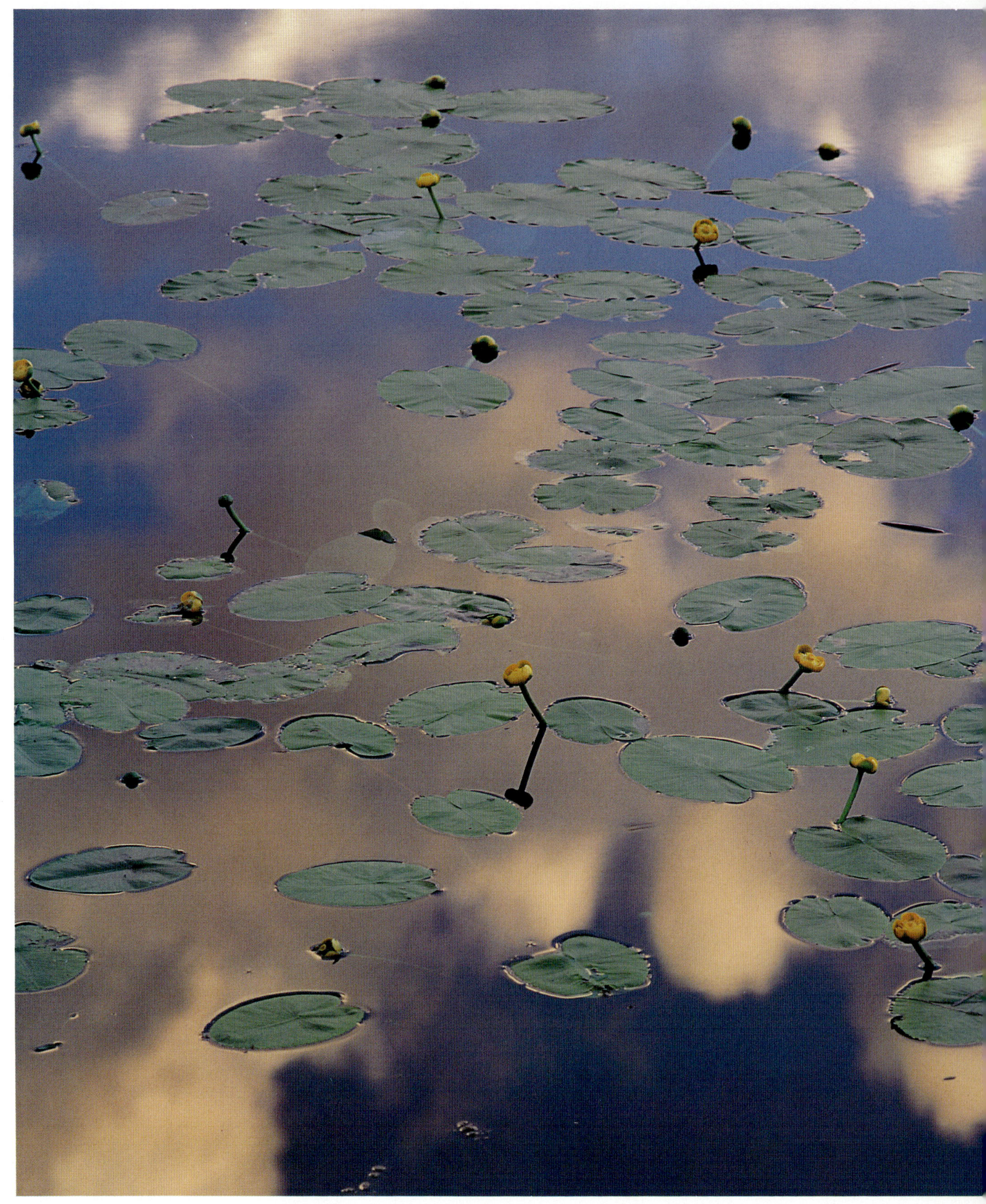

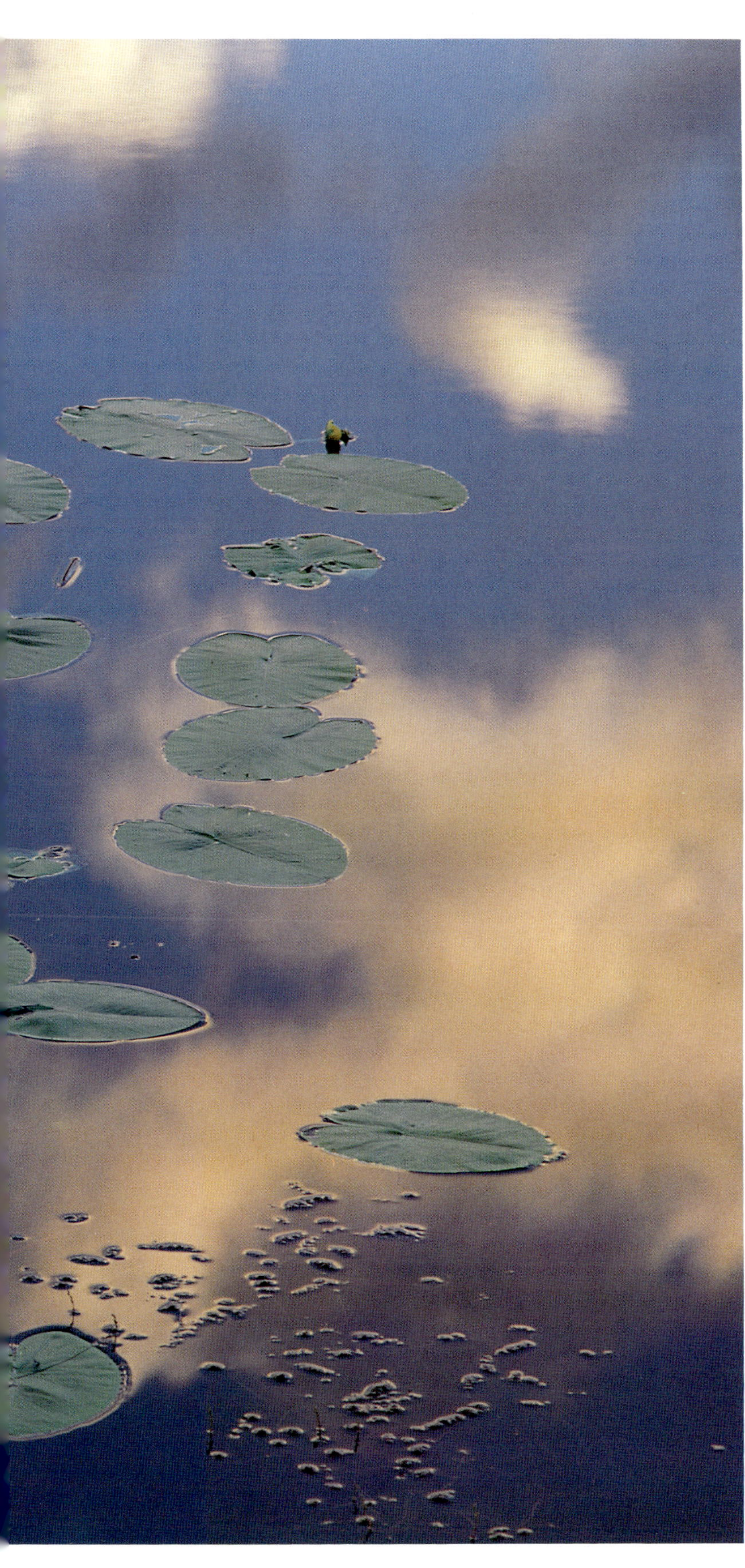

Jan Tove Johansson
Sweden
RUNNER-UP

Yellow Waterlilies

"I thought the cloud reflections
on the water amongst the yellow
lilypads would make a symbolic
picture: between heaven,
reflected on the water, and the
depths of the lake life has a
chance - life as exemplified by the
waterlilies, their roots in the
depths of the lake and their
flowers towards heaven and the
summer clouds."

Pentax 645 with 120mm macro lens;
tripod; f32 at 1/4 sec; Fujichrome Velvia

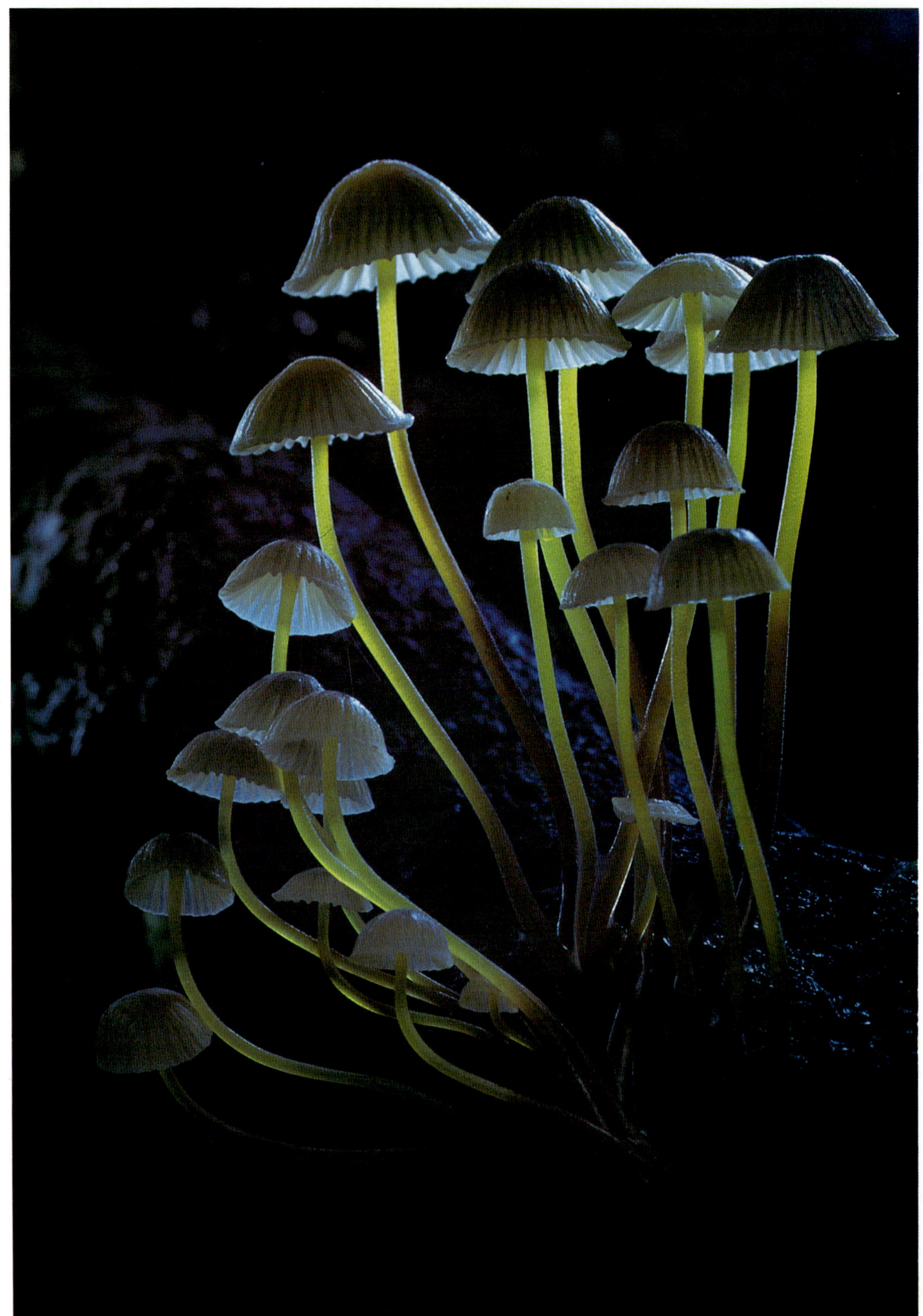

Gary Speer
New Zealand
SPECIALLY COMMENDED

Mycena Toadstools

*"When photographing fungi I aim to highlight their delicate structure and colours. These toadstools **Mycena subviscosa**, were found growing on rotting wood in Peel Forest, North Otago."*

Canon T90 with 50mm macro lens; tripod; reflector; f22 at 10 secs; Fujichrome 50 Professional

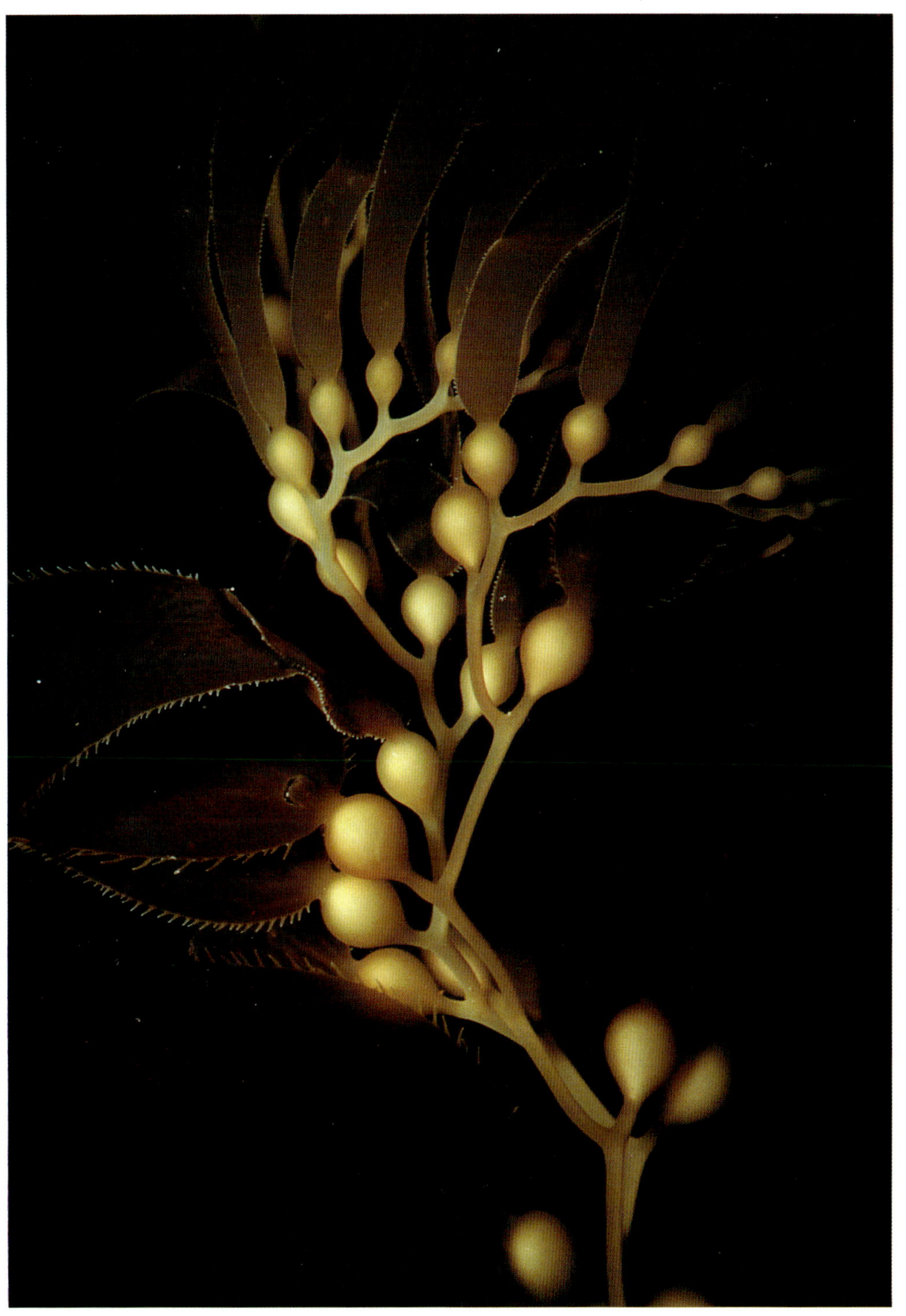

Norbert Wu
United States of America
HIGHLY COMMENDED

Kelp

*"It is the gas-filled bulbs of the
giant kelp plant that keep it
growing to the surface, to catch
sunlight. Ironically, kelp is very
difficult to photograph just
because it 'sucks up' light
so well."*

Nikonos V with 28mm lens; strobes;
Kodachrome 64

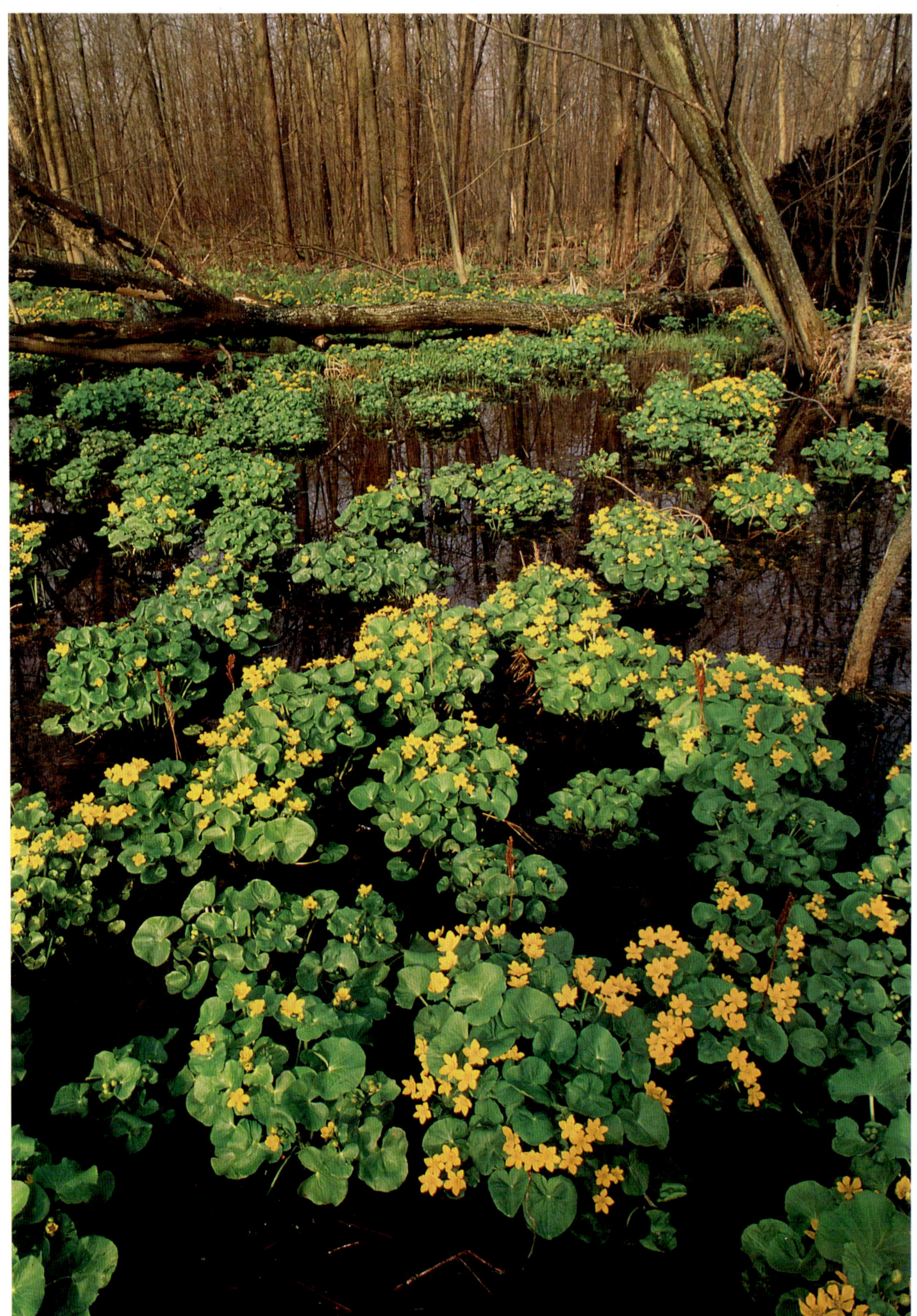

Doug Locke
United States of America
HIGHLY COMMENDED

Marsh Marigolds

"This is the best place I've ever seen for marsh marigolds. Last year, I stumbled on the area, at Seven Ponds Nature Center in Michigan, and so this year I went back at the same time of year, knowing the flowers would be in bloom, and hoping for a really calm overcast day. I took the photograph in the first hour after sunrise, standing knee-deep in the bog."

Nikon 8008 with 24mm lens; f22 at 2 secs; Fujichrome Velvia

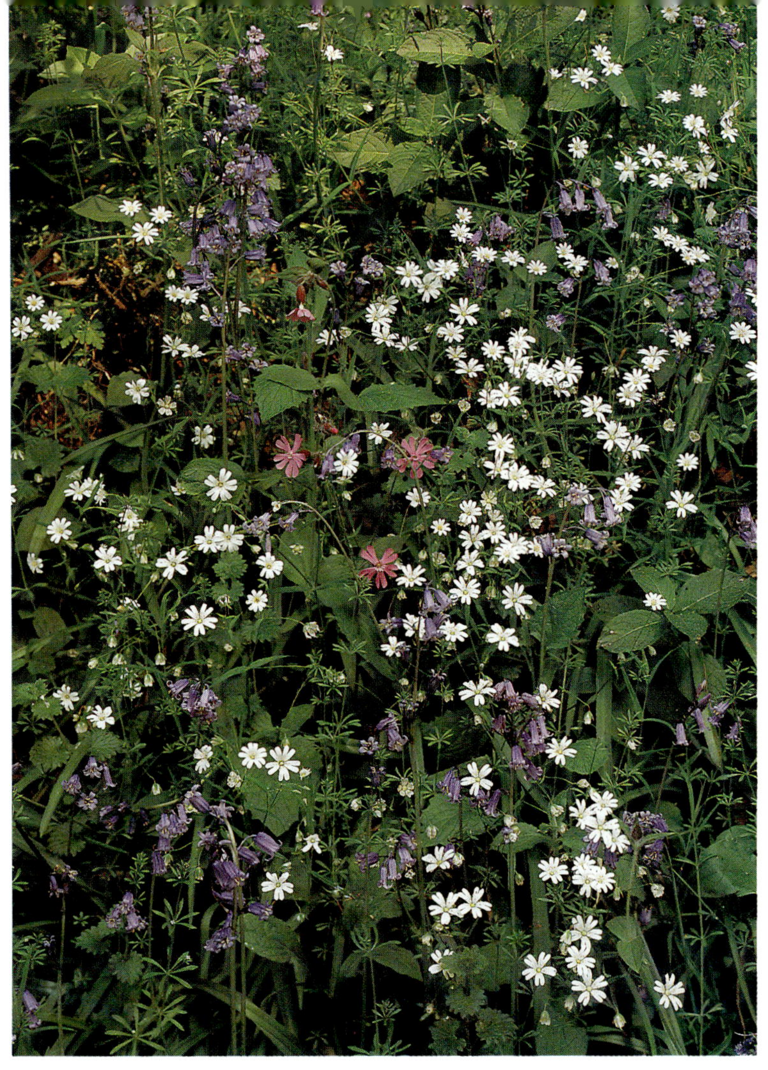

Christopher Gallagher
United Kingdom
HIGHLY COMMENDED

Bluebells and Stichwort

*"No special preparations were
involved in this picture of a
spring woodland understorey in
the Conway valley, North Wales,
beyond taking the time necessary
when working to stop looking
and start seeing."*

Wista 5×4 field camera with
210mm lens; tripod; f22 at 1/2 sec;
Kodak Ektachrome 100

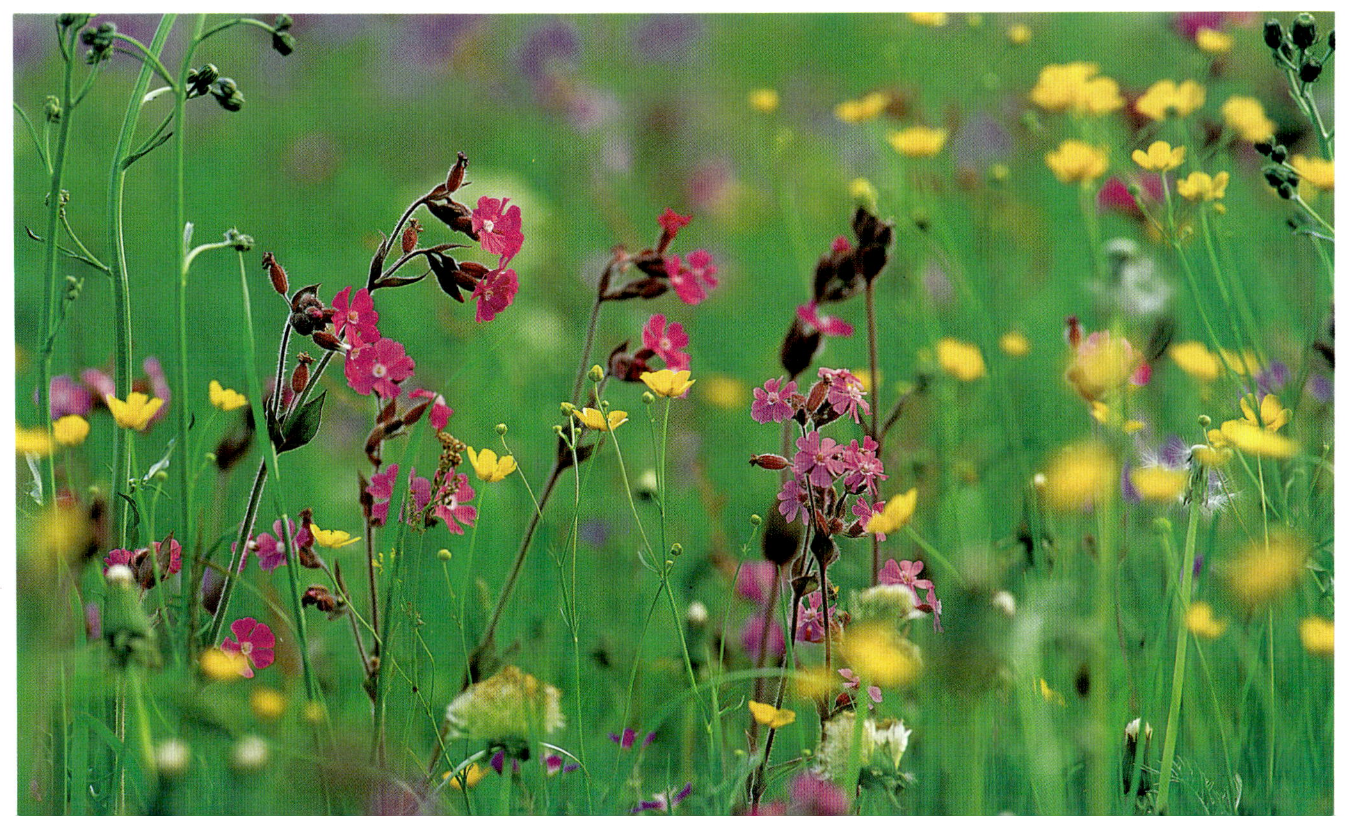

Konrad Wothe
Germany
HIGHLY COMMENDED

Meadow flowers

*"I photographed this meadow in
Bavaria. With so many flowers,
it was difficult to find the
best composition."*

Canon EOS with 300mm lens;
monopod; f5.6 at 1/125 sec

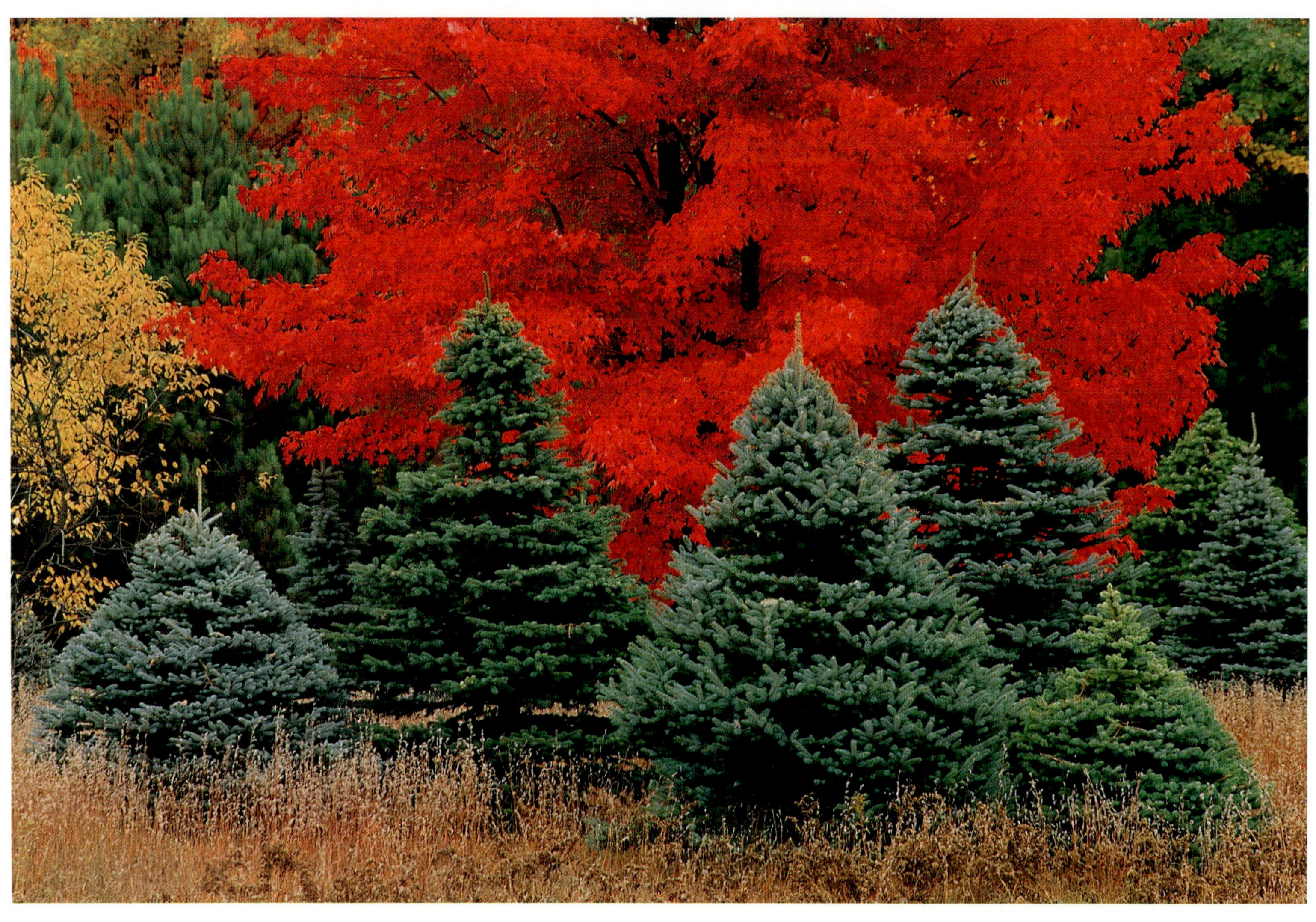

John Shaw
United States of America
HIGHLY COMMENDED

Autumn Maples
and Spruces

*"I always make a point of
photographing autumn colour,
and having once lived in central
Michigan, I knew some good
areas to explore for colour
possibilities. There, I found these
sugar and red maples growing
near spruce."*

Nikon F4 with 50-135mm zoom lens;
tripod; Fujichrome Velvia

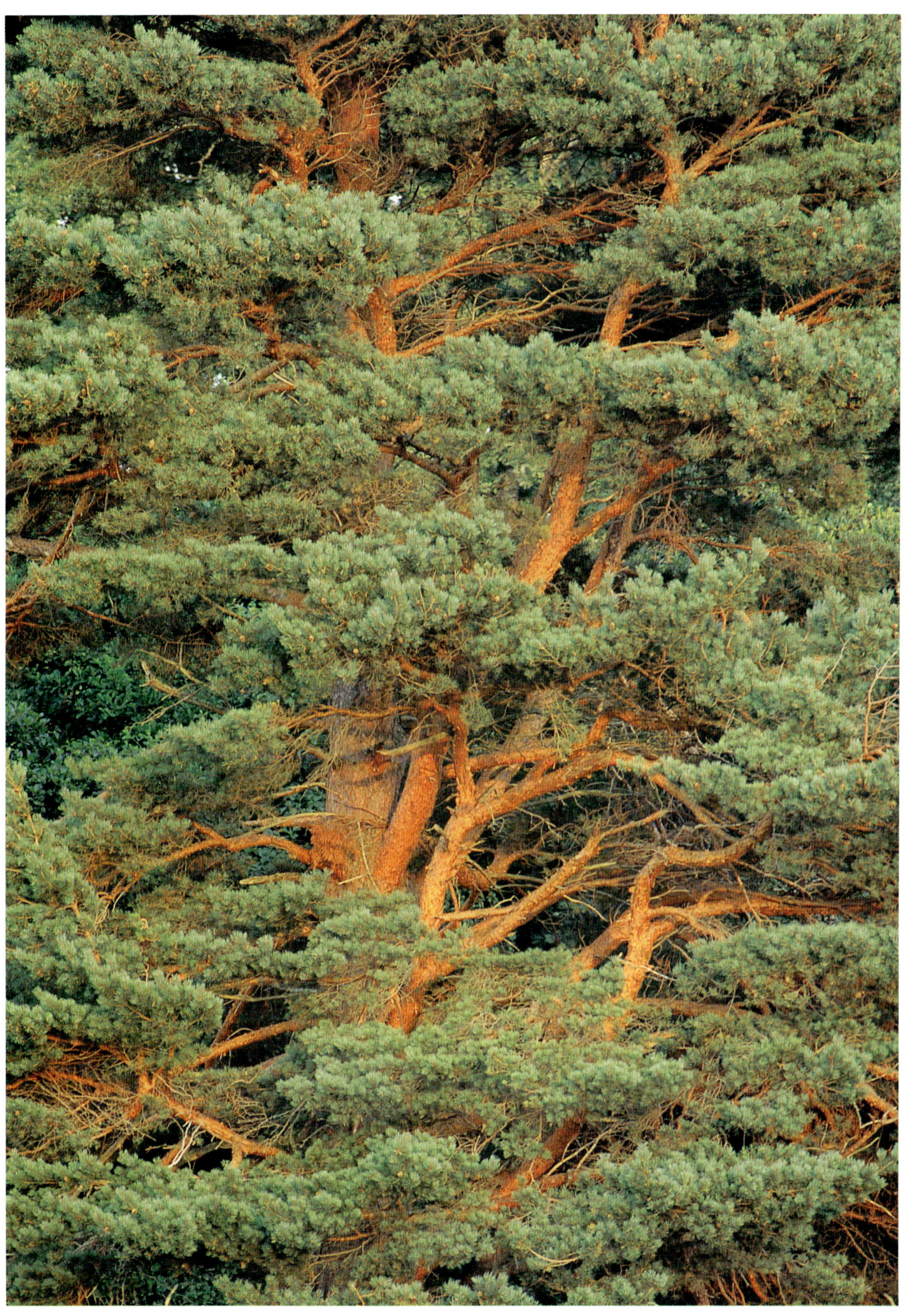

Neil McIntyre
United Kingdom
HIGHLY COMMENDED

Pine tree

''I pass this ancient Caledonian
pine tree every day and have
photographed it many times in
all different light conditions.
This shot shows the lovely
reddish glow on the bark in the
late evening light, which I think
makes the best picture of all.''

Canon T90 with 400mm lens;
f8 at 1/30 sec; Fujichrome Velvia

Marc C Chamberlain
United States of America
HIGHLY COMMENDED

Symbiotic Algae with Bubble Coral

"This picture shows an unusual commensual relationship between bubble coral and algae, not often seen with this species of coral."

Nikon F3 with 55mm lens; underwater housing

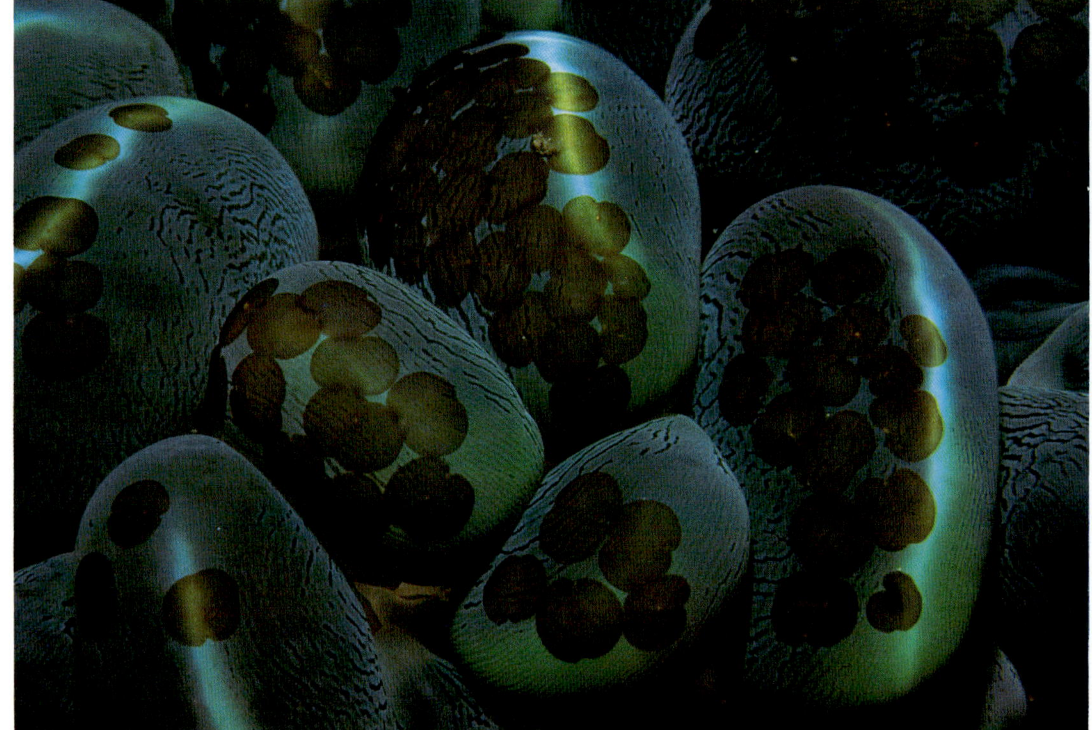

Gerry Ellis
United States of America
HIGHLY COMMENDED

Fly at Rafflesia

"I photographed rafflesia, the world's largest flower, on the rainforested slopes of Mount Kinabalu in Sabah, northern Borneo. It is pollinated by flies which are attracted by its pungent smell. Rafflesias are difficult to find, and very long exposure times are needed to photograph them in the dark conditions they grow in."

Nikon F4 with 85mm lens; tripod; fill-in flash; f8 at 90 secs; Fujichrome 50

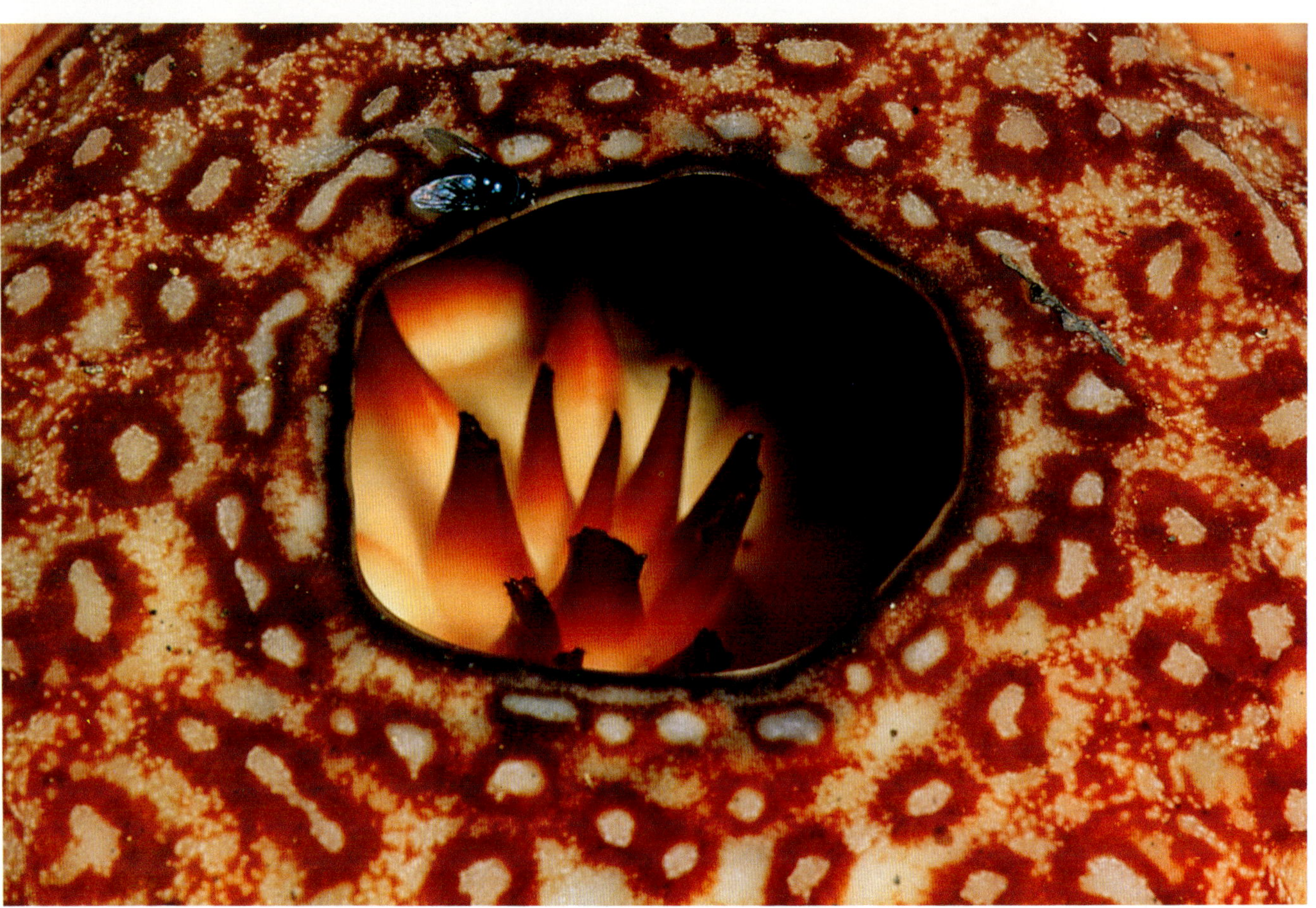

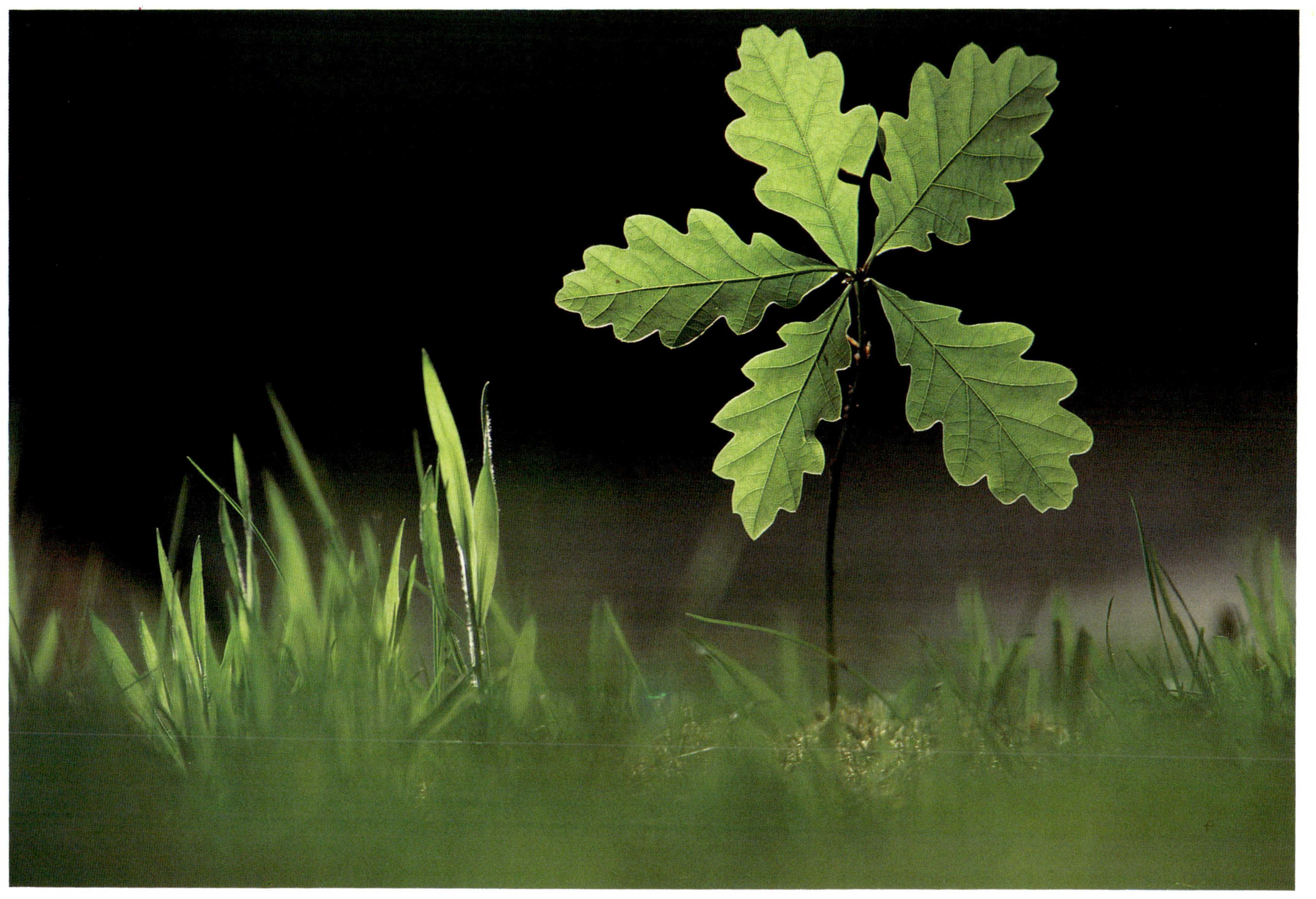

Laurie Campbell
United Kingdom
HIGHLY COMMENDED

Oak seedling
"This picture was taken at 5.30 on a sunny spring morning - an ideal time because of the low-angled light which illuminates the subject from behind."

Nikon F4s with 300mm lens; f2.8 at 1/500 sec; Kodachrome 64

The Underwater World

Photographs for this category have to be taken underwater and can illustrate any freshwater or marine subject.

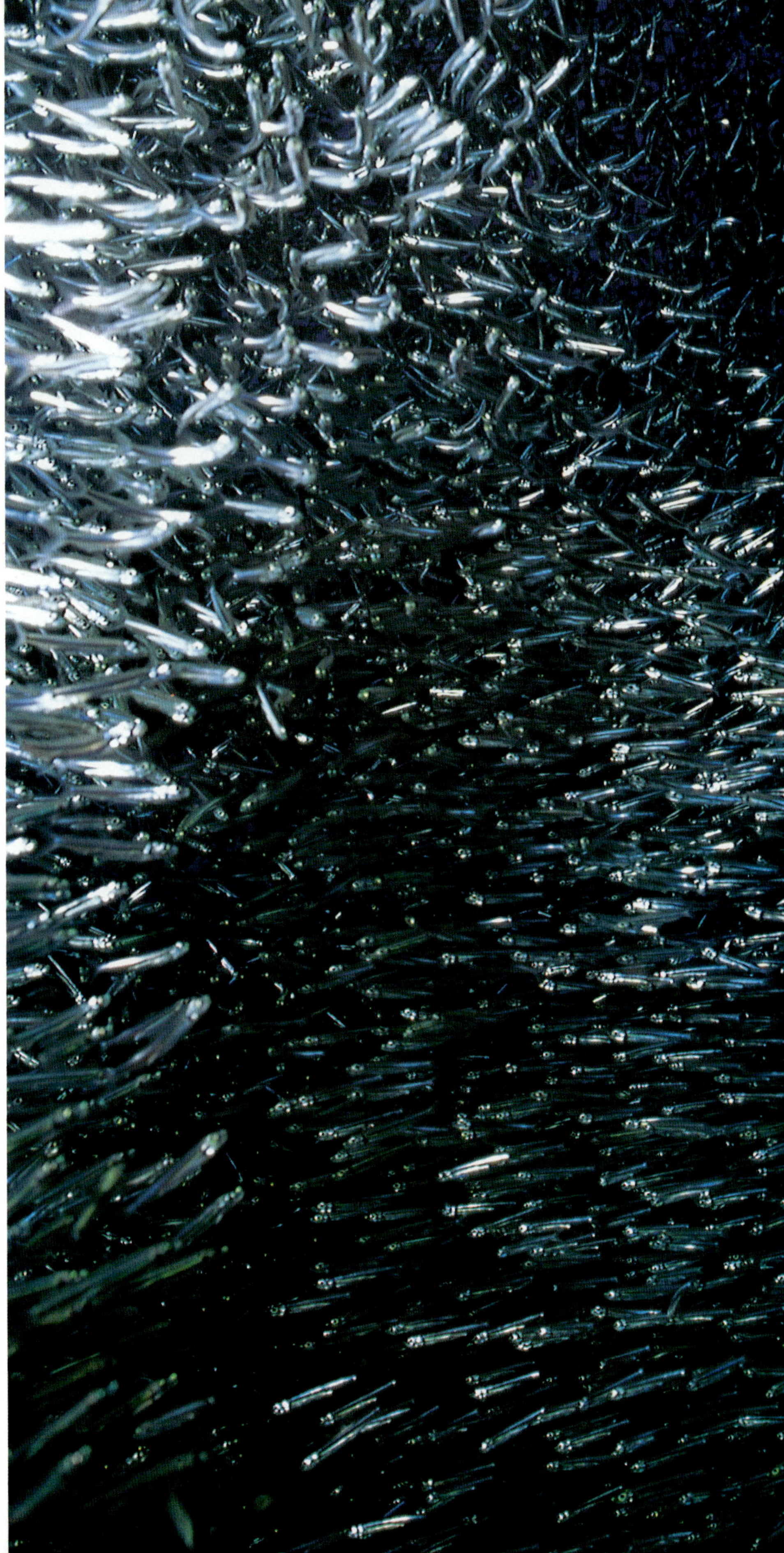

J Michael Kelly
United States of America
WINNER

Tarpon and Silversides

"During the summer months in the Cayman Islands, thousands of small silversides gather together in huge schools in caves and reef formations frequented by the tarpon. It is a wonderful underwater experience to be surrounded by an orchestrated ballet of thousands of schooling fish as they part, flow and contour around you. At night the tarpon and schools of silversides leave the caves to feed at the surface."

Nikonos III with 15mm lens; strobe; f5.6 at 1/60 sec; Fujichrome 50

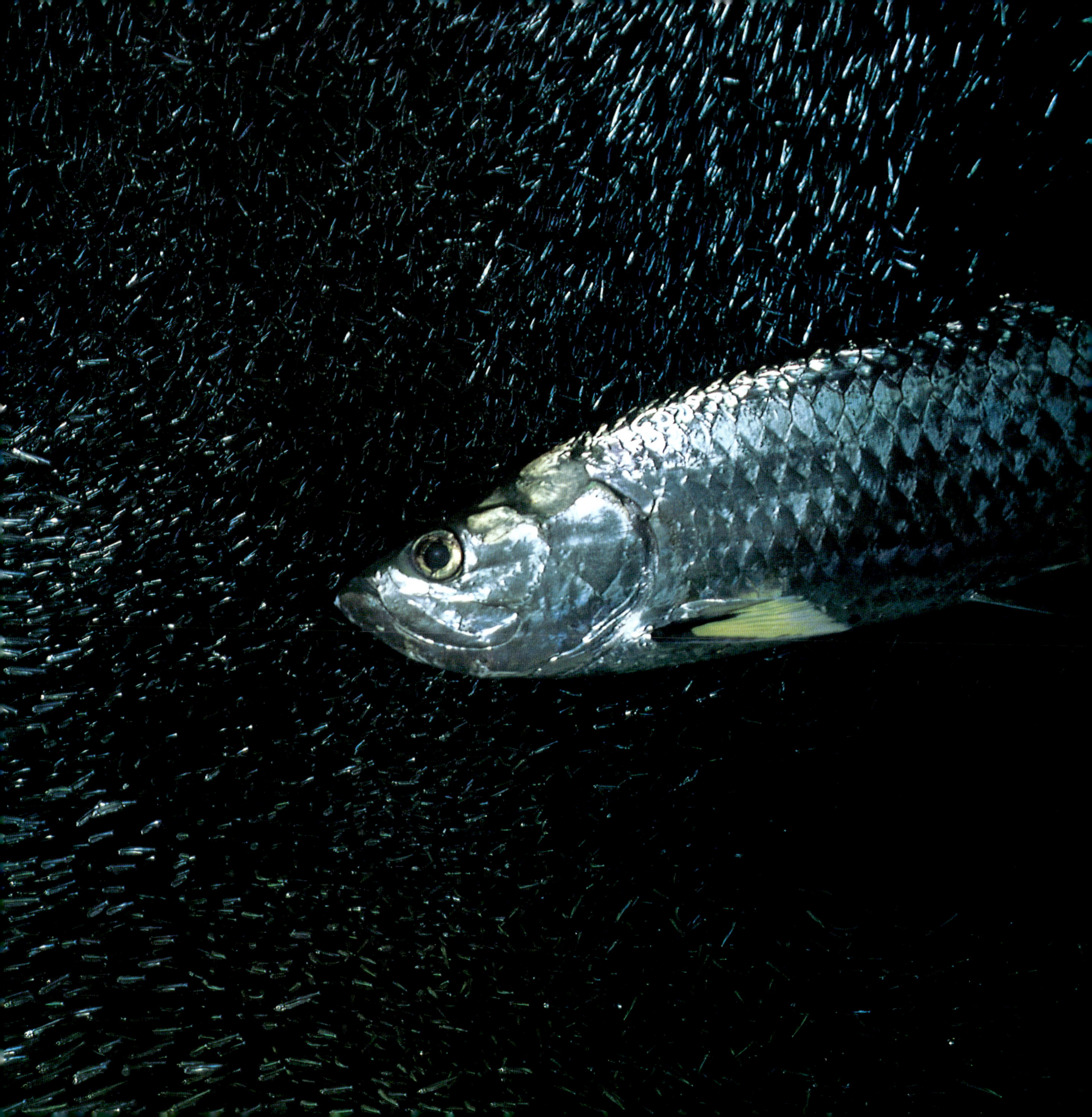

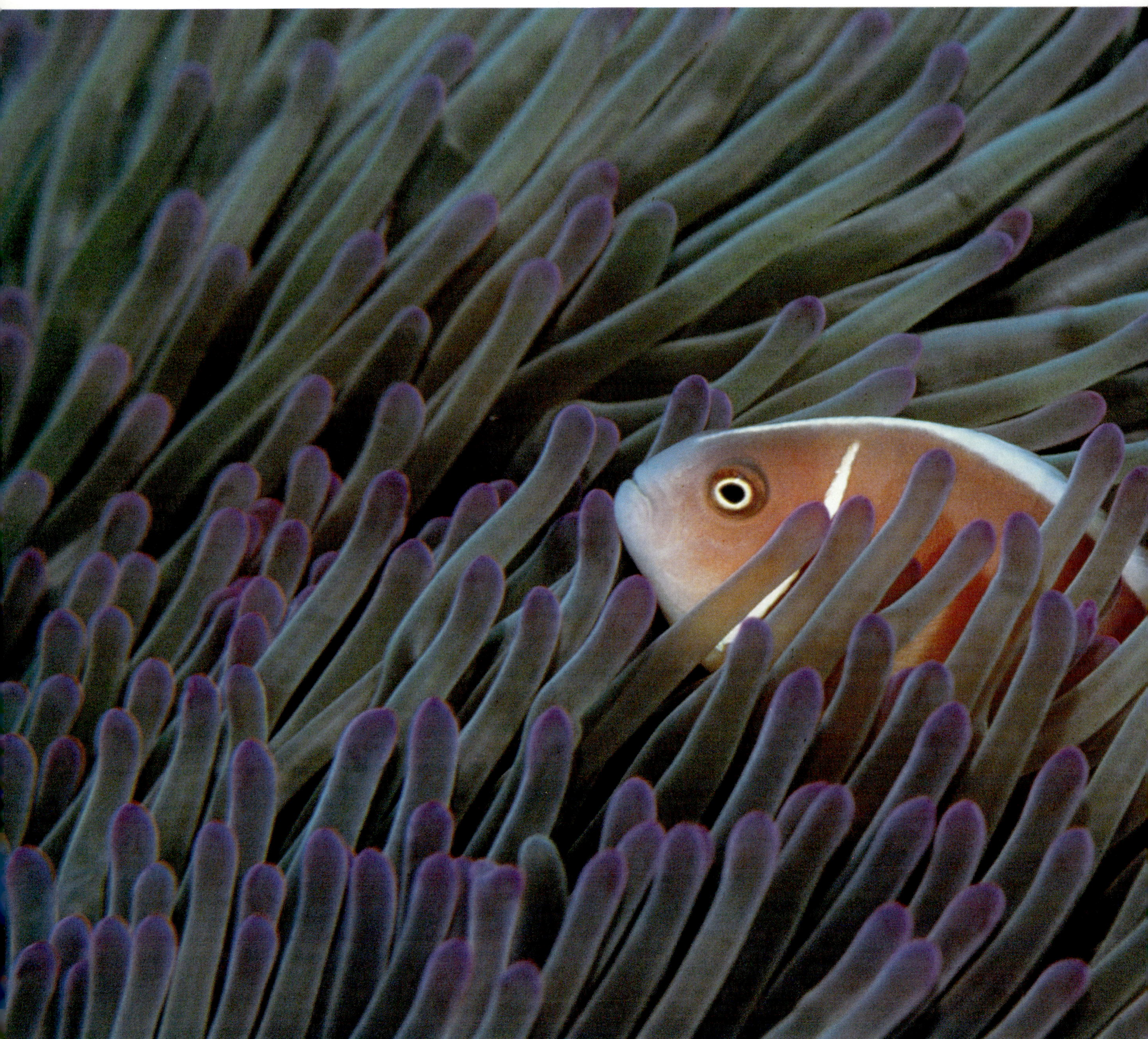

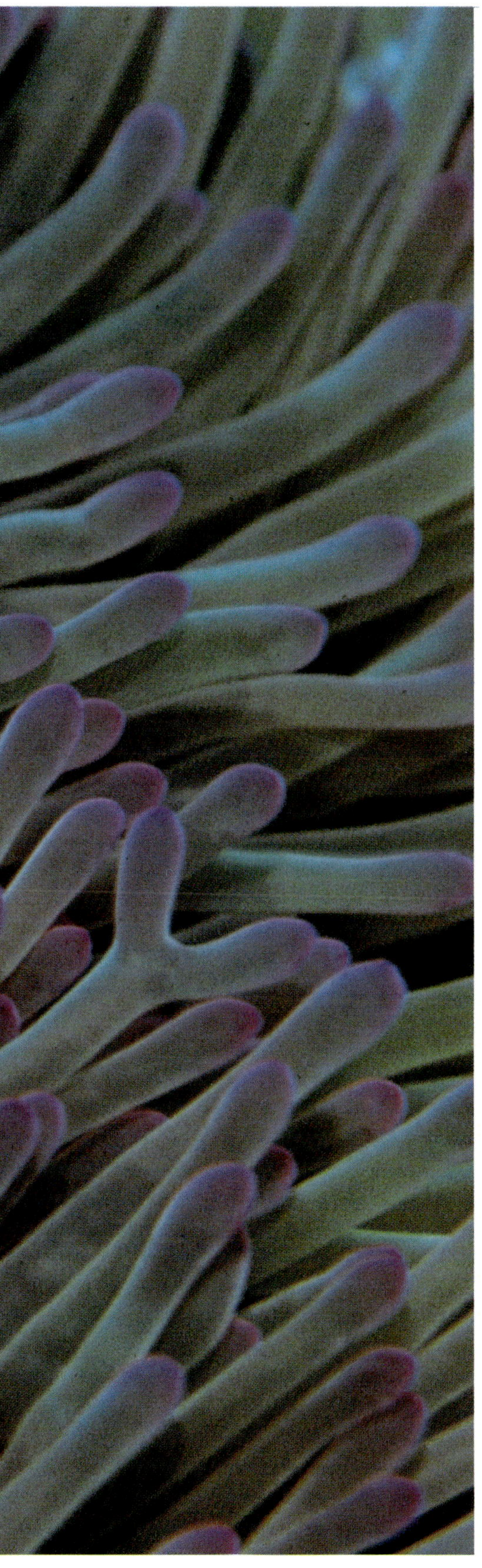

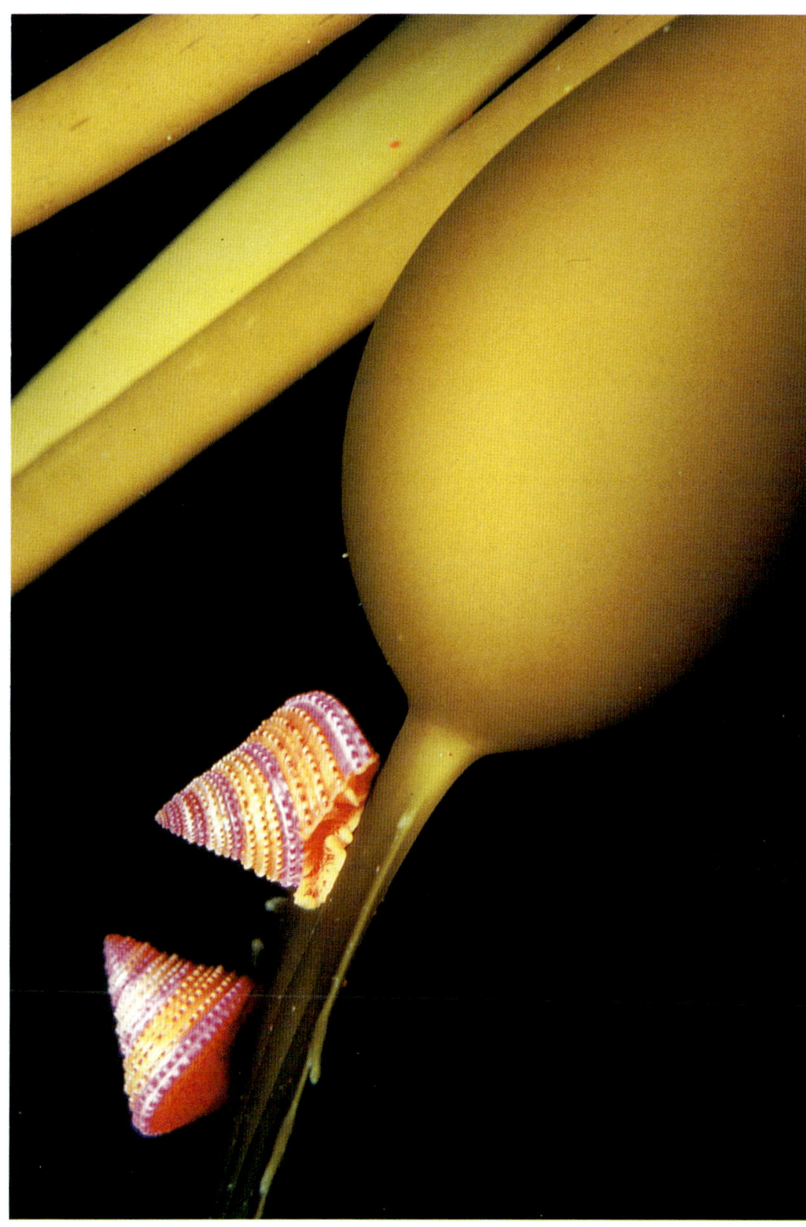

David Hall
United States of America
RUNNER-UP

Pink Clownfish and Anemone

"This picture shows the fascinating relationship between the pink clownfish and a sea anemone. The fish is protected from the anemone's stinging cells by mucus which coats its body. It never strays far from the anemone and seeks protection amongst its tentacles in times of danger. Sadly, this clownfish and its anemone were among the few surviving animals on a reef that had been heavily damaged by dynamite fishing in the Phillipines."

Nikon F with 105mm lens; flash; f11 at 1/60 sec; Kodachrome 25

Norbert Wu
United States of America
SPECIALLY COMMENDED

Jewelled Top Snails and Kelp

"The jewelled top snails are feeding on a blade of giant kelp. They do not actually feed on the plant itself but on other invertebrate life attached to it."

Canon F1 with 50mm macro lens; underwater housing; strobe; f11 at 1/60 sec; Kodachrome 64

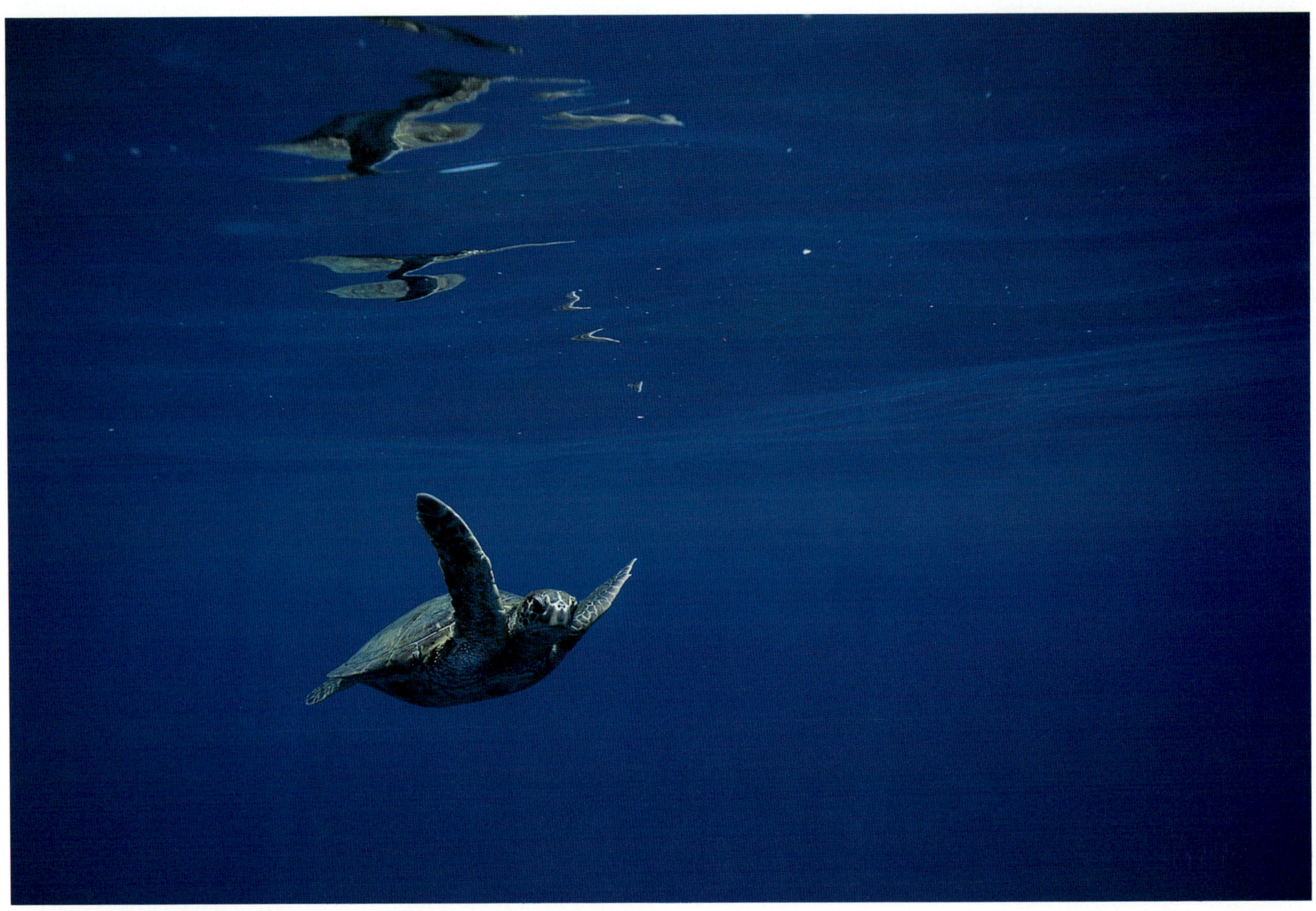

Georgette Douwma
The Netherlands
RUNNER-UP

Green Turtle

"I was with a crew filming lava tubes off Hawaii when this green turtle swam close to our boat. It seemed very interested in us, and so at lunchtime I put on a mask and snorkel and joined it in the water. I must have spent some 45 minutes swimming around it."

Pentax LX with 20mm lens; underwater housing; Kodachrome 64

96

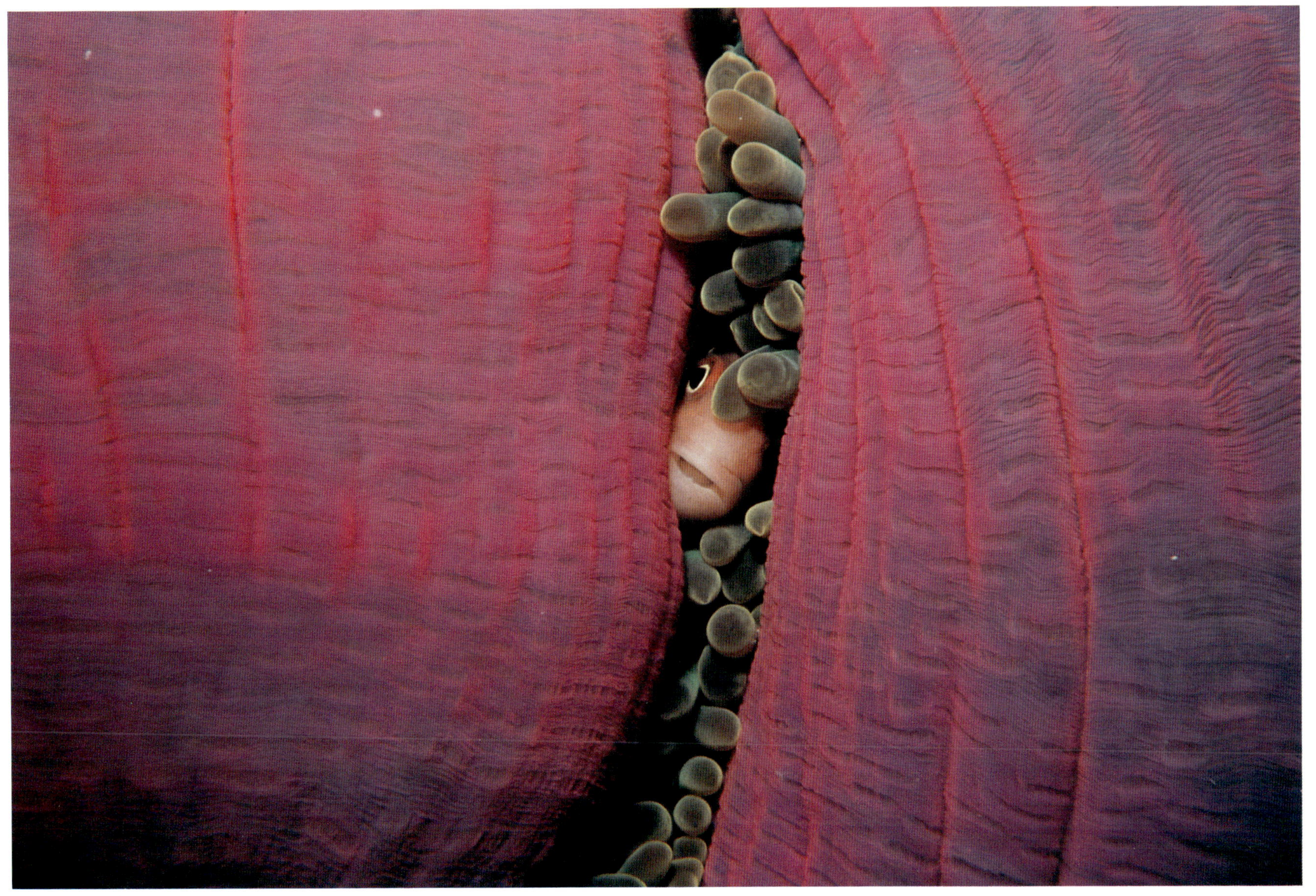

Michele Binder Hall
United States of America
HIGHLY COMMENDED

Peeping Anemone Fish
*"This anemone fish was gazing
at me from the sanctuary of its
host anemone.
Unlike other fish, it is immune to
the stinging hydra of the
anemone's tentacles and so can
live there unharmed."*

Nikonos IV with 35mm lens and
extension tube; strobe; f22 at 1/60 sec;
Kodachrome 64

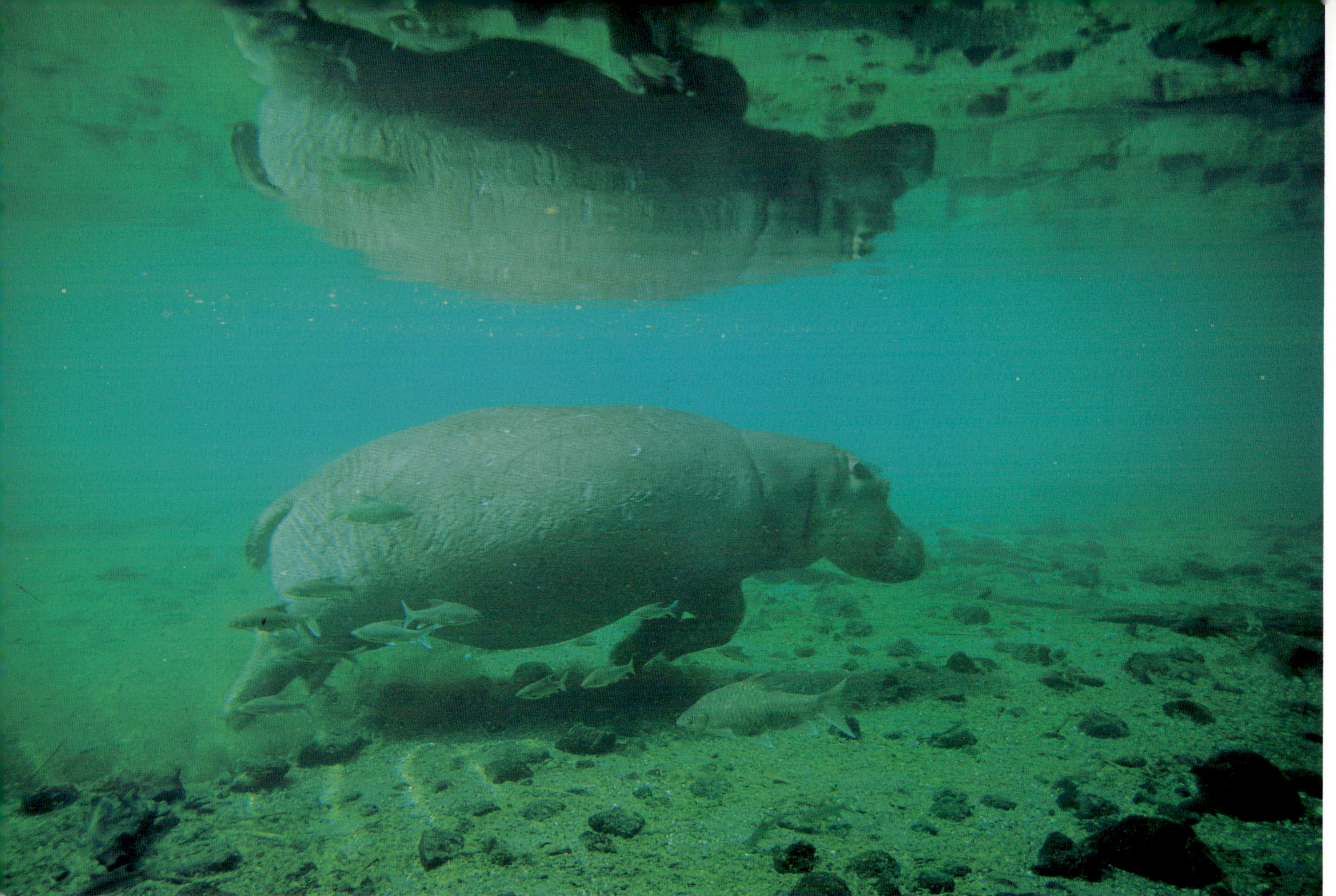

David W Breed
United Kingdom
HIGHLY COMMENDED

Swimming Hippo

"*Mzima Springs in Tsavo West National Park, Kenya, has an underwater viewing chamber where hippos can be photographed at close range. In this shot, the barbels are following the hippo trying to feed on the dung it is churning up from the bottom.*"

Olympus OM4T with 21mm lens:
f3.5 at 1/250 sec; Fujichrome 100

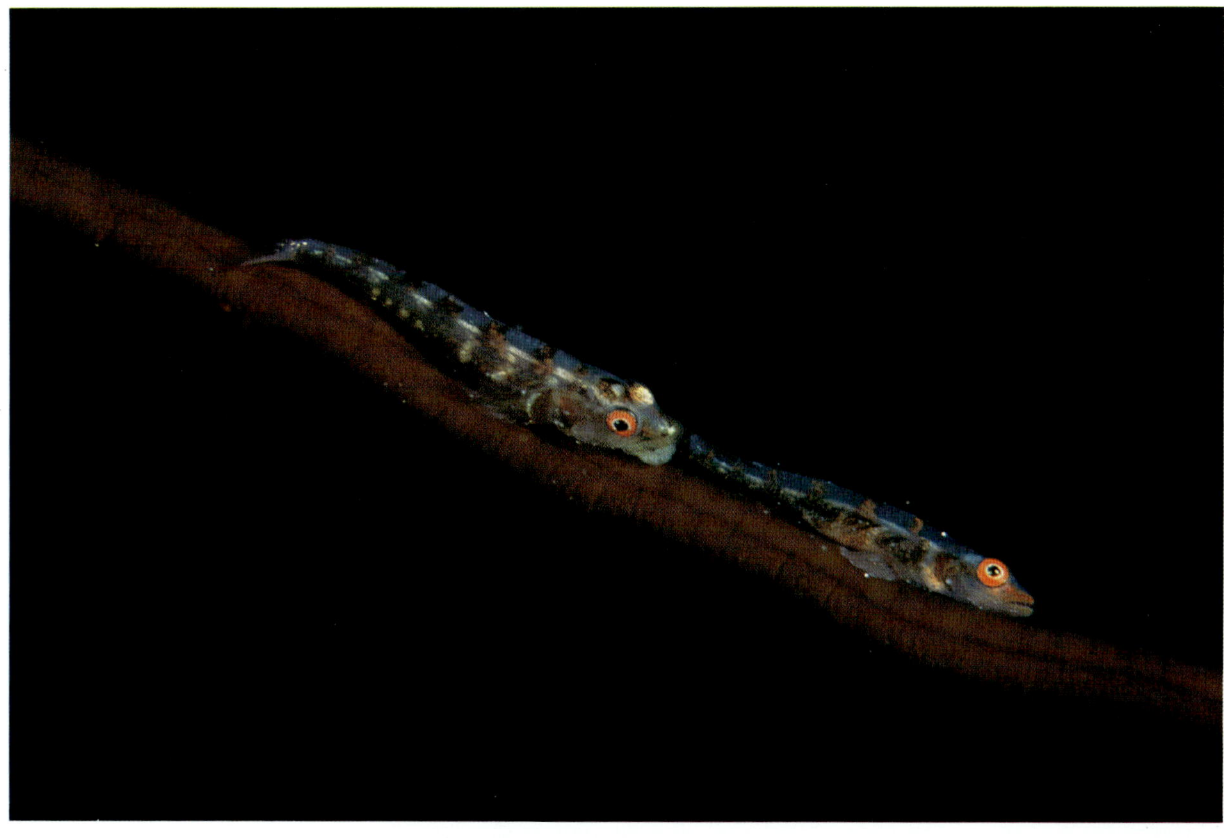

**Burt Jones
& Maurine Shimlock**
United States of America
HIGHLY COMMENDED

Gobies in Wire Coral

"One pair of gobies inhabited the wire corals, but it was difficult to photograph them together. At the same time, we were on a boat confined to harbour in Vanuatu by bad weather."

Nikon F3 with 105mm macro lens; underwater housing; strobes; f22 at 1/60 sec; Fujichrome 50

Peter Hewitt
United Kingdom
HIGHLY COMMENDED

***Cleaner Shrimp on
Sea Slug***

"The Temple, Ras Um Sid, in the Red Sea was the setting for this shot of a cleaner shrimp on the gills of a Spanish dancer sea slug."

Nikonos V with 35mm lens and extension tube; flash; underwater housing; f22 at 1/90 sec; Kodachrome 64

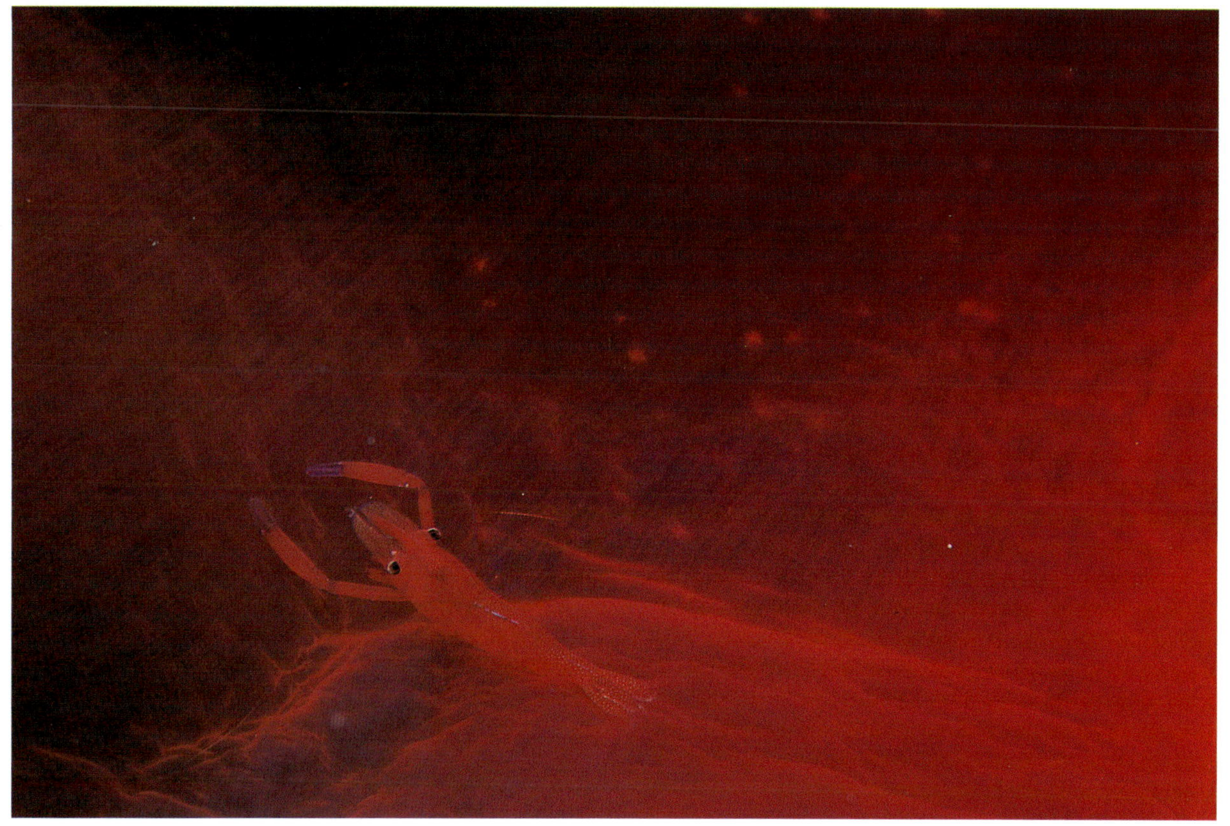

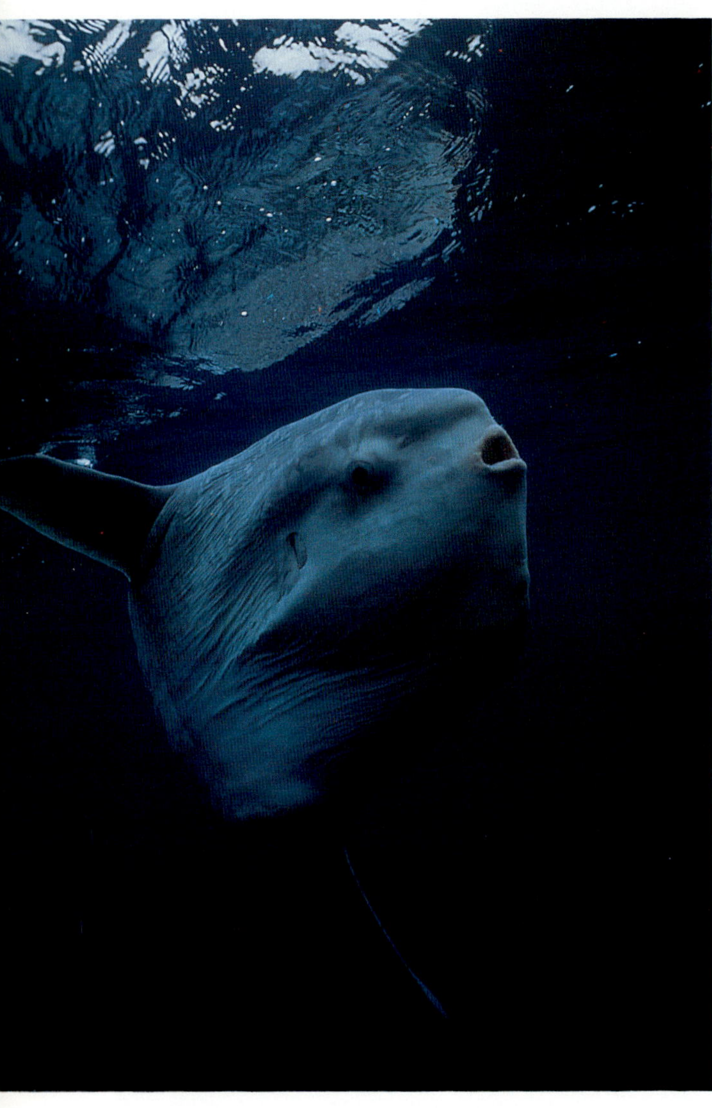

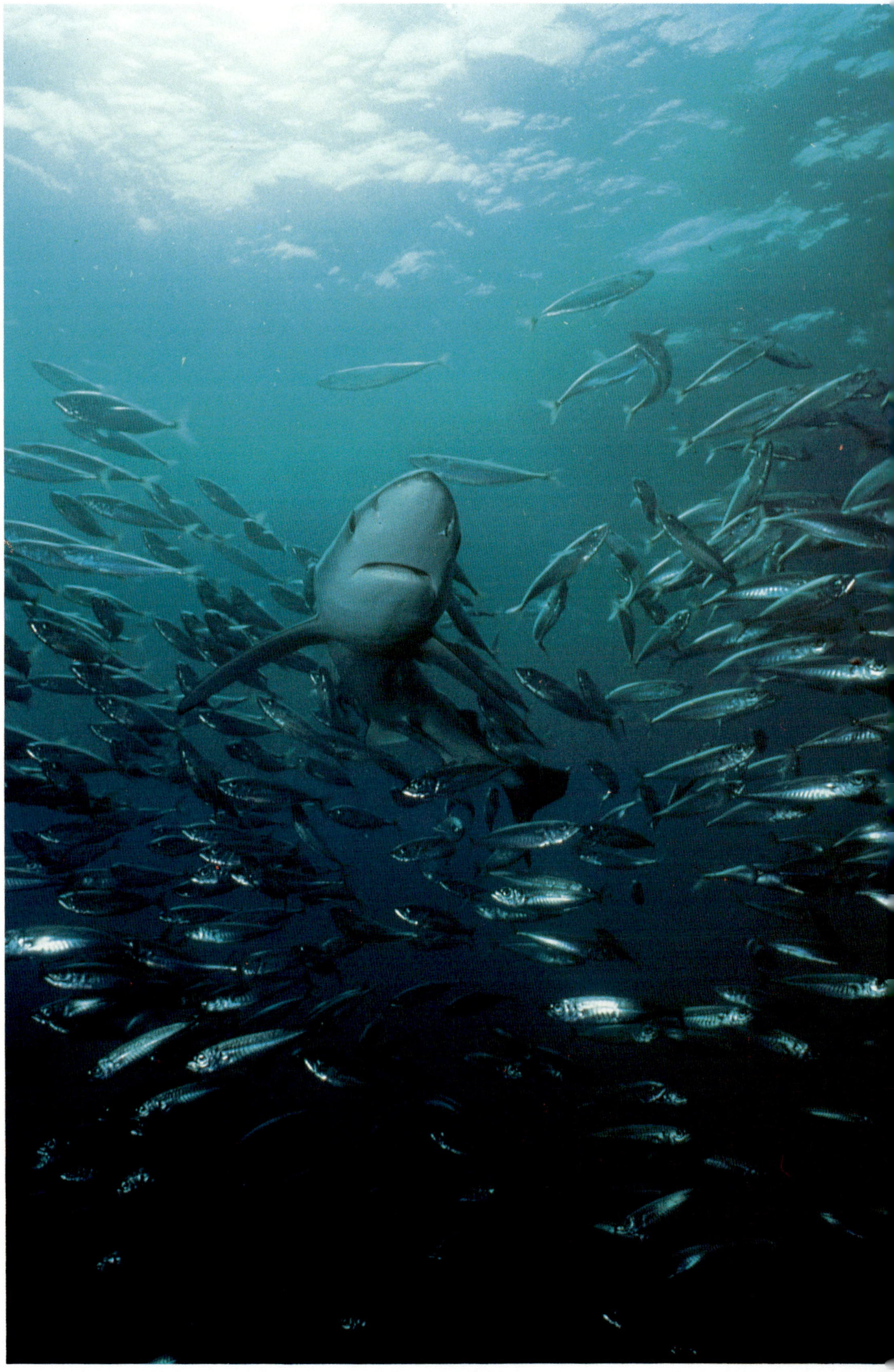

Mike Johnson
United States of America
HIGHLY COMMENDED

Ocean Sunfish

*"While smaller ocean sunfish
are often timid, larger specimens,
such as this one, can be curious
toward the photographer.
I photographed this individual
just beneath the surface 15 miles
off the southern
California coast."*

Nikonos III with 20mm underwater lens;
f8 at 1/60 sec; Fujichrome 50

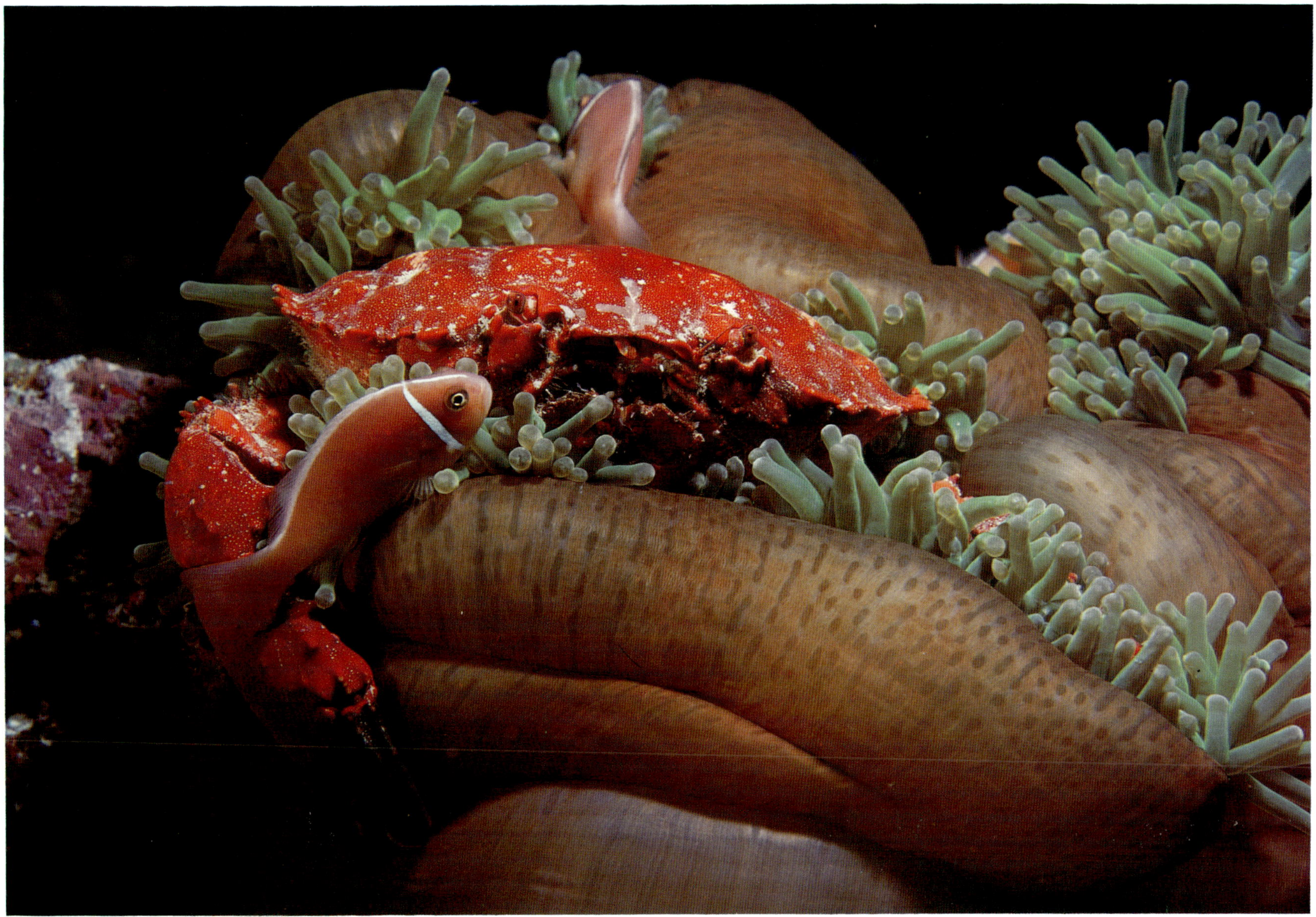

Richard Herrmann
United States of America
HIGHLY COMMENDED

Blue Shark and school of Mackerel

"When a blue shark swims through a school of mackerel, the mackerel will sometimes move in tightly. This bothers the shark, and it will try to shake them off, like a dog with fleas."

Nikonos V with 20mm lens; strobe; Kodachrome 64

Michael Goodwin
United States of America
HIGHLY COMMENDED

Anemone digesting crab

"The crab is ensnared by the anemone and is slowly being drawn in while an anemone fish and shrimp stand by, seeming to watch the commotion. I came across this scene on a night time dive in Papua New Guinea."

Canon F1 with 50mm lens; underwater housing; strobes; f22 at 1/60 sec

From Dusk
to Dawn

Photographs entered for From Dusk to Dawn must
be taken between sunset and sunrise (the sun may
be on but not above the horizon) and must
feature animals.

Laurie Campbell

United Kingdom

WINNER

Red Deer Stag

*"This was a chance encounter on
a night drive in the Strathglass
area last winter. At this time, the
red deer tend to move on to low
ground to feed. This stag was
chewing the cud between
grazing, and was unperturbed
when I stopped to take some
photographs. Further on I saw
the moon and decided to take
another frame on the same
exposure to create this shot. I
then went back and forth a few
times repeating the exercise."*

Nikon F4s; double exposure (stag:
180mm lens; flash; f2.8 at 1/60 sec;
moon: 300mm lens; tripod; f2.8 at
1/500 sec); Kodachrome 64

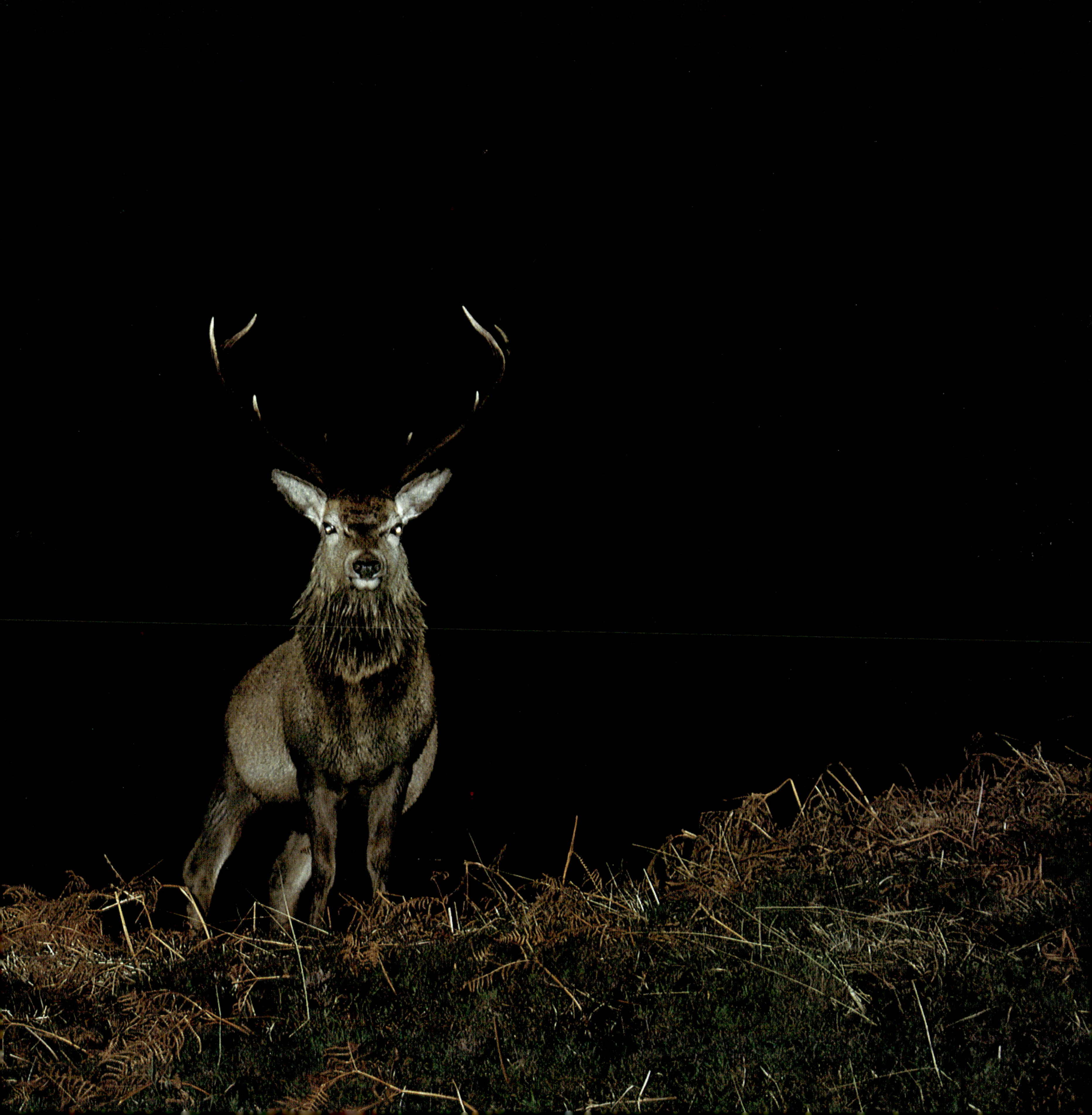

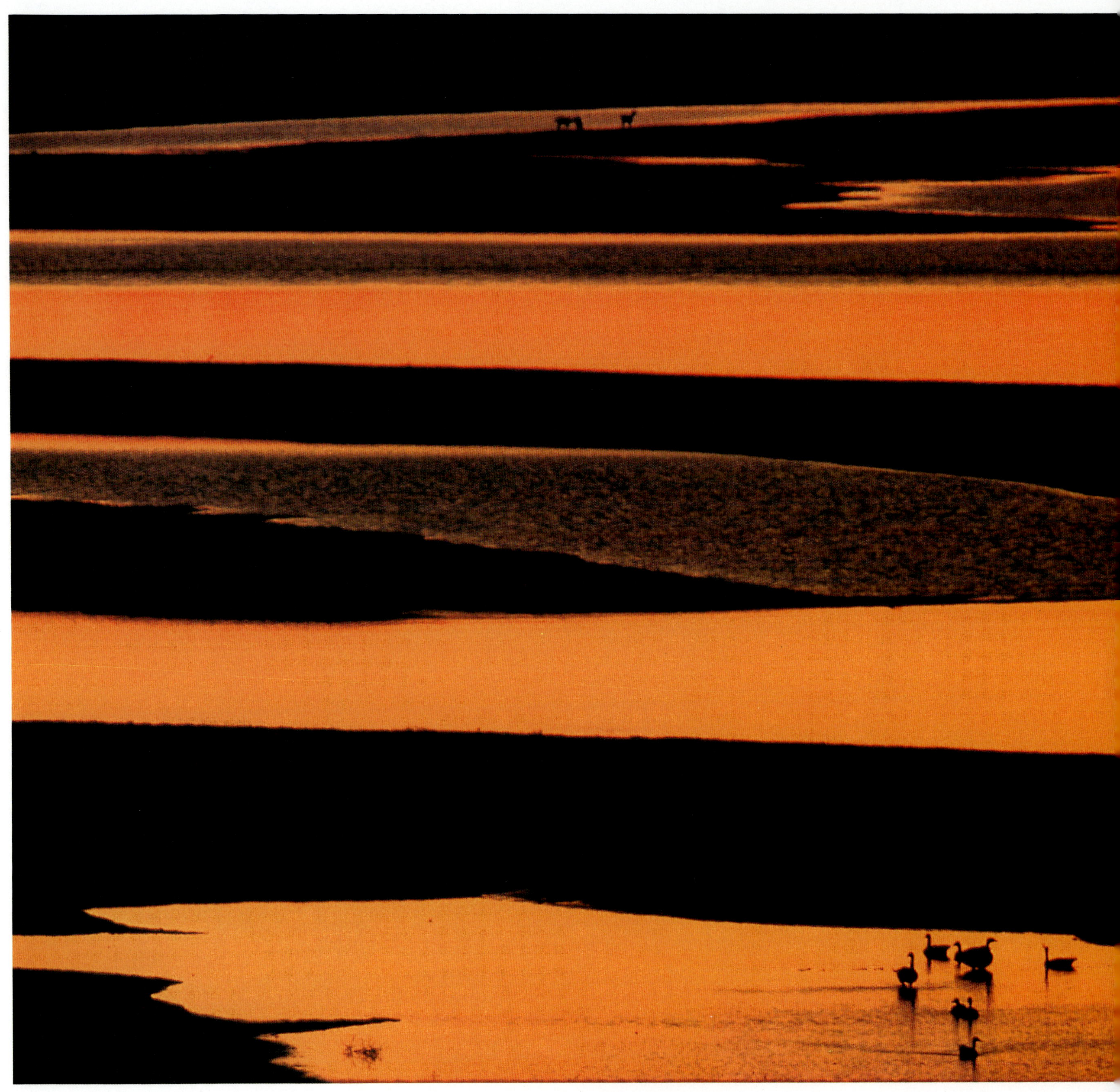

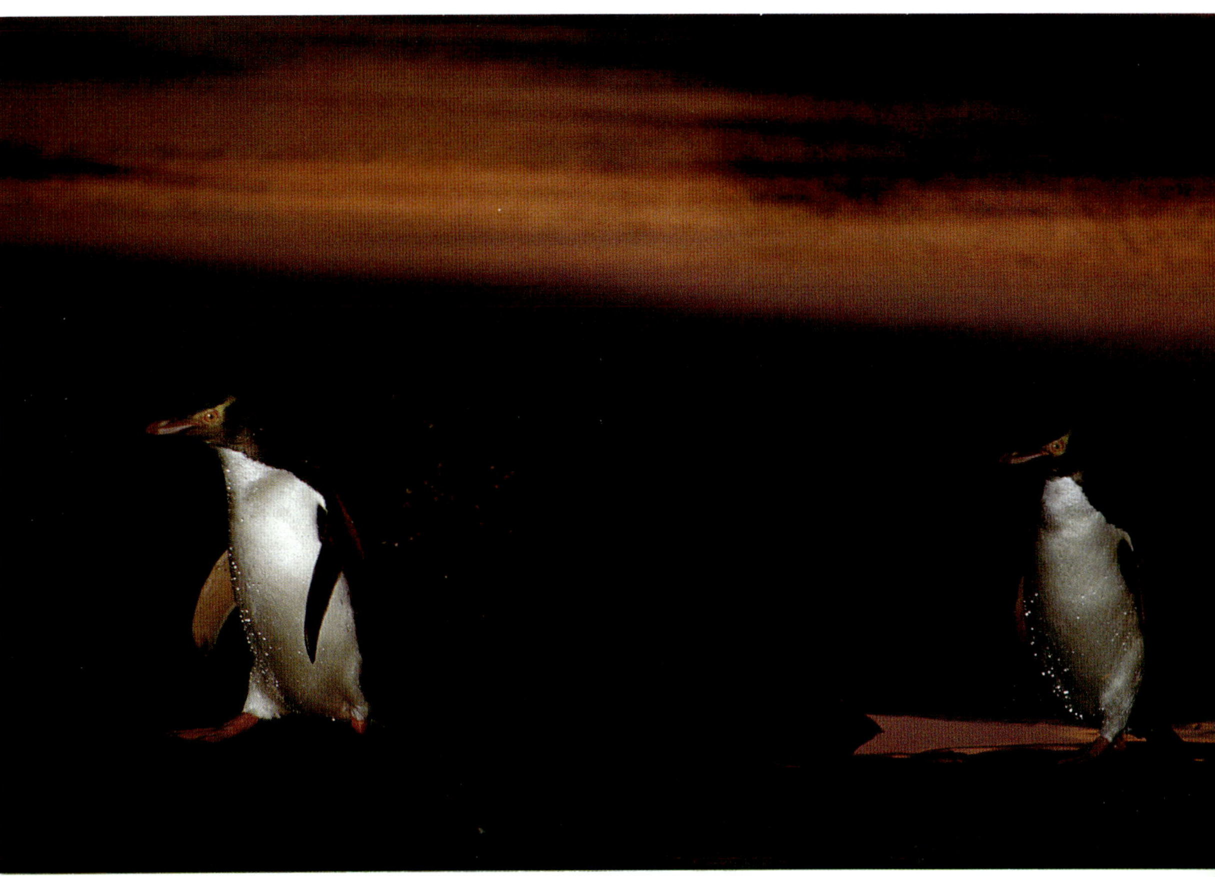

John Eastcott &
Yva Momatiuk
New Zealand &
United States of America
RUNNER-UP

Geese at dusk

"It was just after sunset and we were on a high riverbank looking down on the South Saskatchewan river.
The sky is reflected in the many pools formed by several sandbanks. The Canada geese were in the nearest pool, and two mule deer, which approached as I was taking the pictures, can be seen in the background. The abstract nature of the picture results from using a long lens."

Canon T90 with 300mm lens and ×2 converter; tripod; f8 at 1/30 sec; Kodachrome 64

Gordon Court
Canada
SPECIALLY COMMENDED

Yellow-Eyed Penguins

"Yellow-eyed penguins, the world's rarest penguin, forage at sea by day, returning at dusk to their breeding colonies to roost.
In winter, one can get a close view of the birds from the hides near their landing spots. In this scene, the light of the early evening winter reflects on the wet sand, making a perfect backdrop for the adults leaving the ocean."

Nikon F2A with 80-200mm lens; flash; f4 at 1/90 sec; Agfa 50 Professional

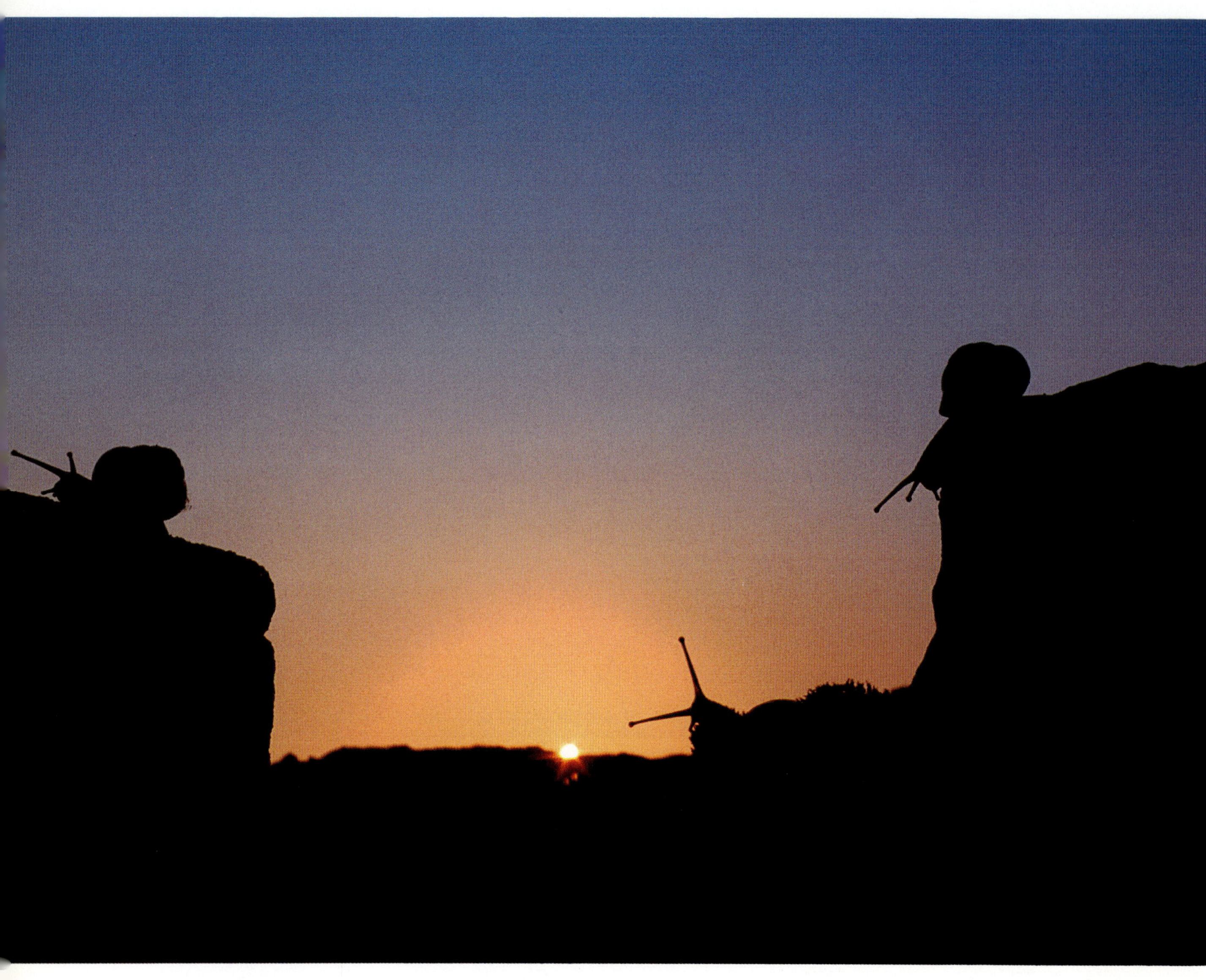

Fritz Pölking
Germany
HIGHLY COMMENDED

Elephant and Zebra

"I came across this African elephant and Burchell's zebra in the Masai Mara. I took the picture for the strong silhouettes they made against the sunrise."

Nikon F4 with 400mm lens; f3.5 auto; Fujichrome 100

Tony Rostron
United Kingdom
HIGHLY COMMENDED

Snail patrol

"I wanted to show snails silhouetted against a bright evening sky. Having noted where the sun had set the day before I put the camera up on a tripod and focused on the top of the wall. I placed some brown-lipped snails on the wall and left them to roam about."

Nikon FE with 24mm lens; tripod; f22 at 1/30 sec; Agfa CT 100

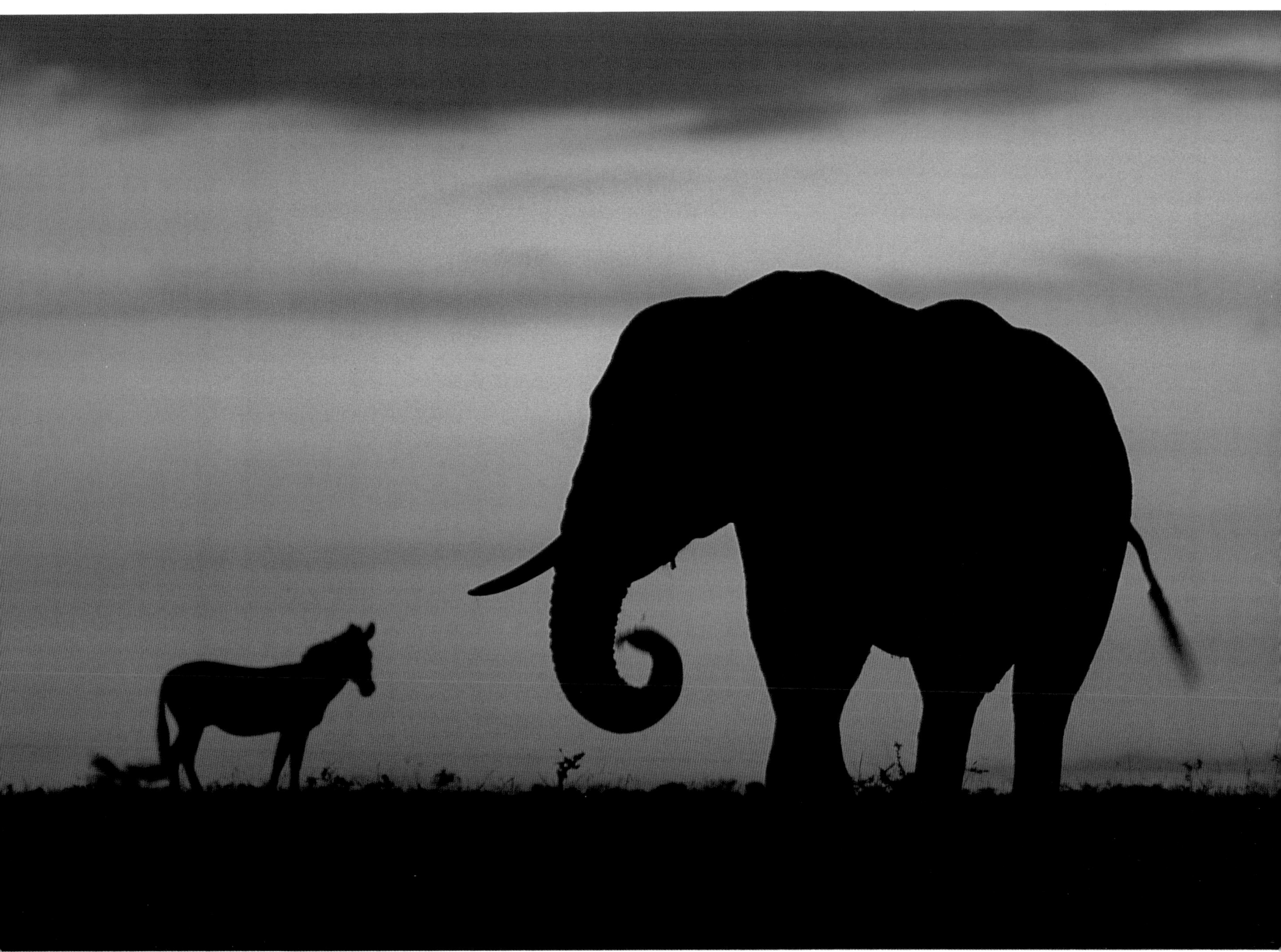

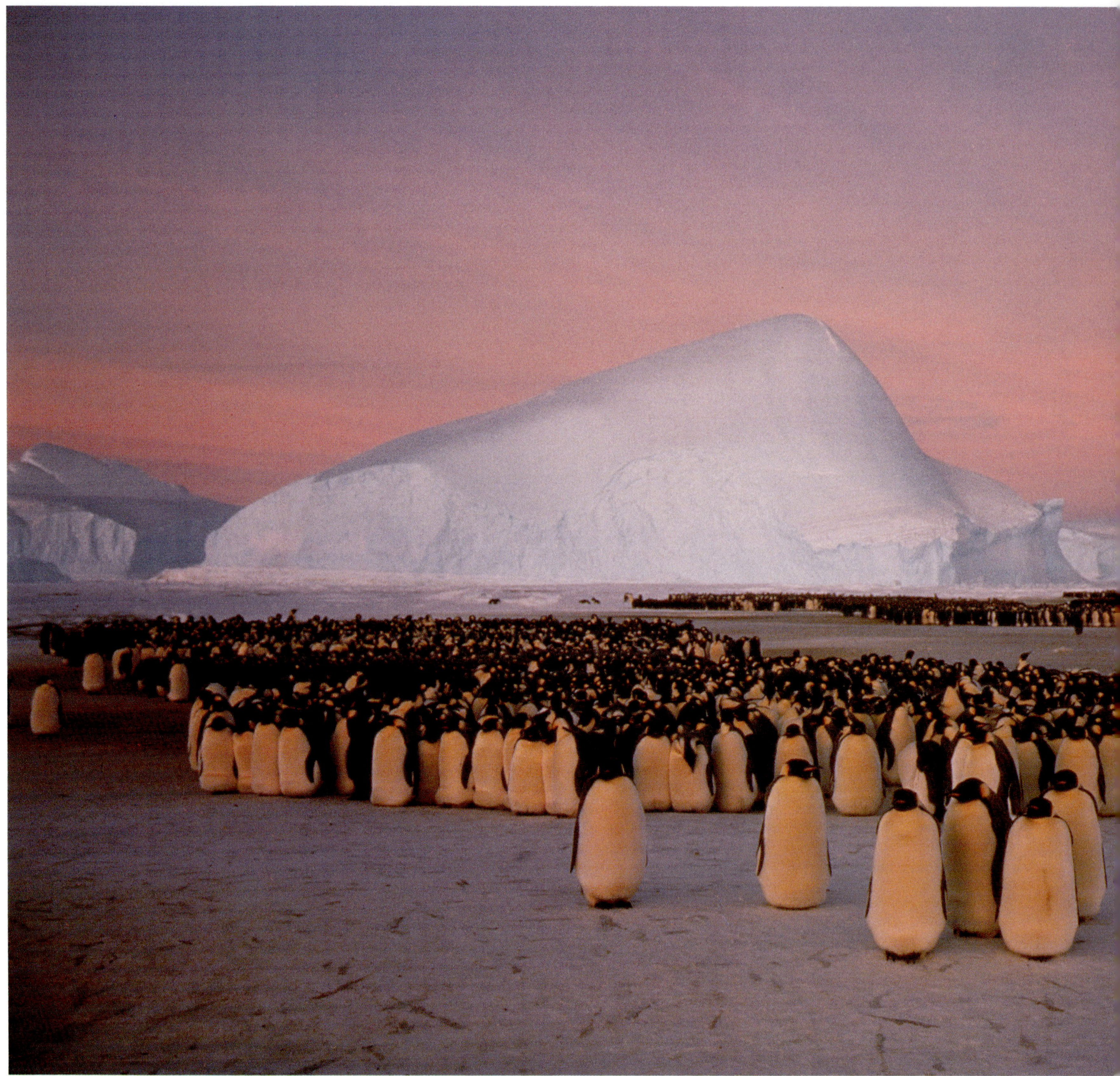

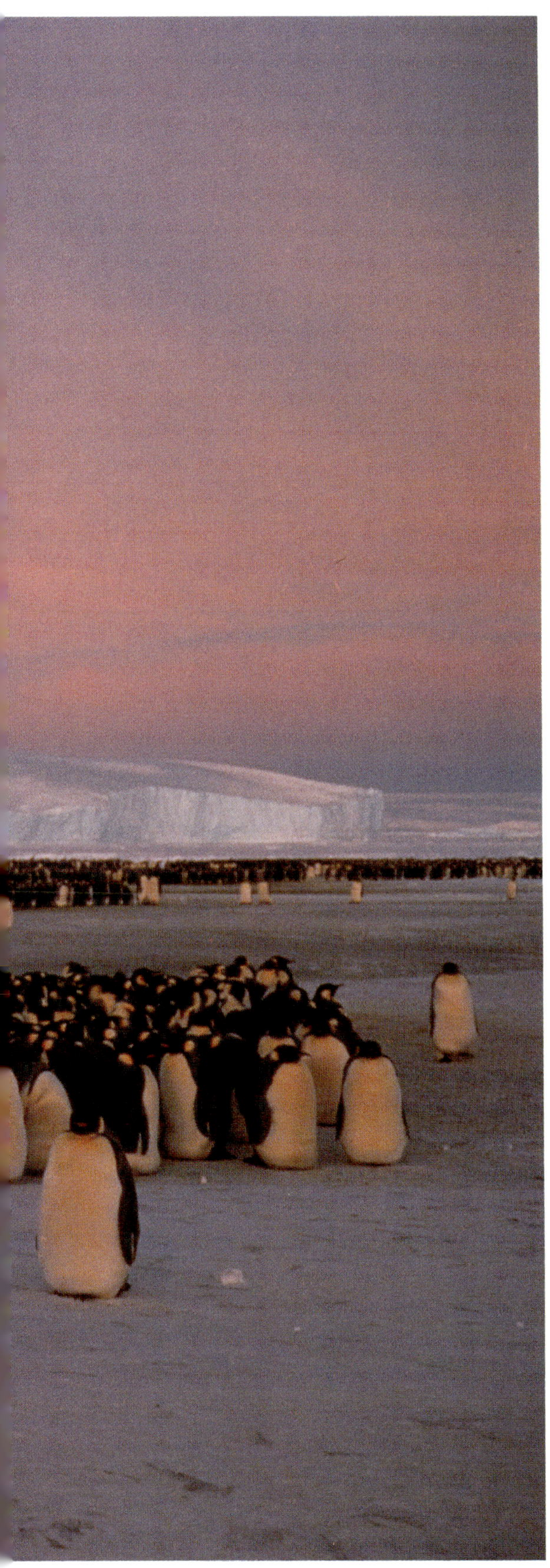

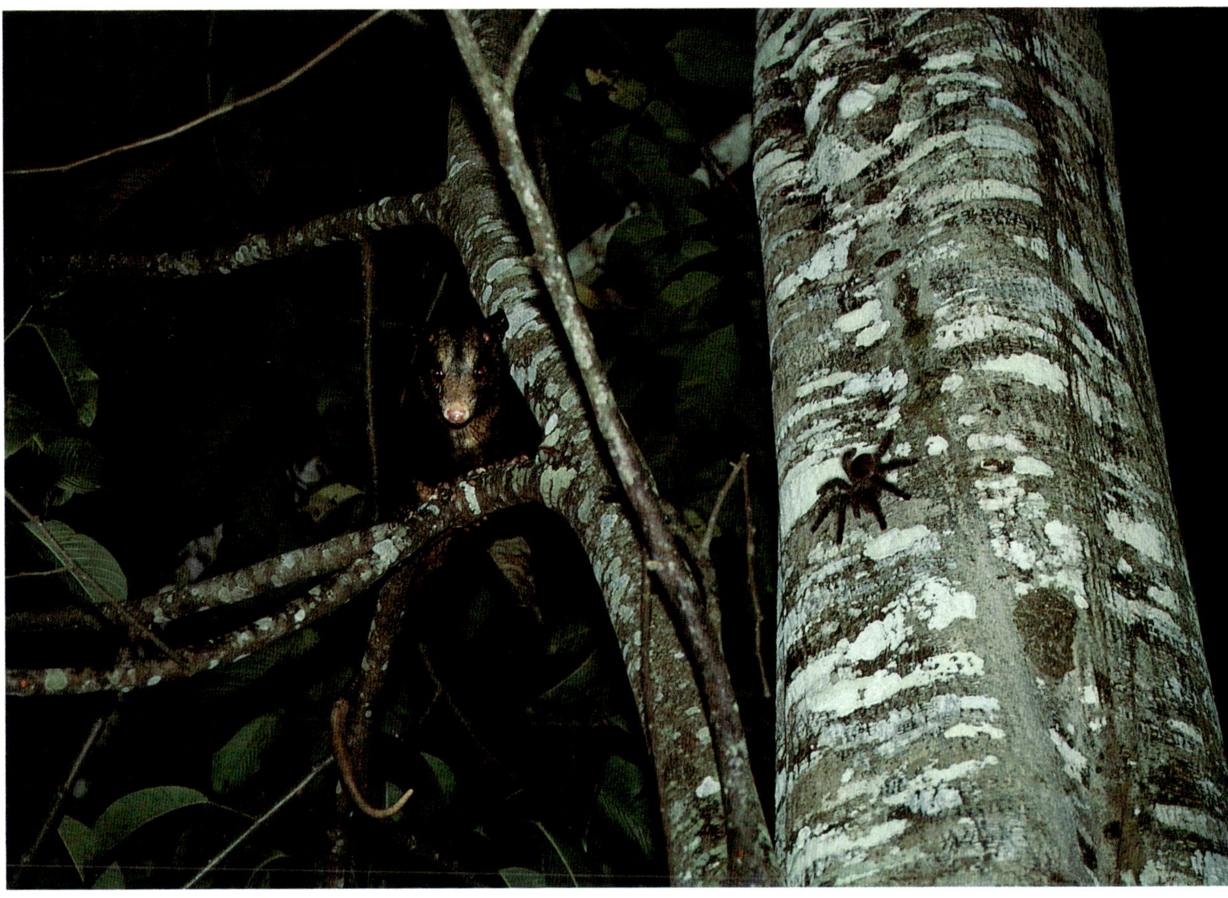

Graham Robertson
Australia
HIGHLY COMMENDED

Emperor Penguins

"For me, this picture epitomises the heart of the Antarctic winter - emperor penguins huddling for warmth, pink twilight skies and dim light. What it doesn't show are the freezing conditions. At −45°C wind chill, the hardest part was getting my equipment to work and my fingers to respond."

Fuji 6×9cm with 90mm lens; tripod; f3.5 at 1/15 sec; Kodachrome 64 Professional

Daniel Fitter Angermeyer
Ecuador
HIGHLY COMMENDED

Opossum hunting Tarantula

"One night in the Ecuadorian jungle as I walked back to my cabin, my torch caught the eye of this grey-tailed opossum hunting tarantulas. He froze in the beam of light, and I was able to take this picture."

Pentax LX with 70-210mm zoom lens; flash; f5.6 at 1/70 sec; Kodachrome 64

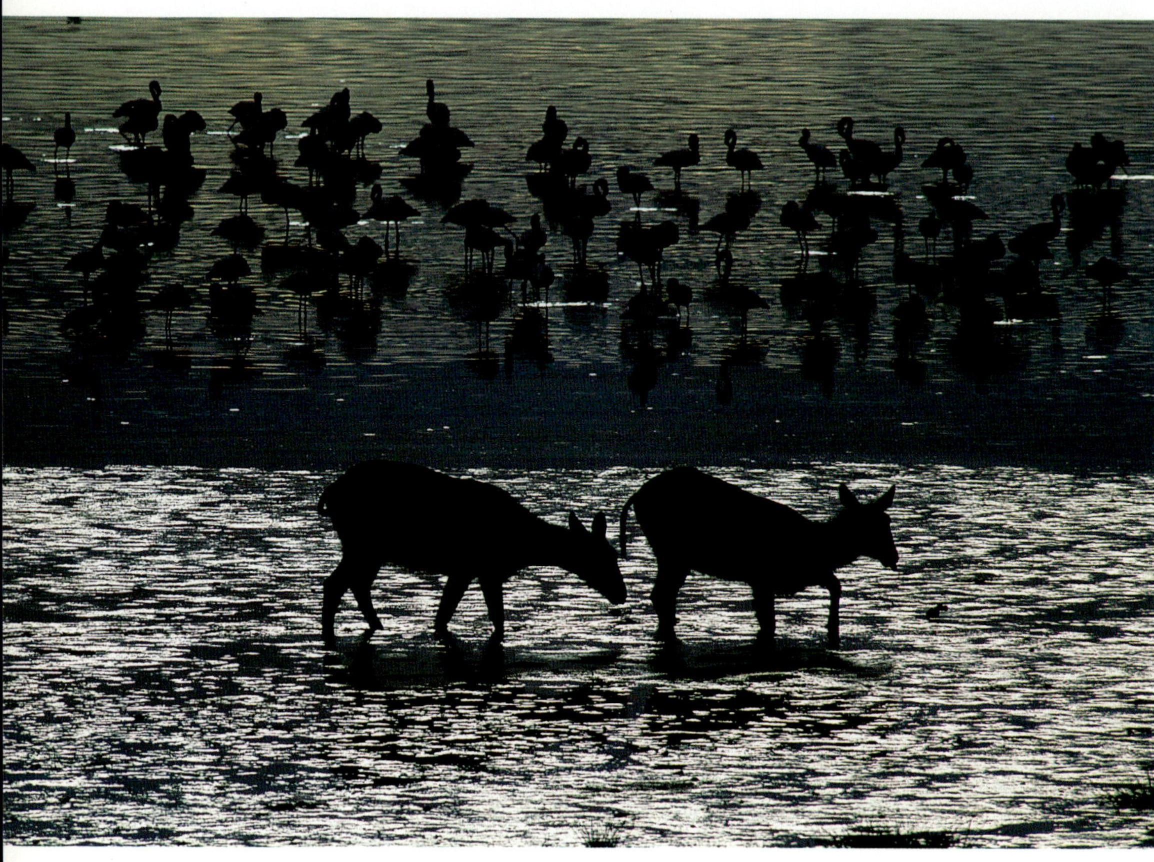

Eberhard Brunner

United States of America

HIGHLY COMMENDED

Waterbuck and Flamingoes

"Waterbuck like the alkaline conditions of Lake Nakuru and tend to feed there in the evening and at night. At the end of the day, I climbed my wobbly tree stand and took as many shots as possible before the light failed."

Nikon F3 with 300mm lens; tripod

Kennan Ward

United States of America

HIGHLY COMMENDED

Brown Bear in Katmai National Park

"In the salmon season, brown bears patrol the lake shore for fish which, after spawning, are flushed downstream and washed ashore. I must have tried this early morning shot a hundred times. Usually, a long exposure would mean a blurred bear, but luckily, on this occasion, the bear hesitated when a fish splashed near the shore."

Nikon F3 with 55mm lens; tripod; Kodachrome 64

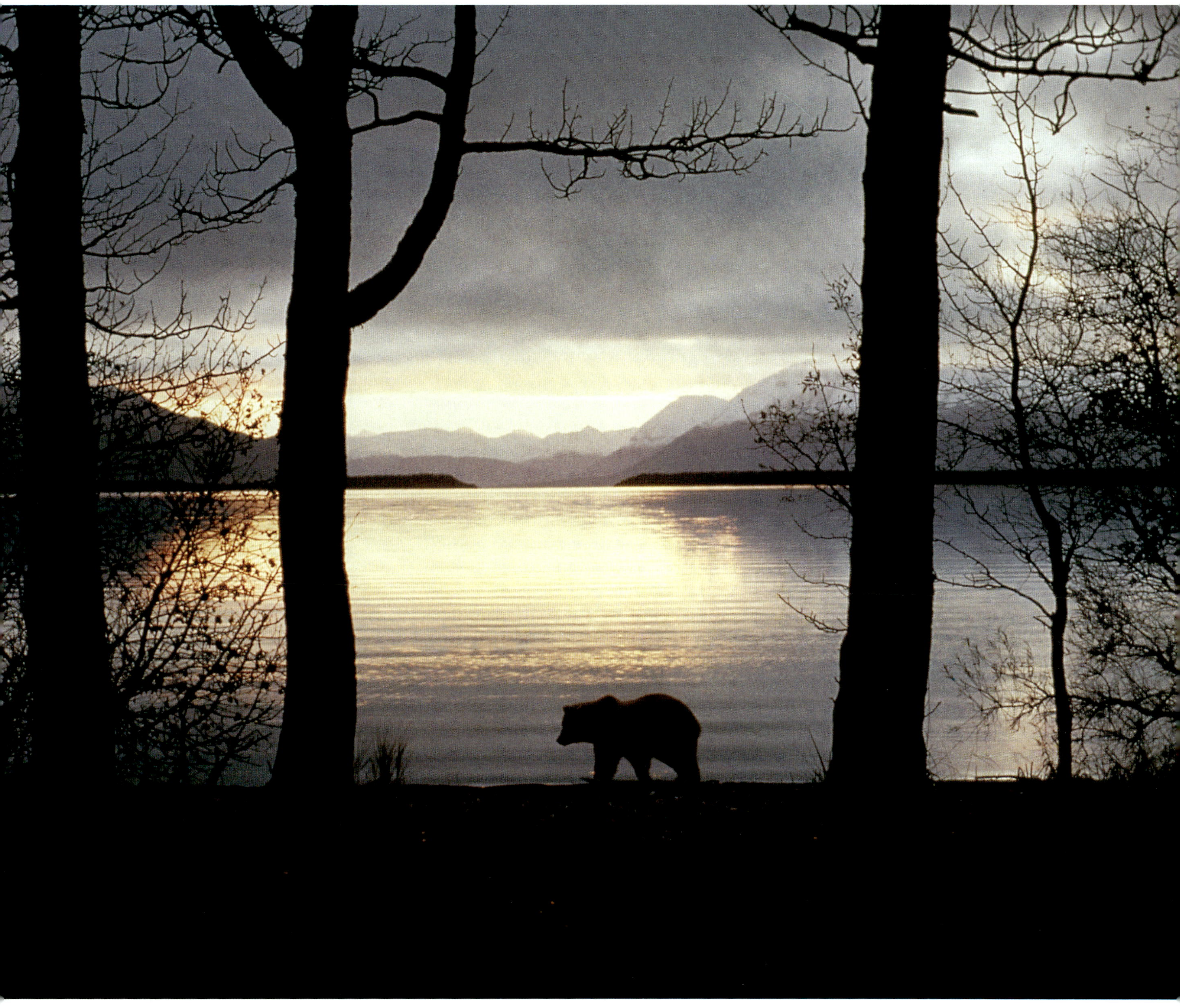

Urban Wildlife

This category is for photographs of plants or animals taken in an urban or man-made setting.

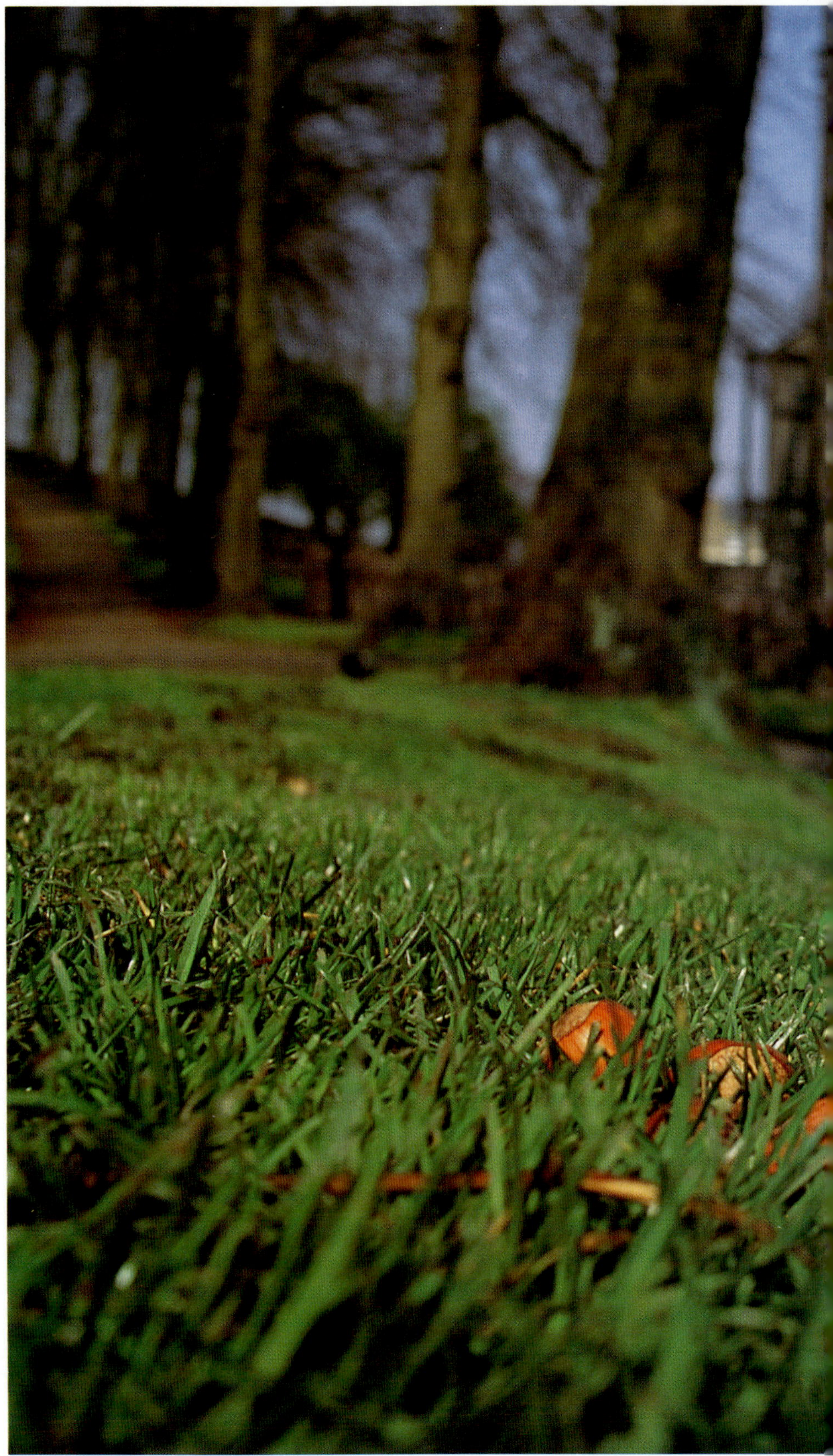

Warwick Sloss
United Kingdom
HIGHLY COMMENDED

Grey Squirrel

"I took this picture to show how squirrels have adapted to our urban environment. I knew of a man who has been feeding squirrels in a park near the centre of Bristol for 30 years. The animals there have become so tame that they will often approach humans in the hope of food. I started by lying flat on the grass and feeding the squirrel from that position. It would come for a nut, run off to hide and then return again. It completely ignored the sound of my motordrive."

Nikon FM2 with 35mm lens; motordrive; Fujichrome Velvia

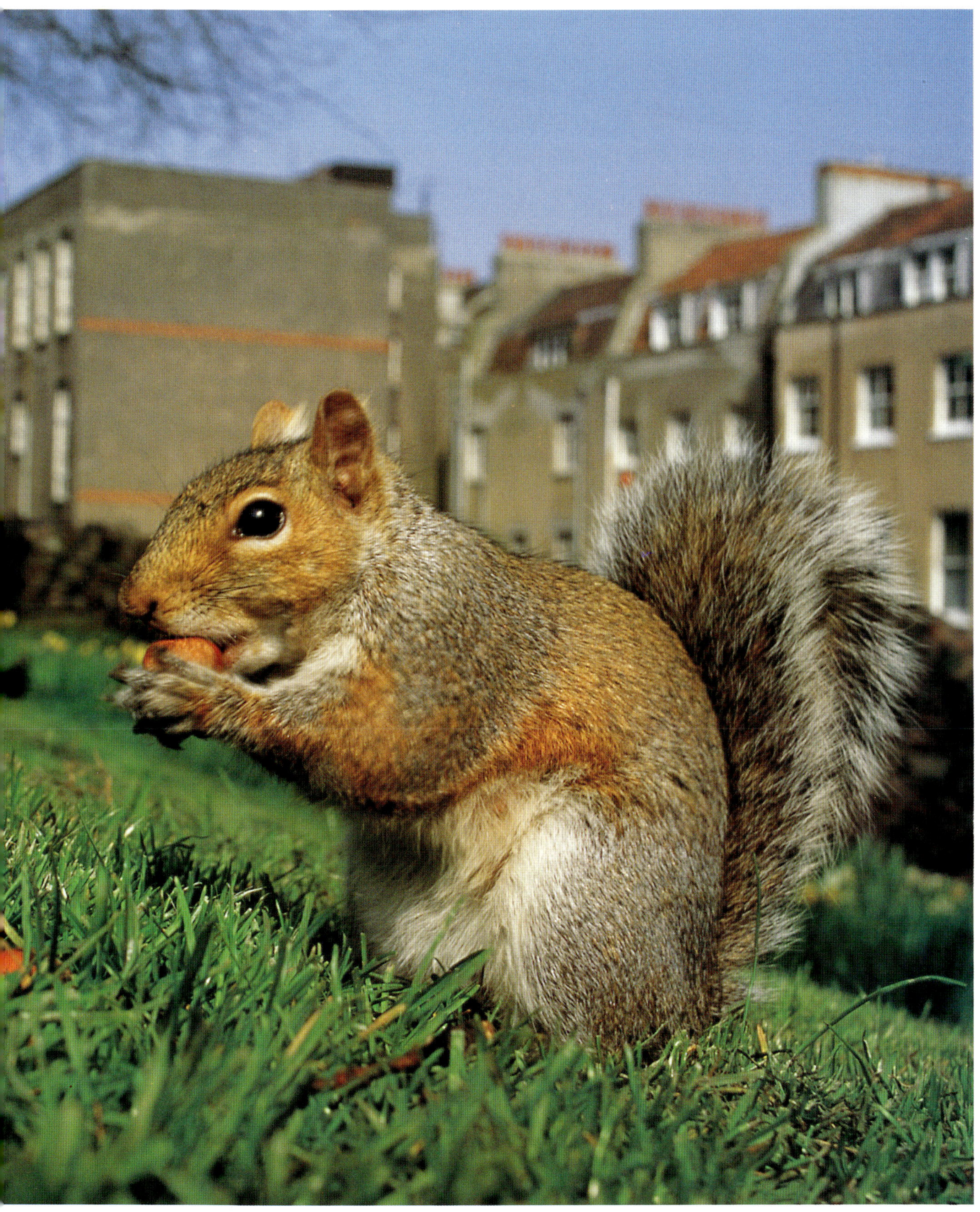

Composition and Form

This category is for photographs which illustrate natural subjects in abstract ways. The pictures are judged on their aesthetic values alone.

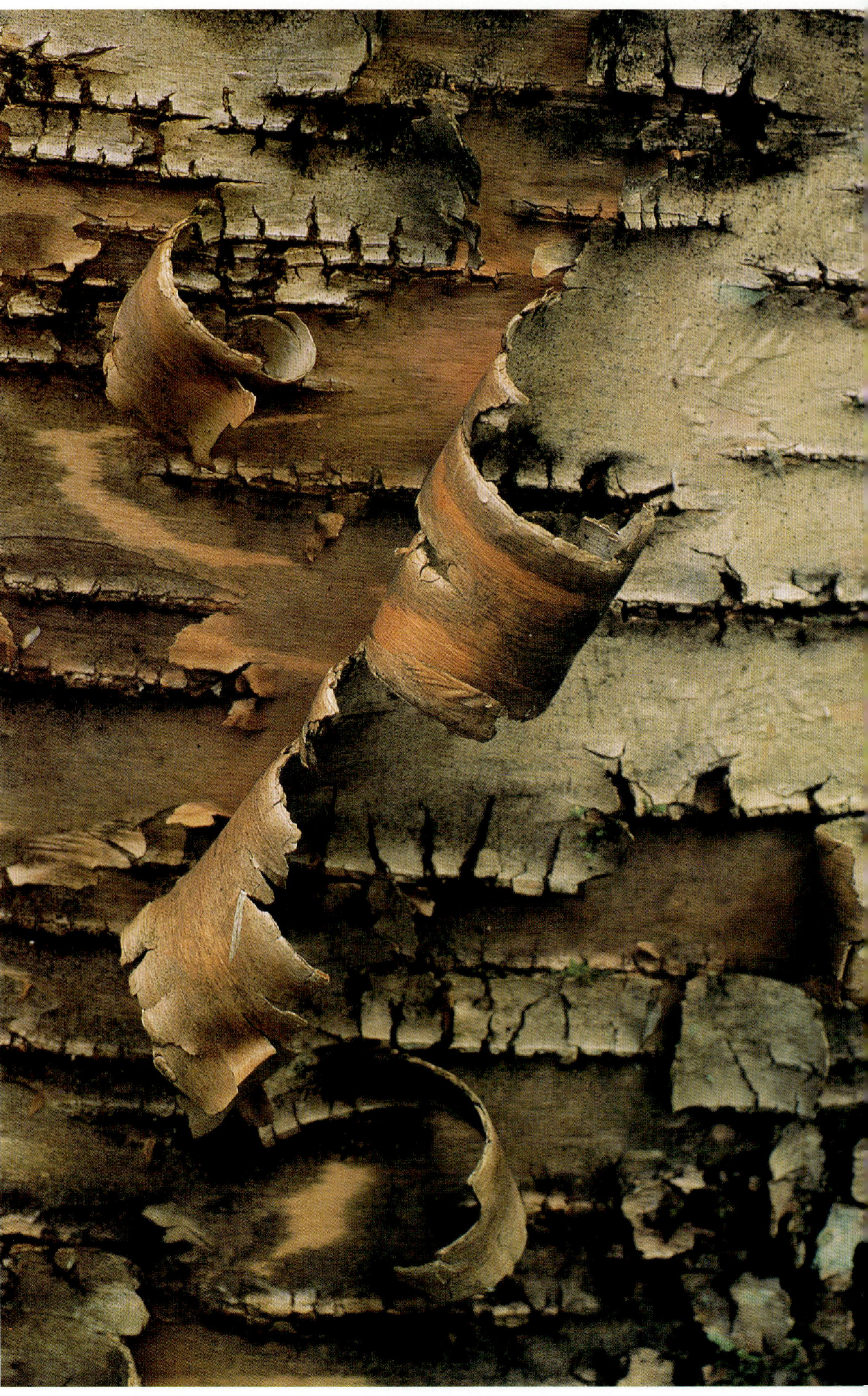

Theresa Thompson
United States of America
JOINT WINNER

Birch bark

"While looking for subjects to photograph in Gorham, New Hampshire, I was drawn to a particular paper birch tree because of the diagonal lines of the peeled bark. The composition I chose was on the shaded side of the tree, so I used a reflector to bounce light on to it."

Nikon FM2 with 105mm macro lens; tripod; reflector; f22 at 4 secs; Fujichrome Velvia

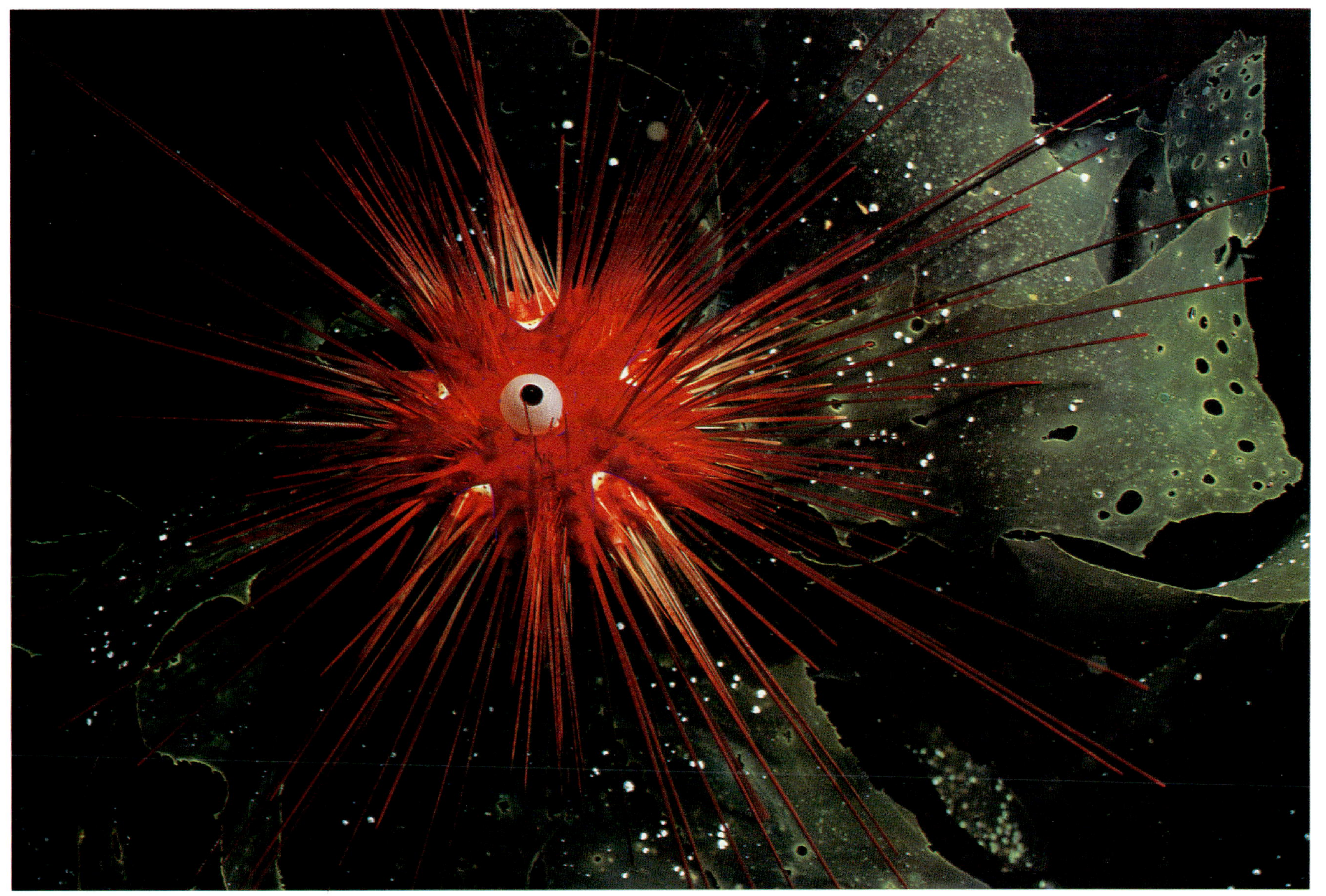

Darryl Torckler
New Zealand
JOINT WINNER

Diadema Sea Urchin and Kelp

"The Diadema is one of the most beautiful sea urchins in the world. Underwater in natural light it looks black, but a torchlight shows it to be brilliant red."

Canon F1 with 50mm macro lens; underwater housing; two strobes; f11 at 1/60 sec; Fujichrome Velvia

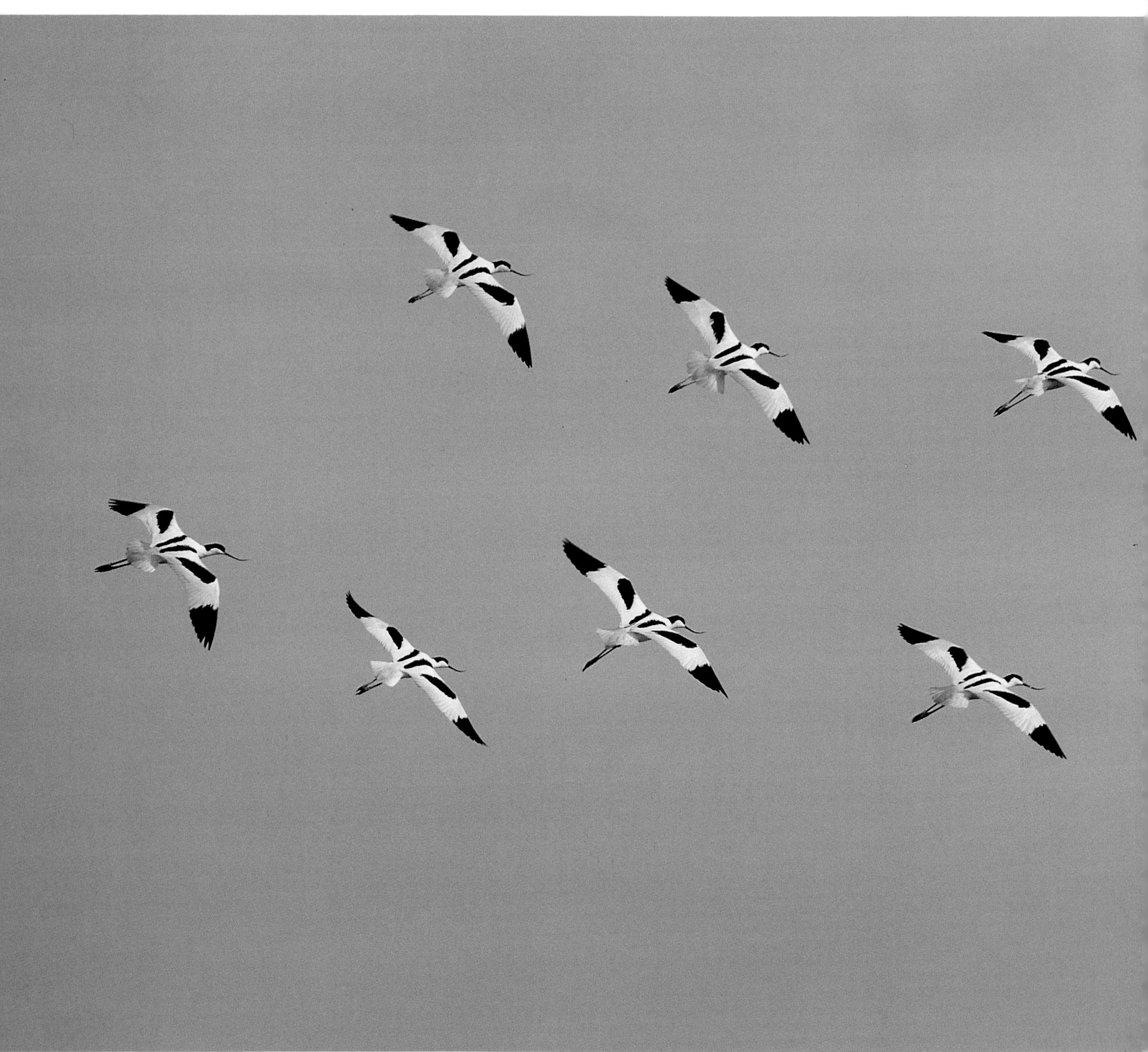

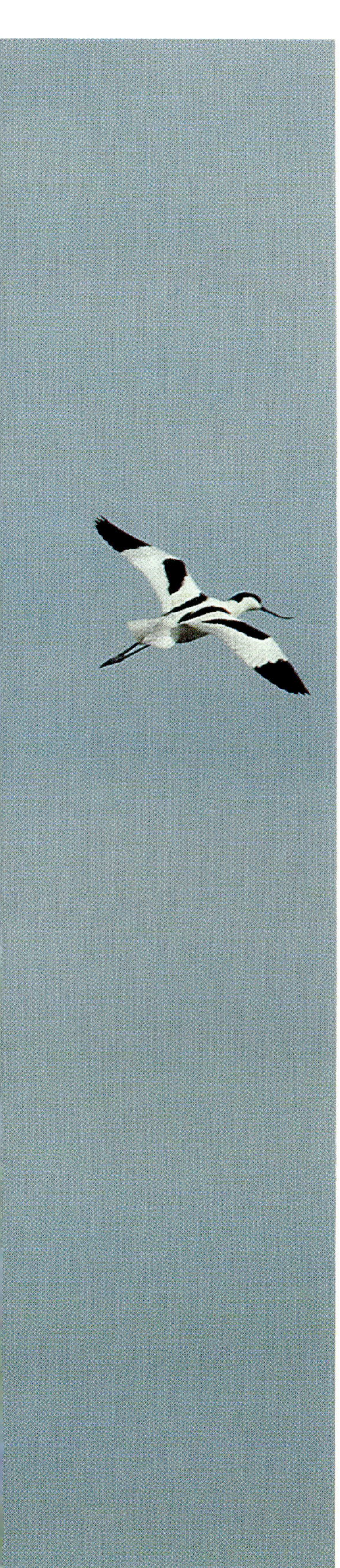

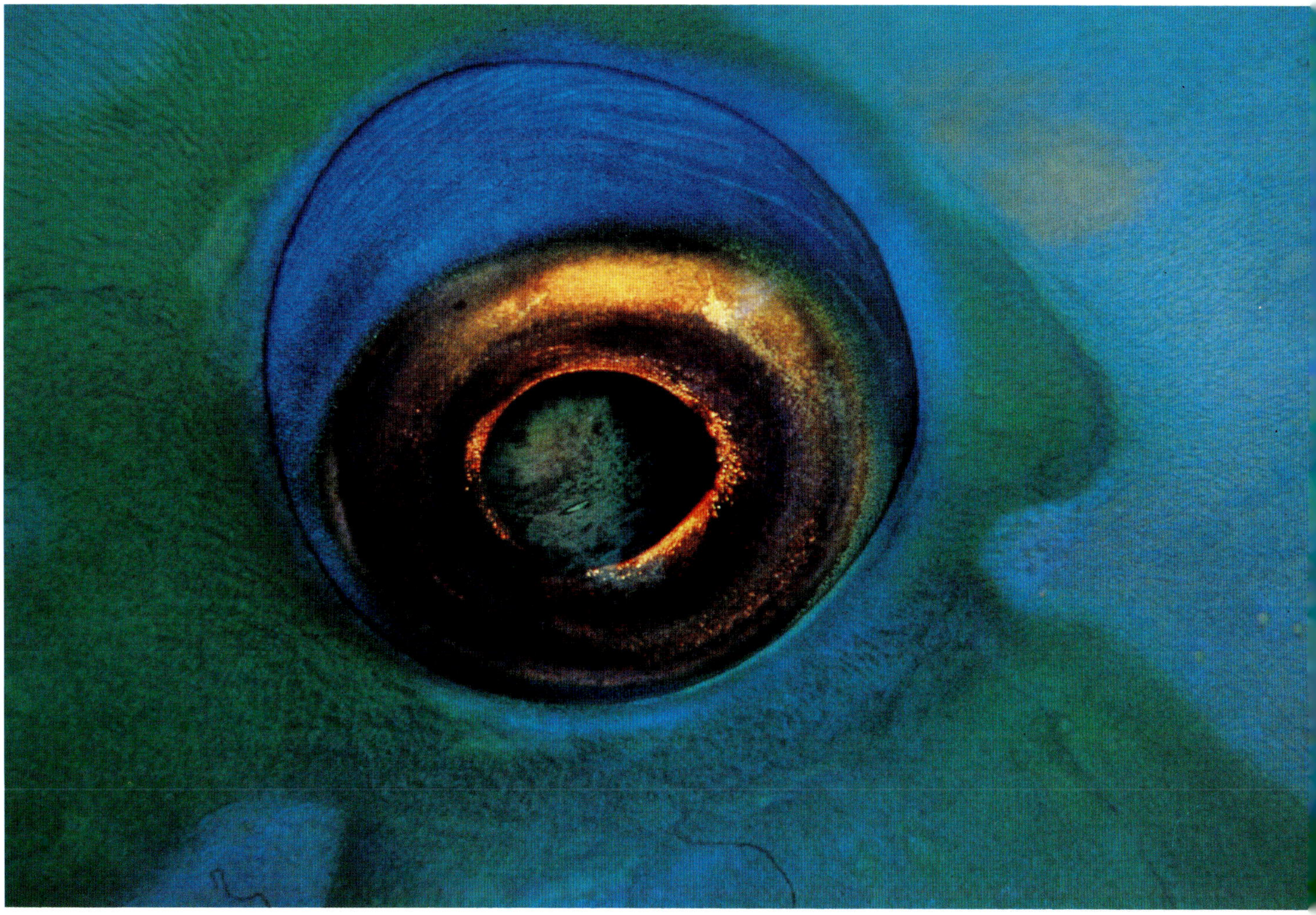

Mike Wilkes
United Kingdom
JOINT RUNNER-UP

Avocets in flight

"We had spent the day
photographing waders at a pool
in southern Spain and had just
packed up our hides when a flock
of avocets flew over.
As they circled to land on the far
side of the pool, I got this shot.
We returned the next day to
photograph them feeding."

Canon EOS 1 with 300mm lens; f4 at
1/1000 sec; Ektachrome 100

Erik Bjurstrom
Sweden
JOINT RUNNER-UP

The eye of a Parrotfish

"The parrotfish was sleeping in a
crevice in the reef. It was night,
and so I had to use a flashlight
mounted on my strobe in order to
focus properly. Although the fish
does not react to light, it is coated
in a thin layer of mucus which is
sensitive to vibrations. I had to
move very carefully to get close
enough for this close-up."

Nikon F3 with macro 105mm lens; two
strobes; f22 at 1/80 sec; Fujichrome 50

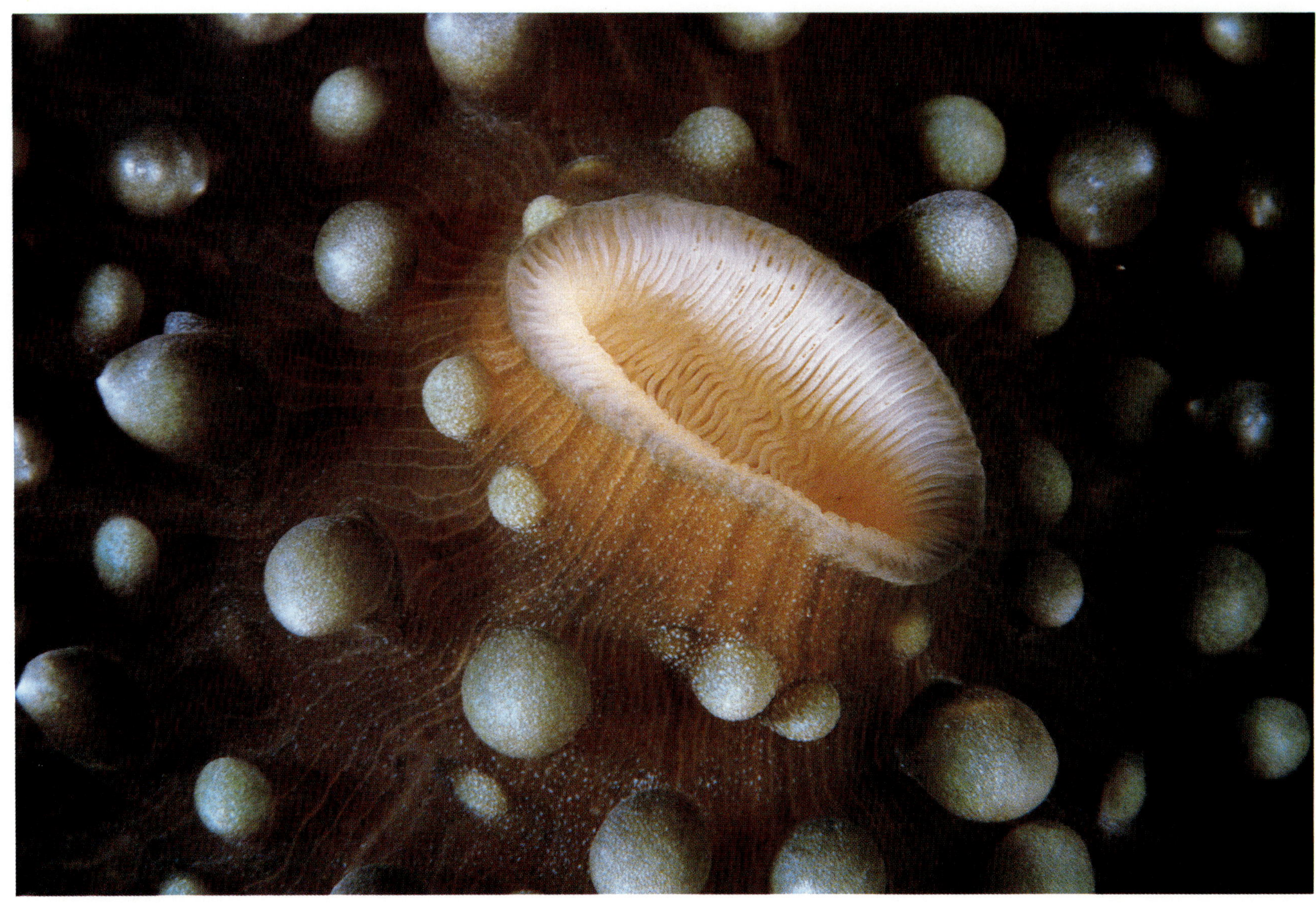

**Burt Jones &
Maurine Shimlock**
United States of America
HIGHLY COMMENDED

Anemone mouth

*"We are always trying to reveal
the unusual and the 'art in the
animal'. Being underwater is like
visiting another planet, and this
anemone, with its mouth slightly
extended for feeding, really
looks like something from
another galaxy."*

Nikon F3 with 105 mm macro lens;
underwater housing; strobes;
f16 at 1/60 sec; Fujichrome 50

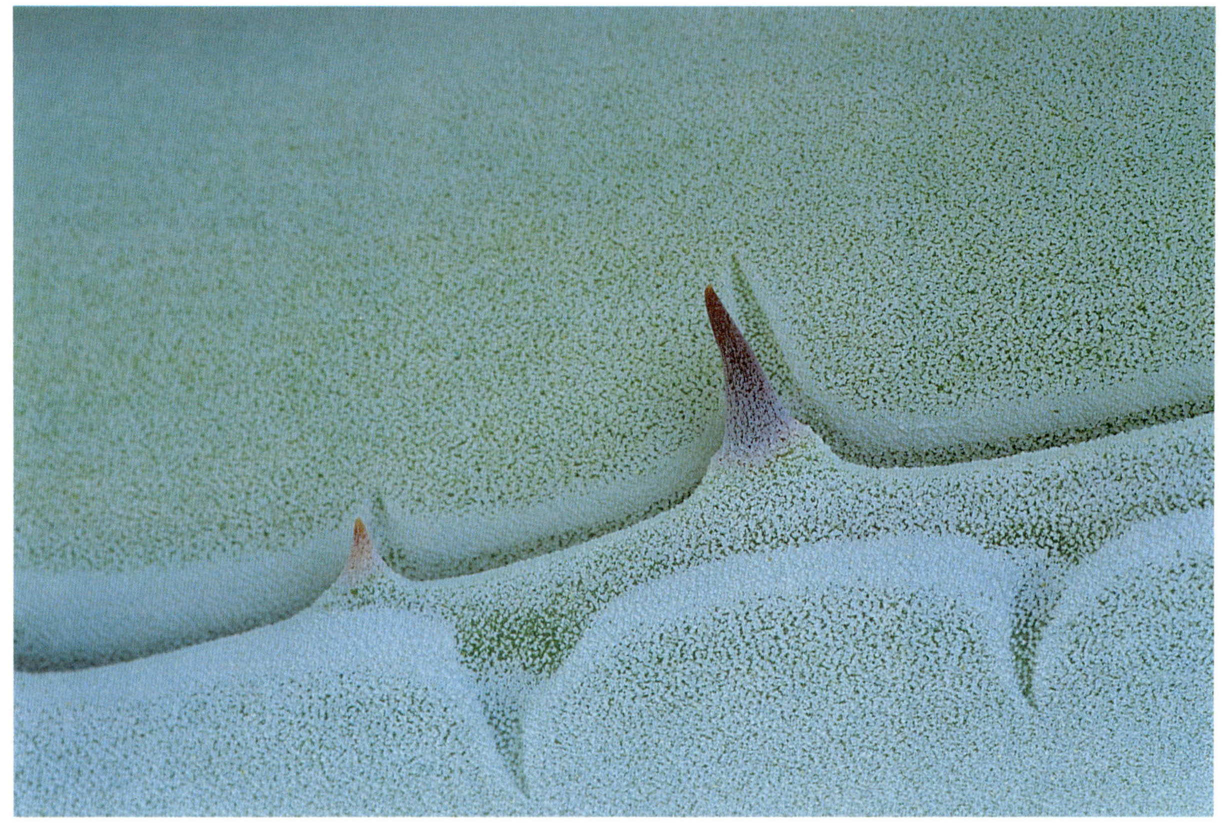

David Welling
United States of America
HIGHLY COMMENDED

Agave in close-up
*"This is a close-up of the spines
and leaf texture of an agave
plant. I was attracted to the
'frost' on the leaves, a powdery
covering of waxy cuticle common
to this type of plant. Presumably
this protects it from the extreme
climatic conditions of its
desert environment."*

Nikon F4s with 105mm macro lens;
tripod; f22 at 1/8 sec; Fujichrome RF 50

Markku Nikki
Finland
HIGHLY COMMENDED

Galaxy
*"I took this shot of algae in the
archipelago of south Finland to
show the special form and colour
of the plant growth."*

Canon F1 with 50mm lens; tripod;
f11 at 1/15 sec; Fujichrome Velvia

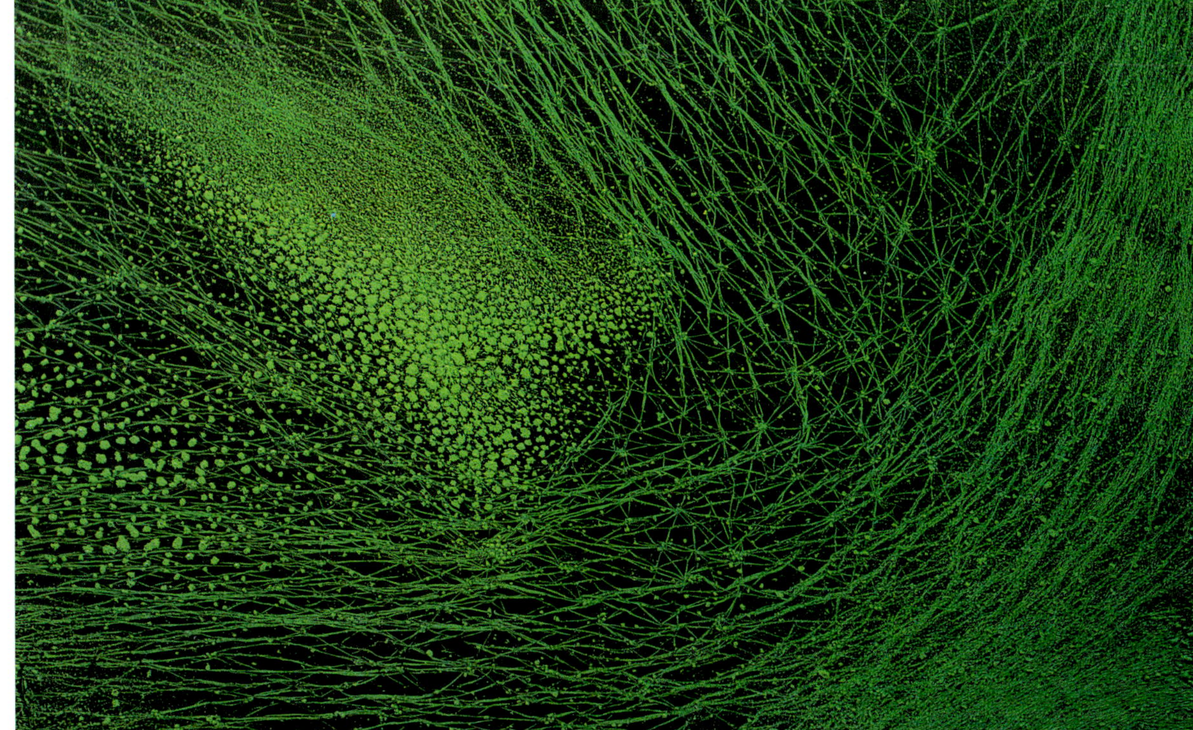

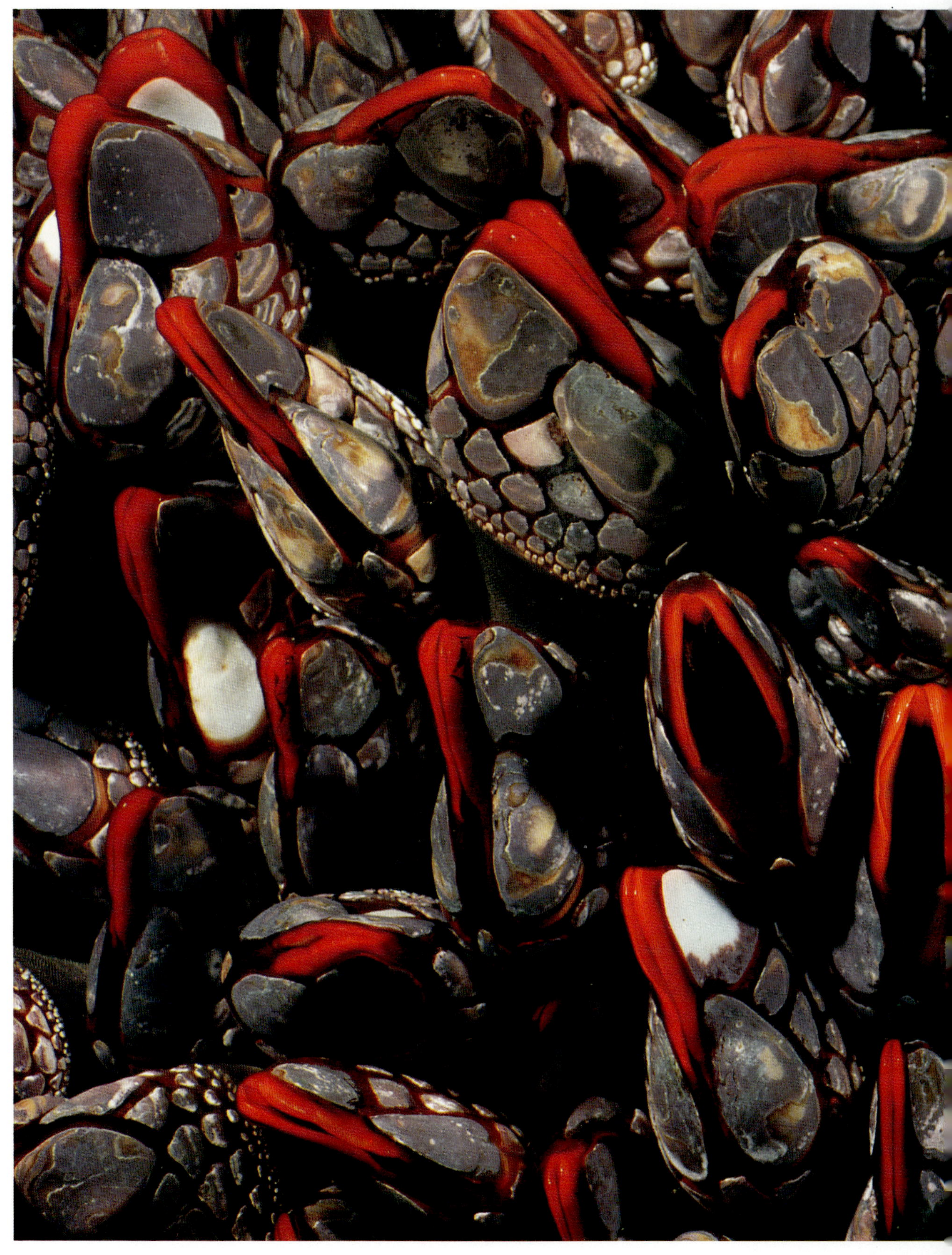

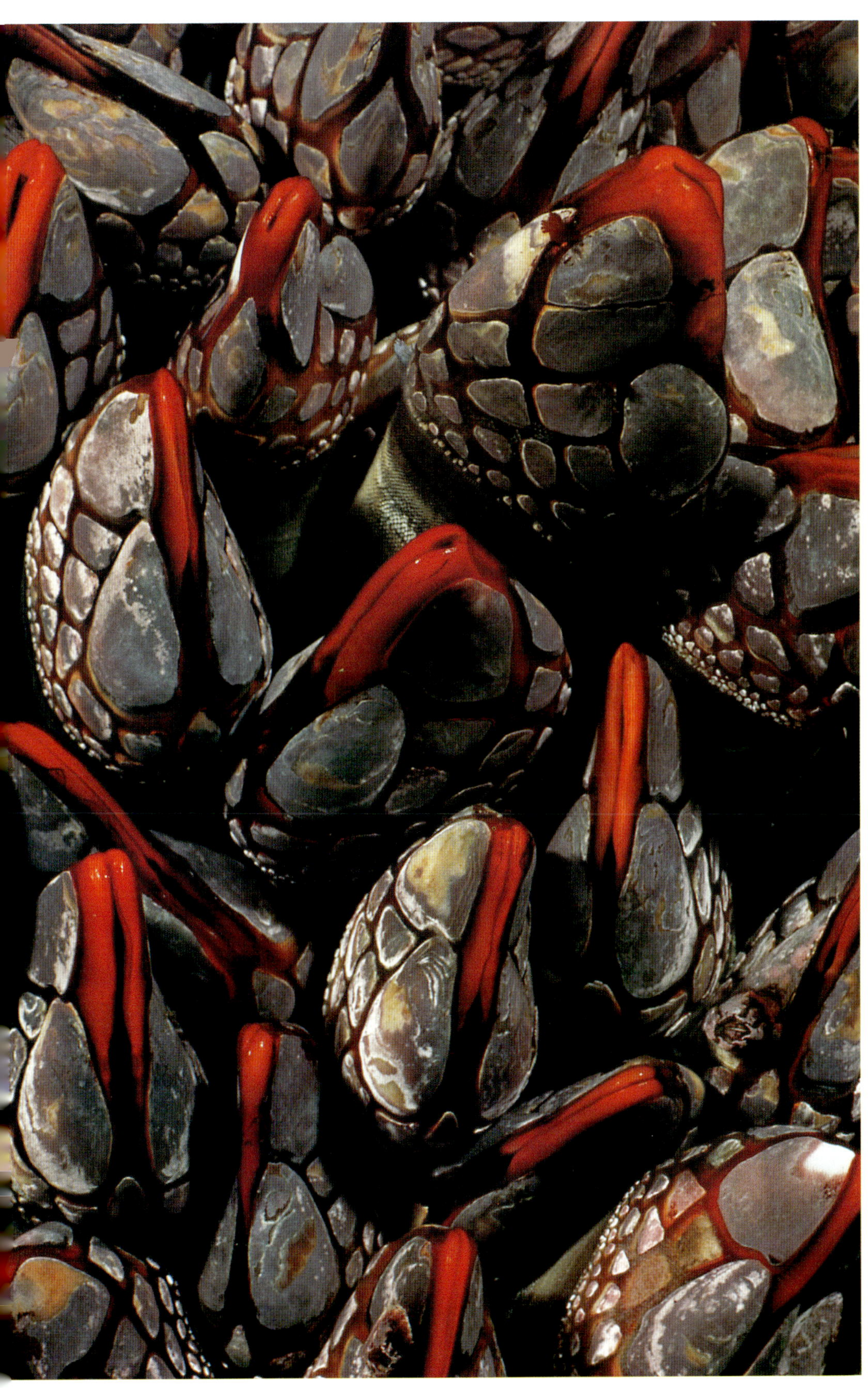

Roger B Mooers
United States of America
HIGHLY COMMENDED

Gooseneck Barnacles
*"The Turret rock on Slingsby
Channel, Canada, where I took
this picture is the only area
where gooseneck barnacles
are red."*

Nikon F3 with 55mm lens;
underwater housing; strobes;
f16 at 1/80 sec; Kodachrome 64

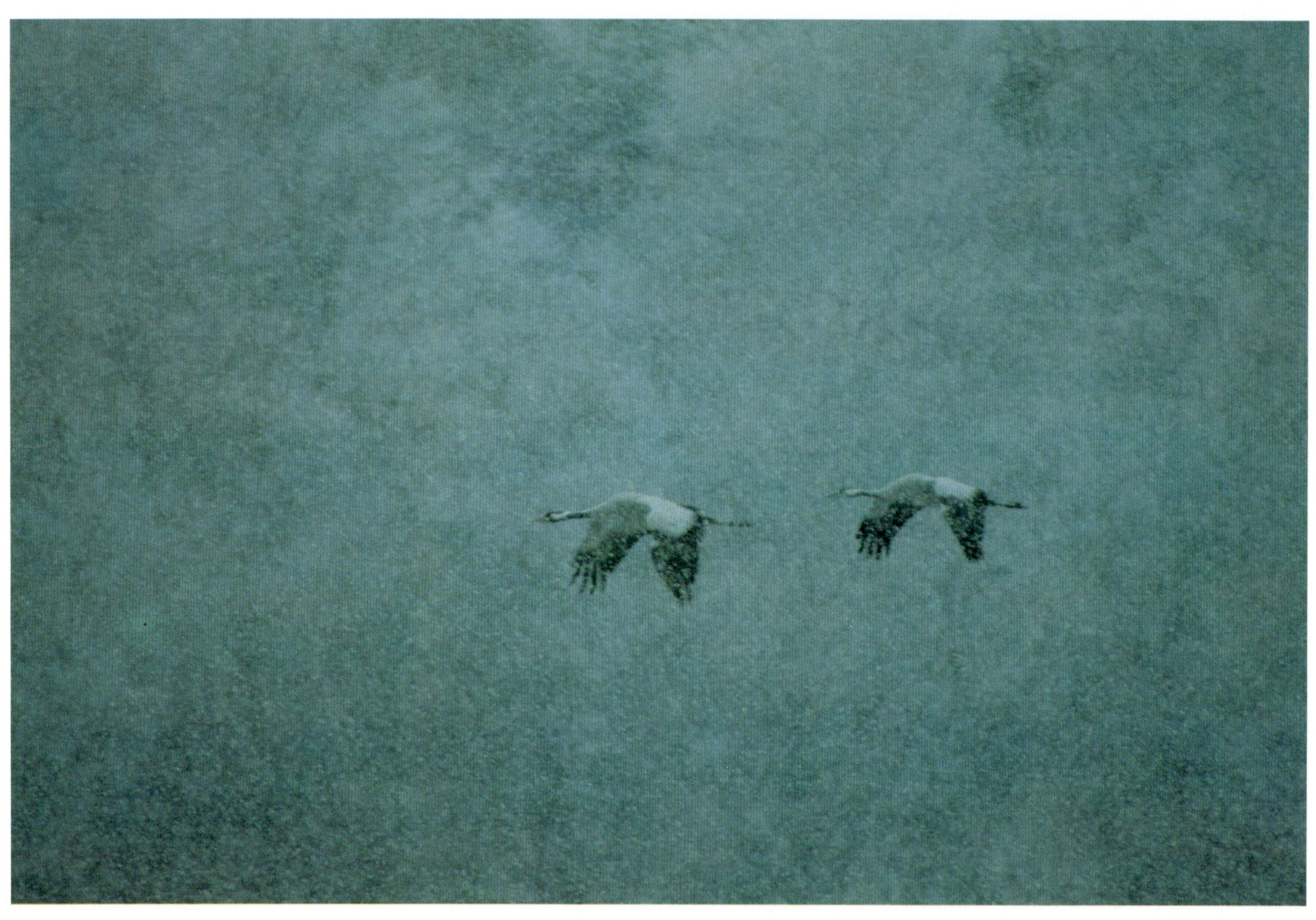

Lennart Mellgren
Sweden
HIGHLY COMMENDED

Cranes in snowstorm

"During April, thousands of cranes arrive at Lake Hornborgasjon, Sweden. My picture shows the heavy snow conditions the birds sometimes meet on arrival."

Nikon F301 with 400mm lens; f5.6 at 1/250 sec; Ektachrome 100

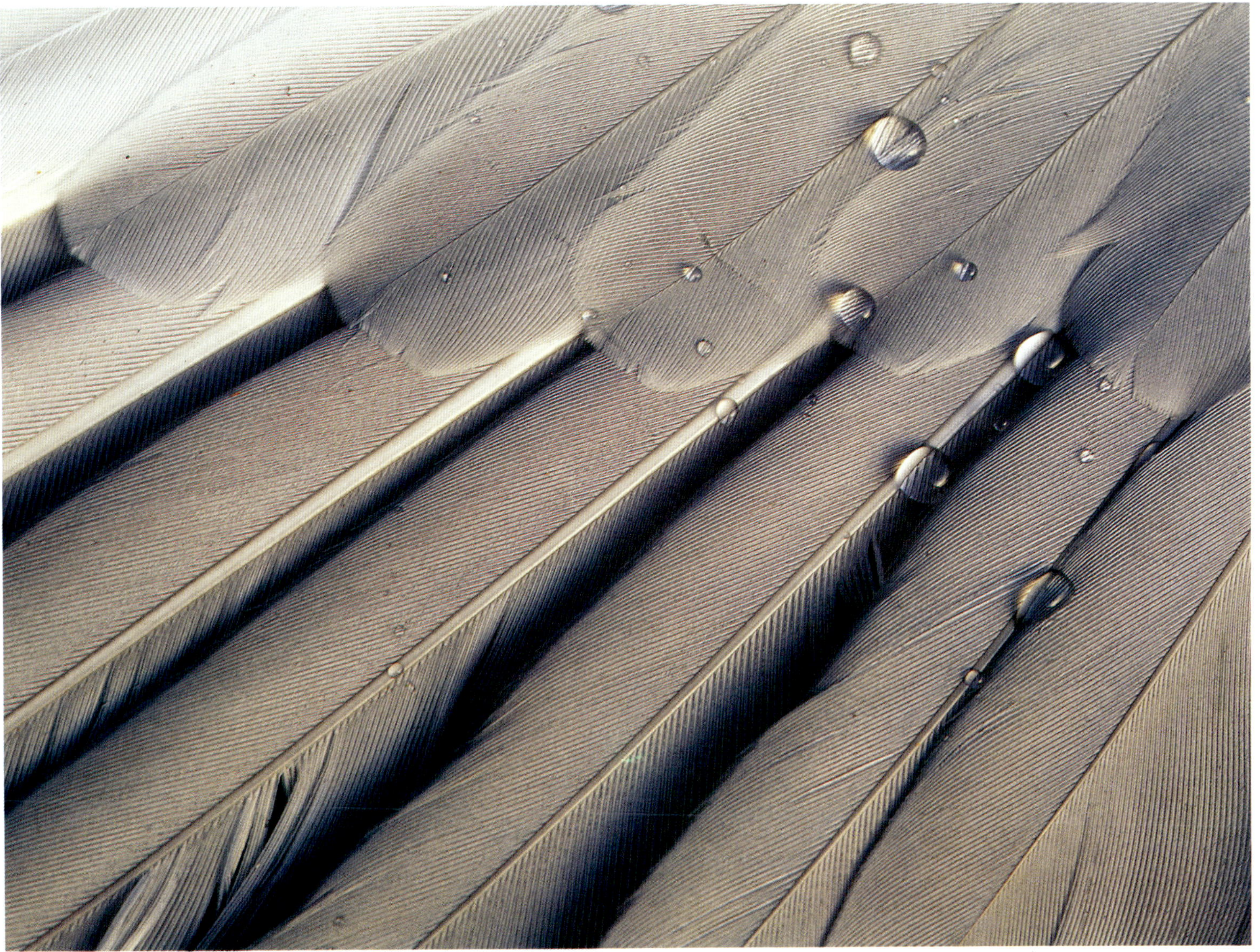

Jan Tove Johansson
Sweden
HIGHLY COMMENDED

Feather detail

"Admiring the shining feathers
of a dead black-headed gull
which I found on the beach,
I decided to take a picture
showing how perfectly the
feathers repel water. I dropped
some lakewater on the wing
which immediately splintered
into small droplets."

Pentax 654 with 120mm macro lens;
tripod; f22 at 1/4 sec; Fujichrome Velvia

Wild Places

Photographs entered for this category should show landscapes which convey a feeling of wildness and create a sense of wonder or awe.

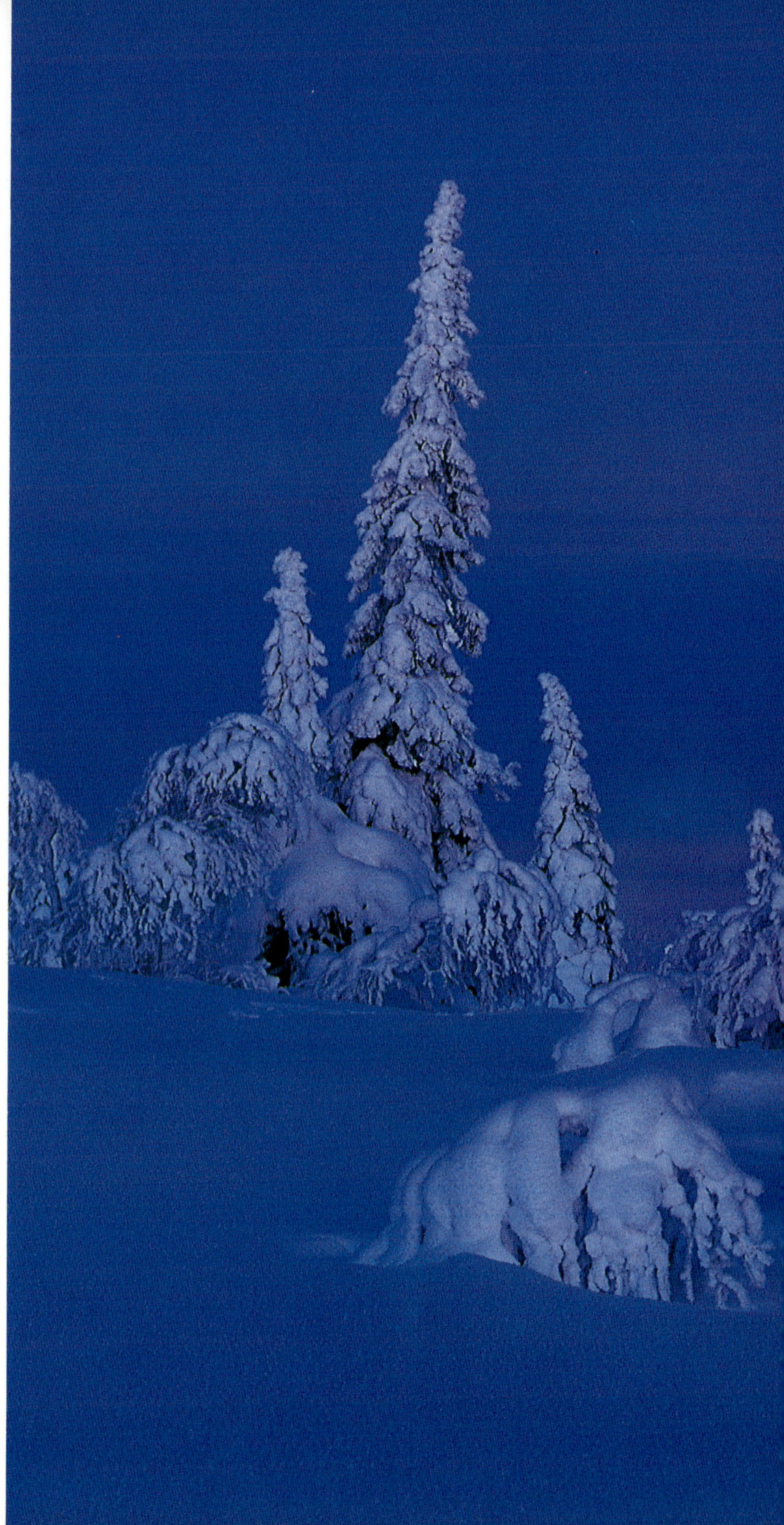

Keijo Penttinen
Finland
WINNER

Winter in Finland

"This photograph of the moon and trees was taken in the Riisitunturi National Park at 9 o'clock one January morning. The blue light is typical of this time of year, when the sun is still below the horizon."

Nikon F4 with 105mm lens; tripod; f11 at 1/15 sec; Fujichrome Velvia

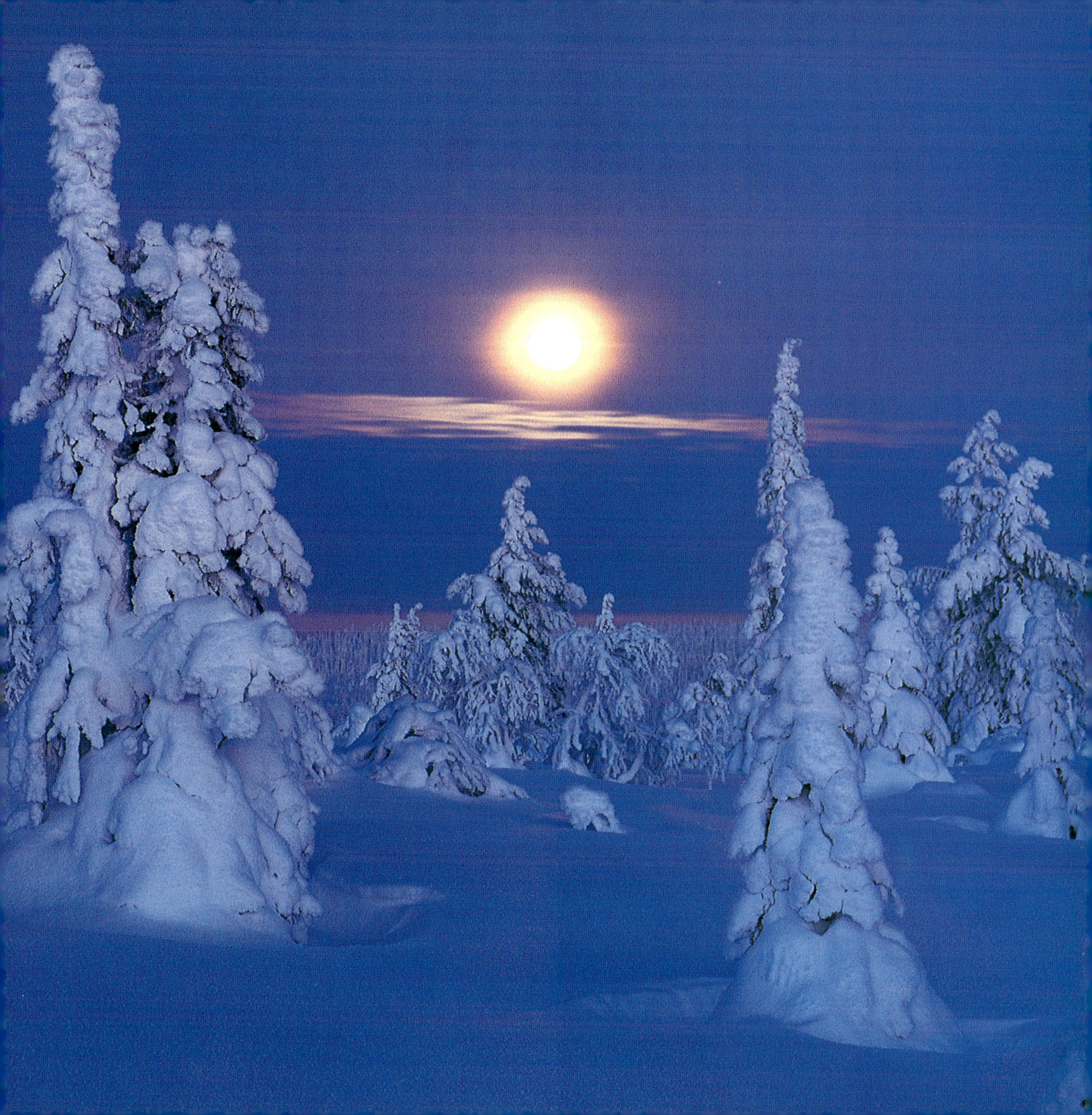

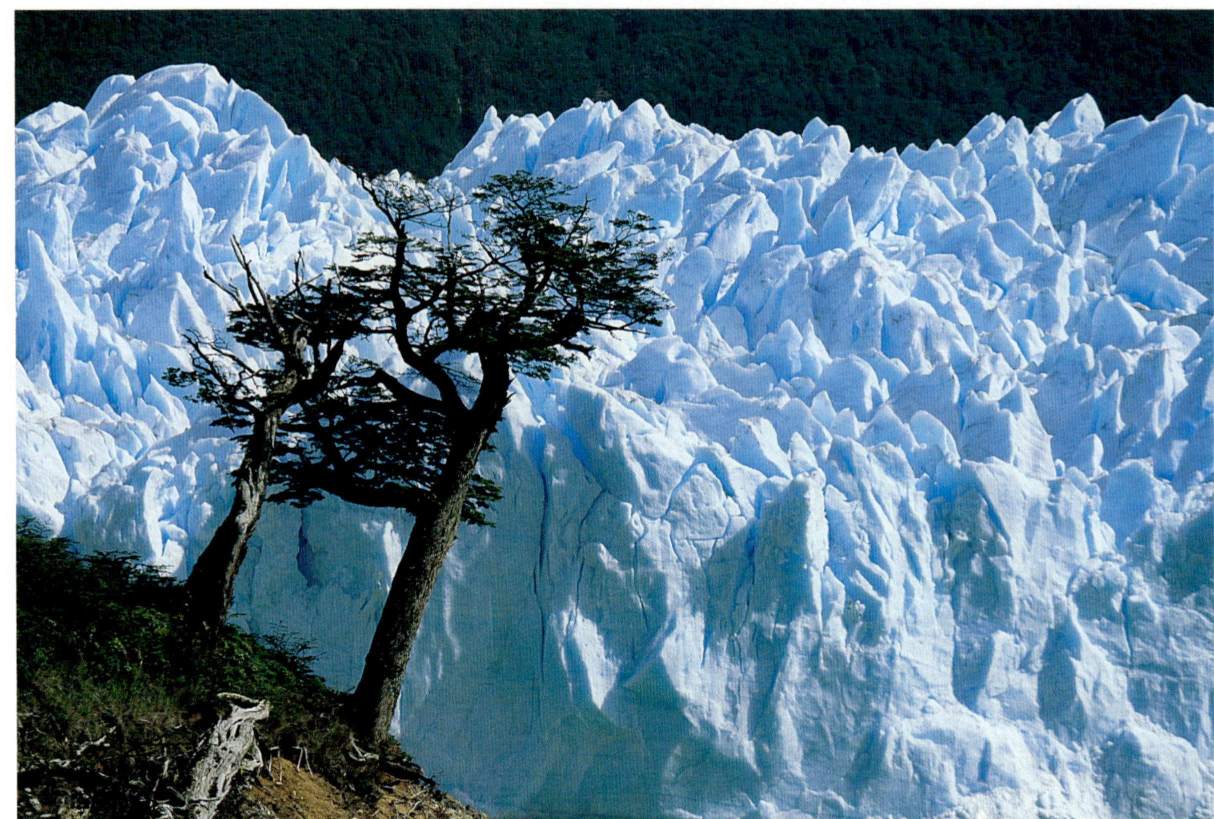

Konrad Wothe
Germany
HIGHLY COMMENDED

Perito Moreno glacier

"This is one of my best pictures from a recent trip to Patagonia and Antarctica, but even so, it doesn't truely represent the breathtaking scenery of this Argentine glacier."

Canon EOS 1 with 80-200mm zoom lens; f6.7 at 1/250 sec; Fujichrome Velvia

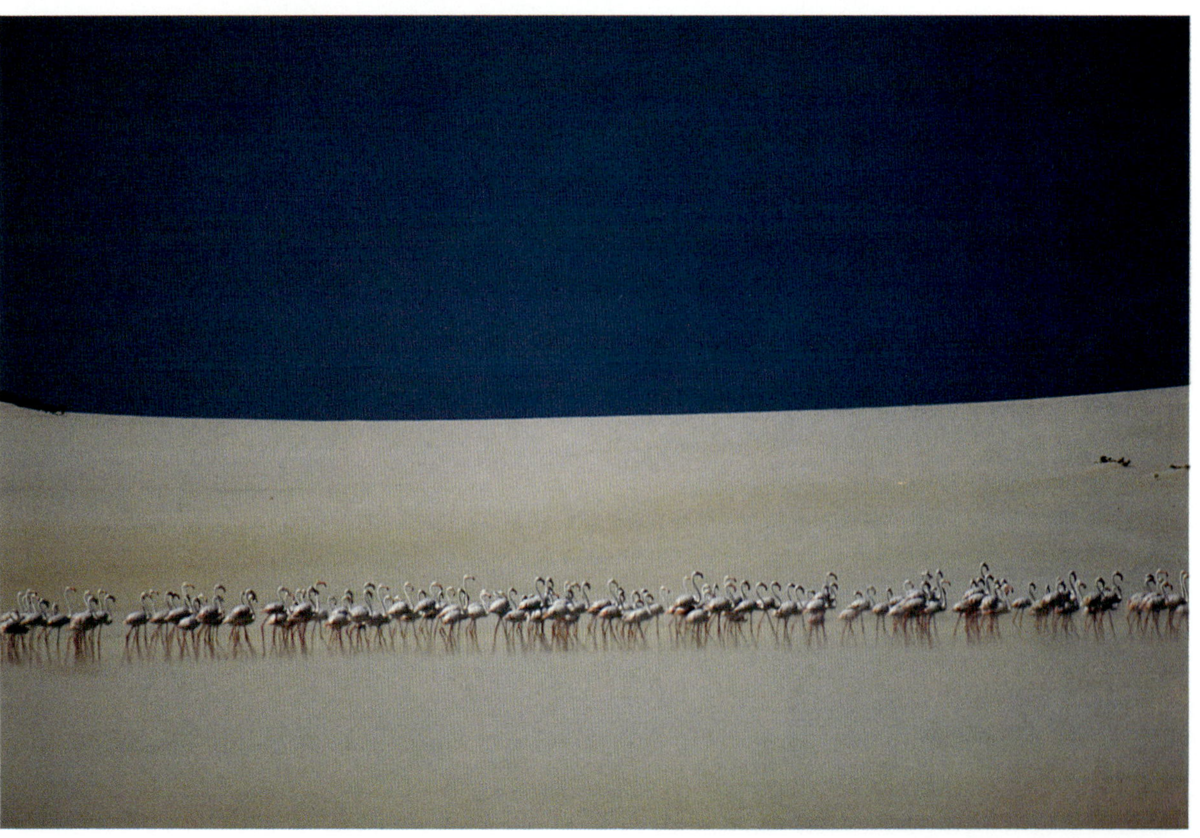

Beverly Joubert
Botswana
HIGHLY COMMENDED

Flamingos

"Greater flamingos congregate on the deserted shores of the Indian Ocean, off the coast of Mozambique. I was exploring the coastline by boat, looking for flocks to photograph, when I saw a splash of pink and white against the sand dunes. Creeping up the shore on my stomach I took four shots before the birds flew off."

Nikon F4 with 500mm lens; f5.6 at 1/500 sec; Fujichrome Velvia

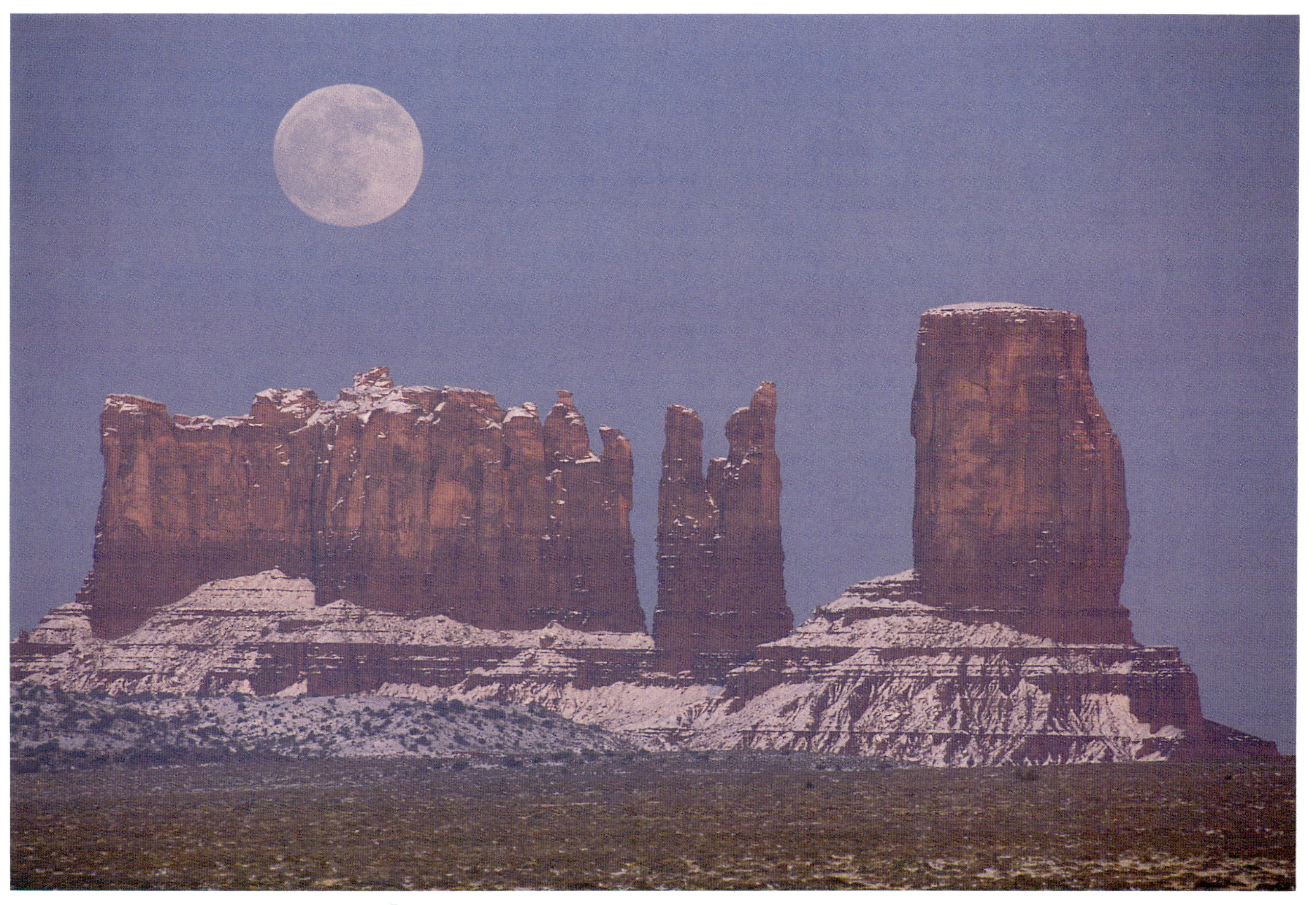

**Wendy Shattil
& Bob Rozinski**
United States of America
HIGHLY COMMENDED

***Moonrise over
Monument Valley***

*"We are partial to shooting
scenics during full moons. This
shot shows the full moon rising
over Monument Valley."*

Canon T90 with 150-600mm lens;
f5.6 at 1/60 sec; Fujichrome 100

Animal Portraits

Photographs for this category should show animals in close-up.

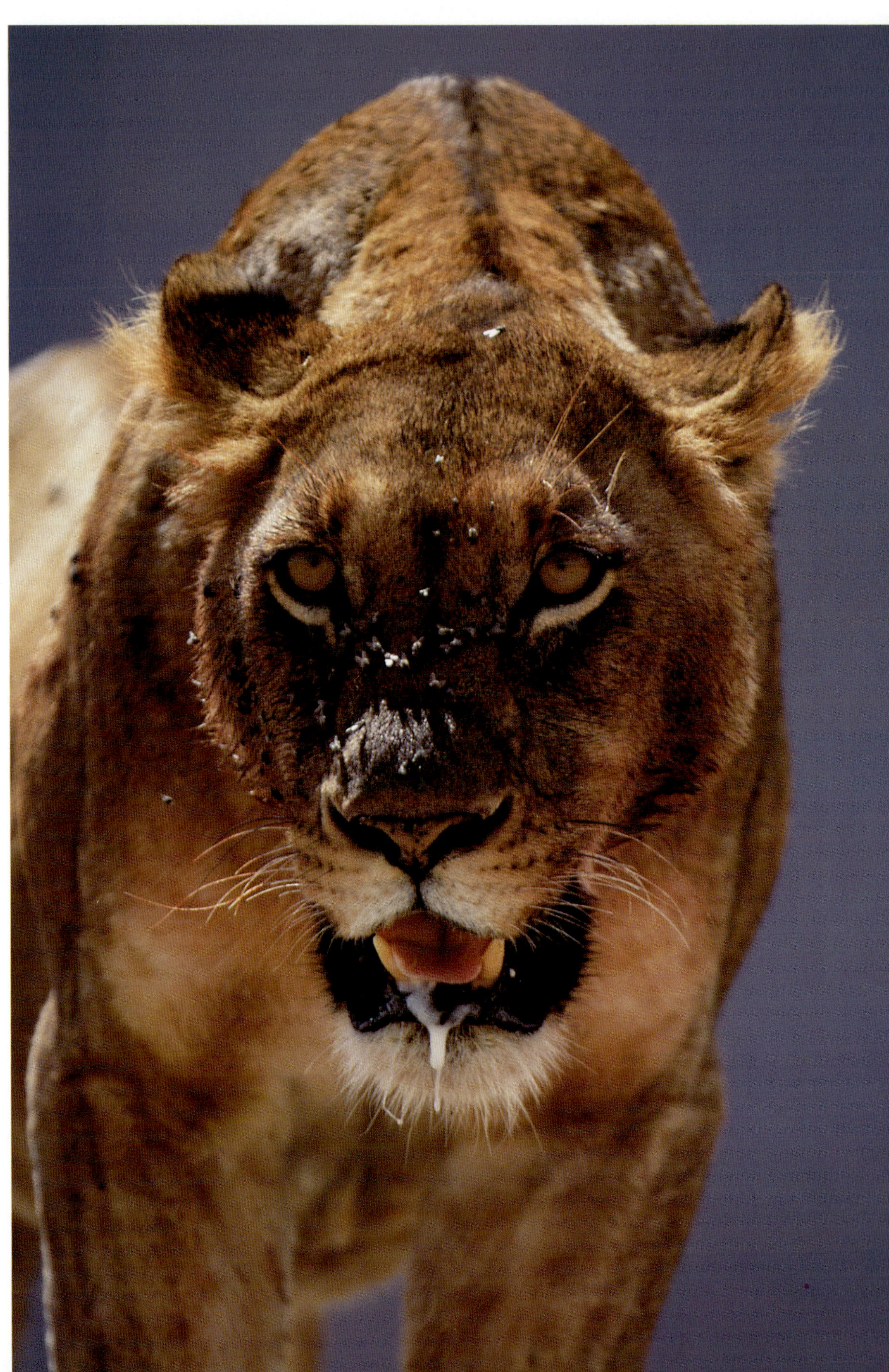

Samantha Purdy
United Kingdom
WINNER

Lioness

"The lioness had walked a long distance during a very hot day in the Ngorongoro Crater, Tanzania, and eventually stopped to rest on a large rock. She was salivating and surrounded by flies, but was also looking around intently, possibly for game or other lions. She was higher than my vehicle, which helped create a more dramatic picture."

Canon EOS 1 with 300mm lens; camera-mount on car door; f5.6 at 1/250 sec; Kodachrome 64

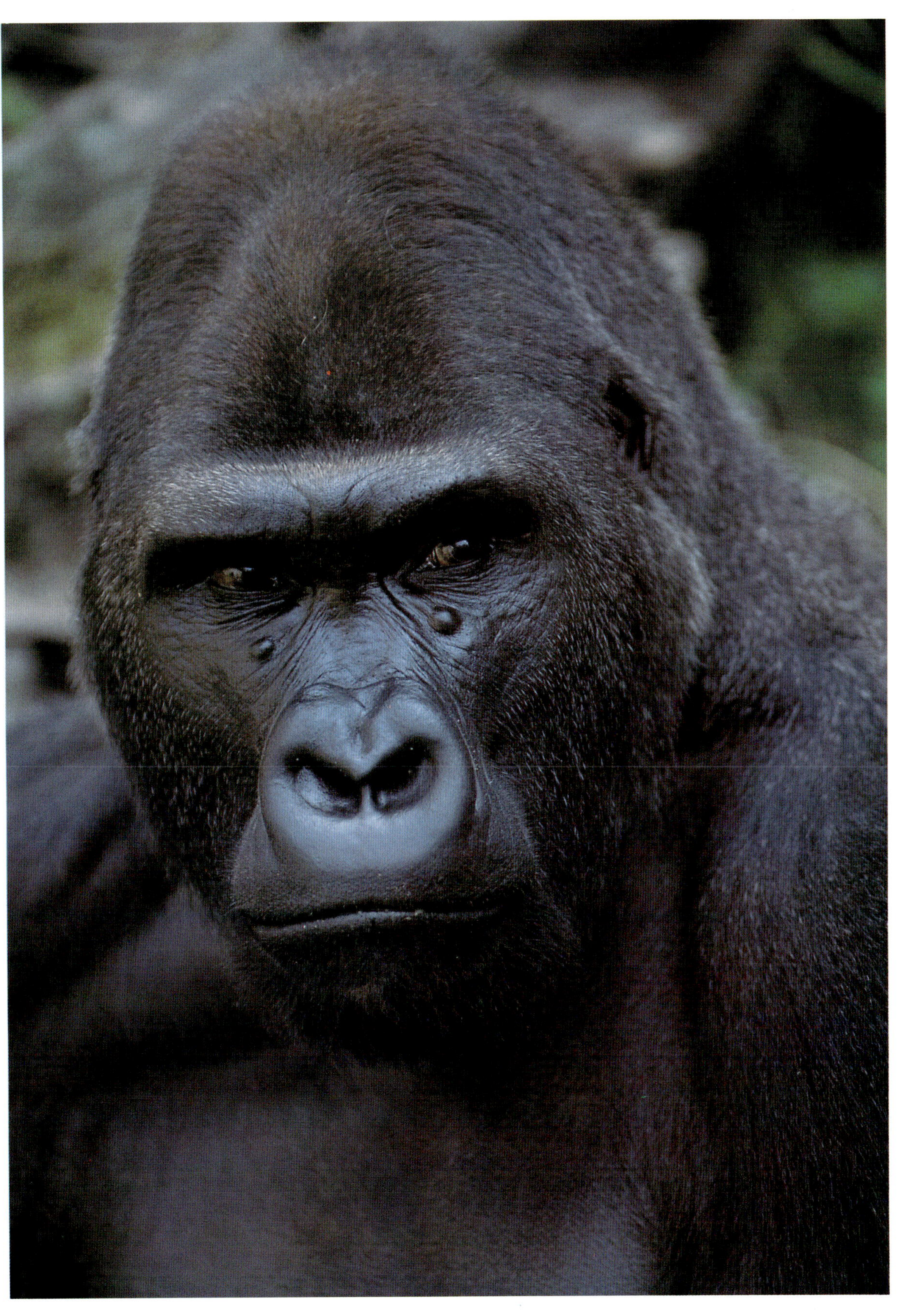

Manfred Klindwort
Germany
RUNNER-UP

Gorilla

"*During summer, the gorillas at Hanover zoo live in a large open enclosure. I spent six hours in front of the enclosure taking many pictures.*
It was a warm day and there were many visitors. This individual seemed very interested in their voices - I wonder what he was thinking."

Canon EOS 1 with 300mm lens; monopod; auto at 1/250; Kodachrome 64 uprated to 80

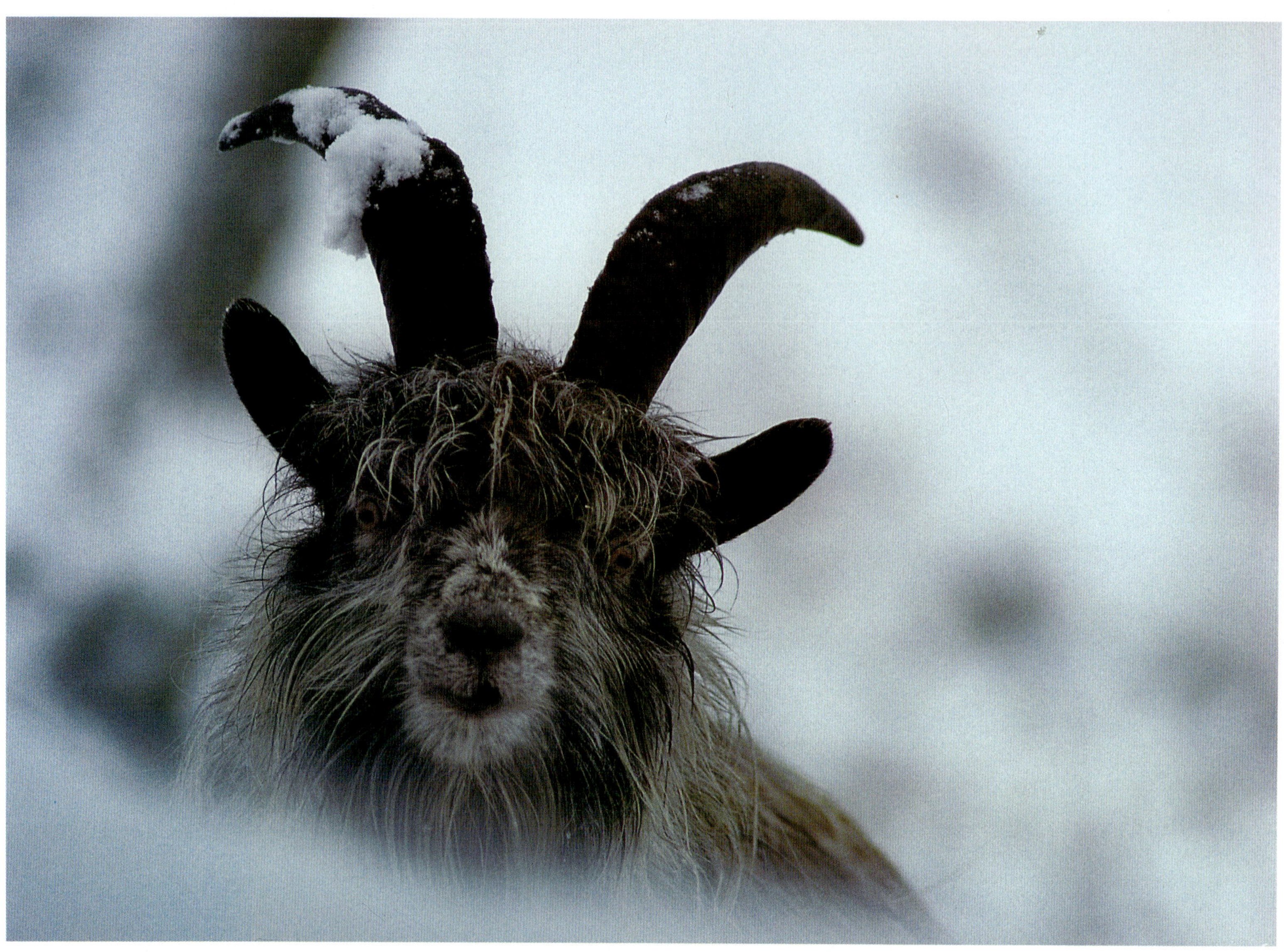

Niall Benvie
United Kingdom
SPECIALLY COMMENDED

Wild Goat
"Heavy snowfall had driven a
tribe of wild goats off the open
hillside into the shelter of a birch
wood. As a rule these goats are
wary of people, a reflection of the
culls that periodically occur.
In this case, I spoke quietly to the
animal and avoided eye contact
until I took the picture."

Nikon FM2 with 300mm lens and ×1.4
converter; beanbag; f4 at 1/60 sec;
Kodachrome 200

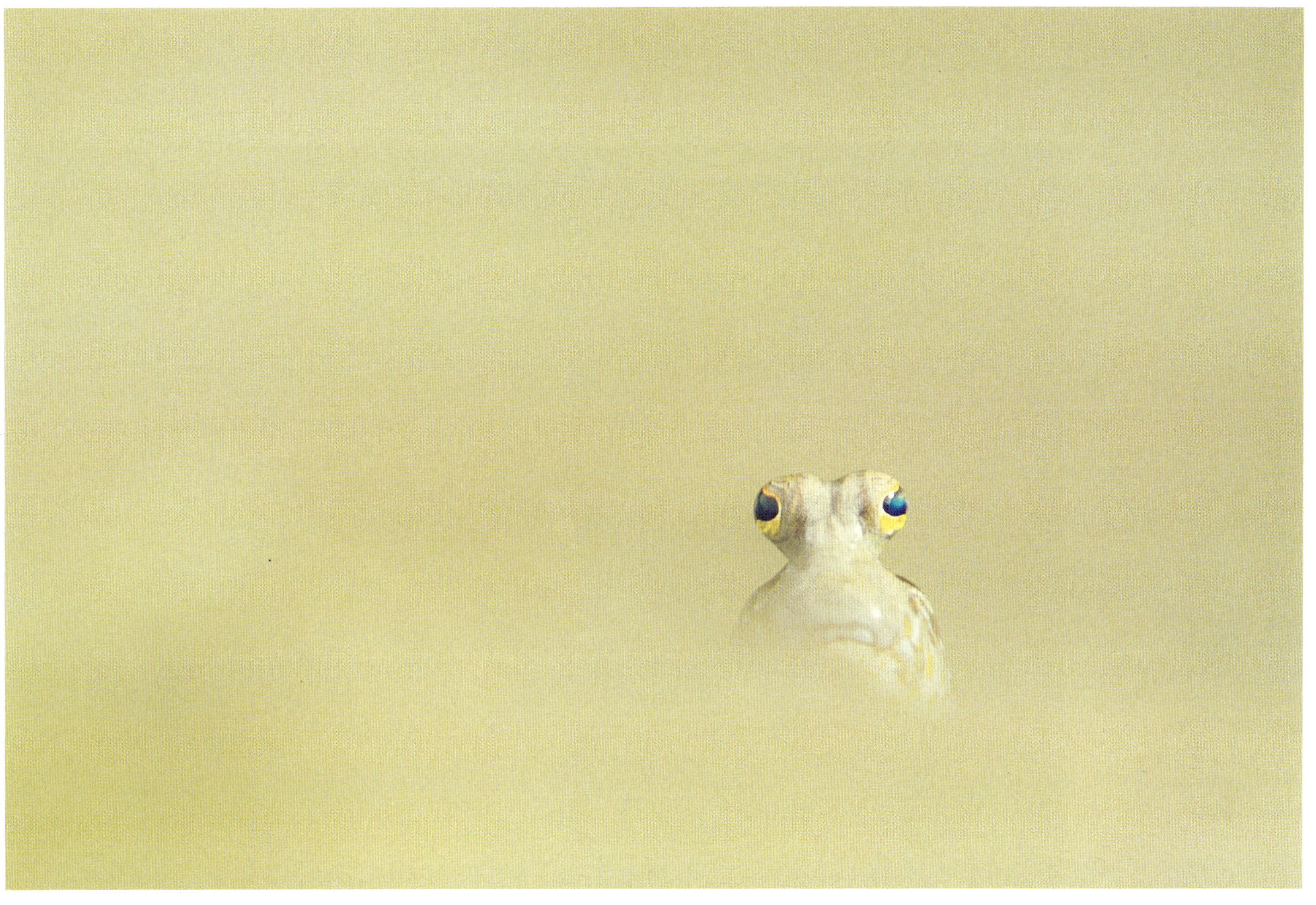

Carsten Broder Hansen
Denmark
HIGHLY COMMENDED

Mudskipper

''I photographed this
mudskipper resting on a rock as
the tide was coming in. These
semi-amphibious fish spend low
tide on mudflats and in tidal
pools feeding on crustaceans.
The picture was taken in the
mangrove swamps of Bako
National Park, Sarawak, where
I spent four months studying
proboscis monkeys.''

Minolta X700 with 80-200mm lens; f8 at
auto; Fujichrome 100

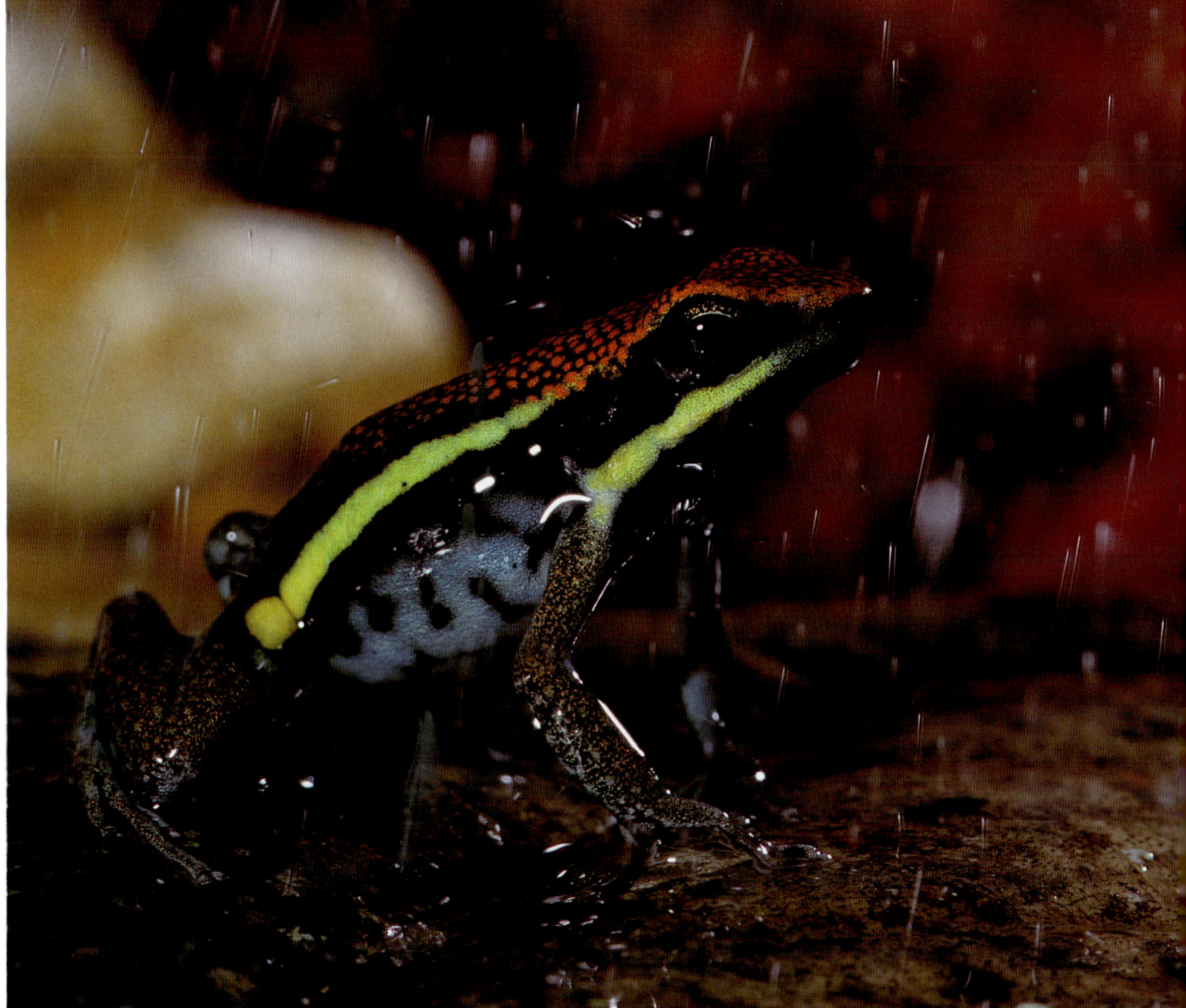

André Bärtschi
Liechtenstein
HIGHLY COMMENDED

Poison-dart Frog

"I found this tiny, brightly coloured male poison-dart frog foraging in the rainforest leaf litter of Manu's biosphere reserve in Peru. He is calling in the rain, either to mark his territory or to attract females. To take this picture, I had to crawl like a reptile on the damp floor, only to see the frog disappearing with lightning speed under some dead leaves. Luckily he returned to his look-out a few minutes later."

Nikon FM2 with 105mm macro lens; flash; Kodachrome 25

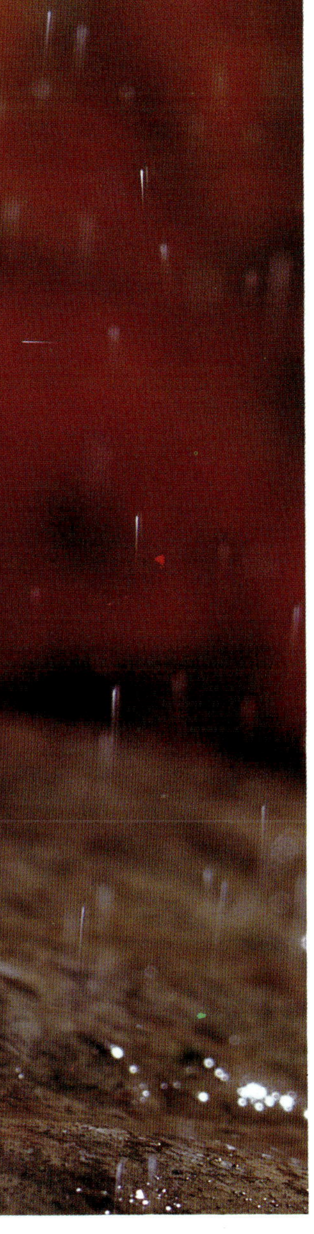

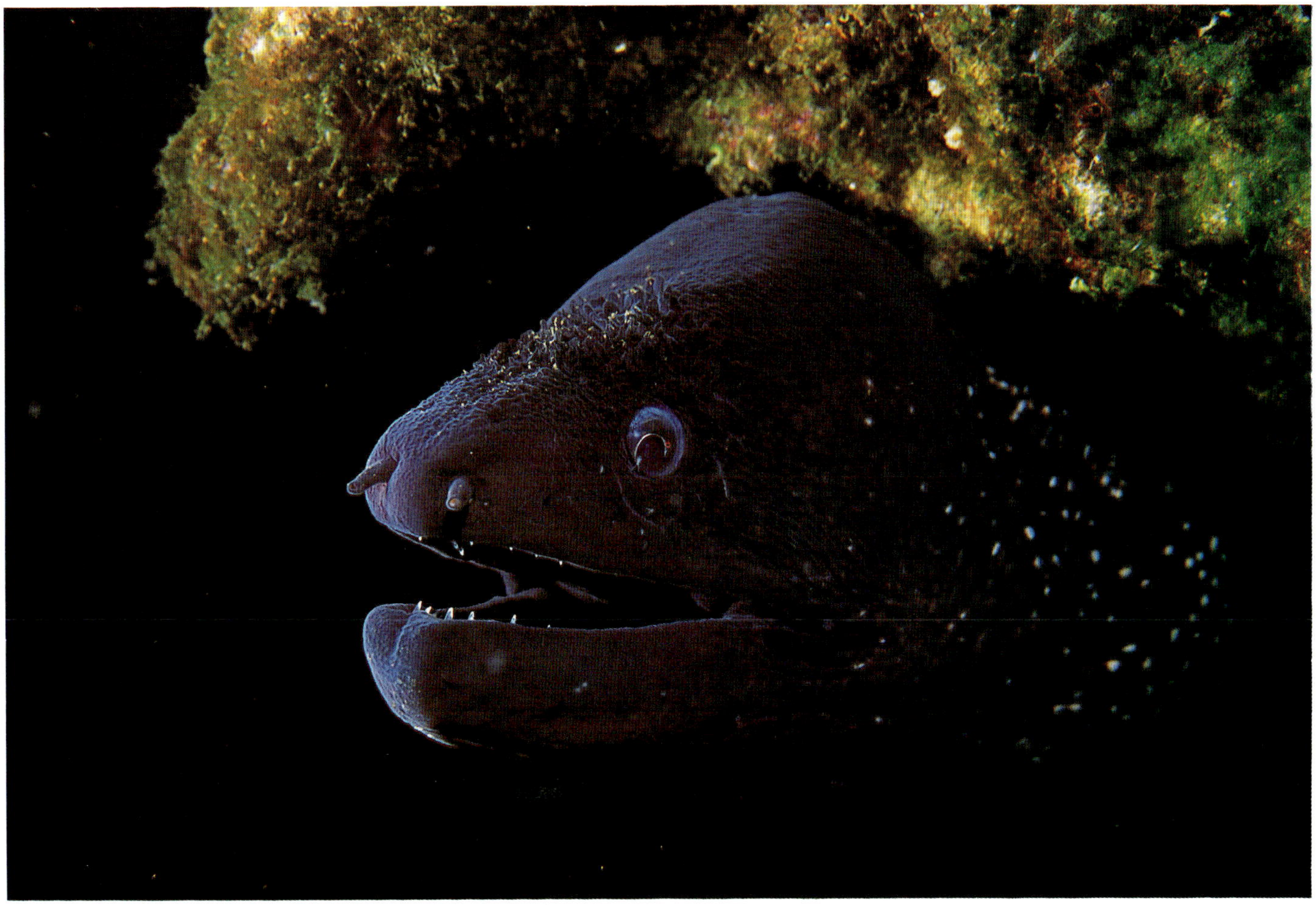

Kurt Amsler
Switzerland
HIGHLY COMMENDED

Moray Eel

"This green moray eel was photographed at the site of the wreck of Antheor in the Mediterranean, near Cannes."

Nikon F4 with 60mm lens; underwater housing; flash; Fujichrome Velvia

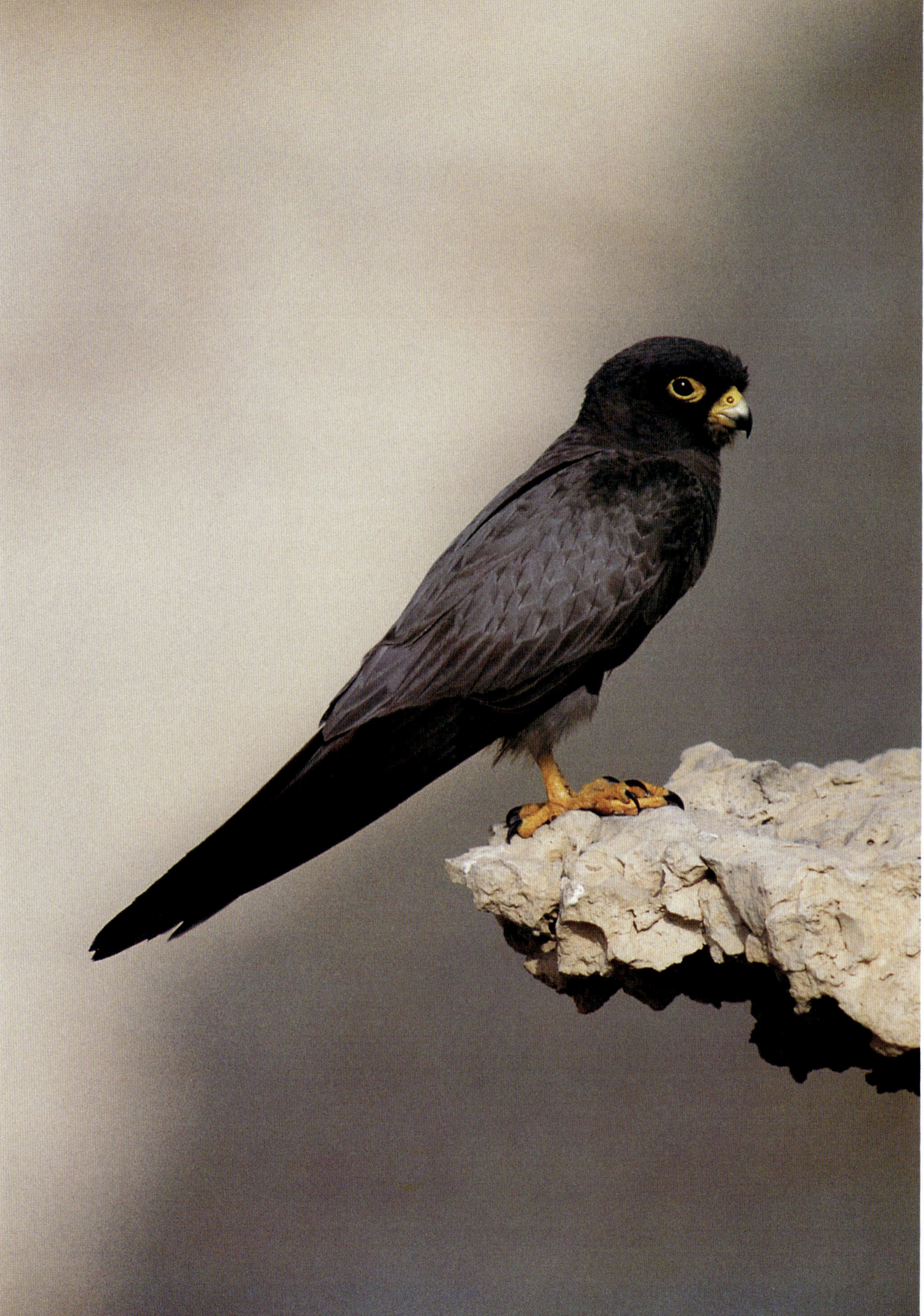

Mike Hill
United Kingdom
HIGHLY COMMENDED

Sooty Falcon

"Sooty falcons have a limited
breeding range and so are not
often photographed. When
working as a consultant to
Oxford Scientific Films
on a film about the natural
history of Bahrain, I found a site
on the Hawar Islands suitable for
filming the birds and took a
few stills."

Nikon F4 with 600mm lens; tripod

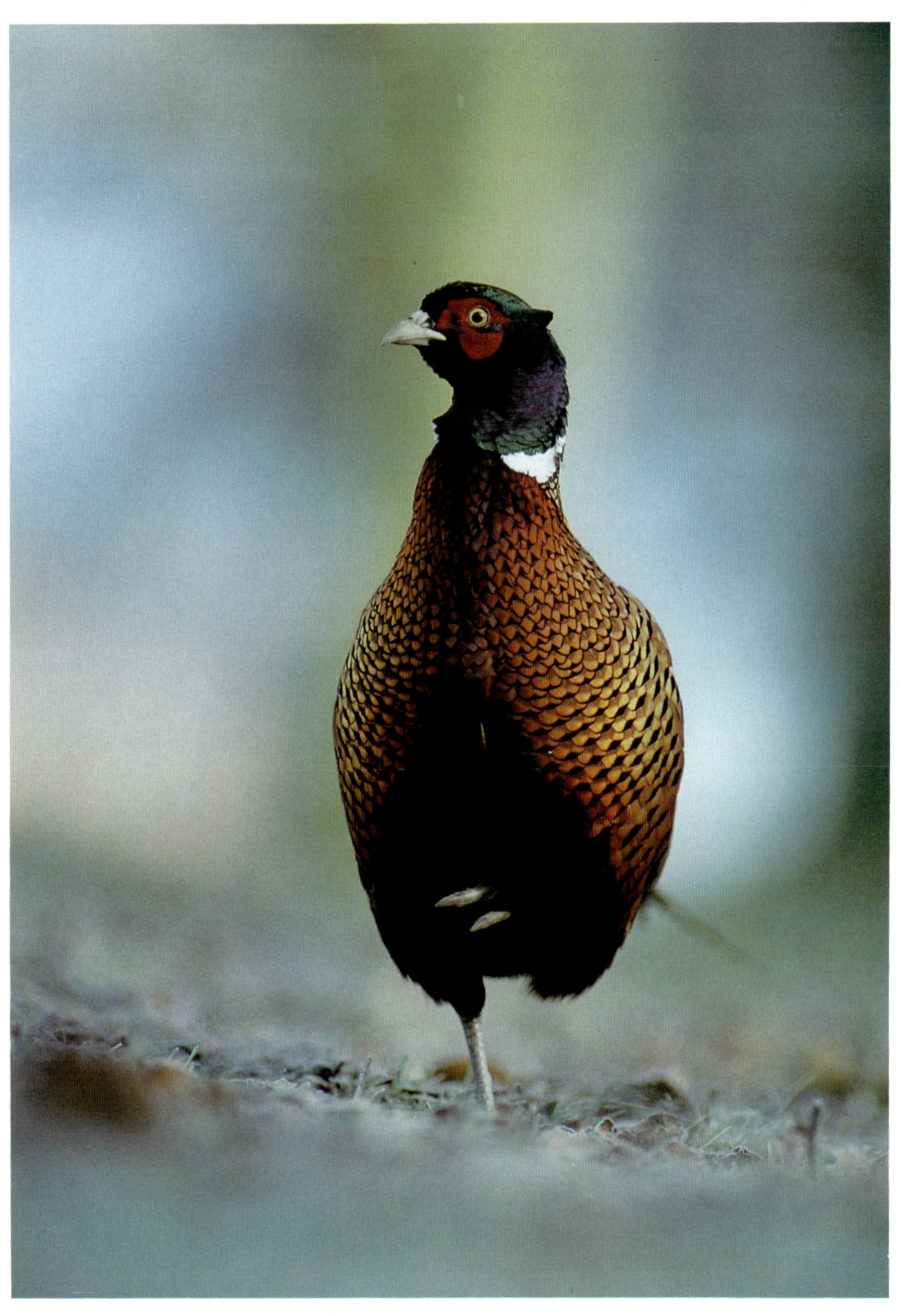

Niall Benvie
United Kingdom
HIGHLY COMMENDED

Cock Pheasant
''The pheasant's interest was
aroused by my bag of grain. It
was a wild bird but was fed
regularly, and so learnt to
recognise the sound of an
imminent dinner.''

Nikon with 300mm lens; beanbag;
f4 at 1/250 sec; Kodachrome 200

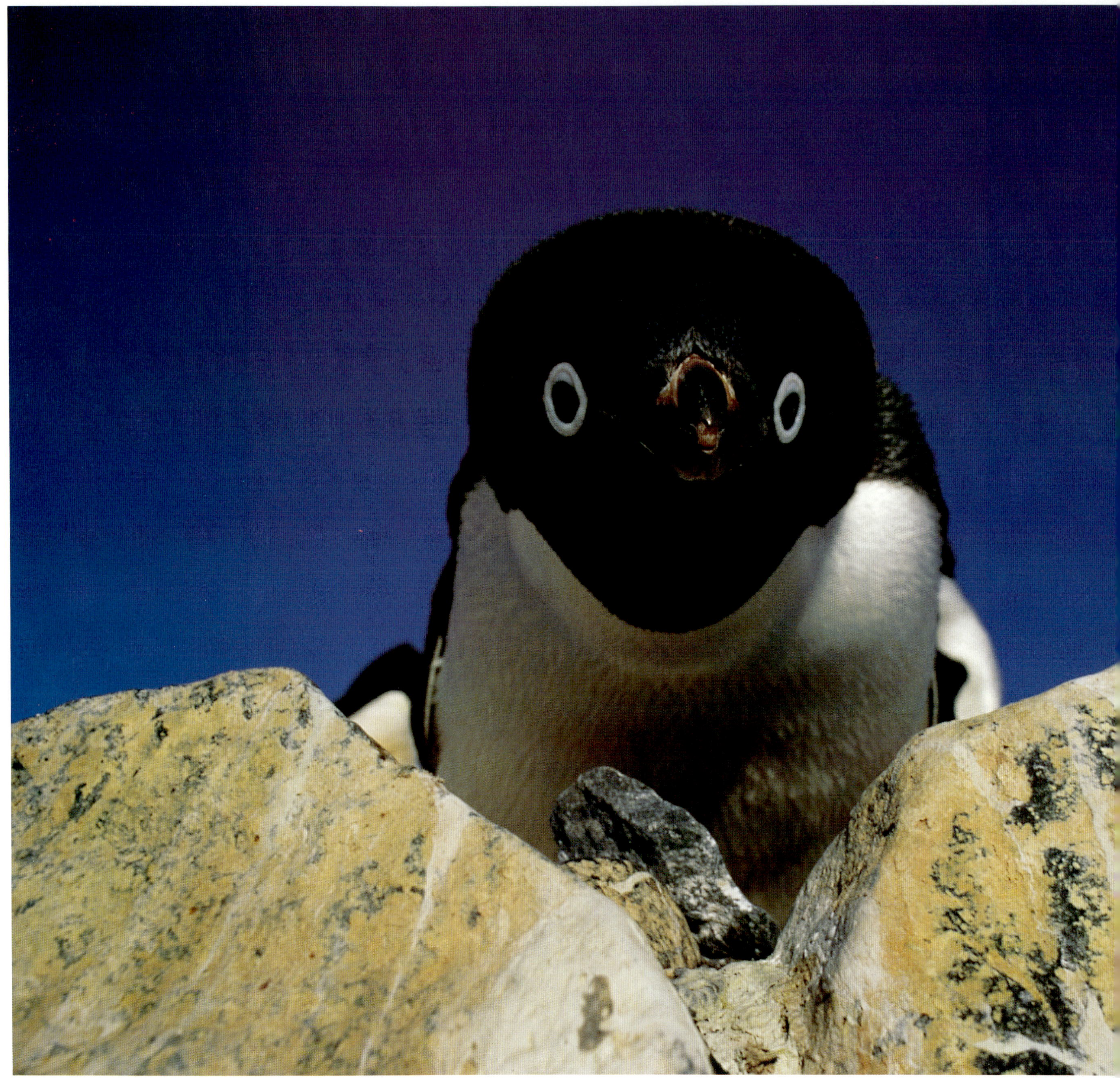

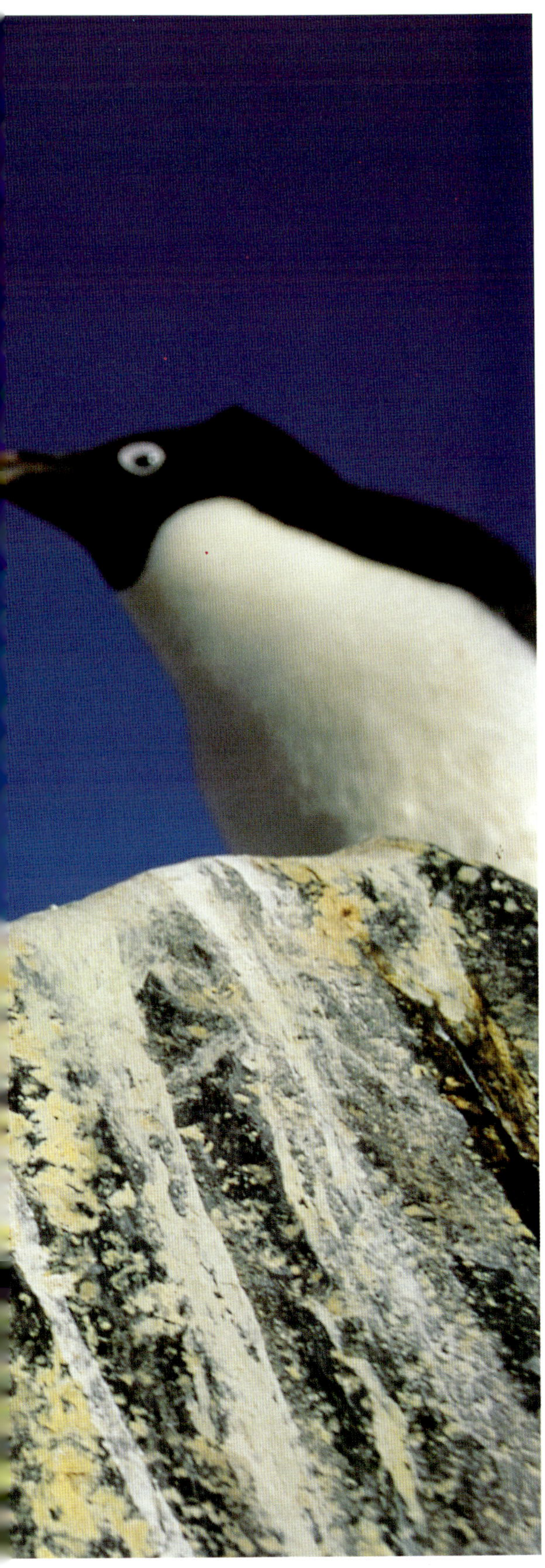

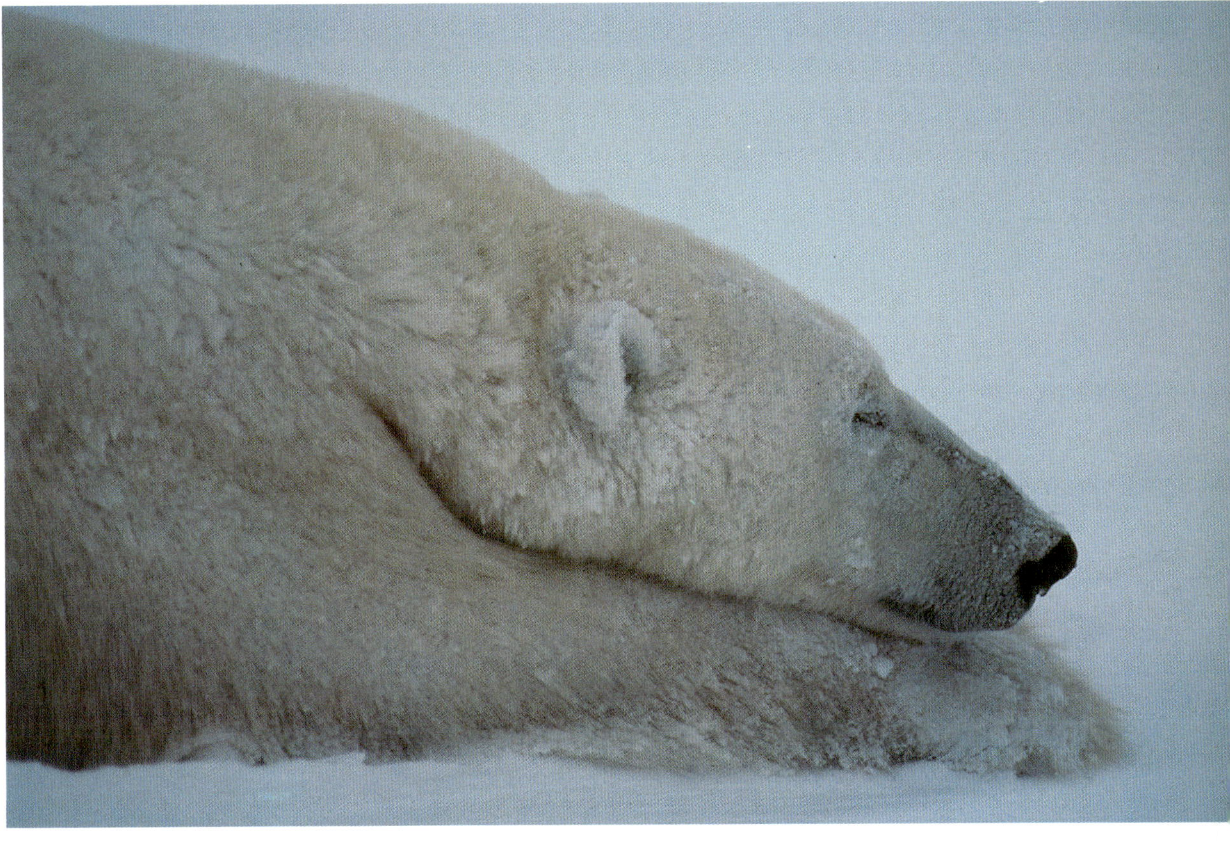

Daniel J Cox
United States of America
HIGHLY COMMENDED

Polar bear in snowstorm

*"This polar bear is sleeping
through a snowstorm on the
frozen shores of Hudson Bay.
The bears gather there each
autumn waiting for the bay to
freeze over, and then move on to
the ice to hunt seals."*

Nikon F4 with 300mm lens;
Kodachrome 64

Gordon Court
Canada
HIGHLY COMMENDED

Adelie Penguin

*"This tame Adelie Penguin
approached as I was seated in a
rookery on Cape Bird,
Antarctica.
It gently billed my boot laces and
pencils, and even my fingers.
I took advantage of its curiosity
by placing a motor-driven
camera at my feet,
pre-focused it at a few
centimetres, and waited for the
bird to look down the lens."*

Nikon F2A with 24mm wide-angle lens;
Fujichrome Velvia

Mark Hamblin
United Kingdom
HIGHLY COMMENDED

Hare in Mayweed

"My father had seen a number of hares in a particular field and we decided to use the car as a 'moveable' hide to get close. The hares remained still until the last moment and I was able to take some attractive portraits, resting my camera on a beanbag on the car window."

Canon T90 with 500mm lens and ×1.4 converter; beanbag; f5.6 at 1/750 sec; Kodachrome 200

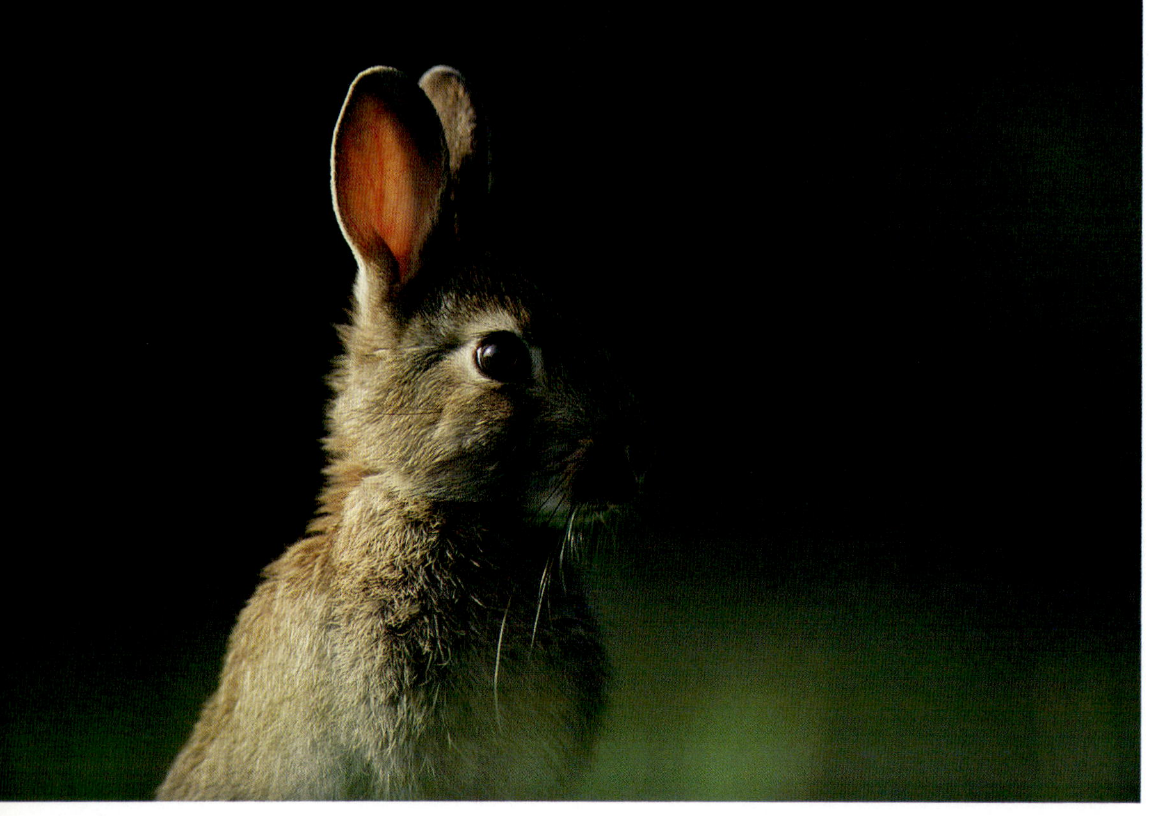

Robert M Canis
United Kingdom
HIGHLY COMMENDED

Young Rabbit

"I took this shot on the North Downs early one evening in May. I wanted to photograph the young rabbits grazing among the buttercups, but this individual came so close that I could hardly focus. It is looking alert because it has just heard a dog bark from across the field."

Nikon F3 with 500mm lens; beanbag; f5.6 at 1/125 sec; Kodachrome 64

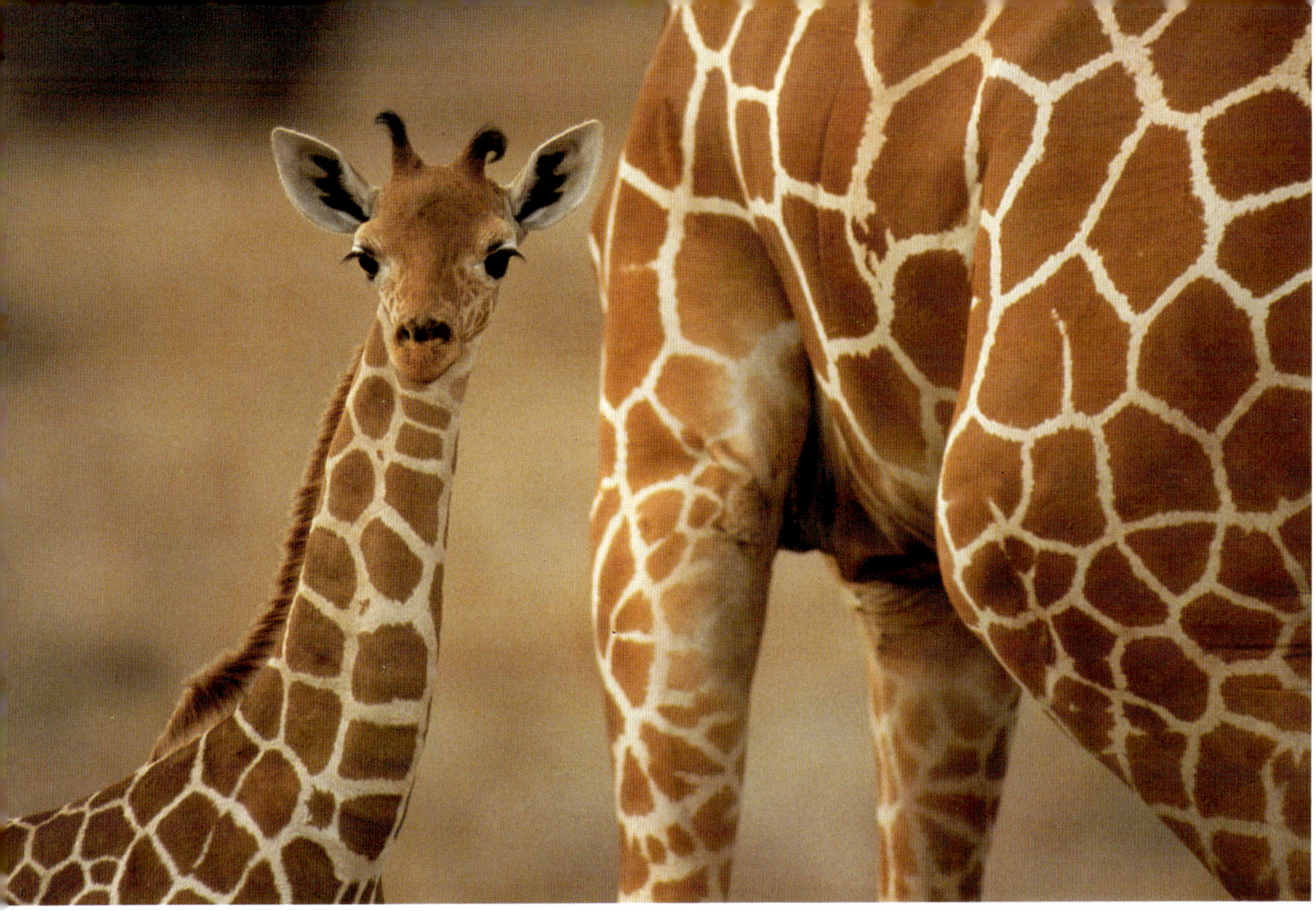

Tim Davis
United States of America
HIGHLY COMMENDED

Baby Reticulated Giraffe

"*I was looking for subjects to photograph in the Samburu National Reserve, Kenya, when I came across a reticulated giraffe and her baby. I have many photos of baby giraffes and was looking for something different. When the the mother moved into the frame for a few seconds, I got this shot.*"

Nikon F4 with 600mm lens; f4 at 1/250 sec; Fujichrome 100

Uwe Anders
Germany
HIGHLY COMMENDED

Baird's Tapir

"*I noticed a tapir's footprints on a river bank in Costa Rica and waited on a fallen tree in the river for his arrival. Tapirs like to take a bath, and this one would come down to a river every afternoon, sniffing the air for hostile smells.*"

Canon T90 with 300mm lens; tripod; f4 at 1/180 sec; Kodachrome 200

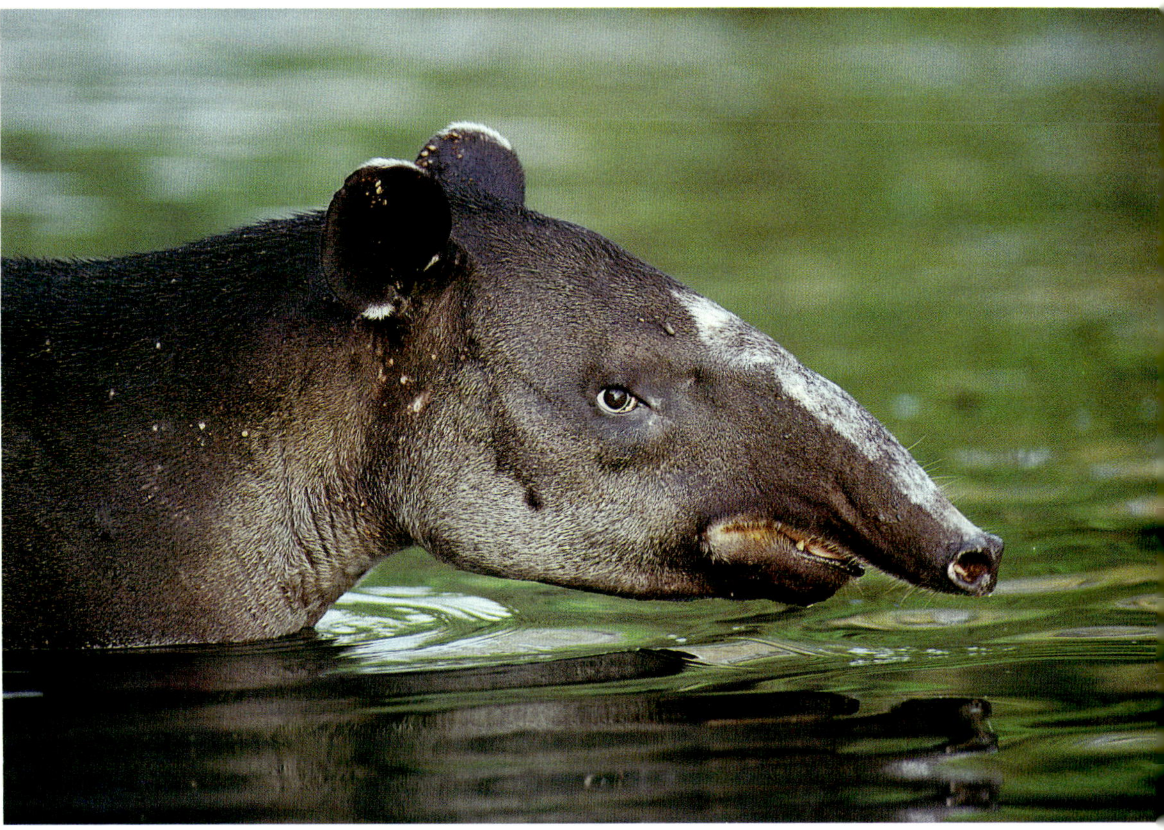

Young Wildlife Photographer of the Year

The Young Wildlife Photographer of the Year
Competition is open to photographers aged 17
years and under and is judged in three separate
age categories. Each photographer can enter up
to three photographs on any wildlife subject.
A first and runner-up prize is awarded in each
category, and the young photographer whose
picture is judged to be the best in the competition
wins the British Gas Award and 'Young Wildlife
Photographer of the Year' title.
Two additional awards were offered in 1992:
the Going Live Award for the best picture of
garden or urban wildlife, and the WWF 'Go Wild'
Club Award for the best picture illustrating the
theme 'wildlife and water'.

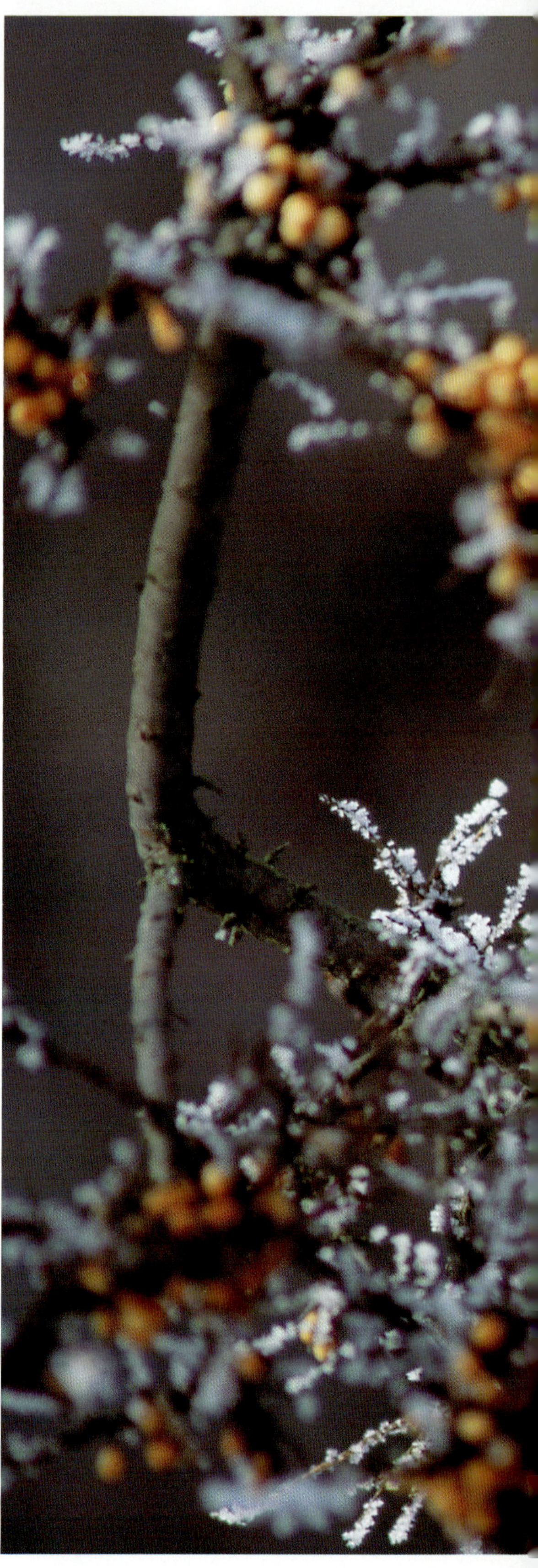

Torsten Brehm

Germany

YOUNG WILDLIFE
PHOTOGRAPHER OF THE
YEAR 1992

Great Tit on frosty morning

*"In the winter the birds in our
area have a difficult time finding
food, so I set up a feeding area in
the middle of some bushes in my
garden. The tit pictured is not
feeding on the berries, but
warming itself up in the early
morning sun after a
frosty night."*

Canon T90 with 300mm lens; tripod; f4
at 1/250 sec; Fujichrome Velvia

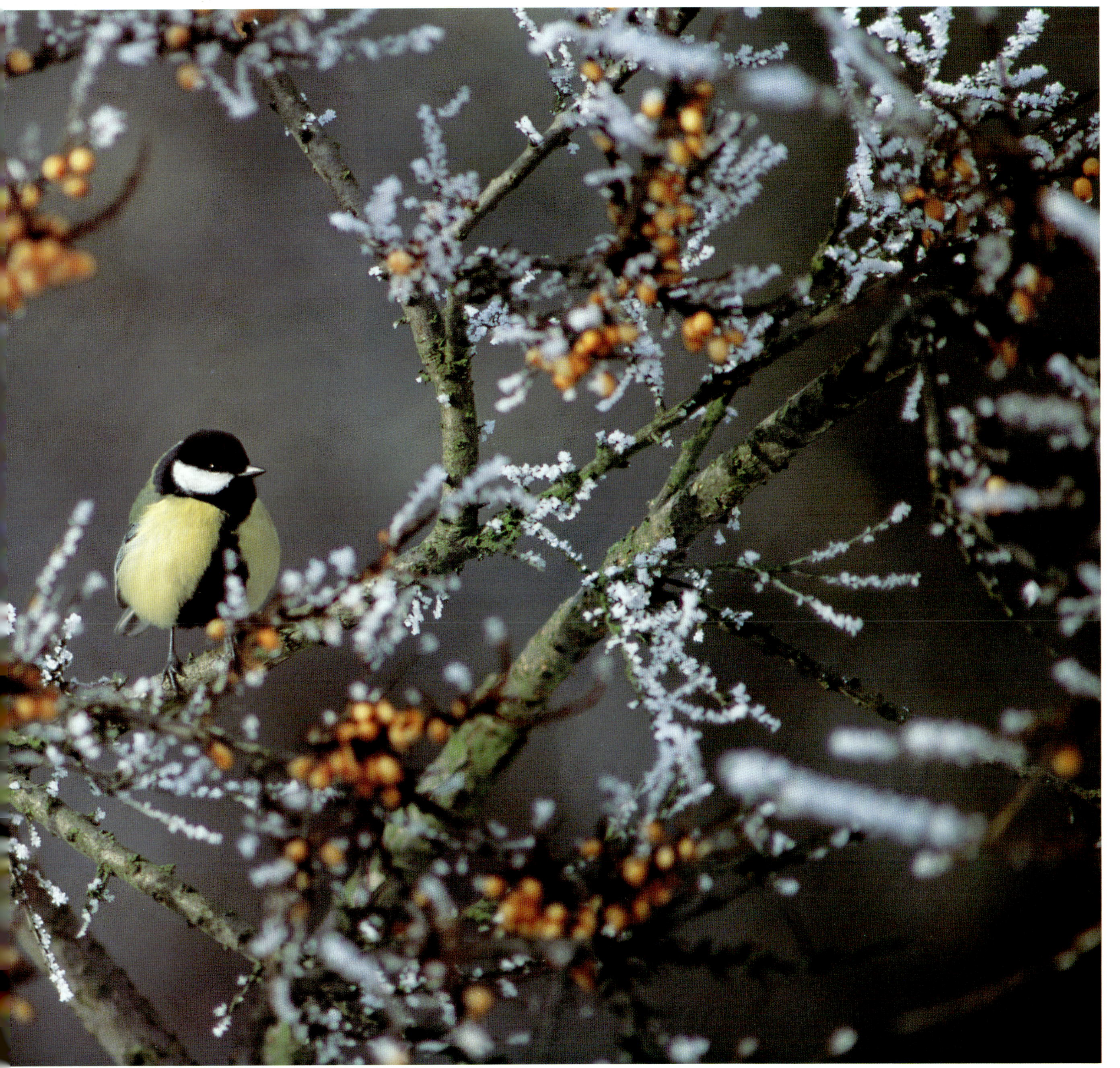

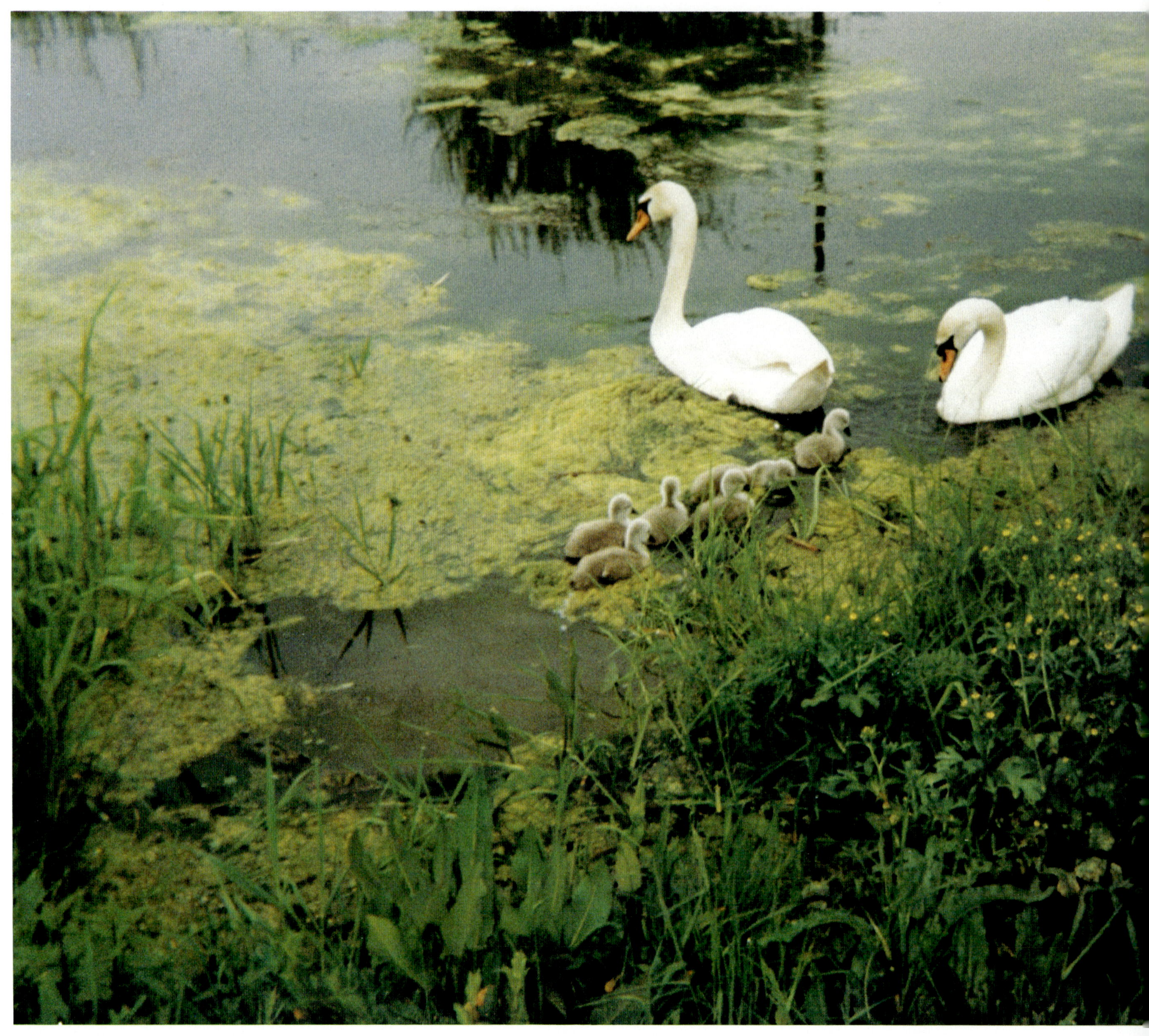

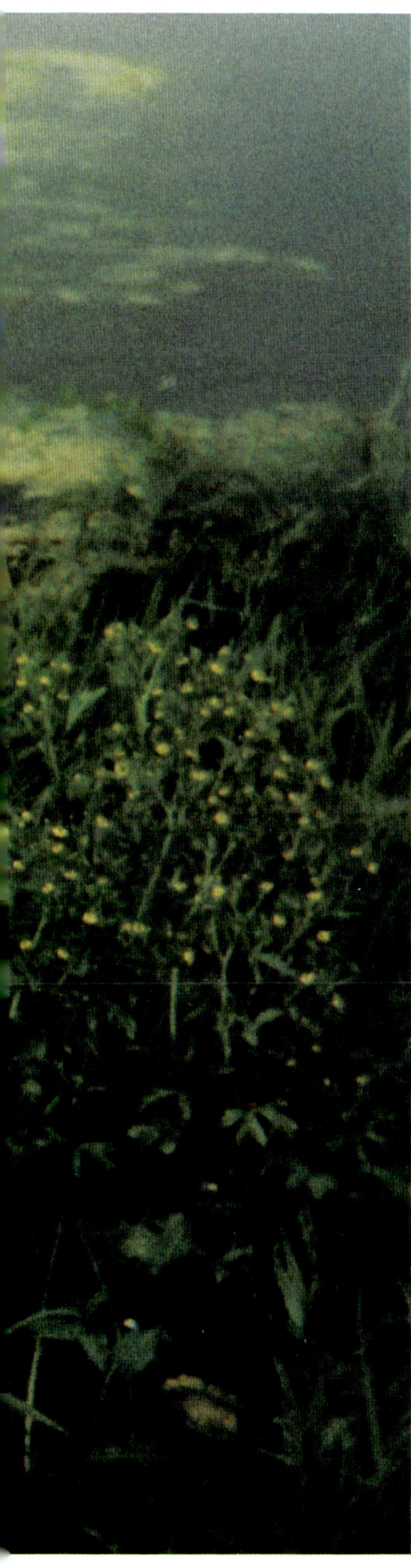

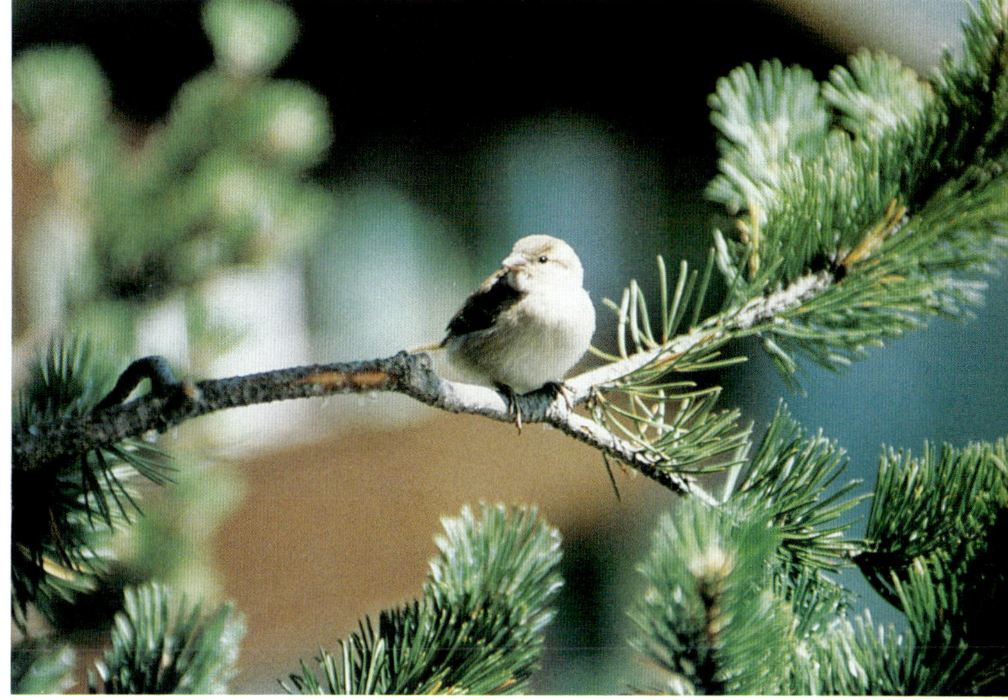

Alex Waterfield

United Kingdom
WINNER
10 YEARS AND UNDER

Swan family

''I had noted where the swans
were nesting on the River Arun
and returned regularly to check
on their progress. After I had
taken this picture, the cygnets
began to scramble on their
mothers back, but my film had
run out!''

Dixons Miranda Solo; Kodak 100

Daniel Andrews

United Kingdom
RUNNER-UP
10 YEARS AND UNDER

House Sparrow

''While on holiday in
Switzerland I saw this sparrow
playing in a pine tree. I took a
chance and pointed my camera
at a branch and waited for a
good shot.''

Praktica MTL3 with 50mm lens; red
filter; f2.8; Supasnaps 200

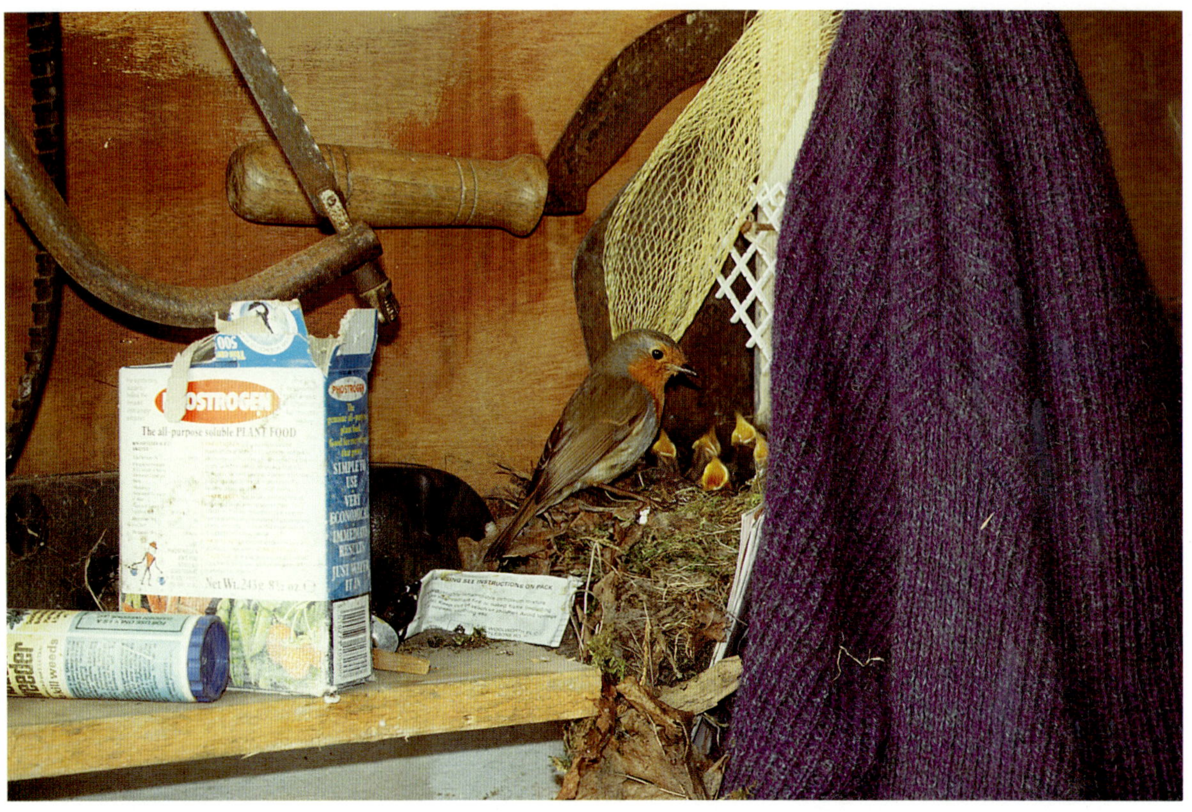

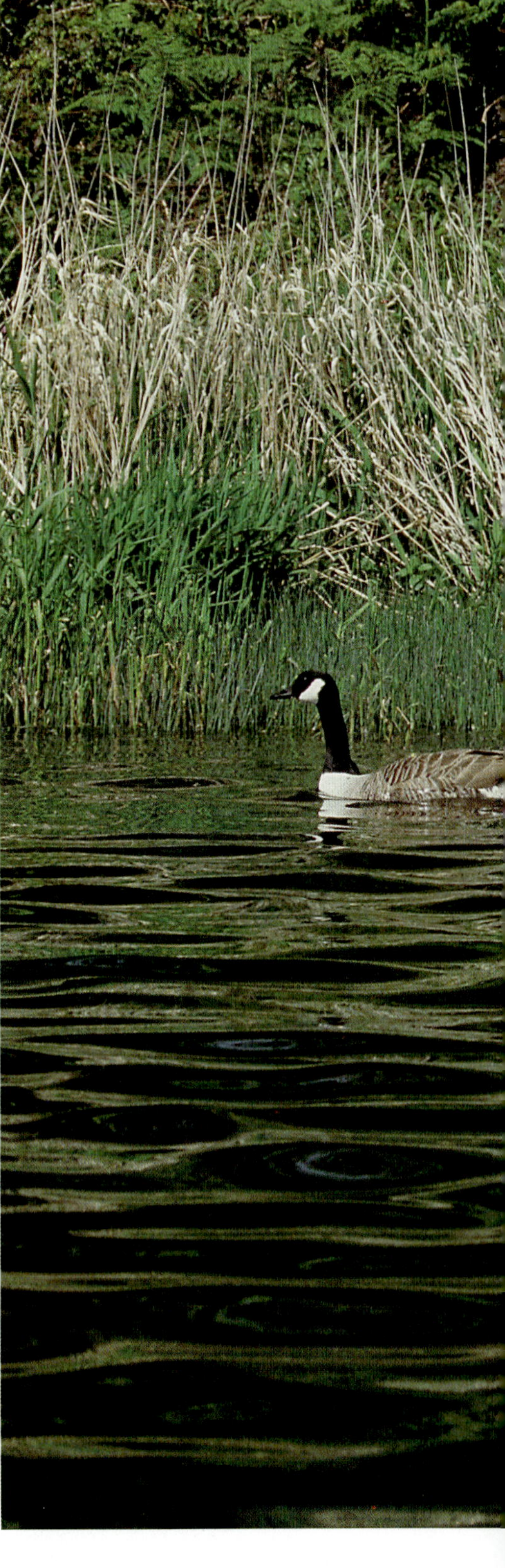

Lucinda Munn
United Kingdom
'GOING LIVE!' AWARD

Robin in garden shed

*"My Grandad told us of a robin
he had nesting in his rickety
garden shed, and for a fortnight
we waited for its eggs to hatch,
fascinated by the bird's activities.
Wanting a picture that my
grandad could remember his
'robin' by, I borrowed a camera
and tripod and set it up in
the shed. An air-release cable
was improvised from elastic
bands which stretched to the
kitchen window, where we waited
for the right moment."*

Canon EOS 100 with 28-80mm lens;
tripod; flash; Fujichrome 100

Louise Dean
United Kingdom
WWF AWARD

Canada Geese

*"I watched this Canada goose
family for some time at Slapton
Ley in Devon.
Whenever they were on the
water, they would form a long
line with one adult at the front
and the other at the back. I took
this picture from a rowing boat,
and although there was quite a
glare, here the sun sets off the
water to great effect."*

Nikon with 75-300mm lens; f11 at 1/500
sec; Kodachrome 200

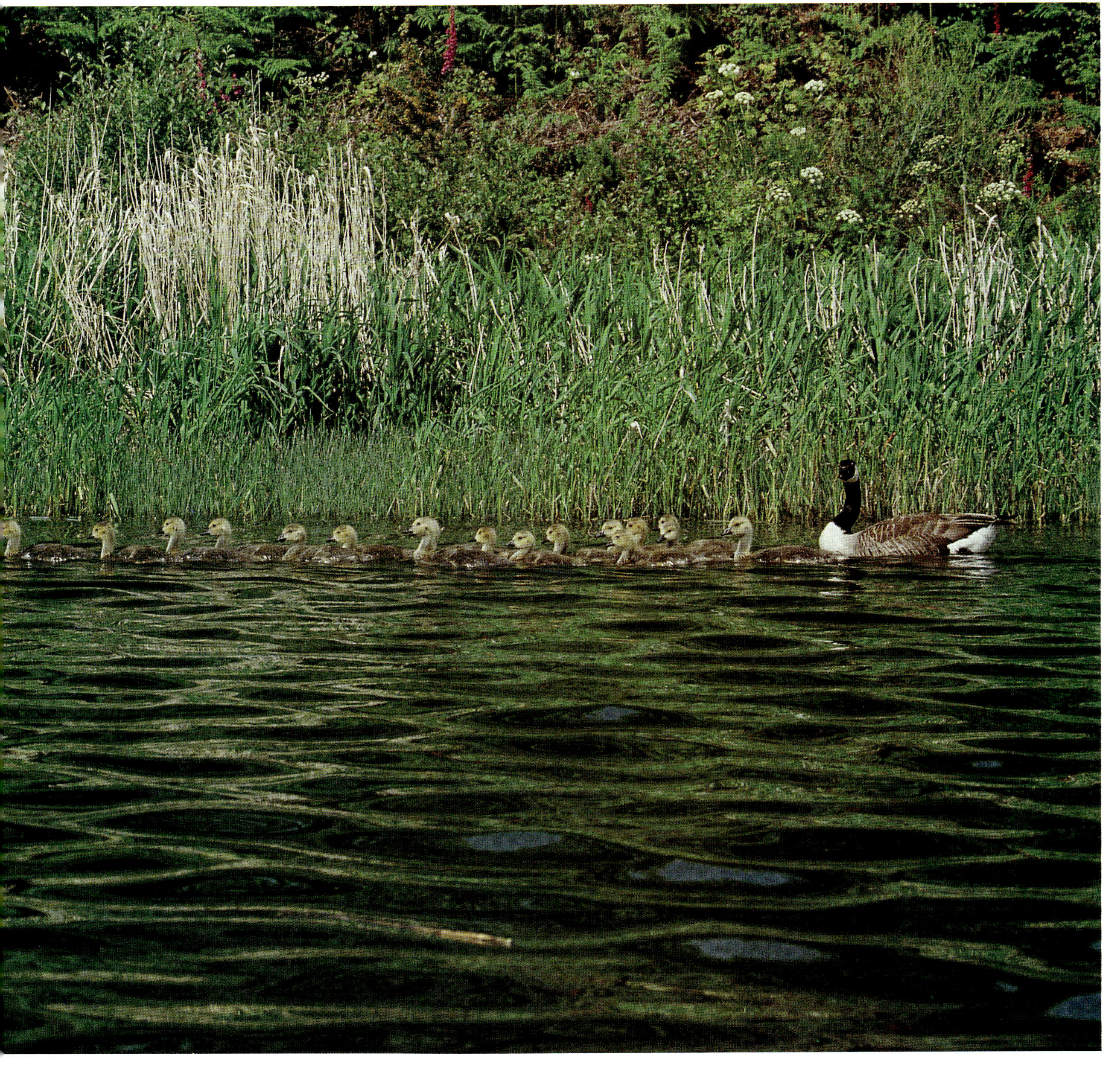

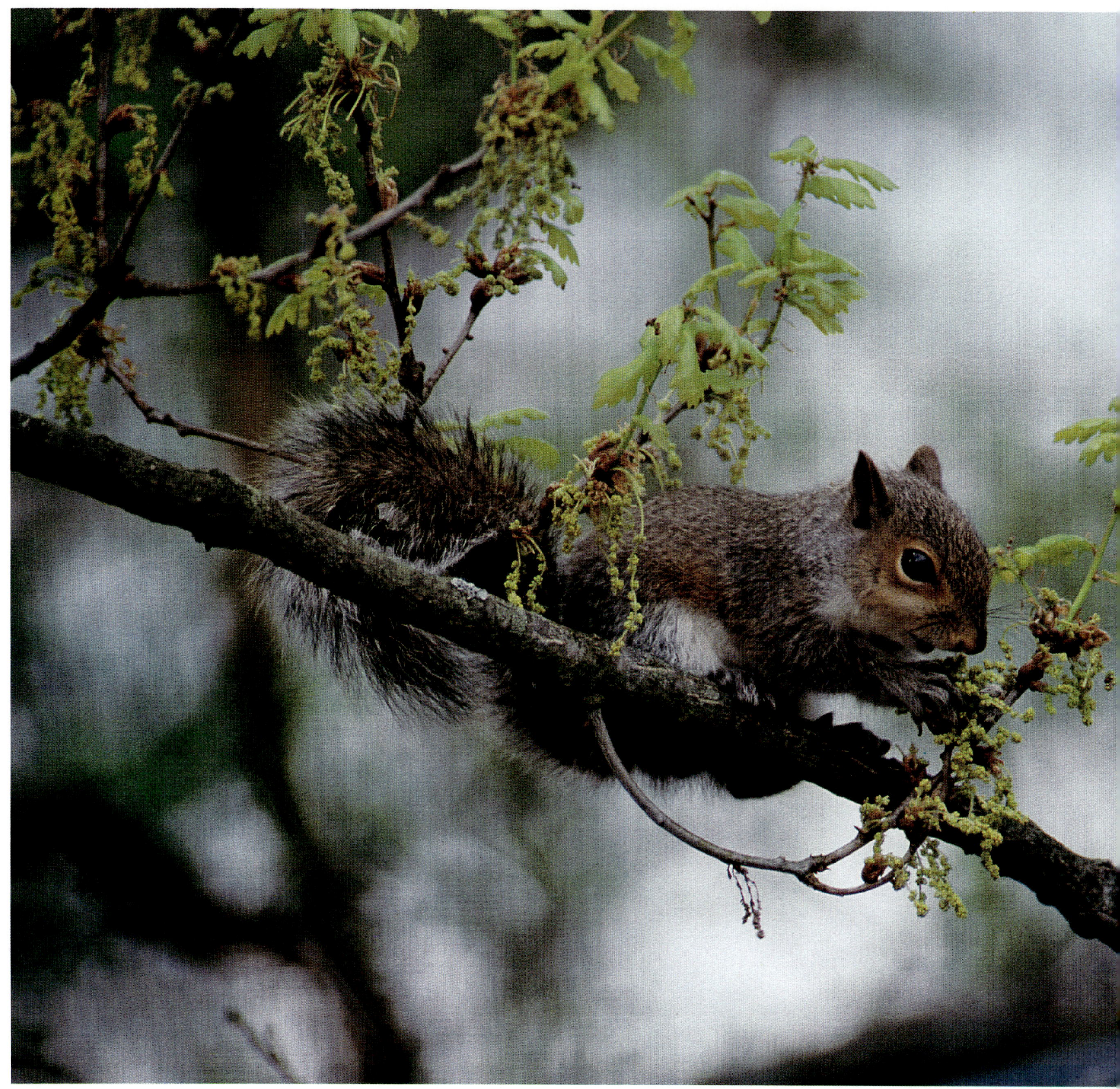

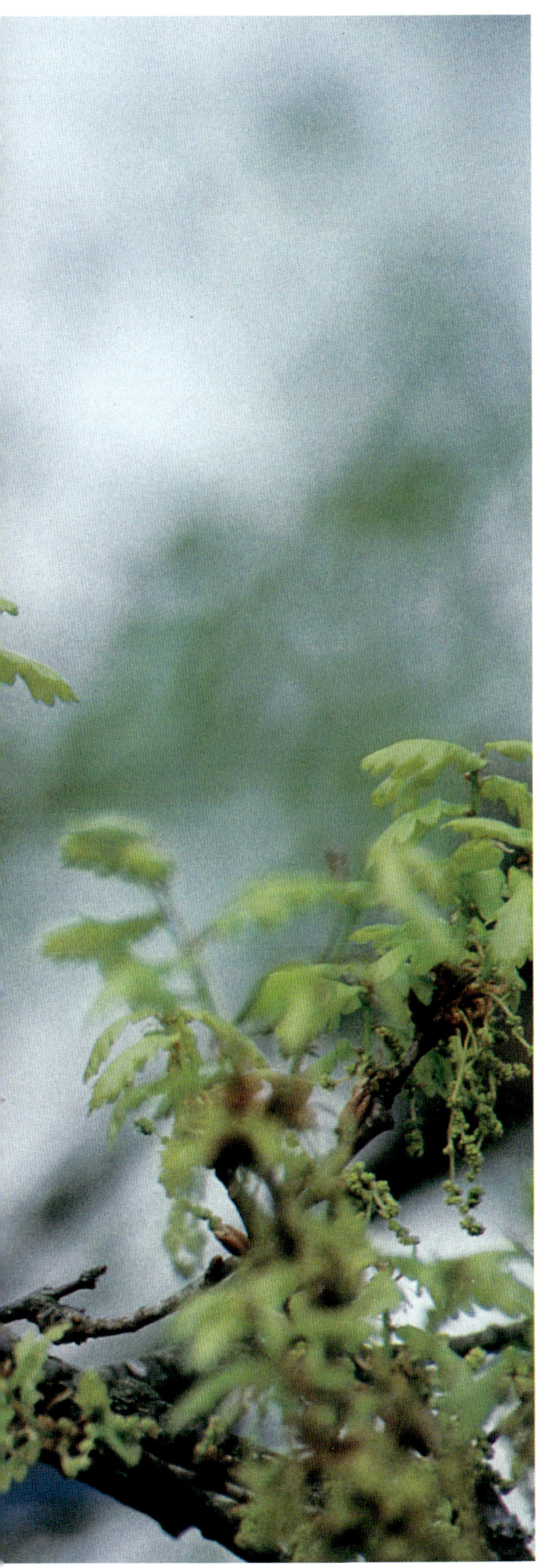

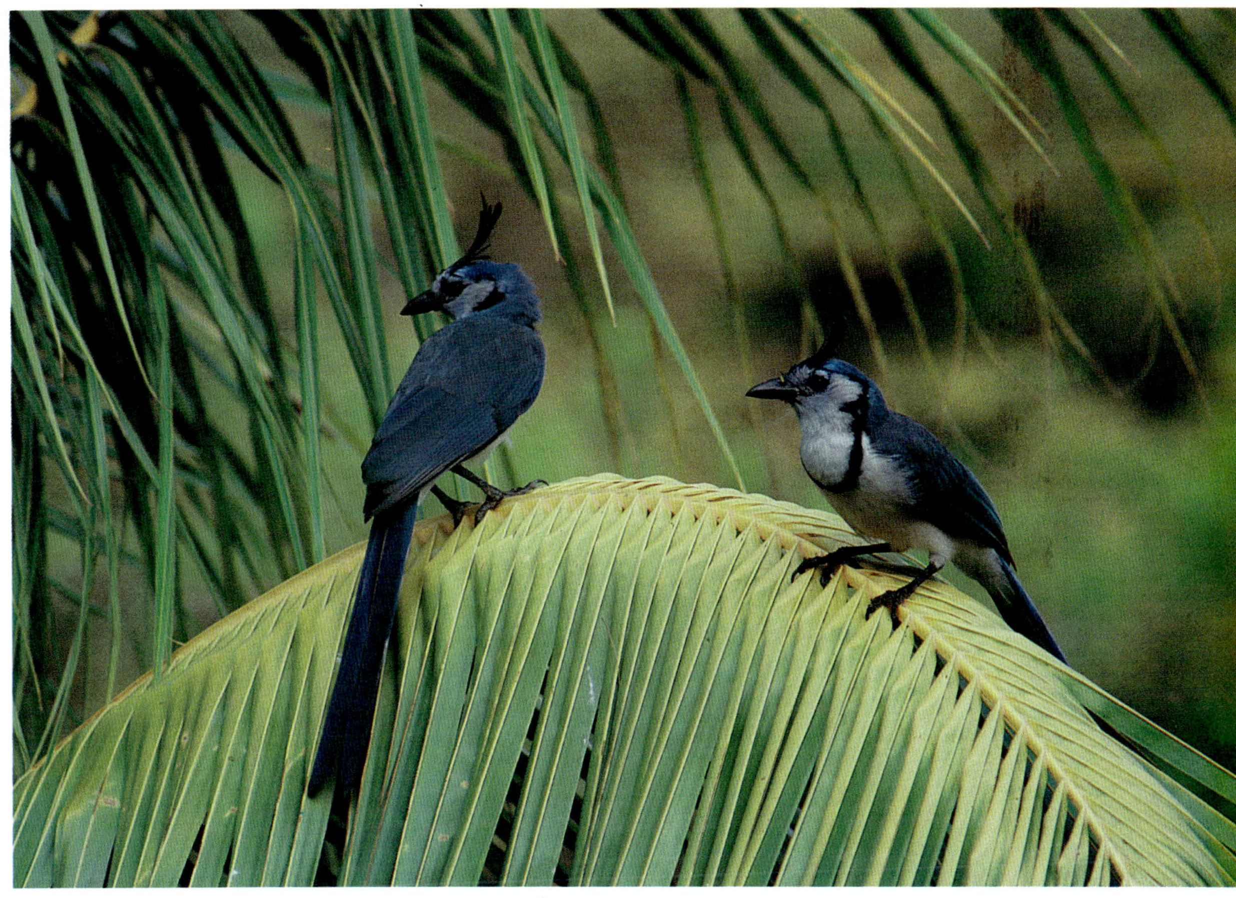

Rosie Bomford
United Kingdom
WINNER 11-14 YEARS

Grey Squirrel feeding on oak blossom

"I spotted this young grey squirrel eating oak blossom from my bedroom window. It was not quite close enough for my camera equipment, so I borrowed my mother's long lens and rigged up a tripod on the back of an armchair. Fortunately the squirrel was still there when I was ready to take its picture."

Canon EOS 620 with 300mm lens and ×2 converter; f5.6 at 1/125 sec; Kodachrome 200

Rebecca Dean
United Kingdom
RUNNER-UP 11-14 YEARS

White-throated Magpie Jays

"As soon as we arrived at the La Pacifica Biological Reserve in Costa Rica, I wanted to photograph the beautiful magpie jays. One day I went back to our hut to find two of them sitting on a palm leaf, but I was only able to get one shot before they flew off. It was the middle of the day and the lighting wasn't very special, but I was pleased with the result."

Olympus OM2n with 300mm lens; f8 at 1/250 sec; Kodachrome 200

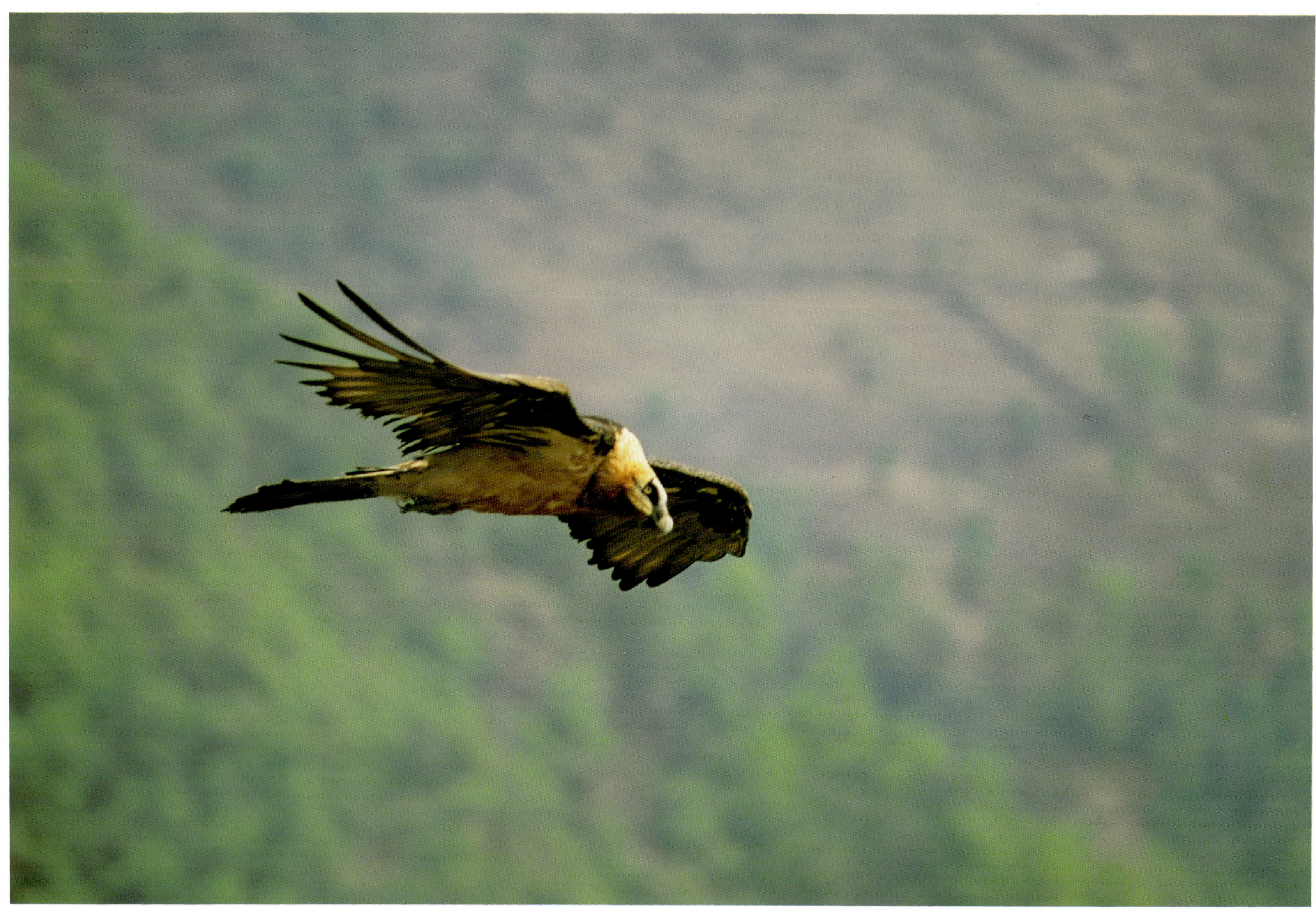

Michael Hill

United Kingdom

SPECIALLY COMMENDED
11-14 YEARS

Lammergeier

*"While on holiday in
Nepal I took this photo of a
lammergeier soaring on the
thermals. The bird feeds mainly
on bones, dropping large ones on
to rocks below to smash them into
more manageable pieces."*

Nikon F3 with 300mm lens; f4 at 1/1000
sec; Fujichrome Velvia

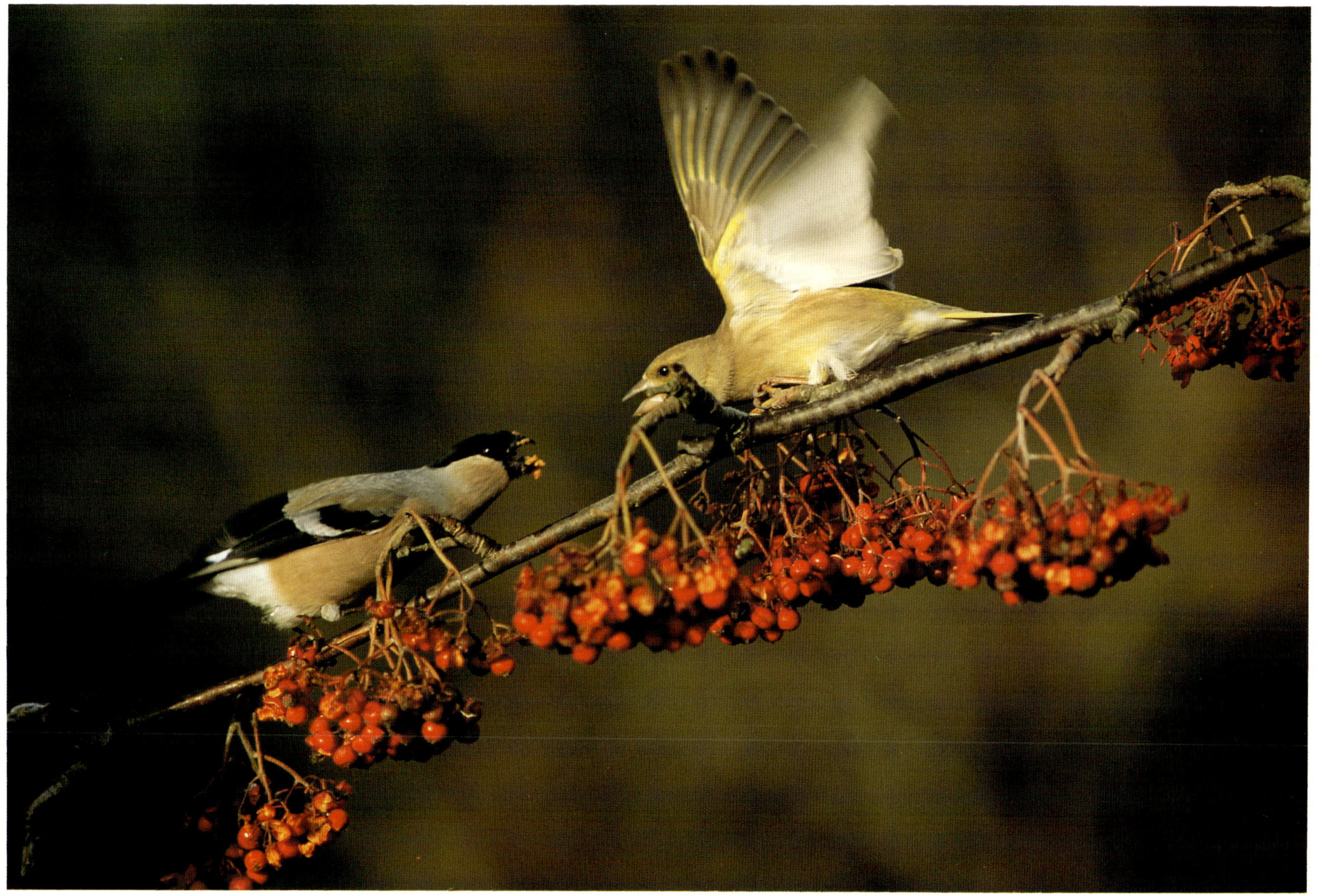

Torsten Brehm
Germany
WINNER 15-17 YEARS

Bullfinch fighting Greenfinch

"Bullfinches and Greenfinches love to eat the berries in our garden. Sometimes, as in this picture, they fight over them. I had trouble taking a sharp picture of such a lively scene, but I finally made it."

Canon T90 with 300mm lens; tripod; hide; f4 at 1/500 sec; Fujichrome Velvia 50

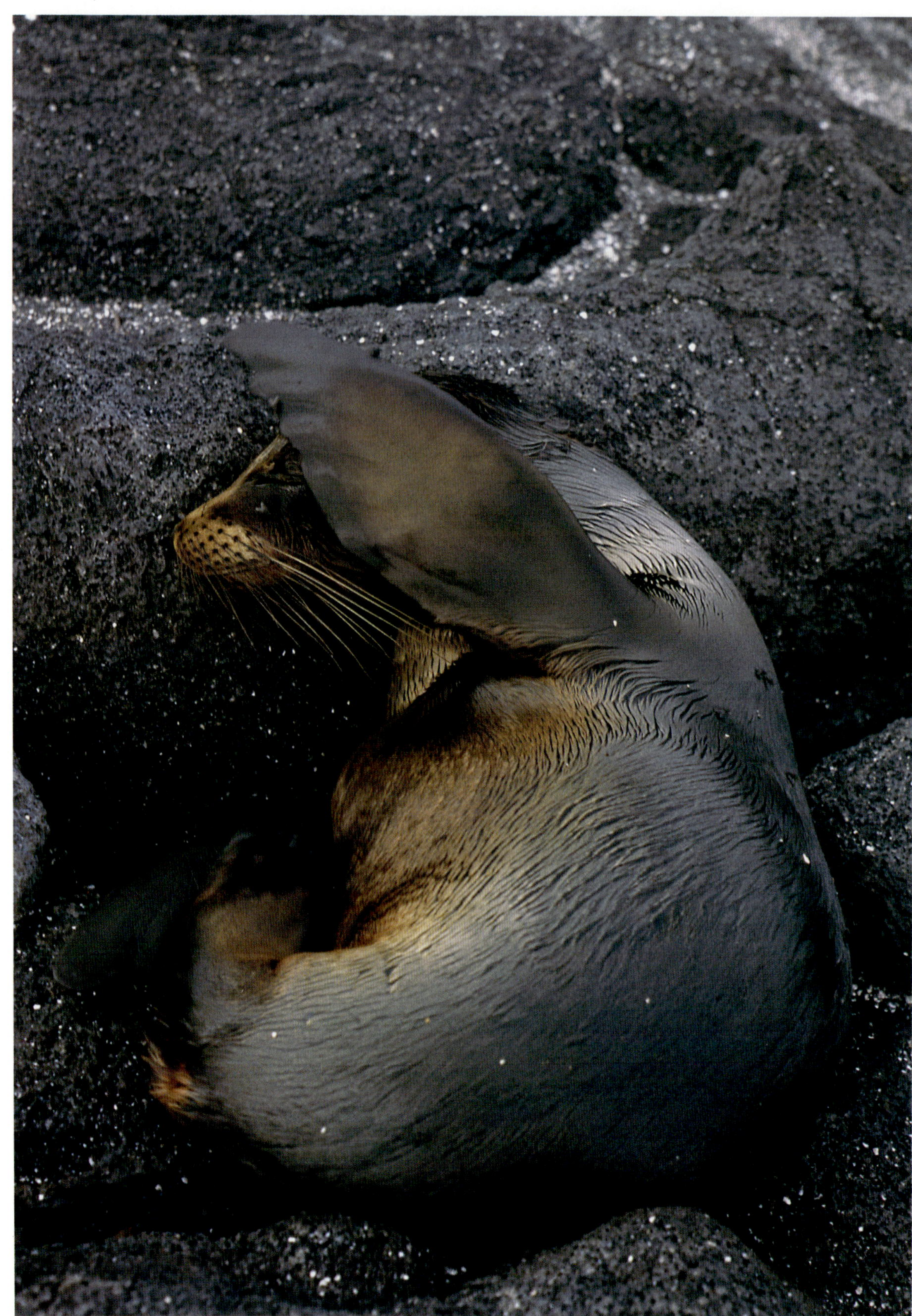

Jutta Sander
Germany
RUNNER-UP 15-17 YEARS

Sealion

"I came across this young female sealion while on holiday in the Galapagos Islands. The pose of the sleeping sealion made a great subject, and the overcast day provided an even light."

Zeiss Ikon with 50mm lens; Agfa CT100

THE NATURAL HISTORY MUSEUM

South Kensington, London

Across the world, the name of the Natural History Museum is synonymous with dinosaurs. But behind the Museum's Victorian facade is a highly complex and sophisticated modern scientific centre.

Without a doubt the dinosaurs will always be a great attraction. This is illustrated by the popularity of the massive new dinosaur exhibition of ancient skeletons and life-size robotic models, which opened in 1992. The exhibition asks whether dinosaurs resembled today's animals - did they care for their young, were they hot- or cold-blooded, and why did they die out? This is in line with all the latest interactive exhibitions, which tackle topical processes of nature such as ecology, evolution and human biology. Also on display are collections of animals, plants, fossils, minerals, rocks and meteorites, providing a dazzling display of the natural world.

The Museum is the home of the nation's natural history collections, which have grown from its origin in 1753 to a current total of over 67 million specimens, 1 million books and many original drawings, prints and paintings.

Unknown to the millions of people that visit each year, there are over 300 scientists working behind the scenes. They have access to an unrivalled fund of data on the natural world against which ecological and geological change can be measured. Every day, these scientists are addressing vital environmental issues such as loss of natural habitats and biological diversity, and the effects of global warming. They are also fighting deadly insect-borne diseases such as bilharzia, which affects at least 200 million people throughout the tropics.

The strength of the Museum's science makes it a leading international institution for the identification and classification of the natural world. Its award-winning displays capture the imagination of visitors of all ages, offering them an enjoyable way to learn. The Natural History Museum is rightly called the home of natural history.

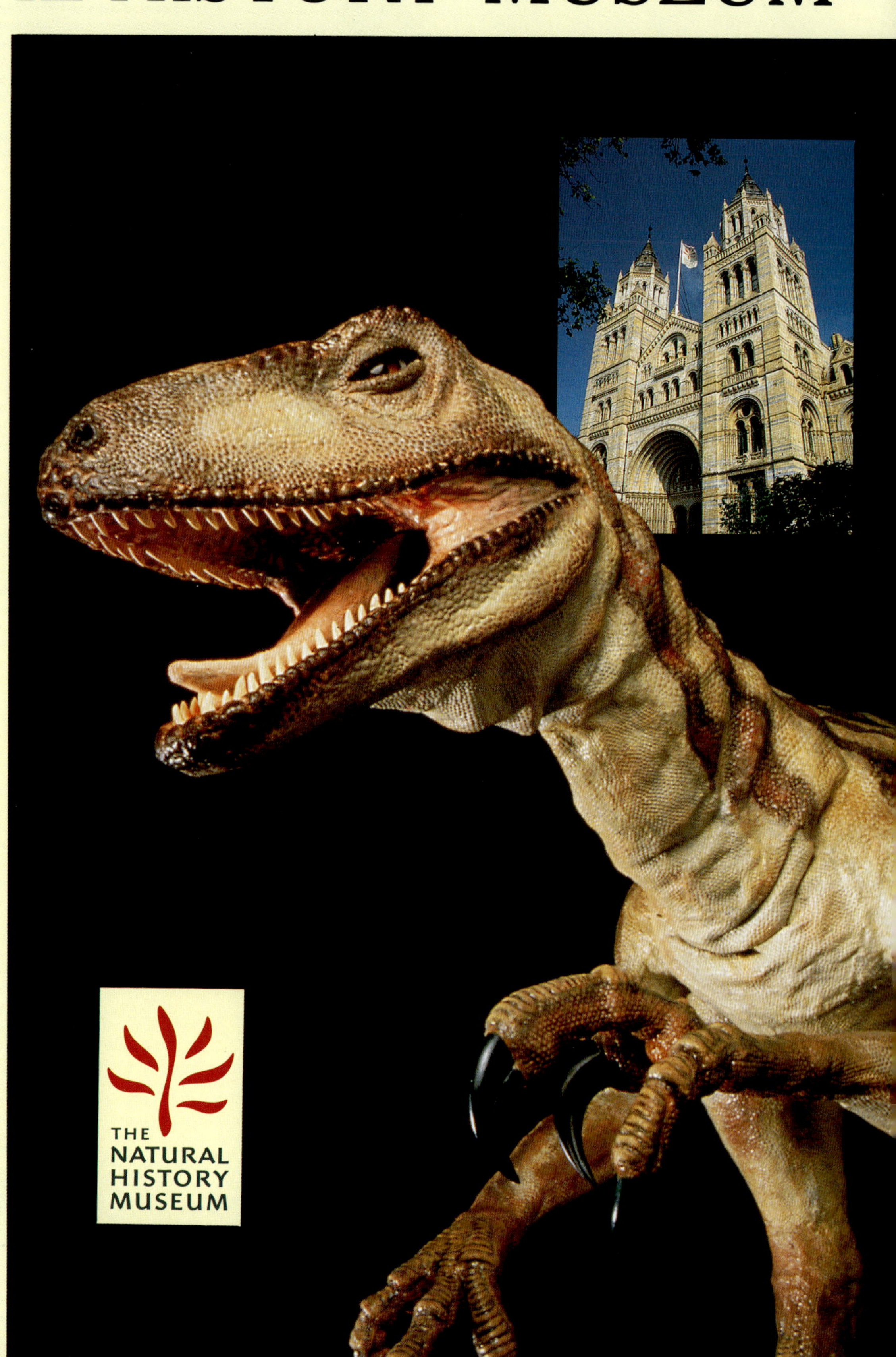

Index of
Photographers

The numbers set in italic type after the photographer's country indicate the pages on which their work can be found.

Markku Aikironiemi

(Finland) *38*

Palkisentie 5
98800 Savukoski
Lapland
Finland

Tel: 9692 41357

Cherry Alexander

(UK) *28/29*

Higher Cottage
Manston
Sturminster Newton
Dorset DT10 1E2

Tel: 0258 73006
Fax: 0747 51474

Karl Amman

(Switzerland) *37, 76/77*

Box 437
Nanyuki
Kenya

Tel: 0176 22448
Fax: 0176 32407 *or*
Nairobi 0275 0035

Kurt Amsler

(Switzerland) *133*

P.O. Box 350
8810 Horgen
Switzerland

Tel: 0041 1 725 8314/725 8172
Fax: 0041 1 725 8314

Uwe Anders

(Germany) *139*

Marienstrasse 1
3300 Braunschweig
Germany

Tel: 0531 796535

Daniel Fitter Angermeyer

(Ecuador) *109*

22 Fountains Mead
Shaftesbury
Dorset SP7 8DE

Tel: 0747 55235
Fax: 0747 55131

Daniel Andrews

(UK) *143*

118 Church Green Road
Bletchley
Milton Keynes MK3 6DD

Tel: 0908 642686

Andre Bärtschi

(Liechtenstein) *8/9, 132*

Bannholzstrasse 10
FL - 9490 Vaduz
Liechtenstein

Tel: 075 232 0338
Fax: 075 232 0339

Agent: Planet Earth Pictures
4 Harcourt Street
London W1H 1DS

Tel: 071-262 4427
Fax: 071-706 4042

Niall Benvie

(UK) *34, 130, 135*

Heughhead
Friockheim by Arbroath
Angus
Scotland

Tel: 0674 74026

Erik Bjurström

(Sweden) *117*

King Faisal Specialist Hospital
P.O. Box 3354, MBC 70
Riyadh 11211
Saudi Arabia

Tel: 144 26243
Fax: 144 27653

Rosie Bomford

(UK) *146*

Little Cwm
Dulas
Pontrilas
Hereford HR2 0PH

Tel: 0981 240122
Fax: 0981 240930

David W. Breed

(UK) *98*

P.O. Box 20118
Nairobi
Kenya

Tel: 562473

Torsten Brehm

(Germany) *140/141, 149*

W - 7187 Spielbach Nr. 90
Germany

Tel: 07939 389

Eberhard Brunner

(USA) *110*

Robin Bush

(UK) *60*

1 Chess Close
Parkfield
Latimer
Buckinghamshire HP5 1UU

Laurie Campbell

(UK) *49, 91, 102/103*

Rosewell Cottage
Paxton
Berwick upon Tweed
TD15 1TE

Tel: 0289 86736

Robert M. Canis

(UK) *138*

26 Park Avenue
Sittingbourne
Kent ME10 1QY

Tel: 0795 477017

Marc C. Chamberlain

(USA) *90*

1350 Las Flores Drive
Carlsbad
California
USA 92008

Tel: 617 543 3906 *or*
617 729 4124
Fax: 617 543 2643

Richard Chandler

(UK) *39*

2 Rusland Avenue
Orpington
Kent BR6 8AU

Fax: 071-823 8525

Gordon Court

(Canada) *105*

913 Alder Avenue
Sherwood Park
Alberta
Canada T8A 1V7

Tel: 403 467 5153
Fax: 403 467 0927

Daniel J. Cox

(USA) *25, 29, 72*

16595 Brackett Creek Road
Bozeman
Montana
USA 59715

Tel/Fax: 406 686 4448

Tim Davis

(USA) 39, 139

Davis/Lynn Photography
P.O. Box 1278
Palo Alto
CA 94302
USA

Tel: 415 327 4192
Fax: 415 322 5082

Georgette Douwma

(The Netherlands) 96

Louise Dean

(UK) 145

Rebecca Dean

(UK) 147

John Eastcott/
Yva Momatiuk

(New Zealand/USA) 104

Eagles Nest Road
Hurley
NY 12443
USA

Tel: 914 338 4260

British Agent:
Planet Earth Pictures
4 Harcourt Street
London W1A 1DS

Tel:, 071-262 4427
Fax: 071-706 4042

Gerry Ellis

(USA) 42, 75, 90

6208 SW 32nd Street
Portland
Oregon 97201
USA

Tel: 503 245 6024
Fax: 503 452 1914

Christopher Gallagher

(UK) 87

Pwllmonyn
Betws Road
Llanrwst
Gwynedd LL26 0PT

Tel: 0492 641569

Robert Garvey

(Australia) 62, 77

24 Cobb Street
Scarborough
Perth 6019
Western Australia

Tel: 61 9 245 2006
Fax: 61 9 245 2007
Mobile: 018 914 868

Michael Goodwin

(USA) 101

Art, Wet & Wild
P.O. Box 11121
Aspen
CO 81612
USA

Tel: 303 920 3967 or
800 841 5379
Fax: 303 920 9311

Nick Gordon

(UK) 79

Little Erray
Tobermory
Isle of Mull
Scotland PA75 6PS

Tel: 0688 2340
Fax: 0688 2124

Joanna Van Gruisen

(UK) 64/65

B4/108 Safdarjung Enclave
New Delhi 110029
India

Tel: 6884562
Fax: 663272

Janet Haas

(USA) 59

P.O. Box 174
Milford
MI 48381
USA

Tel: 313 685 0684

Michele Binder Hall

(USA) 97

Howard Hall Productions
2171 La Amatista Road
Del Mar
CA 92014
USA

Tel: 619 259 8989
Fax: 619 792 1467

David Hall

(USA) 94

257 Ohayo Mtn. Road
Woodstock
NY 12498
USA

Tel: 914 679 6138
Fax: 914 334 4788

Dr. Mark Hamblin

(UK) 138

63 Waller Road
Walkley Bank
Sheffield S6 5DP

Tel: 0742 333910

Carsten Broder Hansen

(Denmark) 131

Dybbolsgade 17 3.TH
1721 Copenhagen V
Denmark

Tel: 45 3121 0685
Fax: c/o Nepenthes 45 3183 2844

Louise Hartgill

(UK) 78

Hartgill Photography
'Mali'
Salisbury Road
Coombe Bissett
Salisbury
Wiltshire SP5 4JT

Tel: 072 277

Asegir Helgestad

(Norway) 16, 17, 18, 19, 20

Tommerv 11
3622 Svene
Norway

Tel: 0376 2390

Richard Herrmann

(USA) 100

12545 Mustang Drive
Poway
CA 92064
USA

Tel: 619 679 7017
Fax: 619 486 0905

Peter Hewitt

(UK) 99

250 Feltham Hill Road
Ashford
Middlesex TW15 1LN

Michael Hill

(UK) 148

Benson House
Wellington College
Crowthorne
Berkshire RG11 7PU

Dr. Mike Hill

(UK) 52, 134

P.O. Box 25005
Awali
Bahrain
Arabian Gulf

Tel: 756292
Fax: 753624

Gerald Hinde

(South Africa) 22

P.O. Box 2783
Benoni 1500
South Africa

Tel: 0027 11 742 1343
Fax: 0027 11 742 1343

Guy Hobbs

(UK) 54

c/o 130 Rosemill Avenue
Atholhurst 2196
Johannesburg
South Africa

Tel: SA 11 786 5836
Fax: SA 11 786 5837

Ernie Janes

(UK) 27

Commercial Photography
10 Boxwell Road
Berkhamsted
Hertfordshire HP4 3EX

Tel: 0442 871342

Jan Töve Johansson

(Sweden) 82/82, 123

Prästgarden
Härna
52015 Hökerum
Sweden

Tel: 033 274028
Mobile: 010 356319

Mike Johnson

(USA) 100

7985 Dormouse Court
San Diego
CA 92129
USA

Tel: 619 484 1740

**Burt Jones &
Maurine Shimlock**

(USA) 99, 118

P.O. Box 162931
Austin
TX 78716
USA

Tel: 512 328 1201

Beverly Joubert

(Botswana) 126

c/o David McKillop
1145 17th Street NW
Washington DC
USA 20036

Herbert Kehrer

(Germany) 43

Im Brühl 21
7054 Korb
Germany

Tel: 07151 31480

J. Michael Kelly

(USA) 92/93

102 W Moore, Suite 102
Terrell
TX 75160
USA

Tel: 214 563 2515
Fax: 214 563 9170

Manfred Klindwort

(Germany) 129

Köhlerstrasse 30
3252 Bad Münder 2
Germany

Tel: 05042 81654
Fax: 05042 81654

Felix Labhardt

(Switzerland) 41, 53

Bruderholzstrasse 26
CH - 4103 Bottmingen
Switzerland

Tel/Fax: 0041 61 4210516

Gary Lee Lackie

(USA) 63

P.O. Box 110405
Anchorage
Alaska 99511
USA

Tel: 907 345 7603
Fax: 907 274 0636

Antti Leinonen

(Finland) 66

Koirisärkäntie 4 C 10
88900 Kuhmo
Finland

Tel: 986 51775

Brian Lightfoot

(UK) 26

Parkhead Croft by Johnshaven
Montrose DD10 0PU
Scotland

Tel: 0561 62017

Hanne Lindemann

(Denmark) 57

Gronholtvej 35B
DK - 3480 Fredensborg
Denmark

Agent: Biofoto
Vodroffsvej 37
DK - 1900 Frederiksberg C
Denmark

Tel: 45 31313568
Fax: 45 31313512

Doug Locke

(USA) 86

1415 Oakbrook East
Rochester Hills
Michigan 48307
USA

Tel: 313 656 1625

Renee Lynn

(USA) 68

Davis/Lynn Photography
P.O.Box 1278
Palo Alto
CA 94302
USA

Tel: 415 327 4192
Fax: 415 322 5082

Antonio Mazanares

(Spain) 45

Apartado de Correos 97
02400 Hellin
Albacette
Spain

Tel: 967 30 1662
Fax: 967 30 1662

Lennart Mellgren

(Sweden) 122

Bergstigen 7
S - 46832 Vargön
Sweden

Tel: 0521 20918

Roger Mooers

(USA) 120/121

59 Hersom Street
Watertown
Mass 02172
USA

Tel: 617 924 4290

Dr. Mark Moffett

(USA) 50, 71

Museum of Comparative Zoology
Harvard University
26 Oxford Street
Cambridge
MA 021138
USA

Kushal Mookherjee

(India) 69

146 Rash Behari Avenue
Calcutta 700029
India

The Wildlife Photographer of the Year Competition is an annual event. Entry forms for the 1993 competition can be found in the spring issues of BBC Wildlife Magazine. Overseas photographers can write for further details to: Wildlife Photographer of the Year Competition, c/o BBC Wildlife Magazine, Broadcasting House, Whiteladies Road, Bristol BS8 2LR.